INNOVATION
AND ITS ENEMIES

"A must read for anyone who wishes to engage in disruption themselves."

— *Sir Richard J. Roberts*
Nobel Laureate in Physiology or Medicine and Chief Scientific Officer,
New England Biolabs

"A very well-researched account of innovation and its enemies, not to be missed by scholars and the public, both for historical perspectives and readiness for future innovations."

— *Professor Yongyuth Yuthavong*
Former Deputy Prime Minister and Minister of Science and Technology,
Thailand

"This book is a timely one. We owe a deep debt of gratitude to Dr. Calestous Juma for his labor of love for the progress of human wellbeing through scientific innovations."

— *M. S. Swaminathan*
World Food Prize Laureate, and Founder Chairman, M. S. Swaminathan
Research Foundation

"This is a good read and an invaluable reference work for those working on new technologies, especially those needed to meet the grand challenges of the twenty-first century."

— *Lord Alec Broers*
British House of Lords and Former Vice Chancellor of the University of
Cambridge

"An excellent analysis of forces that oppose new innovative products and services. A must read for entrepreneurs, policy framers and academicians."

— *N. R. Narayana Murthy*
Founder, Infosys

"Juma's insight is to see how the appropriate deployment of political capital and a deeper understanding of how the average citizen can confuse hazard and risk can make crucial differences to outcomes. Scientific and political leaders need this book."

— *Ian Blatchford*
Director and Chief Executive of the Science Museum Group, the United
Kingdom

Innovation and Its Enemies

Why People Resist New Technologies

Calestous Juma

OXFORD
UNIVERSITY PRESS

OXFORD

UNIVERSITY PRESS

Oxford University Press is a department of the University of Oxford. It furthers
the University's objective of excellence in research, scholarship, and education
by publishing worldwide. Oxford is a registered trade mark of Oxford University
Press in the UK and certain other countries.

Published in the United States of America by Oxford University Press
198 Madison Avenue, New York, NY 10016, United States of America.

© Oxford University Press 2016

Library of Congress Cataloging-in-Publication Data
Names: Juma, Calestous, author.
Title: Innovation and its enemies : why people resist new technologies /
Calestous Juma.
Description: First edition. | Oxford ; New York : Oxford University Press, 2016. |
Includes bibliographical references and index.
Identifiers: LCCN 2015043807 (print) | LCCN 2015048125 (ebook) |
ISBN 978-0-19-046703-6 (hardcover : alk. paper) |
ISBN 978-0-19-046704-3 (Updf) | ISBN 978-0-19-046705-0 (Epub)
Subjects: LCSH: Technological innovations—History. | Technology and civilization. |
Technology—Social aspects.
Classification: LCC HC79.T4 J8178 2016 (print) | LCC HC79.T4 (ebook) |
DDC 338/.064—dc23
LC record available at http://lccn.loc.gov/2015043807

9 8 7 6 5 4 3 2
Printed by Sheridan Books, Inc., United States of America

To my son Eric

Contents

Acknowledgments

This book has benefited from many people who have offered me guidance, research, insights and comments. The book was written over sixteen years, and so it will not be possible to acknowledge everyone who supported me over the period. In fact, I can trace some of the ideas in the book back to the early 1980s when I worked under the late Nobel Peace Prize winner Wangari Maathai at the Nairobi-based Environment Liaison Centre (ELC). The preceding oil crises and environmental concerns had inspired considerable interest in clean energy, which culminated in the convening of the United Nations Conference on New and Renewable Energy Sources in Nairobi in 1981. It became clear then that seemingly basic ideas such as tree planting encounter numerous social obstacles. While at ELC my thinking about technology and the environment was shaped by the guidance of Gary Gallon and the inspirational leadership of Mostafa Tolba, then Executive Director of the United Nations Environment Programme.

Along my intellectual journey I benefited immensely from inspirational support, suggestions, and comments from many colleagues. The list is too long to be exhaustive here, but I will mention just a few. They include Philipp Aerni, Bruce Alberts, Graham Allison, Lewis Branscomb, John Browne, Norman Clark, Abdallah Daar, Henry Etzkowitz, Leonel Antonio Fernández,

Michael Fischer, Archon Fung, Kelly Sims Gallagher, Val Giddings, Alexandra Golikov, Zakri Abdul Hamid, Mohamed Hassan, John Holdren, David King, Victor Konde, Sheldon Krimsky, Kiyoshi Kurokawa, Yee-Cheong Lee, Francis Mangeni, Franklin Moore, Venky Narayanamurti, Joe Nye, John Ouma-Mugabe, Frederick Pardee, Peter Raven, Martin Rees, Andrew Reynolds, Matt W. Ridley, John Ruggie, Jeffrey Sachs, Vicente Sanchez, Barbara Schaal, F.M. Scherer, Susan Sechler, Cyriaque Sendashonga, Raj Shah, Gustave Speth, Kirsten Stendahl, Chikako Takase, Eric Topol, Harold Varmus, Charles Vest, Thomas Yongo, Yongyuth Yuthavong, and Dorothy Zinberg.

A book of this breadth can only be completed with continuous sources of inspiration through words and works. For this I am thankful to Martin Abraham, Aggrey Ambali, Allison Archambault, W. Brian Arthur, Andrew Barnett, Martin Bauer, John Beddington, Sujata Bhatia, Rosina Bierbaum, Johan Bodegård, John Boright, Brantley Browning, Thomas Burke, Gordon Conway, Paul David, Mateja Dermastia, Elizabeth Dowdeswell, Nina Fedoroff, Deborah Fitzgerald, Susanne Freidberg, Lynn Frewer, Sakiko Fukuda-Parr, Frank Geels, Kimo Goree, Philip Greenish, Brian Grottkau, Anil K. Gupta, Eric von Hippel, Heping Jia, Donald Kaberuka, Travis Kalanick, Yusuf Keshavjee, Jennifer Kuzma, Gary Marchant, R. A. Mashelkar, Janet Maughan, Robert May, Erik Millstone, Joel Mokyr, Romain Murenzi, Bernarditas de Castro Muller, Adil Najam, Nicholas Negroponte, Alan Olmstead, Owen Paterson, Samantha Power, Fernando Quezada, Atta ur Rahman, Adrian Randall, Fil Randazzo, Firoz Rasul, Gregory Robbins, Nathan Rosenberg, Marc Saner, Peter Johan Schei, Bruce Scott, Joseph Schwab, Rinn Self, Lecia Sequist, Ismail Serageldin, Peter Singer, Chris Smart, M. S. Swaminathan, and Caroline Wagner.

I am very grateful to my colleagues on the jury of the £1 million Queen Elizabeth Prize for Engineering under the inspirational leadership of Alec Broers for their practical insights into the dynamics of technological innovation. I want to thank Frances Arnold, Brian

Cox, Lynn Gladden, Reinhard Huettl, John Hennessy, Narayana Murthy, Hiroshi Komiyama, Christopher Snowden, Choon Fong Shih, Dan Mote, Viola Vogel, and Paul Westbury.

A few people have read the manuscript, and I am grateful for their comments and additional information. They include Klaus Ammann, Alison Van Eenennaam, Jamal Elias, Elliot Entis, Robert Frosch, Anne Glover, Robert Langer, Dutch Leonard, Silas Lwakabamba, Robert Paarlberg, and J. Craig Venter. Devon Maylie provided me with diligent editorial support and invaluable comments.

Over the gestation of this book I have had the opportunity to present the contents to a variety of audiences. I am indebted to my students who helped me to shape the material for a more scholarly audience. I would like to pay special tribute to students in courses I have taught on innovation and sustainability at Harvard Kennedy School, Harvard College, and the School of Forestry and Environmental Studies at Yale University. Their critical comments and insights helped to improve the structure and contents of this book.

A book project of this scope can hardly be accomplished without diligent research support. For this I am deeply grateful first to Muriel Calo, whose intellectual curiosity and thoroughness helped to unearth the initial material that helped to shape the tone of the book. The same level of research support and project management was provided by Hezekiah Agwara, Bob Bell Jr., Allison DiSenso, Greg Durham, Samantha Fang, Andrea Haffty, Derya Honça, Jo Kim, Katharina Lix, Mahat Somane, and Brian Torpy. I wish to give special credit to Katherine Gordon for not only overseeing the completion of this book project, but also for her additional research support. Her meticulous attention to detail helped to significantly improve the quality of this book.

Parts of this book were written with the financial support of the Sustainability Science Program at Harvard Kennedy School. I am indebted to William Clark and Nancy Dickson for the support and patience. I finalized this book during my 2014–2015 appointment as Dr. Martin Luther King Jr. Visiting Professor in the

Department of Urban Studies and Planning at the Massachusetts Institute of Technology (MIT). I am grateful for the opportunity accorded to me by MIT and would like specifically mention the support I received from Eran Ben-Joseph, Edmund Bertschinger, Phil Budden, Phillip Clay, Wesley Harris, Philip Khoury, Richard Larson, Fiona Murray, Kenneth Oye, Richard Samuels, Bish Sanyal, Lawrence Susskind, and Leon Trilling.

I am deeply indebted to my reviewers. Their candor and rigor helped me to appreciate even more the importance of the debate over anonymity in the review process. The first round of review was as passionately divided as the material covered in the book.

I made the final edits of this book while recovering from back surgery at Massachusetts General Hospital under the care of outstanding doctors, nurses, nursing assistants, and staff and supported by the latest medical technologies ever developed. Without this timely intervention, this book would have not have been published as planned.

Finally, I want to thank my wife Alison and son Eric for their patience and support. There were moments when it looked like this book would never be finished, but I owe it to their encouragement that I have completed it.

INNOVATION
AND ITS ENEMIES

Introduction

New ideas are not only the enemy of old ones; they also appear often in an extremely unacceptable form.

CARL GUSTAV JUNG

The quickest way to find out who your enemies are is to try doing something new. This book explores the dynamics of social opposition to innovation.[1] In his pioneering work, the Austrian economist Joseph Schumpeter identified innovation as the central force in economic transformation. Much of the scholarly elaboration of his work has focused on how innovation drives economic evolution and the critical role that entrepreneurs play in the process. Innovation, according to Schumpeter, is the creation of new combinations that represent a departure from established practices. Schumpeter noted that resistance to innovation is experienced by the innovator, businesses, and the wider economy. He observed that deviation from the norm elicits astonishment and pressure on developers of new technologies and entrepreneurs seeking to bring them to market. He added that it may "even come to social ostracism and finally to physical prevention or to direct attack."[2]

Resistance to new technologies is often frowned upon as a temporary phenomenon that is inevitably overcome by technological progress. In fact, Schumpeter himself suggested that the "opposition is stronger in primitive states of culture than in others."[3] He was acutely aware of the forces of incumbency and acknowledged that "all knowledge and habit once acquired becomes as firmly rooted in ourselves as a railway embankment in the earth. It does not require to be continually renewed and consciously reproduced, but sinks into the strata of subconciousness."[4] This metaphor sets the stage for a deeper analysis of controversies surrounding the adoption of new technologies.

This book examines the sources of such drastic responses to innovation as noted above. It looks especially at conflicts between proponents of new technologies and incumbent industries. Many of the dominant technologies that we take for granted have weathered moments of social tension and threats of succession. In fact, technological failure is the norm.[5] We celebrate the few technologies that have changed the world but hardly remember those that have fallen by the wayside, not to mention the social tensions that surrounded their demise. We read more about inventions that changed the world than those that did not.[6] Between the successes and failures lies a large territory of contestation that deserves deeper exploration.

Consider the case of cell phones. In 1983 cell phones made their commercial debut in the United States and were rapidly adopted despite early concerns that they could cause cancer. Regulators even adopted supportive policies for the diffusion of cell phones. Their carcinogenic risks were acknowledged and early models came with warning labels. At the height of the debate in Europe in 2001 newspapers "advised that minors should take precautionary steps such as holding the phone at a distance while dialing and sending text messages."[7] Despite the debates surrounding the technology, its adoption has been universal, and it has been the platform for the development of new services such as banking, health, education, security, and social interaction. Perceptions of the benefits of mobile communication have by far overshadowed its risks.[8]

The same year that cell phones debuted, European researchers demonstrated that genes and their functions could be transferred from one species to another. Their work made it possible for farmers around the world to grow transgenic crops that resist pests and diseases, reduce pesticide use, and tolerate extreme climatic variations. Yet agricultural biotechnology has been marked by controversy that resulted in international treaties negotiated to regulate trade in transgenic crops and the associated exchange of genetic material under the United Nations Convention on Biological Diversity.

In 2013 the World Food Prize was awarded to Marc Van Montagu, Mary-Dell Chilton, and Robert T. Fraley for their breakthrough achievements in agricultural biotechnology. But the announcement was criticized by opponents of the role of biotechnology and large corporations in global agriculture. A group called Occupy the World Food Prize organized marches in which they castigated the prize committee for honoring individuals connected to industrial agriculture in general and the Monsanto Corporation in particular. The demonstrators represented a different agricultural approach that favored agro-ecological farming systems. The same year, the inaugural Queen Elizabeth Prize for Engineering was awarded to pioneers who developed the Internet and the Web. The £1 million prize was launched to reward and celebrate those responsible for groundbreaking innovations of global benefit to humanity. Robert Kahn, Vinton Cerf, and Louis Pouzin pioneered the development of protocols that constituted the fundamental architecture of the Internet, while Tim Berners-Lee created the World Wide Web and greatly stretched the use of the Internet beyond file transfer and email. Marc Andreessen, while a student in collaboration with colleagues, wrote the Mosaic browser, which was extensively distributed and popularized worldwide web access.

These pioneering engineering achievements revolutionized the way humans communicate. They allowed for the creation of new species of industries that could not have been developed using previously existing technologies. Today, more than a third of the world's population uses the Internet, and the Web has become as essential to today's digital society as railroads were to the early industrial age. These engineering achievements were adopted with little public debate, but they would later become a source of major public controversies, including access to information, property rights, privacy, espionage, and moral values.

Such concerns are a common feature of cultural evolution. This is evident in the creative wonder and extraordinary qualities among deities in Greek mythology. The Greeks had Hephaestus, the god of engineering and technology, who owned his own palace on Mount Olympus containing his workshop and machine tools. His creations were magnificent and included Achilles's armor, Aegis's breastplate, Agamemnon's official staff, Aphrodite's legendary girdle, Eros's bow and arrows, Helios's chariot, Heracles's bronze clappers, and Hermes's winged helmet and sandals. He also created metal automatons to help him, such as tripods that walked to and from Mount Olympus. And of course he created all the thrones in the Palace of Olympus. It was from Hephaestus's forge that Prometheus would steal the fire he gave to humans. To even out the power wielded by Hephaestus, Greek mythology ensured that he was not perfect. Hephaestus is thus the only Olympian with a physical disability.

I first thought of writing this book in the late 1990s when I served as executive secretary of the United Nations Convention on Biological Diversity. In that position I was, among other things, responsible for overseeing the start of the negotiations that resulted in the adoption of the Cartagena Protocol on Biosafety. The international treaty was negotiated specifically to regulate trade in agricultural biotechnology. The negotiations were contentious to say the least. Countries were divided along a wide range of technical, economic, social, environmental, and political fault lines.

As a manager of the negotiating process I observed great divergence among countries in the way they perceived the risks and benefits of a new technology. I would later characterize these perceptions as follows:

In the United States products are safe until proven risky.
In France products are risky until proven safe.
In the United Kingdom products are risky even when proven safe.

In India products are safe even when proven risky.
In Canada products are neither safe nor risky.
In Japan products are either safe or risky.
In Brazil products are both safe and risky.
In sub-Saharan Africa products are risky even if they do not
exist.

This caricature of carefully considered positions by diplomats set me on a research path that resulted in this book. While technological controversies through the ages share many common features, today's debates have a number of distinctive features. First, the pace of technological innovation is discernibly fast. This creates intense anxiety leading to efforts to slow down the adoption of technology. Second, the global nature of technological trends and the conspicuous disparities between individuals, social groups, and nations add to concerns over social inequities. New technologies and the associated business models are implicated in the rising tensions. Finally, modern controversies are occurring in an age of growing public distrust in public and private institutions. These factors are adding to the general gloom arising from a disappointing record in dealing with grand challenges such as meeting human needs, promoting inclusive economic development, and addressing global ecological problems such as climate change.

This book argues that technological controversies often arise from tensions between the need to innovate and the pressure to maintain continuity, social order, and stability. These tensions are compounded by exponential growth in scientific, technological, and engineering advances. The book examines the role of technological succession in understanding the sources of social responses to innovation. The tension between novelty and stability arising from transformational innovation is a leading source of public controversies and policy challenges.[9] Society cannot evolve and respond to change without generating variety in its adaptive capabilities, as illustrated by the case of the sustainability transition.[10]

But society will not function without a certain degree of institutional continuity and social stability. Managing the interactions between change and continuity remains one of the most critical functions of government.

Public debates over new technologies engendering tensions between innovation and incumbency can rage for decades if not centuries. For example, debates over coffee spanned the Old World from Mecca through London to Stockholm and lasted nearly three hundred years. Echoes of the margarine controversy can still be heard in countries such as Canada today. New technologies such as genetic engineering and smart grids have triggered debates over a variety of concerns. Similarly, efforts to address climate change by introducing renewable energy sources such as wind power have generated intense public concern in many parts of the world.

Many of these debates over new technologies are framed in the context of risks to moral values, human health, and environmental safety. But behind these genuine concerns often lie deeper, but unacknowledged, socioeconomic considerations. This book demonstrates the extent to which those factors shape and influence technological controversies, with specific emphasis on the role of social institutions. It shows how new technologies emerge, take root, and create new institutional ecologies that favor their establishment in the marketplace. What starts off as a process of innovation and discontinuity is often followed by technological dominance and incumbency.

Socioeconomic evolution is often associated with continuous adjustments in technology and institutions. It builds on the concept of "self-organization" and differs from the classical Darwinian view where innovation arises from mutations whose survival is only guaranteed by the selection environment of the market.[11] This view grants greater agency to the mutant, which in its own right shapes the environment to suit its needs. Technology and institutions are as inseparable as institutions and technology. There is no institution without an element of technology, and the reverse is equally true.

The face-off between the established technological order and new aspirants leads to controversies. Most of the controversies are driven by uncertainties associated with risks and benefits and are expressed in the form of perceptions. Technological controversies occur in time and in space. First, perceptions about immediate risks and long-term distribution of benefits influence the intensity of concerns over new technologies. Second, society is most likely to oppose a new technology if it perceives that the risks are likely to occur in the short run and the benefits will only accrue in the long run. Technological tensions are often heightened by perceptions that the benefits of innovation will accrue only to small sections of society, while the risks will be more widely distributed. Third, innovations that threaten to alter cultural identities tend to generate intense social concern. As such, societies that exhibit great economic and political inequities are likely to experience heightened technological controversies.

The process of socioeconomic change is largely a footnote on social learning, and public debates about new technologies are analogous to debates about new ideas. Those who can grasp this idea are more likely to better manage the dynamics of socioeconomic change and organize the instruments of government as if they were learning institutions. It is this critical element of social learning that has resulted in the focus on science and innovation advice. The debates are mostly about perception of risks, not necessarily about the impact of the risks themselves.[12]

Two observations arise from the history of technological controversies. The first is the role of leaders in acting as risk-takers on behalf of the public. It is in the nature of leadership to chart new paths while at the same time maintaining continuity, social order, and stability. The way leaders—at all levels—deal with the tensions between innovation and continuity may determine the fate of society. In this respect, leaders bear a primary responsibility to muddle through uncertainty but to do so with the best available advice. It is for this reason that scientific advisory bodies are increasingly important components of democratic governance.

Second, public engagement on scientific and technological matters is becoming a central aspect of democratic discourse. But it must be conducted with a deeper understanding of the wider sources of social tension.[13] Effective risk management practices are as dependent on technical assessments as they are on public engagement. Risk communication is therefore emerging as an important aspect of democratic governance. This is particularly important given rising scientific literacy around the world and the role of information and communications technologies in expanding popular access to scientific and technological information.

Drawing from nearly 600 years of technology history, this book identifies the tension between the need for innovation and the pressure to maintain continuity, social order, and stability as one of today's biggest policy challenges. It reveals the extent to which modern technological controversies grow out of distrust in public and private institutions. The book is divided into three parts. The first part (chapter 1) presents a framework for understanding the relationships between technological innovation and social change. It outlines key global challenges that cannot be addressed without significant technological innovation. It stresses the importance of uncertainty and incumbency as key factors in technological controversies. The chapter shows how prevailing social structures can either intensify or act as moderating forces in moments of radical technological change.

The second part (chapters 2–10) of the book presents historical instances in which tensions over innovation challenged the legitimacy of new technologies. These include the introduction of coffee, the printing press, margarine, farm mechanization, electricity, mechanical refrigeration, recorded music, transgenic crops, and transgenic salmon. The chapters offer a wide range of illustrations of how different social systems responded to new technologies and how these coevolved with social institutions. More specifically, the chapters seek to tease out those salient social responses to innovation: demonization of new technologies, efforts to restrict their use through seemingly legitimate measures such as laws, and efforts to introduce outright bans on new technologies. In addition, the chapters show how advocates of innovation respond to social changes by altering political and policy environments. In other words, the chapters show how technological innovation and institutional adjustments coevolve.

The final part (chapter 11) presents the key conclusions and lessons learned from the case studies and outlines policy options for managing the tensions. It emphasizes the role of science and innovation advice (as well as a responsive education system) in managing the coevolution between technology and social institutions as part of broader governance. The main focus of the chapter is to stress the importance of reordering modern governance systems to effectively manage the process of technological change and the associated institutional adjustments. It notes the importance of a more informed and conscious approach to technology management and the governance of innovation.

As global challenges mount, there is a real risk that governments could retreat from supporting certain technologies—not because they cannot solve societal challenges, but because they are unlikely to enjoy public support for a variety of reasons that include national security. Nuclear power is an example.[14] This book uses case studies of technologies that were initially the subject of intense social opposition but later became widely accepted. The choice of the cases does not diminish the importance of genuine concerns arising from harmful products and technologies that have either been banned or restricted.

There are a large number of such products and technologies, ranging from tobacco to DDT to incandescent light bulbs, many of which have been extensively studied.[15] The phasing out of some of these products has often been accompanied by concerted efforts by incumbent industries to selectively use scientific knowledge to cast doubt on the balance of evidence and the need for policy action.[16] Some of the studies on these experiences have led to scholarship supporting termination of not just the products, but the associated policies as well.[17] The overall body of knowledge suggests that the risks of new or incumbent technologies should be assessed on an individual basis and should not be generalized except where a case for substantial equivalence can be made. This book is not about passing judgment on the safety or risks of a specific product. Instead, it seeks to draw lessons from the case studies and consider how to address social tensions arising from the introduction of new technologies.

Many of the lessons detailed in this book have parallels beyond the domain of technological innovation. They apply to social innovation more broadly. Social responses to new technologies offer a rich source of heuristics that can help us to gain deeper understanding of the dynamics of sociocultural evolution.

1

Gales of Creative Destruction

People are very open-minded about new things—as long as they're exactly like the old ones.

CHARLES KETTERING

The new millennium brought a rising tide of economic, social, and ecological challenges. Meeting basic needs in less developed nations, addressing economic slowdown in industrialized nations, and responding to climate change loomed large on the global political landscape. The new millennium was also marked by technological optimism driven by dramatic advances in science, technology, and engineering and a belief that these advances could solve some of the world's most pressing challenges.

This chapter stresses that while rapid technological adoption in response to mounting global challenges is welcomed by large sections of society, it also triggers societal responses that seek to slow down the influence of technological change. The fear of loss, not novelty, underlies social tension over technologies, some of which takes the form of outright opposition by segments of society against change. Fear of loss can lead individuals or groups to avoid change brought by innovation even if that means forgoing gains.[1] But much of the concern is driven by perceptions of loss, not necessarily by concrete evidence of loss. The fear or perception of loss may take material forms, but it also includes intellectual and psychological factors such as challenges to established worldviews or identity.

Technology, Innovation, and Global Challenges

The world faces a number of grand challenges that are gaining public attention. According to the US National Academy of Engineering, these challenges fall into four main categories: sustainability, health, security, and life enrichment. Sustainability encompasses the need to make solar energy economical, provide energy from fusion, develop carbon sequestration methods, and manage the nitrogen cycle. For improved health, there must be access to clean water, the engineering of better medicines, advancement in health informatics, and work done to reverse engineer the brain. The challenges to security will require actions to secure cyberspace, prevent nuclear terror, and restore and improve urban infrastructure. The challenge to life enrichment requires work to enhance virtual reality, advance personalized learning, and engineer the tools for scientific discovery.[2] As the world's challenges have evolved, so has society's view of technological innovation, and this has implications for technological adoption.

Human understanding of the role of technological innovation in society is changing for three major reasons. Historically, technological innovation was a slow process. Today, many new technologies and engineering solutions are generated at a rate faster than society can design new complementary institutions. The faster pace of innovation has far-reaching social implications, as reflected by the public reaction to the erosion of privacy due to improved technology for data collection. Second, many fields have seen a considerable shortening of innovation cycles. This enables new products to reach the market at a faster rate than was the case in preceding decades. Third, globalization has created new opportunities for the rapid diffusion of new technology and engineering practices.

Shorter time frames between research and product release have changed the nature of technology forecasting, requiring anticipatory regulatory approaches.[3] The exponential growth in scientific and technological knowledge, diversity of cultural activities, and geographical proximity afforded by advances in communications technologies have contributed to the shorter time frame.[4]

The exponential growth in technical knowledge is making it possible to find low-cost, high-technology engineering solutions to persistent problems. These technologies are reshaping the political landscape in unprecedented ways, opening up new technological opportunities through combinatorial evolution.[5]

Advances in science, technology, and engineering will therefore make it possible for humanity to devise solutions that previously existed only in the realms of imagination. This is not a deterministic view of society but an observation of the growth in the global ecology of knowledge and the feasibility of new technical combinations that are elicited by social consciousness. The developing world has the potential to access more scientific and technical knowledge than the more advanced countries had in their early stages of industrialization. The pace at which latecomer economies such as China have been able to leapfrog in certain technologies underscores the possibilities.[6]

There are growing concerns over the implications of these developments for employment. Self-driving cars will restructure transportation through new ownership patterns, insurance arrangements, and business models. Computer-aided diagnosis, robotic surgery, and myriad medical devices are already changing the role of doctors and how medical care is provided.[7] Artificial intelligence and computer algorithms are influencing the way basic decisions are made. Battlefields are being automated with drones and other autonomous vehicles doing the work that used to be performed by a wide range of military personnel. Some of the advances are already shifting the locus of product development. Data-based firms such as Google and IBM are moving into pharmaceutical research. Sharing services such as Uber are acquiring robotics and other engineering capabilities. The implications of exponential growth will continue to elude political leaders if they persist in operating with linear worldviews.

These trends have added new elements of uncertainty in human relations in general and in the economy in particular. As Nicholas Carr writes in his book *The Glass Cage*, "Automation severs ends from means. It makes getting what we want easier, but it distances us from the work of knowing."[8] Such uncertainty may encompass basic societal trends, from the inability to foresee the impact of new technologies to extreme social responses driven by the fear of loss.[9]

There are also numerous cases where society has underestimated the risks posed by new technologies or adopted them without adequate knowledge about their risks. Modern agriculture was made possible through the extensive use of a family of chemicals that now falls under the umbrella of persistent organic pollutants. Early evocations of the danger the chemicals pose were captured by the works of pioneers such as Rachel Carson, whose vivid imagery in *Silent Spring* inspired the emergence of the environmental movement.[10] Increases in scientific knowledge revealed the detrimental health and environmental impacts of a wide range of chemicals, leading to their being banned or restricted.

The rapid expansion of technological diversity as reflected in the range of traded products engenders even greater creativity through new product combinations and integration of technological and engineering systems, but the same process compounds perceptions about risks. Other technological improvements have come from the ability of scientists and engineers to work with smaller and smaller units of matter. The rise of the field of nanotechnology creates greater technological variety and helps industry to introduce new attributes in existing products. This development, however, has resulted in concerns about the ability of countries to regulate the new technologies, as people doubt the adequacy of existing institutional arrangements in safeguarding human health and environmental integrity.[11]

Technological and engineering advancements themselves are a major source of answers to many controversies. For example, safety concerns regarding early mechanical refrigeration could not be addressed without advances in technology. Similarly, the rapid rate at which early tractors were improved helped to foster their adoption. Recent concerns about obtaining stem cells from human embryos have been addressed by innovative approaches that helped to identify other sources.

A combination of technological abundance, continuous improvement, and greater involvement of users in innovation will help to create new avenues for resolving the technological controversies that arise from immature technologies. This is illustrated by the English army's shift from the longbow to firearms. By most eighteenth-century accounts the longbow was superior to the early flintlock musket. The former could be discharged more rapidly than bullets and cost less. In fact the musket was so inaccurate that soldiers were advised not to "shoot until you see the whites of [enemies'] eyes."[12] Among other factors, however, archery required extensive training compared to firearms, and its decline was associated with the allocation of time to other sports.

In 1591 Queen Elizabeth made a spirited effort to revive archery by issuing a decree prohibiting those games that were not essential for the defense of the country. She saw archery as "that kind of weapon whereby our nation in times past has gotten so great honor may be kept in use."[13] She also decreed that "such poor men whose stay of living with their whole families do chiefly depend thereon, as bowyers, fletchers, stringers, arrowhead makers, being many in number throughout the realm, may be maintained and set to work according to their vocations."[14] Technological and engineering advances in firearms would eventually relegate archery to a sport whose military potential continued to decline with the passage of time.

On the whole, a wide range of societal factors interact to define the place and adoption of acceptable new technologies. As Lynn White observed in *Medieval Technology and Social Change*, "The acceptance or rejection of an invention, or the extent to which its implications are realized if it is accepted, depends quite as much upon the conditions of society, and upon the imagination of its leaders, as upon the nature of the technological item itself."[15]

Schumpeter, Innovation, and Social Transformation

The preceding discussion illustrates "creative destruction," a term coined by Austrian economist Joseph Schumpeter in his 1942 book *Capitalism, Socialism and Democracy*. Schumpeter believed that capitalism is a system that must always evolve, and with the evolution comes change. The change requires the destruction of something old, replaced by something new, such as the gun replacing archery and the mobile phone replacing the landline. To fully grasp the implications and scope of the process of creative destruction, we need to return to Schumpeter's original thinking, as laid out in his 1911 book *The Theory of Economic Development*, about innovation as "creative construction" or the carrying out of new combinations. This task, according to Schumpeter, is undertaken by the entrepreneur. In his original view, innovation constitutes five areas: the introduction of new production, development of new processes, opening up of new markets, sourcing of new materials and semimanufactured goods, and finally the reorganization of an industrial sector.[16]

The term can be applied to any of the five areas of innovation identified by Schumpeter. As elaborated by Swedberg, creative destruction and the associated resistance to innovation can be identified in any of those five areas and any additional ones that expand the categories of new combinations.[17] Creative destruction explains why segments of society fear change; at the same time the concept can help individuals embrace innovation.

The concept of creative destruction as articulated by Schumpeter gained currency largely because it has universal appeal.[18] It manifests itself in a variety of forms across cultures and it is therefore easily applied without precise definition.[19] By thinking of the economy as an integrated whole akin to an ecosystem, Schumpeter was able to identify the forces of economic transformation that resulted from waves of technological succession as illustrated by the impact of the introduction of railroads.[20] For him, "The essential point to grasp is that in dealing with capitalism we are dealing with an evolutionary process,"[21] which he elaborates as the "process of industrial mutation ... that incessantly revolutionizes the economic structure *from within*, incessantly destroying the old one, incessantly creating a new one. This process of Creative Destruction is the essential fact about capitalism."[22]

Schumpeter challenged the idea of economic equilibrium using non-Darwinian evolutionary thinking.[23] He focuses on transformations arising from the creation of new combinations. Using his classic reference case, he said: "Railroads have not emerged because any consumers took the initiative in displaying an effective demand for their service in preference to the services of mail coaches."[24] He added other examples: "Nor did the consumers display any such initiative wish to have electric lamps or rayon stockings, or to travel by motorcar or airplane, or to listen to radio, or to chew gum."[25] In fact, "The great majority of changes in commodities consumed have been forced by producers on consumers who, more often than not, have resisted the change and have had to be educated up by elaborate psychotechnics of advertising."[26]

One of the key features of the concept of creative destruction is technological discontinuity. A popular derivative of the thinking is the concept of "disruptive innovation."[27] As noted by Christensen in his original formulation of the theory, disruptive innovation is distinguished from sustaining technologies that "improve the performance of established products, along the dimensions that mainstream customers in major markets have traditionally valued."[28] Disruptive technologies, however, may start off underperforming relative to established technologies. Through technological improvement and marketing, the disruptive technologies eventually end up dominating the market. They are "typically cheaper, simpler, smaller, and, frequently, more convenient to use."[29]

The term "disruptive innovation" is generally used to cover technological innovation as well as business models.[30] This makes it difficult to assess its wider societal implications. Other approaches have tended to focus on the distinction between radical and incremental technological change. These labels are usually attached to outcomes rather than processes and so have limited analytical value.[31] They often fail to account for the fact that seemingly minor technical improvements could have far-reaching systemic consequences.[32]

A promising approach could be to focus on technological discontinuities and their societal implications.[33] Under this evolutionary outlook, "A technological breakthrough, or discontinuity, initiates an era of intense technical variation and selection, culminating in a single dominant design. This era of ferment is followed by a period of incremental technical progress, which may be broken by a subsequent technological discontinuity."[34] The discontinuities may arise from a variety of sources, which include change in products, processes, new markets, organization, and raw materials. The focus should be on the extent to which innovation in these and other areas results in transformations that change the balance of winners and losers, leading to public controversies.

The idea of disruptive technologies offers a starting point in understanding technological succession at the firm and market level, with emphasis on the failure of incumbent enterprises.[35] One of the solutions to stem such failure is to restrict the application of new technologies to start-ups.[36] This view can be extended to accommodate slightly wider perspectives of sociotechnical and innovation systems. These are defined as "articulated ensembles of social and technical elements which interact with each other in distinct ways, are distinguishable from their environment, have developed specific forms of knowledge production, knowledge utilization and innovation, and which are oriented toward specific purposes in society and economy."[37]

There are many examples that, strictly speaking, do not conform to the original "disruptive technologies" framework developed by Christensen.[38] The case of Uber, which started in high-end markets, is an illustration of the need to broaden the analytic framework for market disruption without the need to stretch Christensen's definition beyond its original meaning. The process of market niche expansion is sufficiently complex as to demand openness in analytical approaches to suit different research purposes.

The challenge, however, is to extend the logic of disruption from specific technologies to the wider society to illuminate the tensions between innovation and incumbency. This entails adopting open approaches that do not distinguish between sociotechnical and innovation systems and the environment in which they are embedded. Through improvement and marketing, some new technologies move up the performance ladder to eventually become dominant by displacing previous technologies. But they do more than just replace incumbent technologies. They reorder the socioeconomic terrain by coevolving with new institutional arrangements and organizational structures. It is this wider societal transformation that generates tensions between innovation and incumbency. For this reason the book will focus on transformational innovation because of its wider societal impact. This may or may not incorporate disruptive technologies as defined by Christensen and other formulations of sociotechnical systems. In fact, in most cases the impetus for transformative innovation arises from disruptive technologies. But there are other sources of transformation that do not conform to the Christensen formulation. All references to innovation in this book, unless stated otherwise, will be assumed to be transformational in the sense of Schumpeterian "creative destruction."

There is a classical outlook that simply defines institutions as the glue that keeps society together. This static view ignores the role that institutions play in the process of innovation, especially in the complex and dynamic interactions between technology, engineering, and society. A functional view of the role of institutions in innovation reveals distinct activities that include providing information and reducing uncertainty, managing conflicts and cooperation, providing incentives for action, channeling resources, and maintaining continuity.[39]

Social institutions perform at least six major functions. The first is to enable society to *adapt to change*. This is often achieved through the generation and diffusion of new knowledge and technologies. Institutions that promote innovation therefore play a critical role in socioeconomic evolution.

Society undertakes a variety of tasks to survive. These range from producing food to maintaining national security. Doing so involves considerable coordination. Thus, the second function of social institutions is to *coordinate* activities and promote cooperation among divergent actors to achieve specific goals. Such tasks are implemented through specific organizations ranging from government ministries to private enterprises.

Coordination involves bringing together individuals with diverse knowledge, skills, interests, and perspectives to achieve a specific task. But the requisite diversity needed to guarantee success is often a source of conflict among different actors. Society therefore designs a third function of institutions—*managing conflict* between different actors.

Not much can be achieved without the availability of resources, of which human capabilities and finance are among the most prominent. To get things done, every society creates institutions whose main function is to generate, mobilize, and *allocate necessary resources*. Among the most common of such institutions are funding agencies that allocate resources to support research in emerging fields.

But having resources is not enough to motivate people to perform at the highest level. To achieve this, society creates institutions with the fifth function of providing the *incentive* needed to achieve certain goals. Such incentives could take the form of intellectual property rights, rebates for research funding, or prizes given to pioneers in fields of social relevance.

When society develops practices that guarantee its survival, there is considerable pressure to ensure that they are reproduced as widely as possible and last from generation to generation. *Maintenance of continuity* is the final function of institutions. The rule of law, policing, housing codes, and a variety of social customs are examples of institutions designed to maintain continuity. One of the main outcomes of maintaining continuity is the phenomenon of path dependence or lock-in, where past events tend to define the trajectory of future developments.[40] The associated inertia in the political system sets the stage for tensions between those promoting innovation through the generation of novelty and incumbent forces seeking to maintain the continuity of the status quo.[41]

Most of the functions outlined above are in fact complementary and are implemented through organizations created to perform certain functions. All of them, for example, fall within the job descriptions of various managers in corporations or government departments. At a wider societal level, however, the need to adapt to change through innovation and the pressure to maintain continuity are sources of considerable tension. By definition, innovation seeks to reorder society. It quickly comes in conflict with the need to maintain continuity. This book explores the tensions arising from the two functions. The institutional uncertainties resulting from transformational change often lead to public debates. Society does not oppose change as such, but its concerns over new technologies are a result of perceptions of loss arising from innovation. New technologies present uncertain futures that could reorder the distribution of benefits and losses among individuals and social groups.

The role of technology in society is the subject of extensive discussion and confusion. As defined by W. Brian Arthur in *The Nature of Technology*, technology can be viewed in at least three hierarchical ways. First, it is simply a way by which human beings leverage natural phenomena to meet human needs.[42] Such phenomena can range from stimulants in plants to gravity to magnetism. Flight, for example, is achieved through the combined application of phenomena such as thrust, lift, and gravity. The discovery that rotating a magnet in the middle of a wire coil generates electricity has resulted in the creation of new industries that were unimaginable before the phenomenon was observed.

Second, technology can be understood as a collection of assemblies that form functioning systems. An airplane, for example, is a collection of assemblies for systems and associated subsystems. Each of the subsystems leverages certain natural phenomena that are brought together to achieve a certain function.[43]

Finally, technology exists as "the entire *collection of devices and engineering practices available to a culture.*"[44] The aviation industry meets the human need for travel, but it is also a collection of a wide range of physical assemblies and institutional arrangements. Human needs inspire the search for new technological solutions. Conversely, new technologies lead to the emergence of new needs. The simple rules about demand and supply do not apply neatly in dynamic social systems—where new technologies change the character of the economy just as much as the economy leads to the creation of new technological systems.

The emergence of the aviation industry has been a long process by which natural phenomena have been leveraged to create artifacts, which in turn have been used to create industrial systems and subsystems. This process coevolved with the creation of new standards, rules, social norms, and organizations associated with air travel. A wide range of regulatory institutions and organizations have coevolved with the industry at different levels of local, national, and international social organization.

The introduction of flight has coevolved with the aviation industry, which has transformed economies around the world. It displaced other preexisting modes of transportation such as railroads and many associated industries as well as forces of social organization. Innovation is essentially the transformation of the economy through the introduction of new forms of economic organization. The economy is thus the unfolding expression of the underlying technologies.[45]

Viewed this way, technologies can exist in laboratories or museums independently of the economy, irrespective of whether they were developed in response to social needs. However, economies cannot exist independently of the technological assemblies created to meet human needs. New technologies often bring with them new forms of socioeconomic organization. Technology, the economy, and the associated institutions coevolve as integrated systems. Change in technology often requires complementary changes in social institutions.

Understanding the coevolutionary dynamics associated with technological and economic change is essential for grasping the forces that influence socioeconomic inertia and skepticism about new technologies. A traditional farming economy is an assembly of technological systems and social organization that largely perpetuates itself, generating only relatively slow change. The replacement of basic farm implements with a tractor is not a simple act of technological substitution but a radical reorganization of the overall socioeconomic system. The adoption of the tractor coevolves with new industries and social institutions.

Social Responses to Innovation

Intuitive Factors

The adoption of new technologies is largely a process of social learning. Public education plays an important role in determining the pace and patterns of adoption. Public perceptions about the benefits and risks of new technologies cannot be fully understood without paying attention to intuitive aspects of human psychology. Advocates of new technologies have tended to focus largely on scientific and technical matters. There is growing evidence, however, that "intuitive expectations about the world render the human mind vulnerable to particular misinterpretations" of new technologies.[46] In the absence of relevant reference points or trusted authorities, individuals tend to fall back on intuitive responses that appear irrational but reflect patterns of automatic behavior that rely on deeper evolutionary roots of our fears and phobias.[47]

Such intuitive responses to new technologies are often reinforced by social norms of disgust that have evolved among people as self-protection from contact with potential sources of pathogens.[48] This behavior readily extends to new technologies such as new foods that may be seen as potentially threatening to human health. Or it may be extended to the moral level to provide norms that protect society in general.[49] Society may also automatically question new technologies on the basis of their essential attributes, which are considered wholesome. In other cases new technologies may elicit negative responses because they appear to challenge the perceptive view of the natural world or the intentionality of parts of it. Arguments against "playing God" fall in this latter category.[50]

There may be cultural concern that a new technology is impure or dangerous because it does not fit into accepted social or ecological patterns.[51] It is treated with initial caution partly because of the lack of knowledge about how to control it. Such technologies are generally considered monsters. Notions of purity and danger have found their way into many aspects of risk management. This is particularly true in the food sector, which has had a long history of "pure foods" movements.[52] Much of the opposition to the use of chemicals in agriculture is also rooted in the appeal to purity. To a large extent the introduction of new technologies over which society does not appear to have full control is perceived and treated as the domestication of monsters.[53]

These deeply rooted psychological and cultural factors frame the initial response to new technologies. They serve as the foundations upon which socioeconomic factors are articulated. It is possible to undertake acceptable calculations of risks and demonstrate that they are negligible. But the real discrepancies between acceptable scientific risks and the adoption of new products cannot be addressed simply by providing additional information or logical reasoning.

Dismissing new products as "irrational" does not help either. It has been demonstrated that trying to counter myths or use scientific evidence on a community that is relying on such psychological or cultural responses only helps to entrench prior beliefs.[54] Furthermore, beliefs that may appear irrational or be classified as pseudoscience tend to tap into cognitive intuitions in ways evidence-based positions do not. Indeed, pseudoscience "can achieve widespread acceptance by tapping into evolved cognitive mechanisms, thus sacrificing intellectual integrity for intuitive appeal. Science, by contrast, defies those deeply held intuitions precisely because it is institutionally arranged to track objective patterns in the world, and the world does not care much about our intuitions."[55]

Vested Interests

One vivid historical account of the tensions over innovation is illustrated by the case of Luddites in England.[56] In fact, concerns about mechanization predate the Luddites.[57] The popular narrative portrays Luddites as machine breakers who were simply opposed to change. But the situation was more complex than just opposition to new technology—it represented a clash of competing economic worldviews and moral values.[58] In many cases responses to new technologies depend on the extent to which they transform or reinforce established worldviews, values, or doctrines. This is as true of the wider society as it is within sections of society, such as the military, where technologies coevolve with specific doctrines as well as organizational structures.[59] Attempts to change existing technologies are likely to encourage opposition irrespective of their obvious benefits.[60]

The story of the Luddites captures the systemic nature of technological transformation. The introduction of labor-saving weaving machinery in Britain during the Industrial Revolution resulted in violent opposition from textile artisans. The new machinery allowed employers to replace high-skilled textile artisans with cheaper low-skilled labor. Fearing the loss of their livelihoods, textile artisans throughout Britain destroyed weaving machinery and other parts of their employers' property, beginning in 1811 in Nottingham. The goal of this "collective bargaining by riot" was to force the end of mechanization in the textile industry.[61]

General public sentiment at the time opposed both the new machinery and the replacement of high-skilled workers with low-skilled labor in Britain, which made it possible for the Luddites to slow down the mechanization process. Public opposition to weaving machines came from various parts of society, such as shop owners and other businessmen who feared that the replacement of labor with machinery and the emergence of large factories would not be limited to the textile industry but would spill over to their industries as well. Prior to the Industrial Revolution, the British economy consisted mainly of small, independent, domestic businesses scattered across the country.[62]

In spite of public opposition, the new weaving technology achieved market penetration through gradual increases in government support for profit-seeking entrepreneurs. Ad hoc laws and court rulings increasingly favored entrepreneurs and employers rather than workers, so that by the late 1860s the new weaving machinery and textile factories had become commonplace. Though not effective on a large scale, the riots slowed down the mechanization of the textile industry and built solidarity among workers, laying the foundation for labor unions in Britain.[63] This case illustrates that tensions over new technologies often originate from fear of system-wide impacts and the associated uncertainties in complex economic systems.[64]

The dynamics of the debate during the Industrial Revolution are echoed in today's discourses in fields such as nuclear power, information technology, biotechnology, and artificial intelligence.[65] The common view that resistance to new technology is futile is a misreading of history. Only a small proportion of new technologies reach the market. There are many factors that influence the process of technology adoption.

Schumpeter pioneered the application of complex systems thinking to economic development. He was interested in change over time, which is why he adopted an evolutionary approach that recognized the importance of history. Schumpeter applied complexity thinking and put change in an evolutionary context. In contrast, his critics used economic models that relied on static equilibrium notions even though in practice they sought to depart from them. He said, "It is not possible to explain *economic* change by previous *economic* conditions alone. For the economic state of a people does not emerge simply from the preceding economic conditions, but only from the preceding total situation."[66]

Also evident in this formulation is the fact that economic evolution is a nonlinear or discontinuous process with emergent properties. Schumpeter saw "that kind of change arising from within the system *which so displaces its equilibrium point that the new one cannot be reached from the old one by infinitesimal steps.* Add successively as many mail coaches as you please, you will never get a railway thereby."[67] This theme is explicit in his notion of the generation of variety through new combinations as well as their selection and retention.

A systems approach would make it easier, both conceptually and practically, to address the ecological implications of development.

So far the dominant approaches to environmental issues come from the traditional conservation movement that assumes that the environment is better protected by excluding human activities. Efforts to promote sustainable development can hardly be advanced without a greater use of innovation.[68]

Economies are self-organizing systems that seek to preserve themselves by precluding transformative ideas.[69] This is necessary to prevent the system from devolving into chaos. Indeed, Darwinian selection requires that not every mutation be tried. Limiting selection, however, is not always optimal, as favorable mutations will sometimes be overlooked. Technological systems, such as economies and all cultural systems, have some built-in stability, but every self-organizing system has "mechanisms that can overcome or fool the forces of inertia."[70] Such inertia also applies to fundamental intellectual constructs, as demonstrated in the long history of resistance to basic concepts such as the number zero, which was considered "so abhorrent to some cultures that they chose to live without it."[71] For most cultures the idea of zero clashed with the deeply held view that there was no void. As the British mathematician and philosopher Alfred North Whitehead put it, the "point about zero is that we do not need to use it in our daily operations. No one goes out to buy zero fish."[72] For many traditional cultures the idea of zero also denoted the ultimate exclusion or impoverishment. It did not sit well with the traditional sense of community and belonging.

The fundamental question, then, is one of overcoming forces of inertia. Free-market economies are generally better at overcoming these forces than are command economies because "centralized bureaucracies . . . breed conformity."[73] The challenge lies in balancing between the long-term benefits arising from innovation and the short-term benefits of maintaining the status quo. Both carry risks, and the final outcome cannot be readily derived from an assessment of contemporary technological options. Innovation is by definition an unfolding process whose outcomes are uncertain.

Because they are uncertain, they can go either way. This explains to some degree why technological debates may take generations to settle. The debates are largely about the final outcomes, with the processes of debate being an attempt to anticipate how the risks and benefits are likely to be distributed in the end. The current debate over the potential impact of robots on employment illustrates this sense of uncertainty, reflecting both anxiety and promise.

Much of the concern over new technology derives from the workforce, where changes to technology hurt those who may have accumulated status and prestige, and from employers who fear "having to run to stay in place."[74] While economic factors underlie most negative responses to innovation, objections are usually expressed through nonmarket mechanisms (e.g., legal mechanisms such as regulatory capture and safety regulations, as well as extralegal means such as arson, personal violence, and riots), with some anticompetitive market behavior (e.g., denial of credit to innovators and entrepreneurs).

Three elements typically affect the likelihood of an innovation succeeding. First is the intensity of the motivation: that is, the more valuable the thing being made obsolete, the stronger the challenge to the innovation; or the greater the benefit of the innovation to society, the more the innovation is promoted. A historical example of this is tension over the printing press by the scribes' guilds in the 1460s. "As the social benefits were vast and the scribes did have presumably alternative occupations as clerks, challenges to printing did not last long. Yet the printers' guilds that protected the new status quo were far more powerful and managed to freeze printing technology until the Industrial Revolution. As late as 1772, the Basel master printers' guilds legally restrained Wilhelm Haas from constructing a heavier press made of metal parts."[75]

The second element concerns the distribution of winners and losers. While producers are usually concentrated, consumers tend to be more widely distributed. Such a structure may confer more benefits to the producers, but it also exposes them to collective action by consumer groups. A contemporary example is the seed sector, which is dominated by a few large firms serving diverse markets of farmers. Challenges to agricultural biotechnology were championed by other groups, not directly by the farmers themselves.[76]

Finally, the role of authority is an important factor in technological controversies. Whether the authority favors the status quo or the new innovation has significant implications—take, for example, France's shift from protectionism of the ancien régime (1730) to a protechnology approach (1830). In France, large trade organizations (*compagnonnages*) controlled means of production and challenged innovation, using extralegal means to successfully deter innovation in industries such as papermaking and the manufacturing of muskets and flatware. As a result they drove innovators to Britain or the United States.[77]

Another example of the role of authority in technological controversies comprised attempts by "practical electricians" in the late 1880s to suppress James Maxwell's equation of electrodynamics. In the clash, intellectual authority shifted from "practical" men who believed that electricity flowed through wires the way water flowed through pipes to theoretical mathematicians whose experiments showed that electricity flowed in a field around the conducting wire. Suppressing publications by Maxwellians did little to undermine the power of theories expressed through new electrical applications, and experiments by luminaries such as Heinrich Hertz. Finally, authority shifted to academically trained electrical engineers.[78]

Another example of the clash of authority involved fifteen years of opposition to obstetric anesthesia. Opponents of the technology advanced a variety of arguments despite the gruesome practices of childbirth at the time. The main reasons for the opposition were physiological and focused on the role of pain. Some eminent surgeons claimed that pain served as a survival mechanism as well as a diagnostic signal to help surgeons determine how far labor had progressed. Other objections were nonmedical and centered on moral grounds: "Analogies with drunkenness, references to the freeing of sexual inhibitions under anaesthesia, and chauvinistic appeals to men's views on how they would like their own wives to behave, formed the bases of the 'moral' approach."[79] In the end, the scientific appeal of anesthesia prevailed.[80]

Intellectual Responses

There are at least four sources of intellectual challenges to technological change, identified by risk aversion, negative externalities, correlation between technology and political and social uses, and philosophical objection to the manipulation of nature for human benefit.[81]

The first intellectual challenge is risk aversion. Some technologies, such as asbestos, have turned out to be harmful, with higher ex post costs than benefits. Thus some intellectual movements cite safety concerns as a reason to push back against new technologies, stressing uncertainty and possibilities of unknown risks. The overall assumption underlying such concerns is that most of the unintended consequences of new technologies are likely to be negative.[82]

Negative externalities comprise the second type of intellectual challenge: the assumption that new technologies use too many natural resources and require assignment of property rights to goods previously treated as free. One of the most ambitious global efforts to address negative externalities is emissions trading, which was enshrined in the Kyoto Protocol to the United Nations Framework Convention on Climate Change. The treaty has been likened by some to a form of enclosure that creates a new market out of climate change, which is considered a serious source of global economic damage.[83] Technological innovation, on the other hand, can help solve such negative externalities. An example of such an approach is the creation of an international regime on reducing ozone-depleting substances through international technology and engineering cooperation.[84]

Third, there is a correlation between technology and both political and social uses: weapons are more destructive, therefore more lives are taken; the development of the assembly line caused work to become boring and rote; and technology and engineering are often associated with foreign domination. The uncertain nature of technological applications therefore creates both anxiety and promise, which are magnified by the power of the technology and engineering. Today there is intense debate over the military use of drones,[85] but the same technology is increasingly being deployed for humanitarian as well as civilian applications.

Fourth, the medieval and Renaissance eras saw a rise in human exploitation of natural resources, which evolved into a concern for future generations. The intellectual movement in Victorian Britain saw technology as "dehumanizing," leading to the reification of pastoral and peasant life in medieval Europe. Some of these views persist today. They have found refuge in sections of the environmental movement that assert that nature is better preserved by excluding human activity.[86] Proponents of this view maintain that rapid technological innovation is the main source of ecological degradation and that efforts should be made to slow it down. This view, though credible at face value, confuses technological advancement with the impacts of specific technologies. A rigid adherence to the view would preclude the use of technology and engineering in key areas where it is essential for environmental management. For example, chemistry has given the world industries that have resulted in ecological damage. But many of the same scientific foundations are now being used in "green chemistry."

Sociopsychological Factors

Psychological challenge to innovation is not a rational process. Contrary to what classical economics long assumed, people do not conduct a rational assessment of the risks and benefits associated with each new technology and make a decision based on that analysis. Instead, decisions are made in the face of uncertainty with the help of mental shortcuts or established routines.[87] The biases that result from these shortcuts often give rise to decisions that are considered irrational in hindsight. Decisions about whether or not to adopt new technologies that are often associated with risks and uncertainty are subject to these biases.

Research into the psychology of decisionmaking and behavioral economics has identified three main factors that drive psychological challenge to innovation: people's reluctance to break out of existing habits or routines; the perceived risks associated with innovation; and public attitudes toward the technology in question.

Humans are creatures of habit. Most everyday decisions are based on habits that are sustained without being consciously noticed. Bad habits, such as smoking or overeating, can be changed through repeatedly engaging in the more desired behavior and gradually replacing the old bad habit with a new one. Moreover, most habits are based on social norms. When perception of the norms that govern our social environment changes, so do the habits that are based on these perceptions. For example, in 1984, 86 percent of Americans did not regularly wear seatbelts. In 2010, 85 percent of Americans did buckle up on a regular basis. The reason for this complete reversal of habit was that societal norms regarding personal safety in traffic changed. This change was aided by the enforcement of stricter legislation and safety campaigns in some states.[88]

New technologies encounter more challenges based on both how many of our existing habits they promise to alter and the strength of these habits. Lasting behavioral change must occur through existing habits rather than attempts to alter them. People are likely to adopt innovations only if they improve rather than destroy their existing habits, in the same way that electronic calculators made mathematical computations faster. Thus, public policy should encourage behavioral change by targeting the least-ingrained habits.[89] For example, developing countries could encourage increased protein consumption by offering new high-protein beverages rather than new types of high-protein foods.

The second major factor that leads to challenges to innovation is the perceived risks associated with the new technology. Three common types of risks that are particularly important in this context are aversion to physical, social, or economic consequences of the new technology; performance uncertainty; and perceived side effects. Innovation that has the highest perceived risks and aims to alter the strongest habits usually faces the biggest challenge. Social programs that aim to alter people's choices regarding health and nutrition fall into this category. The most radical technological innovations, on the other hand, are challenged because of the high risks associated with them. They encourage us to form new habits rather than break existing ones.[90]

People have a strong tendency to avoid risks. According to prospect theory, potential losses always loom larger than potential gains.[91] In general, people are more risk seeking when the outcomes of their choices are expressed in terms of what they will gain rather than in terms of what they will lose. Thus the fear of loss leads people to make risk-averse choices, while when faced with potential gains, they tend to make more risk-seeking choices. This is because people make decisions based on the perceived value of a potential gain or loss compared to the current situation (i.e., reference point), rather than solely based on the absolute value of each outcome. These decisions are not solely based on expected value calculations for each outcome but on losses and gains that are triggered by different expression of outcomes.[92]

These insights into people's failure to make decisions in accordance with classical economic models of expected utility form one of the foundations for the field of behavioral economics. Risks and potential losses associated with new technologies often loom much larger than the potential benefits, leading to challenges to innovation.

The tendency to place more weight on potential losses than potential gains leads to two common behavioral biases that explain the frequent failure to adopt new technologies. The first is "status quo bias" and the second is "omission bias."[93] The former describes the disproportionate tendency to stick with the status quo when choosing between alternatives.[94] For example, when asked to decide whether or not to participate in an organ donation program, offering the default option "yes" on the relevant insurance forms produces much higher participation rates than offering "no" as the default option and asking people to take action through opting into the program.[95] New technologies that alter not only social habits but also what is perceived to be the status quo lead to negative responses because they threaten the customs that people have grown comfortable with.

Loss aversion also causes people to underestimate the risks of doing nothing and sticking with the status quo. The tendency to favor inaction over action is called omission bias. This bias prevails even when people know the outcomes of omission and commission. For example, people tend to think that it is worse to vaccinate a child when the vaccination could cause harm than not to vaccinate, even though delivering the vaccination could significantly reduce the risk of harm through disease to the overall population and probably to the individual child as well. People report that by deciding to deliver a vaccination that has a small probability of harm, they would feel as if they caused death if the negative side effects occurred.[96]

Harm that results from taking action seems to produce greater feelings of regret and responsibility than identical harm that results from doing nothing. People are not always subject to this bias, however. In fact, they tend to be too quick rather than too reluctant to act when they are in positions of responsibility.[97] However, especially in the political process surrounding innovations such as vaccinations or transgenic organisms, a few people who value omission over commission can obstruct the advancement of innovations and hinder the social cooperation necessary for their adoption.

People seem to put more effort into reducing risk when the risk is relatively unknown and small, as is the case for transgenic organisms, than when the risk is well known and large, as in the case of radon.[98] In other words, people evaluate risk cognitively but react emotionally.[99] This speaks to the third key factor that drives skepticism toward innovation: attitudes. Attitudes toward innovations have a cognitive and an affective component. The cognitive component of attitude encompasses our evaluations of the specific aspects of a technology, whereas the affective component describes how much we like the technology overall. People's cognitive attitudes toward the technology predict the extent to which they adopt the technology after short exposure to it, while affective attitudes do not. Attitudes are much easier to change than habits because they are socially contagious. Thus, communication that encourages a positive cognitive approach to new technologies—for example, through emphasizing benefits of specific aspects of the technology—can increase the likelihood that people will accept the technology.[100]

It follows that challenges to innovation can be reduced by three psychological factors. First, new ideas are more easily adopted if they work through existing or entirely new habits rather than attempt to break existing ones. Second, framing the potential outcomes of new technologies in terms of gains or losses has a significant impact on whether loss aversion will produce risk-seeking or risk-avoiding behavior.[101] Third, people are more likely to adopt a new technology when communication encourages positive attitudes toward it—for example, by empha-sizing the concrete benefits of specific aspects of the technology.

An equally important psychological factor in defining the chal-lenge to new technologies is political empathy. Social movements use framing as "strategic versions of reality for mobilizing audi-ences, conferring meanings that include causes and solutions."[102] Political empathy not only helps social movements to focus atten-tion on victimization but also creates a basis to mobilize support from other fields that share common concerns. Political empathy has in recent years made it possible for opponents and proponents of new technologies in specific locations to use social media and other information and communications tools to create global movements.

Innovation, Uncertainty, and Loss

Technologies are often associated with competing claims about their economic impacts. In many cases new technologies are exces-sively touted by their promoters, while critics maintain skepticism. Underlying such claims is a usual state of uncertainty that makes it difficult to predict the ultimate evolution of the technology and its socioeconomic impacts. The inability to foresee the long-term impacts of new technologies often arises from the narrowness with which they are defined and often fails to account for factors such as future improvements, innovations in complementary technologies, influences on the emergence of new technological systems, and the development of new applications.[103] The confluence of these factors makes it difficult to predict the pace, direction, and impact of new technologies.

One of the ways to deal with uncertainties associated with new technologies is to conduct economic impact studies, often in comparison with existing technologies. Such studies, however, often ignore the scope for improvement, while the prospects for improving new technologies are potentially large because they are usually in their infancy when studied. Such comparisons may therefore understate the long-term impacts of new technologies. Indeed, the promise of new technologies over existing ones lies largely in the long-term prospects for improvement, not necessarily in the initial technical or economic advantages.

Probably one of the most critical aspects of uncertainty is the failure to see the potential for widespread or universal applications. The successful adoption of gas-powered trucks instead of electric trucks in the United States was closely associated with their universal applicability. Supportive factors such as military procurement made a difference, but such measures were possible precisely because the technology was suited to a wide range of applications beyond urban trucking activities.[104] Perceptions about universal applicability not only shape the emergence of supportive institutions but also influence initial commitments to specific technological directions.

Perceptions regarding universal applicability played an important role in the displacement of gas by electricity in Britain, but not without adaptive responses by the gas industry. In the 1930s, gas power was still used in a majority of homes despite the availability of electricity. A wide range of socioeconomic institutions had emerged over time to support the integration of the gas supply into society. Installing mains for electricity was a viable option only for the wealthy few, thus preserving the gas market.

Gas companies, however, were concerned about the possible erosion of their market with the advent of electrical appliances, whose emergence and diffusion they could neither predict nor control. But when appliances emerged, the gas industry sought to respond with a competing product.

The gas company responded to the electrical radio—which at that time required the use of an unwieldy lead-acid accumulator that had to be taken to a store to be recharged—by producing a gas-powered version. Attaix (Southampton, England) sold a current-generating device based on the thermoelectric effect. The difference in temperatures between the two ends of a circuit generated a current that powered the appliance. The output was modest but sufficient to power radios of that time. By 1939, the integrated gas-powered radio became available. Henry Milnes of the Milnes Electrical Engineering Company produced radios that contained thermoelectric generators inside the same cabinet as the speakers and radio. Gas radios were cheaper than electric radios, and those in the gas industry used this fact to market their product as being more accessible. In addition, they promoted the heating capability of the gas radio.[105]

Following this trend, other appliances were developed to use gas, including the washing machine, dishwasher, gramophone, and vacuum cleaner. What was most important was not selling more gas but preventing the diffusion of electricity. As electrical appliances become more prolific, however, it became increasingly important to have electricity in the house, which entailed increased production and the creation of grid networks that helped to reduce the cost of power generation. Ultimately, electricity prevailed as the most practical energy source. Gas-powered appliances never found popular use.

The ability to identify emerging technological opportunities and harness their benefits is an essential aspect of entrepreneurship, business development, and public policy. New technologies may initially appear to be unreliable and prone to failure, which may in turn result in unfavorable public perceptions. For example, early tractors were not as reliable as horses in the same way that early muskets were inferior to the crossbow. But in both cases the potential for technological improvement favored the adoption of seemingly inferior but nascent technologies with steep but rewarding learning curves ahead of them. This is the essential feature of technological succession and creative destruction.[106]

Economic comparisons between emerging and incumbent technologies are therefore not very helpful because they often fail to account for the potential for improvement in new technologies.

Put another way, the marginal benefits of investment in improving emerging technologies are likely to be higher than in their traditional counterparts. Engineers could upgrade tractors faster than breeders could improve horse performance. What is important, therefore, is to adopt business strategies and policies that take into account the importance of emerging technological opportunities.

What often appears as technological competition may lead to technological convergence, thus giving incumbent technologies new markets. The advent of television, for example, was seen as a replacement of radio broadcasting. The rise of the Internet, on the other hand, resulted in activities such as podcasting that saw radio broadcasting migrate to the Web. This convergence resulted in new business opportunities as well as novel institutional arrangements.[107]

Technological risks are becoming part of the public discourse worldwide. New technologies are credited with the creation of new industrial opportunities but also with the destruction of the status quo. While investors focus on the benefits of new technologies, others worry about their risks. Modern concerns range from perceived risks of new technologies on human health, such as transgenic foods and mobile phones, to wider fears about the impact of technology on society. In the past, technological risks were confined to countries in which new technologies emerged or even to specific sectors where they were applied.

Concerns in the 1970s over the use of microprocessors in industry were restricted to the possible impact on labor displacement in the manufacturing sectors. Workers and labor organizations around the world protested the use of this emerging technology. Echoes of these debates are heard today in discussions on "de-skilling" of the labor force and erosion of human capital. "The opportunities for conflict are much wider when we consider human capital. Skills and experience are acquired over a lifetime, but the ability to learn new skills declines over the life cycle. Workers beyond the student or apprentice stage can be expected to question new techniques insofar as innovation makes their skills obsolete and thus irreversibly reduces their expected lifespan earnings."[108] Fear that using computers as educational tools in schools would displace teachers is still in public consciousness, despite the rapid adoption of this technology for teaching purposes.

Although interest in the impact of microelectronics on employment was expressed in many parts of the world, it did not become a mass movement involving a wide range of social groups for at least two reasons. First, discussions on the risks of job displacement were accompanied by consideration of the benefits of raising industrial productivity. The shifts were also associated with changes in the power of workers.[109] Second, the global economy was not as integrated as it is today, and many of these debates were localized to countries, industries, or regions. Globalization, however, has changed that and has created international forms of organized challenges to innovation.[110] Globalization gives technological risk a wider meaning and turns seemingly local debates over certain products into mass movements.

Challenges to new technologies are not limited to consumers or workers. There are numerous examples where enterprises have suppressed their own technologies because they threaten incumbent product lines. For example, in the early 1930s Bell Labs developed and used a highly advanced magnetic audio recording system.[111] But senior management suppressed its commercialization for more than a decade because they feared that its use would make customers reluctant to use their telephone system. This would then undercut Bell Labs' "universal service" concept.

The fear was expressed in two ways. "First, if conversations became matters of record in the same way as letters or other contracts, managers felt that customers would abandon the telephone for critical negotiations and return to the mail, where a slip of the tongue would not prove fatal."[112] Second, "If conversations could be recorded, matters of an illegal or immoral nature, which some executives estimated made up as much as one third of all calls, would no longer be discussed by phone. The net result of this perceived loss of privacy would be a great reduction in the number of calls and a reduction in the trust individuals placed in the phone system, meaning a loss in both revenue and prestige for AT&T."[113]

The firm was clearly unwilling to let the modest benefits of magnetic recording undermine its reputation and trust among consumers. It is notable that these decisions were made during a period of great public concern over privacy following the 1928 US Supreme Court's ruling in *Olmstead v. United States* that wiretapping was legal, a decision that was overturned in 1967 in *Katz v. United States*. This example illustrates that uncertainty and associated anxieties can lead to decisions to delay or suppress the introduction of new technologies. This is particularly true when people perceive that such uncertainties can result in loss of income, identity, sense of community, worldview, and privacy.

Conclusions

This chapter has sought to articulate a view of both technological success and challenges to innovation that builds on Schumpeter's seminal concept of creative destruction. The kinds of technological transitions needed to address today's global grand challenges will inherently build on rapid momentum generated by exponential growth in scientific and technological knowledge. The pace and scope of such transformation will most likely trigger societal responses aimed at maintaining the status quo. The dynamics are as much technological as they are political. In fact, understanding and seeking to resolve the tensions require an explicit application of political thought as illustrated by the drama surrounding the transition to low-carbon energy sources.[114]

The ensuing tensions between innovation and incumbency are often associated with public debates about technological succession. These dynamics are not unique to technological change but reflect the very nature of cultural change itself. They have been widely documented and discussed in other fields such as the succession of scientific paradigms.[115]

The rest of this book looks back in history to identify lessons than can generate heuristic devices for addressing future technological controversies. The aim is not to provide templates for action, but to stimulate intellectual curiosity so that current and future generations can have historical reference points as they seek to solve their own problems. History does not repeat itself, but its echoes can be heard all around us. The aim of the following chapters is to amplify the echo so that readers can decide which of the narratives might be suitable sources of inspiration for their own creative responses to the challenges they currently face. The case studies show how new technologies coevolve with the wider environment. They create the conditions for their own niche survival and expansion. The tensions between innovation and incumbency are echoes of this dynamic interplay.

2

Brewing Trouble

Coffee

Every great movement must experience three stages: Ridicule, discussion, adoption.

JOHN STUART MILL

In 2003 the Department of Pharmacy at the Italian University of Federico II di Napoli hosted an unusual mock trial. The accused was coffee. The trial in the southern Italian town of Naples sought to settle a long-standing dispute: is drinking coffee good or bad for one's health? Some argue that coffee protects against some diseases, while others claim it leads to "impotence, anxiety and insomnia."[1]

Law professors from various Italian universities presided over the case in a city where coffee has cult status. Twelve expert witnesses from health and culinary fields testified. After the professors did a quick review of the evidence, they cleared coffee of all charges but ordered users to moderate consumption. The Italian judge presiding over the court, Dini Cristiani, "explained that coffee had been redeemed by the stimulating effect it has on the brain, limiting tiredness, and making people more productive, thus counteracting the disruptive effect of the number of breaks it encourages during the working day."[2]

Behind this seemingly comedic lawsuit is recapitulation of one of history's oldest examples of the tension between technological innovation and incumbency. Coffee is one of the world's oldest transformative innovations. Today coffee beans are one of the most important tropical export commodities providing livelihoods for millions of people. It has become an integral part of most cultures around the world. Yet debates over the benefits and risks to consuming the beverage continue to appear frequently in medical journals.

This chapter sets the stage for deeper examination of tension between innovation and socioeconomic incumbency as reflected in the defense of preexisting products and their place in cultural ecologies, using coffee as a case study. The introduction of coffee transformed the complex social fabrics that were woven together by earlier beverages such as wine and beer. Coffee tore their economies apart and served as a purveyor to new routines and new business practices. These ranged from the creation of global coffee chains such as Starbucks Coffee to niche coffee roasters. The public response to the change coffee brought ranged from demonization, bans, and restrictions on trade to novel compromises between competing business interests. Since the fifteenth century coffee has been the subject of extensive legislative interventions, and debates about its impacts on human health rage on today. Behind this seemingly innocent beverage lies one of the world's most colorful technological controversies that spanned centuries and continents.

Grounds for Concern

The story of coffee shows how new innovations coevolve with social institutions that they disrupt and recreate. It also plays to Joseph Schumpeter's rejection of the equilibrium outlook of economic life. He took the rather controversial view that "all change in consumers' tastes is incidental to, and brought about by, producers' actions."[3] Coffee (*Coffea arabica*), native to the highlands of Ethiopia, is such an example. Coffee was used by Ethiopian people for centuries.[4] Most likely this was in the form of whole berries or leaves rather than beans. Its unique addictive properties set it apart from other stimulants. Unlike many other beverages, coffee was consumed largely in the open and not in the privacy of one's home, thereby creating public spaces that fostered social interaction, a phenomenon that continues today.[5] Machines needed to prepare coffee evolved over time and were mostly located in coffeehouses. Technological innovation played a key role in its rise as a beverage. Coffee is literally a manufactured product. "An infusion from green coffee has a decidedly unpleasant taste and hardly any color. Likewise, an underdone roast has a disagreeable 'grassy' flavor; while an overdone roast gives a charred taste."[6]

Social tensions have been a hallmark in this history of coffee's spread from Ethiopia to the Middle East and Western Europe. In his monumental work *All About Coffee*, Ukers says that wherever the drink was introduced, upheavals followed. "It has been the world's most radical drink in that its function has been to make people think. And when the people began to think, they became dangerous to tyrants and to foes of liberty of thought and action."[7] One of the most vivid descriptions of coffee as an *agent agitateur* was written in the 1830s by the French novelist Honoré de Balzac, possibly with the help of the beverage itself:

> Ideas surge forth like battalions of a great army on the field of battle and the combat begins. Memories attack with their banners unfurled. The light cavalry of comparisons develops at a magnificent gallop. The artillery of logic comes to the rescue with its artillerymen and shells. Witticisms appear as sharpshooters. Figures begin to take shape. The paper covers itself with ink, since for the evening begins and ends in torrents of black liquid, just like battlefields in gunpowder.[8]

Coffee consumption stimulated technological innovation in the roasting, grinding, brewing, filtering, and serving of the beverage. With the new technologies and increased consumption also came new manners and customs. The kinds of social interactions it generated helped to imbue civility in society, as opposed to the rowdiness that was often associated with alcohol consumption.[9] The growth of coffeehouses also helped to create spaces for political discourse.[10]

Coffee was not just a product made from beans ground for caffeine, but a Schumpeterian innovation that transformed existing practices and institutional arrangements and engendered the creation of new ones. It was in itself a new product that led to new production processes, the creation of new markets, and new organizational changes in its production and sale. It was the impact of the clustering of techniques and institutions that gave coffee the capacity to restructure social systems and threatened to reduce the consumption of other beverages and associated social institutions.

The controversies over the safety and social impacts of coffee consumption therefore go beyond the impact of the beverage itself and include wider socioeconomic transformation. What is notable, however, is that uncertainties over the impact of coffee on human health became a proxy for discussing discontinuities in society arising from the introduction of coffee and coffeehouses. Underlying this narrative is the story of epic competition between coffee and previously existing beverages and the associated sociocultural evolution.

There Is a New Drink in Town

The spread of coffee was to a large extent aided by its addictive properties. In a few centuries the product moved from its native Ethiopia through the Ottoman Empire and eventually to England.

One of the earliest known instances of coffee cultivation occurred in Yemen in the first part of the fifteenth century. By the early sixteenth century, a drink known as *qahwa* was widely consumed by Sufi sheiks. The drink was initially prepared as a stimulating potion from part of the coffee plant, and by the third quarter of the century the beverage was being made from the coffee bean itself. The communal worship services of the Sufis were usually held at night and included practices intended to produce a trance-like concentration on God. Members of the Sufi orders drank coffee to stay awake during their nighttime devotional exercises.[11]

The adoption of coffee in Yemen had been sustained through a series of judicial rulings in the form of fatwas, mostly by an eminent jurist and scholar, Muhamad al-Dhabani. It is reported that al-Dhabani had personally visited Ethiopia and, witnessing coffee's consumption, claimed it was safe. The standing of al-Dhabani diminished the uncertainty over the safety of coffee in its various uses. He had apparently recovered from an illness after using coffee. He reversed many earlier fatwas issued against coffee consumption. His fatwas, however, were based on the principle of original permissibility—*al-ibaha al-asliya*—under which products were considered acceptable until expressly outlawed. Opponents of coffee, most of whom appealed to the teaching of the prophet Muhammad, claimed that new products—*bid'a*—should be viewed as potentially risky until proven safe. The clash between the two doctrines represented the divergent philosophical approaches to innovation. Yet by the time of al-Dhabani's death around 1470, coffee had been established as a beverage in Yemen.

Members of the Sufi orders were not reclusive holy men; most were of the laity and were men of many trades and occupations. Because these men were integrated into the everyday affairs of Yemeni society, coffee rapidly spread to other sectors, mostly by way of example. The coffeehouse was most likely born from the example of the Sufi gatherings, and from there it proliferated. By 1510, coffee had spread from the Yemeni monasteries into general use in Islamic capitals. Traders and travelers soon recognized coffee as a lucrative commodity. They brought coffee beans to Mecca around the last decade of the fifteenth century.

When coffee spread from Yemen to Mecca, it soon generated social tensions. The first principal opponent of coffee in Mecca was Governor Kha'ir Beg al-Mi'mar. On June 21, 1511, a meeting of the town's leading ulema, or religious scholars, was convened to consider the question of coffee, with an early inclination toward banning it because of concerns that coffeehouses would become sources of social fomentation against religious authority. According to one account, two Persian physicians—one of whom was known to have written passionately against coffee—were present to offer medical evidence. The two physicians claimed the beverage was endowed with vile characteristics and said the governor should receive "great glory and abundant rewards" if he opposed the drink, thus appealing to the governor's desire for legitimacy and power as a ruler.[12] The official account of the story simply reports Kha'ir Beg convening the meeting of jurists on the morning following a nighttime encounter with a group of men reportedly drinking *qahwa* near the Great Mosque. At the meeting he argued vociferously in favor of a ban, which the assembly approved.

Following the 1511 meeting, Kha'ir Beg closed down all the coffeehouses in Mecca and proclaimed a universal ban on coffee. Any coffee found was confiscated and burned in the streets, and those who trafficked in it or consumed it were beaten. Prejudiced medical arguments were given to support the ban. *Qahwa* the drink, rather than *bunn* the beans, which were still routinely chewed, came under attack. Jurists argued that the beans, consumed everywhere, were legal, but the drink, consumed in the coffeehouse, was not.

At the time of the ban, the governor of Mecca was subordinate to the sultan of Cairo, who was a coffee drinker.[13] An official decree came from Cairo that overturned the ban and claimed that nobody would be denied entry into heaven because of drinking coffee. The decree also called into question the knowledge of the physicians and jurists who had added their weight to the judgment. The Persian experts lost their lives under suspicious circumstances, and Kha'ir Beg himself was removed from office two years later on charges of corruption, ending the prospects of another ban. The circumstances of his death on his way back to Cairo remain a mystery. The reprieve of attack on coffeehouses, however, was short-lived.

Under subsequent prohibitions, objections were mounted against activities associated with the coffeehouse that were already prohibited by Islamic law (sharia). Those activities included gambling, whoring, use of drugs such as tobacco, opium, and hashish, and musical entertainment purely for the sake of diversion. In 1525–1526, Mecca's coffeehouses came under fire again, this time by jurist Muhammad ibn al'Arraq from Medina. He directed officials to close down the coffeehouses because of the many kinds of "reprehensible" activities taking place there, of which he had heard upon his arrival in Mecca. Coffee itself was not a target because Ibn al'Arraq had explicitly affirmed its legality. This time it was the coffeehouse that was targeted for prohibition. A year later the jurist passed away, and the coffeehouses promptly reopened. His successors weren't inclined to suppress coffee.

Another leading opponent of coffee was the scholar and preacher Ahmad ibn 'Abd al-Haqq al-Sunbati. He declared the *qahwa* drink forbidden based on what he had been told of gatherings in the coffeehouses and on information from those who had drunk it and repented. His opposition to coffee became quite well known, and many of the religious men in Cairo followed his lead as he emerged as the father of the anticoffee faction in Cairo.

In 1534–1535 he delivered a number of fierce sermons on the subject, the strength of which incited a mob to attack several coffeehouses and beat those they found inside. In response those in favor of the caffeinated drink took to the streets, threatening serious civil disturbance and violence. A Hanafi judge decided to take up the issue and ruled in favor of coffee's legality after consultation with members of Cairo's ulema. Coffee eventually became so popular that a covenant was introduced into the Cairo marriage contract, stipulating a husband must provide his wife with an adequate supply of coffee, and failure to do so was grounds for divorce.[14]

Coffee's critics likened the drink to wine and attempted to outlaw it on this basis repeatedly.[15] The coffee euphoria known as *marqaha* was cited as a reason for prohibition under Hanafi law, one of the four Sunni schools. Debate centered on the legal definition of intoxication and its relationship to wine and other beverages prohibited under Islam. The preferred Hanafi interpretation of the law on this matter prohibits only the consumption of an amount of a particular beverage sufficient to cause intoxication—meaning the substance itself is not forbidden, only overindulgence.

The application of the beverage law in the Hanafi school then became dependent on a definition of drunkenness. On this subject Abu Hanifi offered the following interpretation of the drunk: "one whose mind leaves him and who knows nothing at all."[16] This was later expanded by Ibn Nujaym (d. 1563): the "drunk who is to be punished is one who comprehends nothing at all, and who does not know a man from a woman, or the earth from the heavens."[17] Mulla Khusraw (d. 1480) described drunkenness as "a state that afflicts a man with the filling of his brain with vapors that rise up into it, so that his reason, which distinguished between fine things and foul, ceases to function."[18] Whereas other Sunni schools were less generous with their interpretation of the drunk (considering a mild giddiness to be a sign of intoxication), the Hanafis saw the drunk as senseless, one who had lost all reason, and was practically dead on his feet.

Based on this interpretation, it is difficult to imagine that the *marqaha* experience with coffee could ever be classified as intoxication. Al-Sunbati and others nevertheless made the attempt by claiming that coffee was an intoxicant, and any change in the physical or mental state of the drinker (which coffee was certainly guilty of inducing) cast doubt on the legality of the beverage.

Syrian businessmen Hakm and Shams, who were to amass personal fortunes in reward of their efforts, brought coffee to Constantinople for the first time in 1555. By 1570, during the reign of the Ottoman Empire, Selim II (r. 1566–1574), there were no fewer than six hundred coffee establishments in the city (stalls, shops, and full-fledged houses), and Turks of all kinds frequented them. Tensions between this popular new drink and incumbent social institutions closely followed its introduction.

Selim II outlawed the use of coffee shortly after it arrived in Constantinople, but the ban did not last for long.[19] Murad III, sultan of Constantinople, again closed down the city's coffeehouses in 1580 after murdering his entire family in order to claim the throne. It seems that his bloody rise to power was being discussed in the coffeehouses in rather unflattering terms, brewing sedition. The sultan ordered coffee banned, the coffeehouses shuttered, and the former owners tortured. The religious sanction for the prohibition rested on the discovery, by an orthodox sect of dervishes, that the roasted coffee beans showed a striking resemblance to coals, and anything carbonized was forbidden from human consumption by Muhammad. The prohibition drove coffee drinking into the home, but only until the time that Murad's successor declared that roasted coffee was not coal, and the habit once again became public.

Under the rule of Murad IV (r. 1623–1640), however, coffee and coffeehouses became the subject of yet another ban when the kingdom was involved in a war where revolution was particularly feared.[20] The coffeehouses once again were seen as dens that bred rebellion, and Mahomet Kolpili, Murad's vizier, ordered their closure. When he noted in 1633 that the coffeehouses continued to clandestinely open their doors to customers, he banned coffee altogether along with tobacco and opium and razed the establishments where they had been served on pretext of a fire hazard. The wine taverns of the city were also ordered closed. Finally, as part of an edict making the use of coffee, tobacco, or wine a capital offense— the latter already forbidden under the Koran—Kolpili ordered flogging for coffeehouse customers. Repeat offenders were sewn up in bags and thrown into the Bosphorus River.

These types of prohibitory measures often can be characterized as drivers of moral rectitude. A 1645 campaign against coffee in Iran's capital city of Isfahan was led by Shah 'Abbas II's vizier Khalifeh Soltan (r. 1645–1654). Khalifeh Soltan was a morally upright member of the religious class and a devout scholar. Shortly after coming into power, he launched a campaign designed to rid society of its polluting elements: wine taverns and brothels were first closed, and the coffeehouses were cleansed of their morally dubious elements (although coffee itself was left untouched). Although these public institutions represented the vizier's primary targets, he simultaneously introduced measures to force the country's Jewish population to convert to Islam.[21]

Such prohibitive measures tend to follow the accession of a new ruler to power, and they serve a clear ideological purpose: the establishment of the ruler's moral and divine authority through a show of religious fervor. Besides bolstering the legitimacy of the new ruler, prohibition also served other secondary purposes. For example, it repressed potential challenges to the existing social order by closing down the public spaces and blaming the supposed depravity that prevailed in them for the adversity faced by the state.

From Mecca, the trade of coffee expanded to Cairo in the first decade of the sixteenth century, made its way to Syria a decade later via the pilgrimage caravan, and finally landed in Istanbul by the mid-1500s. Coffee then spread to Europe via India and Indonesia through the commercial activities of the Dutch East India Company, a powerful chartered company set up in 1602 with a twenty-one-year monopoly on trade in Asia. It had quasi-state power that allowed it to establish colonies, make its own coins, negotiate treaties, imprison and execute convicts, and wage war. Moving new crops like coffee around was within its powers. As coffee expanded beyond the Yemeni Sufi worship services and became popular in less pious settings such as the coffeehouse, the drink's reputation as a troublemaking brew developed.

Perhaps most important, the coffeehouse served as a secular forum for conversation that drew people from all social strata, and in this capacity it was a true cultural innovation. The preexisting public institutions included the ill-reputed wine tavern; the bathhouse, reserved for the upper classes and lacking in entertainment; and the mosque, which allowed only limited exchanges before and after worship. None of the existing social venues at the time allowed for the breadth of social discourse that occurred in the coffeehouses. Customers at coffeehouses could engage in the free exchange of ideas, hear the latest news, share grievances and rumors, and air political views. The activities at coffeehouses paved the way for social transformation, and for this reason they profoundly worried the religious and civil authorities. Authorities in Mecca, Isfahan, Cairo, Constantinople, and elsewhere viewed the coffeehouse as a source of dissent and rumors. As a result, coffeehouses were suppressed for nearly two hundred years in these cities.

Europe Smells the Coffee

Coffee's entry into Europe was greeted with negative social responses, mostly inspired by local interests to protect wine, beer, ales, and other beverages. Wine merchants in Italy, for example, were alarmed by the spread of coffee, a drink that had earlier been confined to the premises of universities. Belighi, a sixteenth-century Italian, bemoaned the impact of coffee:

> In Damascus, in Aleppo, in great Cairo
> At every turn is to be found
> That mild fruit which gives so beloved a drink,
> Before coming to court to triumph.
> There this seditious disturber of the world,
> Has, by its unparalleled virtue,
> Supplanted all wines from this blessed day.[22]

Efforts by Italian bishops and priests to argue that coffee consumption violated religious law continued to be ignored by traders and consumers alike.

An appeal to the pontiff by the bishops was the final avenue to purge the drink. But instead of excommunicating coffee, Pope Clement VIII declared in 1600, "Why, this Satan's drink is so delicious . . . it would be a pity to have the infidels have exclusive use of it. We shall fool Satan by baptizing it and making it a truly Christian beverage."[23] The blessing of the substance by the pope himself, a figure of great moral authority in the Christian world, most likely played a central role in the diffusion of coffee in the West and spared Europe the recurring religious quarrels that persisted under Islam for centuries.

The French fascination with coffee goes back to a message that the Italian botanist Onorio Belli sent to the physician, botanist, and traveler Charles de l'Écluse in 1596. Belli referred to "seeds used by the Egyptians to make a liquid they call *cave*."[24] It wasn't until 1644 that Pierre de la Roque brought coffee to Marseilles following a trip to Constantinople and the Levant. The trip, which involved the company of the French ambassador to Constantinople, had all the trappings of technology acquisition. The collection included "all the little implements used about it in Turkey, which were then looked upon as great curiosities in France."[25]

At the time, large parts of the French economy as well as the culture were identified with wine production. The first coffeehouse in Marseilles was established in 1671 and rapidly diffused. Winemakers and doctors formed an alliance to weaken the consumption of coffee by questioning the role of coffee on human health. The public, on the other hand, supported the use of the new beverage. Coffee lovers discredited doctors, who, in turn, attributed numerous ailments to coffee. A public clash ensued.

It was in Marseilles that vintners and a university formed an alliance to challenge the consumption of coffee. Two physicians at the University of Aix assigned a freshman, Colomb, to prepare a thesis titled *Whether the Use of Coffee Is Harmful to the Inhabitants of Marseilles*. Colomb's interdisciplinary work not only covered the impacts of coffee on human health, but it also sought to show that support for coffee was based on self-serving claims by Arab coffee exporters.

Colomb asserted that the "burnt particles, which [coffee] contains in large quantities, have so violent energy that, when they enter the blood, they attract the lymph and dry the kidneys." He also claimed that they were harmful to the brain, and that they "open the pores of the body, with the result that the somniferous animal forces are overcome." The result, he claimed, was one of "general exhaustion, paralysis, and impotence."[26]

Colomb did not have much of an impact on the general public, which continued to hold medical doctors in low esteem. But doctors continued to warn their patients against coffee, attributing a variety of ailments to the beverage and suggesting that it should be consumed only upon prescription. Doctors were also the source of whispers against coffee, spreading rumors that stomach ulcers they found in their patients were the result of the beverage.[27] They also noted that the public preference for wine had declined.

But as coffee spread, the government attempted to capture coffee's economic benefits through a 1692 edict making the sale of coffee a monopoly of the public treasury. When the strategy backfired because of rising prices and the emergence of a black market, the government instead turned to restricting the product's import to the port city of Marseilles, from which a tax could be easily levied.[28] Eventually, compromises were reached that appeased certain economic interests that had suffered in the introduction of this competing product. Notably, café au lait was invented in France in the 1700s, representing a compromise between milk producers and coffee. To this day, this kind of dialogue and compromise within a society with respect to technological innovation remains crucial.

The first record of coffee consumption in England was at Oxford University. An eyewitness account of Nathaniel Conopios drinking coffee was recorded in 1637. Conopios came to study at Oxford after serving as *primore* for the patriarch of the Greek Orthodox Church, Cyrill. He left for England after the patriarch was strangled to death by the vizier. Misfortune seemed to follow Conopios. He was expelled from the university by a "Parliamentary Board of Visitors" following the political troubles of 1648.

The introduction of coffee in England coincided with early efforts to promote the consumption of tea as part of the temperance movement to reduce the social impacts of excessive alcohol consumption. Tea had already been the subject of debate arising from its conflict with beer and other local beverages such as chicory. The economic implications of coffee, however, became self-evident as England strengthened its commercial interests in the product through the British East India Company.[29]

Coffee arrived when Britain was expanding its colonial enterprises, particularly large-scale tea production in India. King Charles II's marriage to Catherine of Braganza in Portugal in 1662 initiated a royal effort to promote tea consumption[30] as a purveyor of temperance, thereby replacing the ales, wines, and spirits. The introduction of tea at home was associated with the creation of new social institutions aimed at strengthening family ties. It was a response to the culture of taverns that kept drinking men from home.

A Lebanese known as Jacob the Jew working for a Turkish dealer established the first coffeehouse in Oxford in 1650.[31] As the habit spread with the coffeehouses, critics credited the beverage with the degradation of academic discourse. Anthony Wood, a historian of Oxford social life, lamented "the decay of study, and consequently of learning" due to coffeehouses, "to which most scholars retire and spend much of the day in hearing and speaking of news, [and] in speaking vily of their superiors."[32] This was followed by efforts by authorities to curtail the consumption of coffee by restricting opening hours for coffeehouses and outlawing the sale of "takeout" coffee to prevent people from drinking it in their houses. Coffeehouses were later established in Cambridge, where similar restrictions were enacted. In 1664 Cambridge University issued a statute decreeing that all students who "go to coffeehouses without their tutors' leave shall be punished according to the statute for the haunters of taverns and ale-houses."[33]

This law did not prevent professors and students from using coffeehouses as a venue for the free exchange of ideas and interdisciplinary discourse. In 1655 students and young fellows urged Arthur Tillyard, a local apothecary, to challenge Oxford and publicly prepare and sell coffee. He responded by creating the Oxford Coffee Club, which would later evolve into the Royal Society of London for the Improvement of Natural Knowledge, which was chartered in 1662 by King Charles II.[34]

The first London coffeehouse was established in 1652 by Pasqua Rosée, a Lebanese trader, advertising the bean as a "simple innocent thing."[35] The London coffeehouses hosted a range of business, political conversations, fights, drinking, and smoking, providing an alternative to the tavern as a place to gather and exchange ideas. Challenges to coffee in England started in the early 1660s with a series of pamphlets critical of the drink. Tavern owners lost business and protested against this "new social center" as well as against coffee itself.[36]

The detractors were as colorful in their depiction of coffee as they were critical. A 1663 broadside entitled *A Cup of Coffee: or, Coffee in its Colours*, derided those who had turned into Turks by drinking coffee. These "Pure English Apes," the author charged, "might learn to eat Spiders." In the same year a pamphlet entitled *The Coffee Man's Grenado Discharged upon the Maiden's Complaint Against Coffee* defended the beverage. This was followed by a 1665 ten-page pamphlet entitled *The Character of a Coffee House, by an Eye and Ear Witness*, offering a positive image of this new institution. In 1672 *A Broad-side Against Coffee, or the Marriage of the Turk*, unleashed one of the fiercest attacks on coffee. These attacks on "Turkey gruel" started to convince the public that coffee was a dangerous drink. The publication characterized Rosée as an ignorant but cunning foreigner misleading the public about benefits of coffee.

In addition to the poetic broadsides and pamphlets against coffee, King Charles II did not conceal his concerns, and in 1672 he sought legal advice on how he could legally shut down coffeehouses. The courts, however, did not close down coffeehouses, and the judges were summoned for consultation. The five that turned up did not agree on what to do. In addition to outlining economic benefits of trade in coffee, some of the judges argued that it would be unwise to issue a command that was likely to be disobeyed. In the end the judges issued an ambiguous statement: "Retailing coffee *might* be an innocent trade as it *might* be exercised; but as it is used at present, in the nature of a common assembly, to the discourse of the matters of State, news and *great Persons*, as they [are] Nurseries of Idleness and Pragmaticalness, and hinder the expense of our native Provisions, they *might* be thought common nuisances."[37]

In 1673 the king sought to influence public opinion against coffee by issuing *The Grand Concern of England explained*, with little success. He asserted:

> As for coffee, tea and chocolate, I know no good they do; only the places where they are sold are convenient for persons to meet in, sit half day and discourse with all companies that come in of State matters, talking of news and broaching of lies, arraigning the judgments and discretion of their governors, censuring all their actions, and insinuating into the ears of the people a prejudice against them; extolling and magnifying their own parts, knowledge and wisdom, and decrying that of their rulers; which if suffered too long, may prove pernicious and destructive.[38]

In 1674 matters came to a boil. An illustrated pamphlet by Rosée titled *A Brief Description of the Excellent Vertues of that Sober and Wholesome Drink called Coffee, and the Incomparable Effects in Preventing and Curing Diseases Incident to Humane Bodies* appeared, presenting the drink as a faster way to cure each disease. He claimed that coffee healed the stomach, sharpened the intellect, rekindled memory, and restored happiness. The publication was in response to *A Broadside against Coffee; Or the Marriage of the Turk*. These claims about the benefits of coffee would soon be overshadowed by a powerful social movement that would pave the way for more government measures.

That same year, *The Women's Petition against Coffee, representing to public consideration the grand inconveniences accruing to their sex from the excessive use of the drying and enfeebling Liquor* charged that men had become as "unfruitful as the *Desarts* whence that unhappy *Berry* is said to be brought."[39] Invoking the fear of impotence, it claimed that coffee would cause the offspring of their "mighty ancestors" to "dwindle into a succession of apes and pigmies." It was not just the health of the people that was at stake, but also their cultural identity.

The petition addressed a wide variety of issues, including the economy. It asserted that the men "spend their *money*, all for a little *base, black, thick, nasty, bitter, stinking, nauseous* puddle-water." It concluded by recommending that coffee consumption be prohibited for people under the age of sixty years and that beer and other spirits be consumed instead.[40]

Tensions over coffee created by the petition gave King Charles II the opportunity to realize his long-standing goal. On December 29, 1675, he issued *A Proclamation for the Suppression of Coffee Houses*, charging that coffeehouses were the source of malicious and scandalous statements devised to defame the king and undermine public order. He directed that coffeehouses be destroyed and the sale of "Coffee, Chocolet, Sherbett or Tea" cease by January 10, 1676. He used national security arguments, thus aligning his interests with those concerned about the economic impacts of coffee on other beverages and the prevailing social order.[41]

The popular protest against the announcement by coffeehouse owners and patrons, who represented a significant economic and social constituency, was so large that the king refrained from closing coffeehouses just two days before the proclamation was set to take effect.[42] The order was replaced by another declaration that allowed coffeehouses to remain open until June 24, 1676. On the surface, the edict appealed to security concerns. The royal family continued to promote tea consumption and the associated cultural practices.

Coffee and coffeehouses reached Germany in the 1670s, and spread to most major German cities by 1721. By the last quarter of the eighteenth century the hot beverage had become entirely adopted across social strata. Prior to its arrival, beer was Germany's dominant drink. Unlike wine, beer was essentially a food, with more nutrients, and was consumed with most meals. It was also consumed in the localities where it was produced. Coffee was dismissed as having no nutritional value. Attempts to respond to the challenge by mixing it with soup did not catch on. Beer producers had such political clout that attempts to tax it in the 1660s were largely ignored.

Economics played a key role in shaping Germany's fierce response to coffee's arrival. "Mercantilism played a prominent role in the polemics, as the growing bill for coffee involved paying considerable sums to neighboring countries, especially Holland."[43] Furthermore, "Protectionism played a related role as the indigenous and well-developed brewery network—including manufacturing, distribution, and sales—reacted to threats by the new rival to the established hegemony of beer and demonstrated a form of liquid nationalism."[45]

Beer was a major export commodity for cities such as Hamburg.[45] Just when coffee reached the Ottoman Empire in the middle of the sixteenth century, beer from Hamburg was invading Holland, Jutland, Sweden, and Russia. This export went well with pickled herrings, which increased the thirst for beer. "Whenever these vessels came to port, there were promoted orgies of beer-drinking and herring-eating. Salted gullets had to be slaked with Hamburg beer."[46]

Prussia and Sweden went through similar experiences. In Prussia, noting the popularity of coffee to the detriment of the country's more traditional drink, Frederick the Great issued a manifesto in 1777 that explicitly addressed the economic implications: "It is disgusting to see the quantity of coffee used by my subjects, and the amount of money that goes out of the country. . . . My people must drink beer."[47] He added that coffee drinkers could not be counted on to defend the country from foreign invasion. Four years later, the king prohibited the roasting of coffee, forcing the poor to turn to coffee substitutes or clandestine roasting. He also employed street sniffers who extracted fines from those caught smelling of coffee. The sniffers kept part of the collection. In 1784 Maximilian Frederick, bishop of Münster (Duchy of Westphalia), decreed the closure of coffee-roasting and coffee-serving places. Private consumption was allowed if it was purchased in quantities of fifty pounds.[48]

Coffee was brought to Sweden through Ottoman contacts but more importantly by adoption of French customs. The first coffee-house was established in Stockholm in the early eighteenth century. This coincided with economic challenges and set the stage for a clash between social classes. At a stormy parliamentary session in 1756, peasants who had been denied the right to distill liquor inflicted their revenge on the upper classes by forcing through a ban on coffee imports. The European trade crisis of the 1760s had severe impacts on Sweden, and the country responded by banning imports, which included coffee.[49]

Coffee consumption in Sweden was punished by the confiscation of cups and dishes. King Gustav III was a leading critic of the drink. He set out to provide evidence that coffee was harmful to human health by authorizing that a convicted murderer be given the drink on a regular basis. His control was another murderer who was given tea instead. The results did not support his hypothesis. The two doctors appointed to oversee the experiment died before the subjects. The king was himself murdered before the research project was completed, and in the end the coffee drinker outlived his control in the experiment.

August 1, 1794, was a day of national mourning in Sweden. In Stockholm, a group of aristocrats assembled for an official burial, ending with the crushing of a sacrificial vessel: a coffee pot. The Swedish government had just enacted its fourth ban on coffee. Between 1756 and 1817, Sweden prohibited the import of coffee in five different decrees, largely motivated by the mercantilist doctrine of the time. In addition, the general crisis in European trade from the 1760s contributed to a reversal of the country's advantageous terms of trade, leading to an effort by the new liberal government to curtail the import of certain luxury commodities such as coffee and silk and impose high taxes on others. The era of free trade had not yet dawned. The last prohibition was lifted in 1822, and in the next thirty years coffee spread beyond the cities and into the country-side, reaching the mass of the people through peddlers, land survey-ors, and other travelers who moved from town to town. Unlike the rest of Europe, the bulk of coffee in Sweden was consumed at home.

In 1855, the Swedish government definitively prohibited the household distilling of alcohol, a move that completed coffee's whole-sale diffusion, as one stimulant replaced another. Campaigning against the evils of alcohol, the Swedish *teetol* movement of the nine-teenth and twentieth centuries was to quickly move against coffee as well, precipitated by people's habit of mixing coffee with liquor.

The chairman of the Swedish National Board of Health in 1860, Magnus Huss, would single-handedly attempt to wipe out the scourge of coffee in his country through the force of his medical expertise. In his book, *On Coffee, Its Use and Abuse*, he said that cof-fee was not a food substance and as such lacked nutritive value; it also functioned as a dangerous stimulant on digestion, the brain, nerves, and circulation. He considered it a luxury. He further alleged that the use and abuse of coffee by women led to two dis-eases. First, it increased stomach acidity in the long run, leading to reduced strength, lowered capacity for work, painful pregnan-cies, and weak babies. Second, its stimulating effects on the brain would become permanent and create a state of hysteria. This led him to claim that families would suffer as a result of women's cof-fee consumption.[50]

Parliament considered imposing new duties on coffee several times between 1870 and 1914, this time not driven by a mercantil-ist philosophy but rather by a desire to restrict through taxation a luxury product still seen as primarily benefiting the upper classes. As the debates raged, coffee consumption increased. The period from 1870 to 1914 coincided with a rapid growth in consumption due to rising income levels, following industrialization in the 1870s and an associated boom in foreign trade that opened up Sweden to foreign commodities. A 1917 pamphlet argued chronic caffeine intoxication had become the most prevalent disease in the country, more serious still than alcoholism. Propaganda efforts finally ceased after World War I, giving way to education and information. Throughout the history of Sweden's long debate over coffee, different sections of society and the legislature used a variety of economic, moral, and health arguments. This underscores the complex nature of the role of this product in society.

Conclusions

The endurance of coffee in public life remains legendary. Much of it is associated with social tensions that reflect the clash between tradition and innovation. The Oromo people of Ethiopia knew it. By custom they would plant a coffee tree on the graves of influential sorcerers. They believed the first coffee bush grew from the tears shed over the dead sorcerer. Indeed, much agony has been associated with the global diffusion of coffee both as a crop and as a social innovation. Its history is a rich well of lessons for contemporary technological controversies, many of which will be elaborated in the following chapters. But five stand out.

The first lesson from the story of coffee relates to time. Inventions invoke considerable fascination. Yet it is after technologies start to have discernible impacts on the economy that their implications for society become clear. In many of these cases, the transformational impact of the technology is less about novelty than about the nature of the new economic combinations. "Indeed the history of twentieth-century technology usefully starts with technology usually seen as old, perhaps even obsolete, merely persisting anachronistically, like camel caravans and donkey carts, or better still horsepower."[51]

Indeed, the time frames for such debates may vary considerably as technologies migrate across countries. It took centuries for coffee's socioeconomic impacts to be felt across continents. It took less than a decade for debates over transgenic crops to engulf the world. Public debates about new technologies are therefore social experiments that involve seeking a new order in light of uncertainty. The uncertainty and vicarious nature of the experiments involves the continuous generation, review, and application of ideas aimed at establishing a new order. Reducing social tensions under such circumstances may require a variety of science, technology, and innovation advisory support for decisionmaking.

The second lesson from the debate is the tendency for opponents and supporters of new products not to reveal the true socioeconomic roots of their position. As Hattox so vividly put it, "What seems to happen is that the prohibitionist, on learning of the drink or the establishment, is first filled with a vague sense of uneasiness about it; it is only then that he sets about to collect the evidence that eventually leads to an official proclamation, a legal opinion, or a mere moral harangue against it."[52] Indeed, "There are other reasons, not explicitly enumerated or detailed, which contribute to the protagonist's initial alarm and subsequent interest [in the product]."[53] Moreover, we "may actually consider these other reasons to be the prime movers toward prohibitionist feelings, more important than the explicitly enunciated arguments by which, through long investigation and perhaps a bit of creative fiddling, the already resolute opponent of [of the product] furnishes himself with legal artillery."[54]

Policymakers must therefore look beyond public concerns or touting of benefits to understand the sources of tension, much of which is mediated through human feeling.[55] Coffee was not just a beverage posing health risks or conferring medical benefits, but also represented a complex ecology of technological innovation, economic interests, and social institutions. Seemingly modest efforts to introduce a new technology could result in major socioeconomic transformation. The uncertain nature of the impact leads to debates and controversies.

The third lesson from the case of coffee is the balance between benefits and risks. Coffee was successful largely because its benefits are dramatically superior to competing stimulants. Whether it is khat (*Catha edulis*) in Yemen or chicory in England and Denmark, coffee had an edge over its competitors as a stimulant. It was a gift to the temperance movement seeking to wean society off alcohol. It has a longer shelf life than many of its competitors and is easier to store and transport.

But it took technological effort and specialized knowledge to extract the caffeine, flavor, and aroma from the beans. Technological and engineering responses to these challenges would lead to the emergence of two complementary developments. First, technological innovation became a necessary accompaniment of the beverage. These new technologies created auxiliary support industries from the early producers of roasting equipment to today's manufacturers of high-end coffee machines. Second, the use of technology resulted in consumption patterns that brought consumers to coffeehouses rather than sending the equipment to homes. These and several other factors would lead to social reorganizations that challenged not only existing businesses but also social orders and flows of political power.

The fourth lesson from the case of coffee is the use of demonization and false analogies to amplify the perception of risks associated with a new product. Such tactics are used to evade the demand for evidence of risk and often rely on false analogies with other products. Such approaches are possible because of the uncertain nature of the risks associated with new technologies and the logical impossibility of proving a negative. Perception of loss was a central theme in the coffee debate. The fear of loss is more evident when expressed in economic terms. But it is not the only form that it takes.

The final lesson of relevance to contemporary technological controversies is that noneconomic factors play a key role in triggering tensions over new products. The consumption of coffee was seen by some as way of turning the English into Turks and was derided as such. In this case beverages and identities could not be separated. It is notable that the same concerns over the loss of identity are at the center of new controversies over the spread of Starbucks cafes in China.[56]

The history of the introduction of coffee was more than the simple introduction of a beverage in a new market. It embodied forces that created uncertainty in the prevailing socioeconomic and cultural order. The perception of risks associated with the innovation shaped the intensity and nature of the public discourse. Although the driving force behind the debate was largely economic, the public discourse itself was framed in terms of wider societal risks such as national security, human health, and cultural identity. The long history of the debate has left us with a wide range of lessons that continue to be replayed in other technological controversies. The rest of the book will explore these themes in depth.

3

Stop the Presses

Printing the Koran

If another Messiah was born he could hardly do so much good as the printing-press.

GEORG C. LICHTENBERG

Some of the epic clashes between tradition and innovation are about transformative technologies that only show their impact long after the battle has been fought. But in the heat of the moment there is usually little appreciation of the long-term implications of the technology. This is partly because the status quo is often the standard against which the new technology is judged. Retrospective studies paint pictures of intransigence and even folly for failing to adopt a new technology in time.

Today's Islamic communities would be unimaginable without printed religious books. But for nearly four hundred years the Ottomans restricted use of the technology for printing religious texts. In 1485 Sultan Bayezid II issued an edict prohibiting the printing of books in Arabic script. In 1508 the Shaykh al-Islam of the Ottoman Empire—the highest-ranking Islamic scholar—issued a fatwa stating that printing using movable type was permitted for non-Muslim communities but not for Muslims.[1] An edict by Sultan Selim I reinforced the ban in 1515.[2] He decreed that "occupying oneself with the science of printing was punishable by death."[3] The reported edicts, not fully authenticated, reflect the prevailing mood among authorities regarding the wider societal implications of the printing press.

This chapter uses the case of initial rejection and slow adoption of printing in the Ottoman Empire to illustrate wider societal factors that influence the pace and direction of innovation. It examines the extent to which the prevailing mode of transmission of information and religious sources of authority influenced attitudes toward the use of the printing press to produce religious texts. It also explores how incumbent modes of book production dependent on scribes provided additional sources of incremental innovation. The subsequent adoption of the printing press and its widespread use were associated with major shifts in society as well as advances in technology that undercut some of the earlier technical objections, especially related to the place of calligraphy.

Society as Whole

In a vivid account of "Islam as a barrier to printing," the British historian Thomas Francis Carter noted that "between the Far East that printed, and Europe where printing was unknown, lay the Moslem world that refused to put its literature in printed form."[4] For him, this geographical and cultural barrier of Islam "between the Far East, where . . . literature was being spread abroad in printed form, and Europe, where ancient manuscripts were being so laboriously copied by hand,"[5] acted as "a barrier rather than a bridge for the transmission of block printing to Europe."[6]

Muslims were familiar with the printing technology in China because they traded extensively with the country. In fact, there were large Muslim populations in China. The answer to the four-hundred-year delay in the adoption of the printing press among Muslims was attributed by Western scholars to conservative values. According to Carter, "It has been suggested that the Moslem suspected hog's bristles in the brush used for cleaning the block, and that to touch the name of Allah with this brush seemed to him the height of blasphemy. It is more probable that mere conservatism was the back of this prejudice."[7] The same view is expressed by Toby E. Huff in *Intellectual Curiosity and the Scientific Revolution*: "The conservative Muslim tradition of opposing new technologies at that time prevented the use of the printing press, both in the Ottoman lands and in Mughal India."[8]

Implicit in the conservative charge is the view that orthodox ulema (Islamic scholars) "ever weary of the possibility of religious innovation (i.e. *bid'a*, the nearest that Islam gets to the Christian concept of heresy) would have been deeply concerned about the introduction of printing."[9] The charge of conservatism extends to the "doubt which many pious Muslims would have felt about associating with *kufr*, with the products on non-Islamic civilizations."[10] These explanations are not consistent with the fact that the Muslim world readily adopted other Western ideas such as military technology, cartography, mechanical clocks, tobacco, electric light, watches, astronomy, and medicine.[11] The adoption of foreign ideas included the use of mechanical metaphors for understanding the world.

Some of the imported technologies struggled to find appropriate uses in society and as a result got off to a rocky start before evolving into institutionalized usages. An example of this was spyglasses, "Galileo's glasses," an early version of binoculars. The first record of the use of such binoculars was in the 1630s when a Venetian merchant was caught using the technology to gaze at the harem of the royal palace. The merchant was hanged for the offense by the impulsive Sultan Murad IV, who in turn used the technology to spy on the nearby French embassy. In the meantime Murad IV introduced searches for spyglasses in imported goods and imprisoned those found with the technology.[12] The technology quickly moved from being used by members of the royal family to spy on citizens in their backyards to being used by the Ottoman navy.

The delay in the printing press adoption is more complicated than the spyglass. A better understanding of the reasons for the delayed adoption of the printing press requires a deeper appreciation of the Muslim worldview regarding knowledge and the systems of thought as well as institutional arrangements associated with the Koran as a source of central organizing doctrines. Resistance that developed toward adopting the printing press took the form of rhetorical devices or narratives for rallying popular support. But they alone hardly explain the delay or the divergent attitudes toward different technologies.

The main explanations lay in more entrenched social values related to the oral mode of the transmission of knowledge and its connection to religious authorities. Related reasons included the manuscript economy that employed a large number of scribes, and the reverence granted to calligraphy, which could not adequately be rendered by the early printing presses. In effect, the reasons could be traced to the coevolution of religion, technology, political power, and social institutions. It is the wider social system that defined the reaction to the printing press, not any one particular source of opposition.

The knowledge system derived from the Koran as an inspirational document helps to explain the specific insistences of technology rejection. But it also provides cultural insights as to why technologies that initially encounter resistance are later adopted with a sense of urgency. Indeed, "When Muslims were under some form of colonial rule, and the threat of the West was more evident, the response was much more rapid, much more urgent. Within two decades of the beginning of the [nineteenth] century the Muslims of Tsarist Russia had seventeen presses in operation. By the 1820s in the Indian sub-continent Muslim reformist leaders were busy printing tracts."[13] Under such conditions printing became a source of entrenching local values and traditions as well as a way to counter colonial influence.

Probably the most important source of interest in regard to printing is the position of oral tradition in Islam. The debate over the supremacy of orality versus transmission of knowledge through written texts can be traced to ambivalence of the recording of the prophet Muhammad's own deeds and sayings, Hadith. Part of the concern was the possibility of misrepresenting the saying or deeds. Later Muhammad granted permission for Hadith to be written down, which made it possible for people to access the contents of the sayings and deeds without committing them to memory. Islamic scholars could look to the Koran and Hadith as sources of jurisprudence, which paved the way for Islamic law to become an integral part of Islamic society.

Despite this decision to record Hadith, orality was the most trusted way of transmitting Muhammad's word contained in the Koran (which means recitation). This changed with the Battle of Yamamah, which started in 632 as part of the Apostate Wars. Numerous carriers of Islamic knowledge perished. It was decreed that the knowledge would be written down. This was under the third caliph of the Muslim community, Uthmān ibn 'Affān (r. 644–656 CE).

Also tied to the early writing of Hadith and the Koran was the emergence of a strong emphasis on calligraphy—the "tongue of the hand"—as part of Islamic written expression and art. Calligraphy helped to standardize pronunciation among Koran readers. This was achieved by adding short vowels to the written text, or "pointing," which ensured the correct pronunciation. Calligraphy came to occupy a key place in Islam partly because of the early encouragement of reading and writing. Calligraphers enjoyed state support. It was considered as an expression of genius and creativity. Printing technologies that could not render calligraphic expressions were viewed as inferior.

Even more importantly, calligraphy was a field where women excelled. Many sultans were themselves calligraphers who had learned the art from their accomplished mothers. In fact, calligraphy and the ability to recite the Koran were exalted as pinnacles of excellence. "The calligrapher who knew the Koran by heart, whether man or woman, was thought to be more trustworthy."[14] In the Ottoman lands female calligraphers were revered. The delicate art of calligraphy evoked poetic feminine images in the Ottoman lands: "Her ink was like the blackness of her hair, her paper was like the tanned skin of her face, her pen was like one of her delicate fingers, and her knife was like the penetrating sword of her sweet looks."[15] Good penwomanship was often equated with beauty: "It was always said that a lucky woman was one who combined the beauty of body and face with that of character and penmanship."[16] These associations created strong bonds between religion, art, and beauty in ways that made it difficult to dislodge one without irrevocably ripping apart the social, aesthetic, and spiritual tapestry. Calligraphy occupied a central place for the few women who had the opportunity to excel in it; they otherwise lived in a world with restricted gender roles.

Calligraphers played a significantly different role than European scribes. They occupied a creative role that is imbued with spirituality. They were artists and custodians of the faith, and they played a key role in enforcing communication standards. The added role of women calligraphers expanded the base for its support. The printing press, on the other hand, was more centralized and lacked broad-based support.

These innovations are intricately linked to the central role of orality in Islam. The Koran occupied a different role in Islam than the Torah or Bible in Jewish or Christian traditions. The Koran is the primary source of lifestyle guidelines for Muslims. "Muslims strive to learn as much of it as possible by heart. They recite it constantly through the daily round, at prayer times, through the passage of the year, most notably in the month of Ramadan, and through all the stages of life."[17]

The words of the Koran for Muslims, as the British missionary Constance Padwick put it so aptly, are "the twigs of the burning bush aflame with God."[18] The words are committed to memory, a learning ritual that starts early in life. The teaching method provides immense rewards for children as they move from verse to verse with chants that fill the air with a sense of attachment to deity. There are pedagogic tools such as rhyme that help memorization. This emphasis on orality creates a sense of trust between those transmitting the knowledge and the recipients. The transmitters commit themselves to intellectual honesty and rigor in memorization, as deviation from the meaning of the text comes with consequences.

The focus of this approach is to hold the transmitter of the knowledge accountable for its accuracy. This approach creates a level of skepticism of the written word. In effect, the written Koran is meant to act as a tool for humans, not a substitute that cannot be held accountable for the true transmission of the word of Allah. In other words, the transmitter of the knowledge from the Koran is simply serving as an extension of the source, not a substitute in the way a book might be perceived to be. The mode of knowledge transmission was therefore intended to be from person to person, which creates new challenges when a medium such as a book is introduced. The Koran in this case is not just a source of knowledge but a learning methodology that focuses on recitation. In the words of Hadith: "You can return to God nothing better than that which came from Him, namely the Recitation [al-qur'ān]."[19]

The quest for knowledge that developed early in Islamic thought entailed traveling to specific sheikhs or authorities to hear them speak their wisdom and accounts and "to obtain their [authorization or *ijaza*] to transmit these in their names. This *ijazah* system of personal rather than institutional certification has served not only for Hadith, but also for transmission of texts of any kind, from history, law, or philology to literature, mysticism, or theology."[20]

The same system of authentication of knowledge was used when material was transferred from memory to text. "The author would dictate his first draft, either from memory or from his own writing; the copyist would then read it back to him. Publication would take place through the copyist reading the text to the author in public, usually in a mosque."[21] After the required changes the author would then give the *ijaza*. In effect, the work may have been written down, but it was transmitted to the author orally. Until any copy of a book had been read back to the author, it had no real authority. The same granting of *ijaza* was used in teaching where pupils read back to the teacher what they have been asked to commit to memory. It was when the teacher was satisfied that the *ijaza* was granted.

The transfer of knowledge from oral transmission to printed media was perceived to create opportunities for endless publication of books, but with a resulting loss of control over the contents of what was being communicated. Religious scholars argued that committing ideas to books created a slippery slope that would lead to the production of book after book. The threat was evident: "Even for secular scholars, the great increase in books . . . made it possible for ignoramuses to infiltrate the ranks of the qualified intellectuals, and actually diminish the quality of books."[22] The concerns were also accompanied by the fear that those capable of producing books would consider their work as the most authoritative source available, potentially overriding oral communication. A related concern was that while orality created a certain level of equitable access, amassing books would give more authority to those who owned or had access to books. These arguments tended to reinforce reliance on the oral transmission of knowledge.

Social order that draws its inspiration from theology and jurisprudence possesses inner forces that guarantee social stability and continuity. These are also the same forces that block or slow the process of introducing new technologies. The existence of practices such as *ijaza* inherently makes society skeptical about the authority of the written word. This may come through as conservatism but is simply a way by which a system manages change. It is therefore not sufficient to look only at the superficial fact that when a book has been written, it can easily be read. It is even more important to look at the modes of the transmission of knowledge and their legitimacy.

Pressing for Change

The dramatic impact of the Reformation on Europe provides an important backdrop against which to review the self-preservation strategies of Ottoman rulers in the face of the printing press. One of the most highly debated issues in the history of the printing press is the extent to which the technology induced large-scale societal transformations. The printing press was known and widely used in Asia long before it made it to the Western world.

The printing press used movable type, which was invented around 1450 by Johannes Gutenberg in Mainz, Germany. Gutenberg's contributions to printing included inventing a process for mass-producing movable type, mechanical movable type, using oil-based ink in book printing, and using a wooden printing press similar to the time's agricultural screw presses and adjustable molds. His first major product was the publication in 1455 of the Gutenberg Bible. In the subsequent fifty years the printing press diffused in much of Europe with limited opposition in some cities.

It is estimated that by 1500 "nearly 8 million books had been printed, most of them religious in nature and printed in Latin— perhaps more than the scribes had produced in the previous millennium."[23] Between 1450 and 1500 book prices dropped by two-thirds, "transforming the way ideas were disseminated and the conditions of intellectual work."[24] The printing press is considered by numerous historians and scholars as the most transformational technology of modern time.[25]

The diffusion of the printing press was concentrated initially in key cities such as Augsburg, Cologne, Leipzig, Nuremburg, and Strasbourg. Gutenberg and his assistants created the first printing workshops, which they controlled as a monopoly before the first printing of the Bible in in Strasbourg in 1459. In the first few decades printing remained in German hands. By the 1470s "printing was controlled by a small group of printer-scholars, educated laymen who ran the printing presses and played a significant role in editing."[26] The printer-scholars, mostly former priests or professors, lived migrant lives across cities and university towns where there was demand for their services. Neither books nor printing presses could be readily moved around. The printing press hubs therefore became important anchors for the emerging information and technology industry of the time. Indeed, cities "that were early adopters of the printing press attracted booksellers, universities, and students. Adoption of the printing press also fostered backward linkages: the printing press attracted paper mills, illuminators, and translators."[27]

Despite its rapid diffusion, the printing press coexisted with scribes for nearly a century.[28] Despite a few reports of opposition, there are no major cases of objections to the printing press by scribes. There are many reasons as to why the introduction of printing in Europe was not associated with social unrest. As pointed out by Neddermeyer, "Gutenberg's invention was no real threat to the existence of scribes. More often than not, the social consequences of the mechanization of book-production were alleviated by the fact that the writers were supported by ecclesiastical institutions, offices or prebends."[29] At the time of the invention of the printing press, "The majority of the manuscripts had not been paid for, often the writer needed the book for himself, or it was meant to enlarge the library of the religious communities he was a member of."[30] The scribes also continued to be paid from writing minutes, letters, inventories, and other documents. In fact, scribes and the associated chancery services were a key employment sector at the time.

There have been attempts to link the introduction of printing to economic development in Europe more broadly. The evidence for this is scant, though printing functioned as an entrepreneurial crucible around which a number of skills clustered related to typesetting, papermaking, equipment maintenance, and business practices. In addition, social organizations such as guilds sprang up to promote and protect the trade. The diffusion of knowledge through books is another factor to take into account.

One of the most interesting themes worth exploring is the extent to which the printing press contributed to the spread of the Reformation in Europe. This is a point of particular interest because the Reformation represents an epic transformation of European history. Its pivotal moment was on October 31, 1517, when Martin Luther nailed his *Ninety-Five Theses on the Power and Efficacy of Indulgences* to the door of All Saints Cathedral at Wittenberg in Germany. Luther was concerned with church abuses as well as the theological stranglehold on society. It is tempting to put too much emphasis on a single factor as a primary trigger for change. It is equally unreasonable to dismiss the idea as a "ridiculous thesis that the Reformation was the child of the printing press."[31] It is the coevolution between social change and technological innovation that shaped political events.

Luther's grievances were initially focused on reforming the church from within, but they found resonance with widespread antipapal sentiments in much of northern Europe. His ideas spread quickly in print form. Luther was not alone in pushing for reform. His efforts were complemented by other reformists such as Huldrych Zwingli (1484–1513) in Switzerland. The Reformation quickly took root in urban areas "through the efforts of a small cadre of learned, literate priests and scholars."[32] The Reformation occurred during a period of widespread ferment that included a series of peasant revolts in rural areas between 1524 and 1526.[33]

The Reformation was a radical transfer of power and in many cases it involved the destruction of church property. Generally after a town accepted the Reformation, "The old privileges and status of the priesthood and hierarchy were removed, followed by the confiscation or destruction of the Church's material wealth."[34] The Protestant movement swept through Europe, often encountering violent pushback from the ruling elites. For example, the Spanish Habsburgs burned nearly two thousand Protestants between 1523 and 1555. The movement became the basis of new political leadership structures in places such as the Netherlands and England. These changes were aided by the spread of the printed word.

The primary print vehicle for the transmission of Protestant material were eight-page pamphlets that were easy to read and easy to transport around. In addition to conveying religious ideas, the pamphlets were powerful tools for planting dissent against the church. This was often done through negative portrayals of the church, including caricaturing and direct insults. The pamphlets were easy to conceal, but there was no transportation network for wider distribution. Spreading the message involved reprints, which required the existence of printing presses.

The printing press was also being used by the church to counter the Reformation movement. In some cases the efforts backfired. The church published and distributed posters of books that needed to be burned. This inadvertently served as advertising as people went out and bought the books. It was all-out war: "All Germany caught fire. Pamphlets filled with the thunder of violence came out on all sides. . . . Every device, not only of the printer's art, but also of illustrations and even caricature, was brought into service."[35] Between 1520 and 1530 more than 630 pamphlets (*Flugschriften* as they were called in German) survived. The pope and the monks were referred to as donkeys and cows. In turn the Lutherans were described as madmen.

The printing press played an important role in the Reformation. Luther fully understood its power and referred to it as "God's highest and ultimate gift of grace by which He would have his Gospel carried forward."[36] Luther was a prolific writer himself. He "wrote thirteen treatises and sold over 300,000 copies between 1517 and 1520."[37] The number of books published rose sharply as the debate intensified. Luther's works are estimated to have represented nearly a third of the German books sold between 1518 and 1525. His famous pamphlet *To the Christian Nobility of the German Nation* was published on August 18, 1520. It had to be reprinted a week later. It sold four thousand copies in three weeks and was reprinted thirteen times in two years.[38]

The extent to which the printing press influenced the Reformation has been widely documented. The causal relationship between the printing press and the Reformation, however, is only being fully appreciated now. According to statistical analysis by Jared Rubin, the "top print cities were more likely (on average) to adopt the Reformation by 1530 and by 1600; 70 percent of the top printing centers of the 1470s and 60 percent of the top printing centers of the 1480s and 1490s adopted the Reformation by 1530, despite only 32.6 percent of German-speaking cities adopting the Reformation by this date."[39]

Indeed, "The mere presence of a printing press prior to 1500 increased the probability that a city would become Protestant in 1530 by 52.1 percentage points, Protestant in 1560 by 41.9 percentage points, and Protestant in 1600 by 29.0 percentage points."[40] It is notable that the church itself was a major user of the printing press and applied the same technology for religious and anti-Turkish propaganda. One of the key impacts of printing was to shift the locus of knowledge generation and conservation to universities, which in turn weakened the role of the church in society.

The role of the printing press and wider economic transformation following the Reformation remains a subject of considerable intellectual interest and study. It is not possible to adopt a deterministic view. Those cities that adopted the printing press may already have contained the entrepreneurial seed for subsequent transformation. Though there has been little evidence of the macroeconomic impact of printing, city-level data show that "between 1500 and 1600, European cities where printing presses were established in the 1400s grew 60 percent faster than otherwise similar cities."[41]

The spread of the Reformation may have been part of a trajectory already set in earlier phases of development. But what is evident is that the confluence of printing, the spread of ideas, and the adoption of more liberal systems set in motion events that would alter the social order irrevocably. The upheavals of the Reformation were felt far and wide. The Ottoman lands that neighbored the regions affected by the Reformation knew about the impact of the printing press, and it would not have been in their interest to risk the adoption of ideas of technologies that had the potential to undermine their own regimes. The backdrop is important when evaluating the reaction of the Ottoman Empire to the printing press.

Trailing Behind

The adoption of the printing press was associated with major social and economic transformations, as witnessed by its adoption in European society. The social and economic changes came with significant shifts in power relations. The biggest losers in the process were those who derived their authority and power from the church. New players such as universities gained in stature as they became the loci of the generation and conservation of knowledge. These changes were obviously known to the Ottomans, who were in competition with the Western world for imperial influence. It is against this background of uncertainty and change that the opposition and slow adoption of the printing press in the Ottoman Empire needs to be understood. The edicts, debates, and social responses to the printing press among the Ottomans illustrate the system-wide dynamics associated with the adoption of new technology. This case is particularly interesting because it has explicit religious elements that are often missing in many other technological controversies.

The delay in the adoption of the printing press was due in part to a lack of familiarity with the technology. Religious minorities were allowed to set up printing presses in Ottoman lands to publish books using non-Arabic characters soon after the technology was invented. In 1493 Jewish immigrants from Portugal and Spain were allowed to set up printing presses in Istanbul for religious and secular works in Hebrew characters. In 1567 an Armenian priest started publishing books in the Armenian alphabet with imported fonts. In 1716 the first book printed in Arabic script in Ottoman lands was issued in Aleppo, Syria. It was a Bible in Arabic translation. In 1488 two Italian traders were given permission to import printed books into the Ottoman Empire, some of which were Christian texts printed in Arabic.[42]

The printing press was therefore not new in the Ottoman lands, but it was operated by non-Ottomans. It would take a Hungarian convert to Islam, İbrahim Müteferrika, to make one of the boldest efforts to introduce the printing press in Istanbul. Müteferrika was born in Kolozsvár in Transylvania. It is claimed, though disputed, that he had been training as a Calvinist minister when he was captured and enslaved by the Turks in 1692 or 1693 in Prince Tekely's war against the Habsburgs. After he converted to Islam he performed a variety of governmental and diplomatic tasks. He published a polemic against papism and disputed the Trinity doctrine. His early accounts reveal a person of remarkable zeal and activism. His birthplace "was the centre of the threefold struggle of Catholicism, Calvinism and Unitarianism."[43] He participated in the Reformation movement and was familiar with its inner workings, especially in regard to using printed material as a way to challenge authority.

In 1726 Müteferrika produced a pamphlet, *The Usefulness of Printing*, in which he listed ten reasons for setting up a printing press. He said printing "would help the propagation and revival of learning among the peoples of Islam; it would facilitate reading and ensure the preservation of a work, since the printed page is legible and durable; it would reduce the cost of new books and thus enable everybody to buy them."[44] He added that "it would facilitate the founding of more libraries; it would put an end to the printing of Islamic books by Europeans who fill them with errors and ugly type-face; it would make the Turks the sole leaders and protectors of learning in the world of Islam."[45]

He submitted a request to establish a printing press to the grand vizier, Nevşehirli Damat İbrahim Paşa, the grand mufti, and Shaykh al-Islam (from whom a fatwa was requested to allow the use of the technology). Later he sent the same request to Sultan Ahmed III. The request was for nonreligious books. He was also assigned traditional proofreaders to ensure that there were no errors in the published books. In 1727 the sultan issued a *ferman* (imperial edit) granting the permission to set up the printing press in Istanbul. Shaykh al-Islam also issued a fatwa. The fatwa was appended with the consent of twelve other religious scholars.[46] "The *ferman*'s regulation entailed a strict prohibition on the printing of Qur'ans, collections of hadiths (sayings of the Prophet Muhammad), and religious works on theology, law and exegesis. For these reasons, dictionaries and books on secular subjects such as history, logic, astronomy, and geography would form the core of Müteferrika's printing efforts."[47]

The main opposition to the edict came from scribes and calligraphers, who demonstrated against the press on grounds of safety and religion.[48] The calligraphers put their inkstands and pencils into coffins and walked to the Sublime Porte (Bâb-ı Âli). The opposition came from the "book guilds protesting the sacrilege of using a machine in producing the word of God and in allowing the use of brushes made of pig bristles in inking the platen."[49] Accounts of the time report that "riots and civil unrest ensued . . . and Ahmet was forced to delay permission for the project until agreement was reached that no religious works would be defiled by the new techniques and tools of the innovator."[50] The scribes were a formidable force: "When the Bolognese scholar Luigi Ferdinando Marsigli (d. 1730) visited Istanbul . . . he said there were eighty thousand copyists in the city."[51]

The protests did not enjoy much support, partly because of the exclusion of religious material from printing. It is notable that Müteferrika himself had excluded religious material from his original request, thereby allaying concerns, especially from the ulema.

In fact, he would not have received permission if his request had included religious books. The opposition soon died out, possibly helped by the perception that secular books represented a small section of the market and the risks of including controversial content would be controlled through those assigned to supervise the printing.

In order to obtain the authority to set up a printing press, Müteferrika used two approaches that turned out to be strategic. First, he demonstrated that he could actually run a printing press. In 1719–1720 he used a woodblock print to create a map of the Sea of Marmara that he presented to the grand vizier, Damat İbrahim Paşa. Müteferrika showed that he had the tools and capacity to print. But equally important was his strategy to present printed material that was valuable. Cartography was one of those fields that enjoyed support from the imperial rulers. He used a seemingly basic technology for his sample, which could have helped to reduce concerns about his ability to print from more sophisticated material, including copper plates. His incremental approach showed that he was aware that he was venturing into a controversial field whose political implications needed to be managed carefully.

The authorities included other beneficiaries in the edict. One was Sai'd Efendi, who had returned from a diplomatic trip to Paris with his father Yirmisekiv Mehmed Çelebi in 1721. Çelebi was a special envoy of the Ottoman Empire to the court of King Louis XV in Paris. During the 1720–1721 tour he visited a wide range of French institutions and gathered extensive information on scientific, technological, and cultural advances in France. The fact that his son would be granted permission to run a printing press is suggestive of the impression the power of publishing made on him.

In the end the introduction of the printing press did not lead to revolutionary change. In fact only seventeen books were published by the time Müteferrika died in 1745. His heirs were granted authority to continue printing, but they managed to produce only seven books before the press closed in 1797 under financial duress.

Most of the supplies such as types and ink needed for the press were imported from Europe, which kept the price of printed books relatively high. The venture did not serve educational institutions partly because of poor marketing and networks, and many of the books were remaindered. Müteferrika did not have resources for advertising and lacked connections with the business community. In fact, the press operated as an official facility sanctioned by the sultan.

The actual impact of Müteferrika's printing press is hard to judge as an activity that is distinct from its religious, cultural, and political context. Narrow assessments based on the number of books sold are an inadequate measure of the inspirational role that this pioneering effort played against remarkable cultural inertia.[52] It took several decades before the prophecy in the sultan's proclamation in the *ferman* was realized, such that "this Western technique will be unveiled like a pride and will not again be hidden. It will be a reason for Muslims to say prayers for you and praise you to the end of time."[53]

Incremental Innovation

The effort by Müteferrika was part of a slow and incremental introduction of the print culture in the Ottoman lands. This pace of adoption was influenced by a wide range of societal factors. The first is the culture of orality that prompted general skepticism toward the authority of the written work. As argued by Robinson, the "problem was that printing attacked the very heart of Islamic systems for the transmission of knowledge; it attacked what was understood to make knowledge trustworthy; what gave it value, what gave it authority."[54]

The primacy of orality could not be easily overcome because it represented the most authentic and legitimate way of transmitting information. Skepticism about printing and the potential of generating errors was real. In fact, this concern would later become evident, especially when books were printed by people not proficient in Arabic or not sensitive to the importance of orality as the most trusted way of transmitting information. The challenge is even greater when one takes into account religious or imperial competition of the day. Under such circumstances, genuine errors in religious texts may be interpreted as lack of respect for Islam or a conspiracy to denigrate the faith of others.

Indeed, "The disturbing manner in which European printers took liberties with the text of the Koran (when compared with the care taken in printing the Gutenberg Bible, for instance) could not but raise doubts among Muslims regarding the virtues of printing when they first came in contact with the new technology."[55] As Mahdi has commented, a "look at the title page of the Koran printed in Hamburg in 1694 ... must have made Muslim readers of the Koran think that only the Devil Himself could have produced such an ugly and faulty version of their Holy Book."[56] Many other prints of the Koran, such as the edition from the 1530s by Alessandro Paganino in Venice, simply mixed up some letters of the Arabic alphabet. The appearance of such poorly produced books reinforced the credibility of the scribes and reduced trust in printed editions.

Despite these challenges, the transition from manuscripts to printed works slowly occurred in the Muslim world. Part of the transition included establishing standards and routines for quality control. In some cases, the quality control measures used in the production of manuscripts was transferred to the world of print. For example, *muṣaḥḥiḥ*, the person in charge of producing the correct version of a book, "performed a task similar to that of the scribe in the manuscript age, that is, he corrected and sometimes revised the language of the manuscript copy before it was sent to the printer."[57] The *muṣaḥḥiḥ* also "contributed to assuring that the proofs were properly corrected and a list of errata was appended to the printed book."[58]

There were four specific issues related to the printing of the Koran that were sources of legal contention. The first was about the purity of the material used to print the Koran. Assurances were needed that parts of animals such as pigs and dogs and other impure material were not used in the printing process. The second point related to whether exerting pressure to print the Koran constituted disrespectful handling of the holy book. The third concern regarded the possibility of introducing errors given the departure from the prescribed ways of producing the Koran. Finally, there was the concern that the printing process would create possibilities for non-Muslims to come in contact with the Koran, which was not allowed. This last point was particularly pertinent given the dearth of Muslims trained in printing. This was the case with the first printing press in Istanbul, which employed the services of a Jew from another press and brought in typesetters from France.[59]

These issues were particularly difficult to resolve because of variations in interpretation among different Islamic followings. For example, the pig belongs to the highest categories of impurities. But there were different interpretations as to whether the classification extended to bones, hair, skin, sweat, or any other parts of the body. There were differences over whether ornaments, including gold, could be added to the Koran. There were also variations in the interpretation of non-Muslims being involved in the production of the Koran. Printing presses located in areas without a steady supply of Muslim workers would hardly survive. The same fate met the Istanbul press when Müteferrika passed away. Not a single Muslim had been trained to operate the press by the time of his death.[60]

It is clear from Müteferrika's example that the introduction of a printing press, despite state support, had to deal with Islamic legal issues. The interpretation of the legal aspects of the printing press itself varied across different Islamic traditions. The uncertainty arising from such conditions is not conducive to the introduction of the technology. This was compounded by the financial outlays needed to run the press. The ensuing debate and the absence of predictable political support required a much stronger basis for survival.

As Ghaly said, "The making use of printing especially for producing religious texts did not represent a public need in Muslim communities. On the contrary, the manuscript culture was cultivated in the Muslim world. Muslims were inclined to buy and obtain books in the manuscript form rather than the printed one."[61] The interplay between the manuscript culture and legal interpretations not only made it hard to introduce printing presses, but also made it easy to reverse printing decisions, as happened in Egypt, where the first printed Koran was sold from 1832 with the stamp of the mufti of Egypt. But with the change of leadership an order was issued in 1853 "to confiscate the printed editions, forbid selling or circulating them and punish those who do not abide."[62] It is not that the errors could not be corrected in subsequent editions. The political weight was on the side of the manuscript culture, at least for that time.

Printed books posed a dilemma for the authorities. On the one hand they provided new knowledge that could help increase economic opportunities. But the same spread of knowledge also made it hard to control the population. This was compounded by the fact that books made knowledge more readily available, thereby undermining religious authorities who transmitted it orally. In this respect, books carried with them the germ of subversion. The "Ottoman sultans and religious establishment feared the creative destruction that would result. Their solution was to forbid them."[63]

The Ottoman Empire eventually saw the wide adoption of the printing press. In 1802 the ban on Islamic subjects was lifted, and lithography was adopted soon after it was invented in Germany. The main driving force in the change in policy was the shift in the source of legitimacy for the rulers. As argued by Coşgel and his colleagues, the "Ottomans regulated the printing press to prevent the loss it would have caused to the ruler's net revenue by undermining the legitimacy provided by religious authorities."[64] Over time, the Ottoman lands went through social changes that reduced the role of religious authorities as sources of legitimacy for the regime.

The role of technology in providing legitimacy to the ruling class would later play out in the case of the telegraph following the Crimean War (1853–1856), when Britain and France sided with the Ottoman Empire in its territorial dispute with Russia. The sultan saw the technologies not as tools for imperial expansion, as Britain did, but as a means to maintain control over the population. Ironically, it was the same technology that would empower the Young Turks with the means to undermine the sultanate, resulting in its abolition in the early twentieth century. Mehmet Talât Paşa, a leading personality of "the Young Turks Revolution, who became minister of the interior and grand vizier (1917–1918), was formerly a mere telegraph clerk."[65] The technology "enabled him to organize and spread the movement in spite of the sultan's spies."[66] In fact, "The effective use of the telegraph was also a key to the success of Kemal Atatürk, the founding father of the Republic of Turkey."[67] As was the case in the social uprisings in Meiji Japan in the 1880s, isolated communities vandalized telegraph wires to draw the attention of central authorities to local grievances. In the end what was originally conceived as a tool for imperial control became a medium for political disintegration.

The liberalization of society shifted power from religious authorities to local leaders whose positions were not threatened by the printing of religious books. Having an alternative source of legitimacy that did not involve control over the transmission of knowledge meant that the state had no incentive to continue supporting the interests of religious leaders by restricting the printing of religious material. In addition, the introduction of the printing press offered additional opportunities for the state to generate revenue. In effect, the balance of costs and benefits of adopting the printing press had gradually but irreversibly changed over time.

A related factor that may have played a part in the evolution of printing in Ottoman lands was the nature of the Arabic script itself. "Printing in Arabic script ... is a more difficult enterprise than printing in Greek, Latin, Hebrew, or Armenian, all of which have discreet block letters. Arabic script loses much of the calligraphic beauty of a hand-copied text, and the cost of equipment for printing is extremely high compared with that required for a manuscript at a time when the cost of labor was very low."[68]

The invention of lithography as a new technological species made it possible to make multiple copies of work while preserving the calligraphic and aesthetic attributes of a manuscript. It overcame the limitation of working with fonts. Whereas the European language fount had around 275 characters, Arabic had over 600 characters. Even though Arabic had as many letters, its cursive nature included initial, medial, final, and independent forms. This made printing in Arabic more expensive. Lithography made it less credible to argue against printing by resolving the aesthetic limitations of previous technology. The new technology, which was cheaper and easier to use, seemed to be exactly what the Arabic script had been waiting for, and with it publishing spread quite rapidly in the Muslim world of India, Persia, the Ottoman Empire, and North Africa.

Conclusions

The first major lesson from this case is the importance of taking a long-term view when assessing the adoption of new technologies. Modern society is accustomed to the rapid uptake of gadgets such as mobile phones, tablets, and the like. Many such technologies ride on the backs of major foundational technologies that took decades or even centuries to build. They can escape controversy partly because their parent infrastructure paved the way for their adoption. Transformational technologies often have to work their way along with other changes in the society that they are located. This is mainly due to the institutional adjustments that need to occur together with the technology. The secularization of the Ottoman Empire was one of such changes. Without it the printing press would probably have remained a technological curiosity in much of the Ottoman lands.

The second lesson from this case is the importance of wider societal shifts in creating opportunities for the adoption of new technologies. This is particularly the case when such shifts alter the balance of the risks and benefits associated with the adoption of new technologies. Such shifts arise from direct policy interventions or gradual changes in society. They can also arise from the efforts of reformers and activists. In some cases, the technologies themselves can serve as triggers of change. One contemporary example is the role that modern information and communications technologies—especially social media—have played in fostering reform in the Middle East. Like the printing press, social media have been the subject of considerable restriction in the Middle East. But they have also been adopted by the ruling classes to support their own propaganda efforts.

In this respect, technologies that confirm legitimacy to the ruling class are likely to be adopted faster than those that threaten its base for support. It is notable that Müteferrika's printing press was set up as an official state activity. This would not have been done if the rulers had not stood to benefit from it. The role of social media was evident in the 2011–2014 Arab Spring uprising in Egypt.[69] To forestall the use of social media by opposition forces, the government authorized the shutting down of the Internet. But the action had broad impacts on the economy, costing nearly US$90 million in five days. The closure not only denied the government revenue, but threatened to alienate the affected business leaders from the state, many of whom were supporters of the government.

This brings us to the fourth lesson related to the broad claim about conservatism. Social responses to new technologies are hardly uniform. The Ottomans readily adopted a wide range of imported technologies. This might appear contradictory, but it calls for close scrutiny of the benefits and risks of the technologies being adopted and the extent to which they confer benefits to society or at least do not add to the risks. There are many contemporary examples of differential adoption of even the same technologies across sectors. A case in point is genetic engineering, which in many countries is readily accepted for medical purposes but frowned upon for agricultural applications. The explanation for this is not inconsistency but a reflection of the distribution of risks and benefits. Calling up the seeming inconsistency is hardly taken seriously.

The final lesson from the case of printing in the Ottoman Empire is the role that technological advancement sometimes plays in eliminating the basis for some of the objections. Early printing presses were ill-equipped to handle the aesthetic and calligraphic aspects of the Arabic script. This was used by opponents of the technology even though their objections may have been influenced by other considerations. The invention of lithography by Alois Senefelder of Munich in 1796 made it possible to print books without compromising aesthetic considerations.

A contemporary example of such trends includes the identification of alternative sources of stem cells, which helped to reduce the intensity of objections from those concerned about obtaining stem cells from human embryos. Another potential example is the use of gene-editing techniques or precision breeding within crop species to address concerns about moving genes across species. Technological solutions alone are not sufficient in many cases without the complementary social change that makes new technologies more acceptable. Without such changes opponents can always find alternative ways of standing their ground.

It is not uncommon for objections to persist long after the change in technology or even in cases where the new technology was never deployed. For example, rumors still persist around the world about the existence of seeds incorporating sterility genes even though the technology was never deployed. The persistence of such rumors is very much influenced by the degree of moral repugnance that they invoke. The thought that the Koran is being printed using derivatives of pigs or that new crops may actually contain pig genes has a chilling effect on Muslims. The invocation of repugnance or disgust is about generating strong, negative emotional reactions toward the new technology irrespective of the supporting evidence.

There is a tendency to consider rumors as ephemeral, yet they can linger on for a long time. They may look ridiculous, so there are levels where they do not need to be corrected. In many cases they simply become part of the unspoken subtext in technological discourse. It is important that they are identified and corrected, even where the act of doing so appears to be unnecessary. Pointing out the persistence of misinformation is a key role of public education and information. It is usually hard to counter myths after they have become part of the popular narrative, especially where they play to unspoken fears or concerns.

The final lesson from this case relates to the role of leadership and its ability to set in motion reforms that may appear on the surface as trivial but could be in the long-run transformational. The commitment of the Ottoman rulers to the press continued despite the initial challenges. Sultan Selim III (r. 1789–1807) purchased the press in 1797 from its previous owners to be used in Mühendishane-i Berr-i Hümâyûn, the newly established military school in Istanbul. The state founded two other printing presses, Üsküdar (Dârüttıbaa) and Takvimhane-i Âmire. This gave printing the continuity and stability that it needed.[70]

The introduction of the first printing press, though approved only for secular books, provided a glimpse into the reformist attitudes of the leaders of the time. The forces of inertia, which they were part of, could hardly provide room for radical changes except where they conferred to them some clear benefits. Under such a deeply entrenched system, one has to contend with long-term, incremental, and uncertain adoption of new technologies.

What appears as short-sightedness is often a window into a more complex world. Technological innovation coevolves with social institutions to create a complex fabric. Separating the technologies from their social context can hardly be done without altering the wider social context in which it is embedded. Similarly, introducing new technologies in such social settings comes with social adjustments that represent a new order.

Smear Campaigns

Margarine

Nothing will ever be attempted, if all possible objections must be first overcome.

SAMUEL JOHNSON

In 1979 Theodore William Schultz of the University of Chicago received the Nobel Memorial Prize for Economic Sciences for his "pioneering research into economic development research with particular consideration of the problems of developing countries." Schultz started his academic career at Iowa State College. In 1943 the economics department he headed published a pamphlet, *Putting Dairying on a Wartime Footing*, which claimed that margarine was "as palatable and nutritious as butter, and more sensible to use during wartime because it requires less manpower."[1] This did not go down well with the dairy lobby. Through the Iowa Farm Bureau the lobby reached out to the college president, who suppressed the pamphlet. Schultz decided to resign, and several of his colleagues in the department followed suit.[2]

The case of Schultz and his colleagues who resigned from Iowa State College was just one example of the worldwide controversies sparked by the invention of margarine. The backlash included protectionist legislation and empowered the creation of strong lobby groups that continue to hold considerable political and social sway today.

This chapter uses margarine as a case study to explore the way resistance to new technologies is articulated through legislative processes. The chapter examines how the US Congress served as a locus for political influence aimed at restricting the spread of margarine and limiting the market for the new product. It also examines how tactics such as false advertising were used to shift public perceptions against margarine. Similar to coffee, margarine was the subject of considerable vilification and slander, and much of the debate focused on its perceived health effects. The chapter then examines how margarine producers were resilient, flexible, and able to counteract the negative campaigning by developing their technology and highlighting the benefits of margarine to ultimately surpass butter consumption by the mid-1900s.

The Fat of the Land

One of the sources of resistance to innovation identified by Schumpeter lay in "the social environment against one who wishes to do something new. This reaction may manifest itself first of all in the existence of legal and political impediments."[3] One of the institutional manifestations of this phenomenon was the rise of the dairy lobby in the United States in response to the emergence of margarine. The dairy lobby that exists today was not always so powerful. Butter also was not so widely consumed. The dairy industry was fragmented and run by small-scale farmers. Over time that changed. The creation of margarine ultimately gave the dairy lobby the additional fuel it needed to become a coordinated and organized group with the ability to influence politicians and social perceptions.

During the second half of the nineteenth century the dairy industry was an entirely decentralized entity consisting of about five million individual producers. The ecological durability of the dairy cow, which could thrive in a variety of climates and on various feeds, allowed farmers across a wide geographical area to successfully raise the animals. The dairy belt stretched from New England westward across New York, Ohio, Illinois, Iowa, Michigan, Wisconsin, and Minnesota.[4]

Dairy products often came from small-scale operations on the same farms that harvested the milk. Many producers were not dairy farmers by trade, but rather owned dairy cows to supply their family's needs. Thus it was only during peak production period, when a surplus was available, that they would enter the market. The small-scale nature of dairy production was largely a result of the technological difficulties of bringing milk to markets. Without refrigeration or pasteurization, milk would quickly sour or become contaminated if not consumed. Furthermore, transportation networks—mostly consisting of railroads—could not support the long-distance movement of dairy products. For these reasons dairy products had to be produced close to their consumers and in relatively small batches.[5]

Butter producers in the United States, who were mainly dairy farmers, ran household operations well into the twentieth century. These included small-scale home production for local markets or for sale to dealers who would repack and sell elsewhere. Like many other food products, butter itself had to overcome significant prejudice to make up for a checkered history dating back to the early 1840s.[6] These scandals included butter adulteration, watering milk, and using questionable colorings and chemicals to improve the taste and look of rancid butter. For example, salicylic acid was employed as a preservative to prevent decomposition in straight butter, and boric acid was added to disguise the presence of rancidity or slow down its advancement.[7] Despite being condemned by authorities as harmful to human health, these chemicals were widely used by butter dealers to "repack and work over sour, strong and cheesy low-grade butter."[8]

Though dairy farmers numbered in the millions, the sector didn't unify and form the politically influential dairy coalition that exists today until individual producers realized they could make money from their products and that they needed to protect their livelihood from competition in the late 1800s. Until that moment, no single producer had the incentive to take on the significant task of organizing a countrywide dairy interest group. Second, late nineteenth-century America had little precedence for the establishment of such an industry lobby, making the initial costs of organization all the more significant. Third, federal and state governments during the late nineteenth century did not intervene in the agriculture sector. The government did not regulate the industry, and it did not provide social programs to protect the dairy farm's profitability. Thus farmers had no role model to follow and also few political battles to fight.

The incentives to form a dairy lobby emerged with the industrialization of butter and cheese production. The introduction of the centrifugal cream separator shortly after the Civil War increased the efficiency of butter production at a factory scale. Factory-manufactured butter and cheese were of higher quality than their farm-produced counterparts. The improved quality drove up the price and increased demand. By the turn of the century, factory-manufactured butter comprised more than 28 percent of total butter production, a far cry from the almost nonexistent industry at the end of the Civil War. Cheese factories grew at an even faster pace. By 1899 more than 94 percent of cheese produced in America was manufactured in a factory.[9]

Though the new butter- and cheese-manufacturing methods were capital-intensive and required certain business and organizational skills, a national lobby still did not form at this time. Its precursors, however, could be found in the formal and informal organizations that arose from the various arms of the factory system. Factory owners and producer associations, boards of trade and produce exchanges, and producer and dealer cartels were all self-organized to promote the expansion of dairy markets before a national lobby took shape.[10]

Factory owners were the catalyst that led to the creation of an industry-wide lobby. Unlike the individual farmer, who was more subsistence-oriented and diversified in his investments, the factory owner's primary interest was to maximize the profitability of dairy products. Factory owners were especially aware of market dynamics and were therefore eager to stave off competition from nondairy products such as margarine. The factory owner was not only a producer, but also a business leader who participated in wholesale markets on the national and international level. This necessitated expertise in all aspects of the industry and knowledge of the problems that might obstruct profits. The relatively small number of factory owners made their organization easier to achieve. Unlike the millions of individual farmers, factory owners maintained contacts with industry leaders across the country. For these reasons, factory owners created an industry-wide strategy and produced a business lobby powerful enough to take on margarine at the national level.

The first dairy associations were formed in the years following the Civil War. Members included factory dairymen and related industry leaders. Their initial aim was not to challenge margarine but to increase demand for dairy products by establishing and protecting reputations for quality among their members. Dairy production during that time was entirely unregulated and rife with poor-quality products. Initial county-level associations gradually expanded to encompass state and regional levels. At first these associations were apolitical. They focused on educating members about national and international market conditions as well as new developments in dairy science. In addition, they encouraged the implementation of new practices and helped prevent dishonest or opportunistic behavior by members.

Margarine Invades America

Just as butter makers realized the commercial potential industrial processing created for them, there soon emerged another technological innovation that introduced a cheaper competitor to the market. Margarine production started in Holland in the early

1870s and spread to other European countries, the United States, and eventually the rest of the world. World production was 100,000 tons in 1875 and grew to 4.8 million tons in the mid-1960s. The per capita consumption of margarine rose steadily in the United States, overtaking butter consumption in the mid-1950s and peaking in the mid-1970s. After that, per capita margarine consumption dropped sharply while butter consumption rose again, overtaking it around 2005. These swings were riddled with intense public debate over safety, misinformation, and legislative intervention.

Margarine originated from a social and political need. Rapid industrialization and urbanization in nineteenth-century Europe posed nutritional problems. The power of the newly influential middle class depended largely on sustaining the laborers and troops. Dietary fat, obtained mainly from meats and dairy products, provided the calories necessary for work and warfare, but as urban populations expanded, the new city dwellers found these options to be too expensive.[11] In France, for instance, the price of butter doubled between 1850 and 1870 beyond the inflation rate. This alarmed French leaders because it threatened social stability.

One underlying reason for the development of margarine, often unacknowledged, is that French leaders were also worried about Otto von Bismarck's increased militarization of what was then Prussia and its implications for industrial labor and military productivity. Deteriorating access to dietary fat among laborers and a looming war with Prussia threatened the industrial base and the security of France. France's survival therefore depended on finding cheaper supplies of dietary fat, mainly a substitute for butter. It was this realization that prompted Emperor Louis Napoleon III to offer a prize during the Paris World Exhibition of 1866 for the development of a reasonably priced alternative to butter.[12]

The French food chemist Hippolyte Mège-Mouriès won the prize in 1869. Mège-Mouriès used margaric acid, a fatty acid component isolated in 1813 by Michael Chevreul. Using the Greek word for pearl, *margarites*, he named his invention "margarine." The patents were later purchased by Dutch interests in 1871 and by Britain, the United States, and Prussia in 1873 and 1874.[13]

The case of margarine is an example of government officials using technology policy to generate desired socioeconomic outcomes. While the French could have relied on market policies such as subsidies and rationing to manage the shortage of butter, they instead launched a challenge to solve their problem through the creation of a new product.[14]

Spreading Opposition

What worked in France to solve the butter problem proved to be more difficult in the United States. Margarine was developed in France to reduce social tension caused by rising butter prices. However, the re-emergence of margarine in the mid-1890s in the United States created a new set of social tensions. Despite a rapid uptake in production and consumption, margarine's entry into the US market was rife with problems.

In 1873, Mège-Mouriès obtained a US patent with the intent to expand his French margarine factory and production in the United States. He sold the patent to the United States Dairy Company, which produced the "artificial butter" between 1871 and 1873. Inventors found ways around the patent and came up with new processes that treated fat using minor ingredients not specified in the original patent to create the same margarine output. Additional process innovations allowed the technology to be adopted widely, and soon margarine production expanded to a number of states and was traded nationwide.

Despite the rapid production uptake, margarine's entry into the United States was a case of bad timing. It occurred in the wake of the economic crisis of 1873, the first severe depression ever to strike the nation's agriculture industry.[15] Farmers faced serious financial problems, often selling their butter at a loss.[16] An additional complication for butter producers was price fluctuation. Because butter claimed residual milk supply, and because low-income families reduced their milk consumption during economic depressions, the milk supply available for butter production increased during depressions and declined during times of prosperity. Thus, butter prices fluctuated sharply. The price problems came on top of over-production and other changes that had already started to affect the dairy industry's profitability.

What emerged from the tension caused by lower-cost margarine and dairy producers' financial troubles was the dairy association. The creation of the dairy association was one of the most important institutional responses to the industry transformation that started in the 1860s in New York, Vermont, and Wisconsin. The associations led to the launch of a number of dairy newspapers that wielded considerable public influence. The *Hoard's Dairyman* of Wisconsin began in 1870 with a circulation of seven hundred, and grew rapidly to a circulation of eleven thousand in 1892 and about seventy thousand by 1918. Its editor, William D. Hoard, was a prominent industry spokesperson and a leading player in the early campaign against margarine. He later became governor of Wisconsin (1888–1891).

In a telling comment published in a 1986 booklet entitled *Oleomargarine and Butterine: A Plain Presentation of the Most Gigantic Swindle of Modern Times*, the New York State Dairy Commission is quoted as saying:

> There never was, nor can there ever be, a more deliberate, outrageous swindle than this bogus butter business. The whole scheme was conceived in iniquity, is nurtured by commercial moonshiners, and carried into execution by desperate men who are careful to appeal to that protection which our laws wisely throw about those charged with crime, in order that the innocent may not unjustly suffer, while they are deliberately, persistently, and willfully

violating the law and profiting by the perpetration of a base fraud upon the people.

The dairy sector began to wield immense political influence with the help of the associations and soon became margarine's biggest opponent. In connection with the Grange movement of the 1870s that encouraged families to band together to promote their agricultural interests and the Populist Party of 1880s and 1890s, dairymen were organized into local and state associations that took active part in supporting or resisting all kinds of laws affecting farmers.[17] In line with public sentiments against adulteration of dairy products, the associations used their influence to obtain legislation aimed directly at margarine as part of a wider campaign against fraud.

Like other substances such as alcohol and narcotics, margarine carried powerful social and cultural connotations that influenced not only market taste but also public policy. By the late nineteenth century, social status rested upon one's ability to consume competitively at an acceptable standard.[18] These "pecuniary canons of taste"[19] pervaded domestic rituals such as the family meal. Any housewife who served margarine therefore "cheapened" the entire family and cast doubts on her husband's ability as a provider. Even margarine's lower price made it seem inferior to butter.[20]

By contrast, butter took on social rectitude, expressing a "pastoral genre" and an appeal to the "good old days."[21] As a competing food alternative, margarine was thus stigmatized as an imposter delivering new dangers and an artificiality that corrupted natural "good food."[22] As a new processed food product of the industrial laboratory, margarine was suspect. Popular figures such as Mark Twain denounced it as another sign of the artificiality of modern life, and Governor Hubbard of Minnesota called "oleomargarine and its kindred abominations" a "mechanical mixture" created by "the ingenuity of depraved human genius."[23] To them, margarine was counterfeit butter, and its manufacturers were swindlers. In fact, opponents carefully designed the term "counterfeit butter" to associate margarine with illegal currency and therefore subject it to similar sanctions. Margarine was vilified and its producers demonized by the dairy associations as a bad and unhealthy imitation of butter. The dairy industry fought margarine on two fronts: legislation and false advertising campaigns.

The Laws against Margarine

In 1877, the New York State Legislature enacted the first antimargarine law as a direct result of lobbying efforts by the New York Dairy Association. New York became the antimargarine legislation launch pad because of unique state attributes, including the large population of working-class and immigrant families who would have had the most to benefit from margarine's lower price. The legislative measures were quickly adopted the following year in California, Connecticut, Maryland, Massachusetts, Missouri, Ohio, and Pennsylvania. The earliest round of legislation was framed as a means to protect the public against corporate falsification. The legislation required manufacturers, stores, hotels, restaurants, and boarding houses to post public notices if they sold or served margarine.[24] Industry leaders advocated for the legislation because they believed consumers would choose butter over margarine if given all the facts. The dairy industry aimed to destroy the margarine industry based on this assumption. State legislatures enacted laws that required proper labeling of the product to call it "oleomargarine" or "butterine" so it could not be confused with butter. They also fixed penalties for violations and, in some cases, required licensing of margarine manufacturers and dealers.

The labeling laws varied in their extremism and extended to packaging. Some variations included requirements for the location, size, and type of lettering used on containers. Some states enacted labeling laws that, in addition to making the contents easily recognizable, apparently were designed to make the packaging unattractive to the eye. For instance, one state required that a three-inch-wide black band be painted around the container, and another state required the use of labels painted in lampblack and oil on all containers of butter substitutes.[25]

In 1886 the US Congress passed the Oleomargarine Act. The 1886 statute and subsequent amendments and laws, however, failed to slow the spread of margarine. Many consumers recognized margarine as providing the same service as butter at a significantly lower price, and that trumped the legislation. Margarine held its market position, and in many instances the voters rejected prohibitive margarine legislations in referendums.

A series of lawsuits were filed against the Oleomargarine Act of 1886. Courts sustained the law as a tax instrument within the federal government's almost-plenary tax power. Lawsuits to invalidate the labeling or licensing requirements were also dismissed. Similar rulings upheld state laws restricting trade in margarine. In 1895, the Supreme Court upheld a Massachusetts law on the absolute prohibition of colored margarine. Laws were also passed to ensure that margarine crossing a state line would be subject to prohibition in the original packaging. Those laws were also upheld by the Supreme Court because they were an expression of the police power of the state.

The dairy industry needed to become more aggressive after it realized that state laws were not meeting its expectations and reducing the consumption of margarine. The dairy industry stepped up its efforts to get more aggressive and damaging legislation passed against margarine. At the dairy industry's recommendation, some states made the laws more severe, while others prohibited the manufacture and sale of margarine altogether. Five states further stipulated that any product manufactured in imitation of butter must be dyed pink.

Federal margarine legislation began with the Oleomargarine Act of 1886. The law imposed a tax of two cents per pound on margarine and required expensive licenses for manufacturers, wholesalers, and retailers of margarine. When the New York State's ban was voided, dairy activists turned their attention to enacting a federal law. In February 1885, dairy interests from twenty-six states convened in New York, resulting in the inauguration of a nationwide campaign to place the dairy industry on an "equal footing with its dangerous competitors."[26]

The campaign was led by the American Agricultural and Dairy Association, successor to the predominantly New York–based cheesemakers' American Dairymen's Association, created in 1866. As a result, Congress received petitions from all parts of the country, culminating in twenty-one bills on food adulteration and misbranding, sixteen of which specifically targeted butter substitutes. The bill included taxation, labeling, and forfeiture and licensing provisions aimed at crippling the industry. In effect, efforts to suppress margarine were portrayed as revenue collection under the federal government's taxation powers and therefore shielded proponents from charges of protectionism and the associated constitutional challenges.

During debate on the bill that would become the Oleomargarine Act, the dairy industry and its supporters in Congress advanced several critiques, most unsubstantiated by evidence and based on protectionist impulses. First, they argued that margarine was unhealthy. There were claims that the product caused Bright's disease (affecting kidneys), dyspepsia, and several other maladies. Second, they alleged that the product contained "diseased or putrid beef, dead horses, dead hogs, dead dogs, mad dogs, and downed sheep."[27] Third, critics sought to show that the ingredients associated with margarine and its methods of production were harmful. The list of ingredients read during the congressional debates included carbolic acid, caustic soda, nitric acid, and sulfuric acid. Though these ingredients were used in the processing of animal fat, they were not used in making the final product. The number of patents held by margarine manufacturers was used as evidence against them. The patents were seen as the idle experiments of "cranks" who set out to produce oleomargarine by intricate methods and with the help of a laboratory, though there was no evidence that these patents were ever used in margarine processing.[28]

During the debates, the bill was frequently referred to by margarine supporters as "protection run mad."[29] Lawmakers used protectionist arguments to weaken the margarine industry and strengthen dairy farmers. Dairy farming was portrayed as a strategic national industry that needed protection from competitors. The protectionist argument was akin to measures adopted by lawmakers against products such as tobacco and alcohol, where the moral rectitude of smoking and drinking was in question. Instead of the morality of margarine, the attackers used terminology to instill fear in consumers. The margarine industry was depicted by critics as "an insidious foe," and "a bad business [to be] exterminated." A congressional member from Wisconsin proclaimed, "I fly the flag of an intent to destroy the manufacture of the noxious compound by taxing it out of existence."[30] The debate was so vitriolic that when President Grover Cleveland received the bill, he said, "Those on both sides of the question whose advocacy or challenge is based upon no broader than local or personal interest have outnumbered all the others."[31]

The commissioner of agriculture in 1886 was an earnest supporter of the bill and a firm believer in the impurity of oleomargarine, and he had many backers in the House. The chair of the Committee on Agriculture, which passed the bill through the House, said, "There is no such thing as oleomargarine that is as wholesome in every respect as pure butter." He went on to say that he didn't agree that margarine could "be made palatable and wholesome as human food."[32]

Ultimately, President Cleveland, from the dairy state of New York, signed the law. He justified his decision to sign the law as a means to increase government revenue. The effect of the law ended up being somewhat counterproductive for the dairy lobby. Its enactment preempted all other prohibitive state laws and recognized margarine as a lawful article of commerce.

The antimargarine law had other blowbacks for the butter industry. In Iowa in November 1886, an Internal Revenue collector impounded sixty-six pounds of rancid butter, mistaking it for oleomargarine. He was subsequently obliged to release the consignment because it was proved to be straight butter, although not fit for table use.[33] The most damning case occurred in Georgia when a quantity of Norwegian butter was seized as oleomargarine. The state chemist analyzed and tested the Norwegian butter under the order of the state agricultural authorities. The chemist pronounced the impounded material as unquestionably oleomargarine. The importers appealed to a laboratory in Washington and provided affidavits from the makers and shippers to subsequently prove "the pedigree of the butter direct from the milk-pail."[34]

Government enacted additional laws and amendments to control margarine production. The 1886 federal law was twice amended to regulate the coloration of margarine. In 1902, the stamp tax levied on margarine, which aimed to make "oleomargarine free from artificial coloration that causes it to look like butter of any shade of yellow," was reduced to one-fourth cent per pound, compared to ten cents a pound on artificially colored margarine.[35] Dealers' license fees were also adjusted to discriminate against yellow margarine. The aim of the coloration amendments was to kill the margarine industry, because lawmakers believed consumers would not buy margarine if it did not look like butter.

Regulators underestimated the resolve of the margarine industry. Around 1909, facing the hostile regulatory environment on artificial yellow coloring, the margarine industry discovered oils that naturally imparted a yellow color to margarine.[36] As a result, they successfully petitioned the court to strike down the ten cents per pound tax on artificially colored margarine because the naturally yellow margarine had no added coloration.

The dairy industry was forced to advocate for more extensive laws that would hurt the industry. Regulators asked Congress to clarify the legislation to distinguish between artificially and naturally colored margarine. The final blow fell on the margarine industry in 1931. A ten-cent tax was levied upon all margarine products that exceeded 1.6 degrees on the scale of yellow.[37] By the early 1940s, two-thirds of US states banned the sale of yellow margarine, and twenty states prohibited the use of butter substitutes in state institutions. The exception was penal institutions in some cases.[38] It wasn't until the late 1960s that the last ban on yellow coloration in margarine disappeared in the United States. They continued in Canada.[39]

The Emergence of the National Dairy Council

Much of the campaign against margarine is credited to the National Dairy Council (NDC). The dairy industry became more sophisticated over time, and NDC emerged and spearheaded the fight against margarine as well as led the promotion of dairy consumption. To maintain pressure on margarine, the dairy industry, operating through the NDC, employed a wide range of disparaging campaigns that spread false information against what it saw as a competitive threat to the profitability of its industry. This marketing effort was more than forceful advertising, however. It was a conscious endeavor to convince the general public not to consume margarine via the dissemination of false information about its contents, nutritional value, and other aspects. The adverse reaction of an incumbent industry toward a new technology that may threaten its market share can do much to illuminate the ways in which technologically advanced applications penetrate the status quo.

To properly understand its reaction, one must first understand the organization. The NDC was established in 1915 for the purpose of promoting and advancing the dairy industry in America. Over the course of almost a century of advocacy the NDC has employed a variety of methods toward that end. By acting as a consolidated voice of the many individual stakeholders within the dairy industry, the NDC is able to support the industry in a way that promotes dairy commodities such as milk and butter in general without being brand specific.

From its inception, the NDC employed a strategy to propagate misleading information to support its goal of maintaining a strong consumer base for dairy products. It positioned itself not as an interest group but rather as an educational and research organization specializing in health and child welfare. It describes itself as a "Leader in Nutrition Research and Education," not as an advocacy group for the dairy industry, even though its mission since its inception has been to advance the cause of dairying in America.

The NDC benefited by framing itself as an education and research organization. The NDC was able to market itself as a neutral actor in the field of nutrition and education, similar to that of a university or government agency rather than as an industry group lobbying the public. As a result, it gained trust from the public. The position also allowed the NDC to seek and secure support from a much broader base than would have been available to a commercially focused interest group. Health, educational, and community organizations that otherwise rejected solicitations from a commercial group were willing to associate themselves with what appeared to be a more altruistic purpose. This granted the National Dairy Council access to schools and unique endorsements from government agencies. Indeed, on the web page for the Department for Health and Human Services today the NDC is listed as an organization that generates nutrition education programs and materials for schoolchildren, consumers, and health professionals. The NDC declares itself a public health organization to further the interests of the dairy industry.

However, going back to the late 1920s, the NDC has appeared to have a very different purpose. The dairy industry was very much aware of the threat that margarine posed and, through the NDC, took actions to destroy margarine's reputation. The majority of claims by the NDC made against margarine concerned the nutritional harms margarine posed to children. For example, in a report entitled *Butter—a Vital Food for Health*, the NDC pronounced as conclusive evidence "that vegetable and animal fat margarines are in no way comparable to butter for promoting growth."[40] The "conclusive evidence" was collected during an incident at an orphanage when a group of only seven children were fed butter for a period of months, then switched to margarine, and then back to butter. During these time periods the children were tracked in terms of height and weight and found to have developed at a relatively slower rate when fed margarine instead of butter.

New York City health officials released the report and later were forced to admit the NDC findings were only a post facto quantitative observation made after the small group of children were accidentally fed the alternating diet of butter and margarine. It was not a conscious decision to perform the experiment, and the validity of the data was discredited. That, however, didn't stop the NDC from disseminating the conclusions of the findings en masse to the public via commercial advertisements and other promotional materials.

The NDC not only embellished experimental results but also fabricated them entirely. In one particular case, an NDC article featured documentation of nutritional experiments that supposedly had been conducted on rats at a university in Cincinnati. The two rats were fed identical diets, except one was fed margarine and the other butter. The results, as the NDC explained, showed that the margarine-fed rat was underdeveloped, exhibited sore eyes, had rough and brittle hair, and a "weakness of skeleton." The butter-fed rat, on the other hand, was larger and had skin of a "splendid condition." The message attached to the end of the article stated, "If mothers wish to protect their children, they will insist that their children receive plenty of nature's real products, butter, for which there is no substitute."[41] When questioned, the university that had purportedly conducted and released the study denied that the experiment had ever taken place. Despite the falsification of its claims, the NDC simply removed the reference to the university but continued to publish this material.

In another instance margarine was decried by the dairy industry as completely lacking in vitamins and other nutrients. The NDC used a study concerning the presence of a high occurrence of xerophthalmia, a disease associated with a poor diet, within the Danish population during World War I. In its publications, the NDC stated that the Danish public's higher rate of margarine consumption was the sole cause of the disorder. When regular availability of butter resumed after the war, the article claimed, the rate of the disorder decreased. But the article failed to mention that those affected by xerophthalmia were very young and most likely consumed neither butter nor margarine. Furthermore, it neglected to mention other dietary aspects that may have contributed to the increased rate of symptoms or the apparent cure. Danish authorities denied the claims made by the industry, and one response to the head of the State Laboratory for Nutritional Research in Copenhagen wrote: "Once during the war ... there were some mothers who gave their small babies only skimmed milk, no whole milk at all. Some few of them got [eye disease]. No, people in Denmark are not stupid. They eat margarine and let the English pay three times as much for our butter."[42]

Other campaigns against margarine included claims that whale oil was being used in the manufacture of margarine. In 1926, the *Nation's Business*, a journal of the US Chamber of Commerce, reported that an "amazing amount of chemical technique and trade strategy have gone into the business of turning stinking inedible whale oil into margarine."[43] In an effort to portray the product in the most unnatural terms, the article stated that the oils must be "deodorized, hardened into fats and the acids removed. After being washed, dressed and perfumed, after a manner of speaking, they present a simulacrum of butter fair to look upon and with good keeping qualities, but at best a pale and insipid substitute for the best creamery prints."[44] Although various government agencies confirmed that no whale products were being used in the manufacture of margarine, public suspicion lingered.

Blending In

Despite the work the antimargarine campaign did to levy legislation and false advertising against the new product, US butter consumption declined by one-third and margarine consumption quadrupled between the early 1920s and 1950s.[45] The margarine industry was forced to innovate, and that contributed to its success.

One technological innovation happened in the late 1800s that particularly helped boost consumer's preference for margarine and limited the effectiveness of the legislative measures taken against the butter substitute. Chemists discovered hydrogenation. Hydrogenation is a chemical process that enabled margarine producers to replace the animal fat in butter with vegetable oil. Hydrogenation opened new opportunities for the industry. By heating inexpensive, inferior oils and exposing them to metal catalysts, a manufacturer could artificially create a solid or semisolid substance that was essentially shelf-stable. Hydrogenation made possible the development of the first two plant products, shortening and margarine, that later replaced their animal counterparts, lard and butter. As butter became increasingly expensive and relatively scarce, margarine became an attractive substitute for consumers. Hydrogenation technology appreciably lowered the price of margarine, reduced the stigma associated with the product, and provided an excellent source of nutrition.[46]

Hydrogenation struck a blow to the antimargarine forces, but it also opened a new battlefront. Margarine had become "un-American" overnight because producers used coconut oil, and the oil was entirely imported from the Philippines. Although the Philippines was a US protectorate, the dairy lobby labeled the innovation an invasion by the foreign "coconut cow."[47]

The imported oil gave the dairy lobby fresh political ammunition and enabled it to call for new protectionist measures. There was a rush in new federal and state margarine legislation, the so-called domestic fat laws. Most southern and western states, which had previously supported margarine, enacted these severe laws. The margarine industry had lost critical constituencies because of its use of coconut oil and hence had to abandon this ingredient despite its proven superiority. Yet this never deterred margarine manufacturers. They soon adopted the "very American" cottonseed and soybean oils to advance their cause.

With the switch, the margarine industry reinvigorated cotton and soybean farming and gained a powerful political ally that crushed the dairy lobby challenge. Cottonseed and soybean oil made up three-fourths of all oils used in margarine in the United States in 1942, representing 12 and 17 percent of total cotton and soybean oil production, respectively.[48] Opposition to margarine began to wane in most states. They provided a political counterweight to the dairy lobby. It was no longer politically tenable for the dairy lobby to discriminate against cotton and soybean farmers to protect the dairy sector. Dairy farmers were already earning average incomes two to four times greater than the average cotton or soybean farmer, and margarine provided these farmers with expanded opportunities to increase their incomes.

Between 1933 and 1935, fifteen states introduced discriminatory taxation on margarine made from "foreign" ingredients. Alabama, for example, imposed a ten-cent excise tax on all oleomargarine except those made from domestic ingredients such as peanut, cottonseed, corn, and soybean oils; oleo oils from cattle; neutral lard from hogs; or milk fat.[49]

Other states closely followed Alabama in enacting new legislation. The introduction of new raw materials into margarine production marked a turning point in the challenge to margarine. Legislation extended to the nondairy southern and western states and provided new ammunition to the dairy lobby to restrict margarine production. The southern states wanted to protect their "domestic" oilseed industries, but this gave dairy producers an excuse to fight margarine. By default, margarine legislation became a potent protectionist tool against interstate trade. Interestingly, the traditional dairy lobbies now faced several powerful opponents.

Continued discrimination against margarine elicited ill feelings and retaliation among groups that felt threatened by the legislation, especially among cotton growers and livestock farmers. For instance, some cotton-growing southern states protested and threatened reprisals immediately after Wisconsin passed a law imposing a tax of fifteen cents per pound of margarine in 1935.[50] In addition to public protests and threats of reprisal made by state governors and commissioners of agriculture, the Mid-South Cotton Growers Association, the Mississippi Wholesale Grocers Association, the Tennessee Federation of Labor, and other agencies protested vigorously.[51]

The margarine industry had other allies too. The Iowa State Grocers Association, for example, argued against the Iowa Farm Bureau and dairy interests. Its work resulted in a bill calling for the sale of yellow margarine. As part of the campaign, samples of yellow margarine were provided to members of the assembly and state officials. The opponents told the Senate that margarine was harmful to human health and claimed that it caused hair loss among men, stunted human growth, and affected sexual health. In support of the bill, Senator George O'Malley closed his remarks saying he had used the product for years and demanded an end to the practice of having to mix it with additives to make it yellow. He stressed that his health was excellent, alerted the senators to his big stock of gray hair, and indicated that he was six feet, three inches tall. He further told the house that he and his wife had ten children, laying to rest the claim that margarine caused impotence. The next day the Senate passed the bill, removing barriers to the sale of margarine.

Vestiges of laws introduced to curtail the spread of margarine can still be found in some US states. In Missouri, for example, a law restricting imitation butter that dates back to 1895 is still on the books. Although it is not enforced, dealers in the product could spend a month in jail and pay a $100 fine. Repeat offenders get six months in jail and pay $500.

Before the end of World War II, margarine returned to the political scene in the United States. The US first lady, Eleanor Roosevelt, featured in commercial ads for margarine in what appeared to be a vindication of Theodore Schultz. The debate dragged on for six years, led to four major hearings, and resulted in some fifty different aborted bills.[52] The explosion in the price of butter in 1947 proved a boon to margarine; the 1902 margarine law was repealed in the House of Representatives in 1949 and in the Senate in 1950, making margarine a normal food product subject to the Food and Drugs Act.[53] After this, margarine steadily edged past butter as the main source of dietary fat.

Blends of the two products are widely marketed today. The debate between butter and margarine, however, has not ended. Claims and counterclaims about the health risks of the products continue to be discussed. Health authorities, however, are using evidence-based decisionmaking to promote safety irrespective of the sources of concern.

This approach allows regulators to use the latest safety information to determine how well to protect consumers, as opposed to protecting specific industries. For example, in 2015, the FDA announced new measures to phase out trans fat used to extend the shelf life of processed foods in three years. The efforts started in 1999 when the FDA required manufacturers to declare the amount of trans fat in their products. The requirement went into effect in 2006, although firms continued to use partially hydrogenated oils in processed foods.

Trans fat can still be found in crackers, cookies, cakes, frozen pies, and other baked goods; snack foods (such as microwave popcorn); frozen pizza; vegetable shortenings and stick margarines; coffee creamers; refrigerated dough products (such as biscuits and cinnamon rolls); and ready-to-use frostings. Measures to eliminate the use of trans fat are expected to prevent an additional seven thousand heart disease deaths per year and up to twenty thousand heart attacks annually. Evidence of the risks of trans fat has led the FDA to argue that trans fat no longer falls in the legal category of substances "generally considered as safe." The measures will apply to all trans fat irrespective of whether it comes from artificial or natural sources.

Conclusions

Margarine represents one of the best examples of incumbent industries using legislative instruments to curtail or extinguish new technologies. A wide range of tactics were used by the dairy industry to block margarine, including false advertising, product disparagement, and the creation of other health scares. Their intent was to maintain public support for legislative restrictions on the product. Several lessons from the case of margarine are relevant to contemporary policy debates over new technologies.

The first main lesson from the margarine case study is how resistance can lead to the rise of lobbying and the use of legislation as a primary instrument to restrict trade in new products. The rise of lobby groups in response to new technologies is an important feature of the changing landscape of the political governance of innovation. Much of the dairy lobby work focused on labeling, segregating production, and limiting interstate trade. The overall strategy was to pass restrictive state laws before pushing for a federal law. Similar strategies have recently been employed in regard to the labeling of transgenic crops, led by advocates of organic foods. It is notable that the creation of market space for margarine was accompanied by the repeal of the laws.

The second lesson is how technical trade barriers to new technologies are still used in subtle forms around the world. Fundamentally, such restrictions are intended to protect existing industries by keeping new products out of the market. The most important of such measures comes in the form of labeling requirements. These requirements are often seen as a way to protect public interest, such as consumer health or environmental well-being. It is usually difficult to distinguish between labeling requirements that seek to protect human health and those that have the underlying motive of protecting incumbent industries. The need to ensure that public health and environmental well-being are protected is a genuine concern. But in many cases not all those who support labeling want to do so for these reasons. As the case of margarine shows, some proponents of legislative restrictions are explicitly interested in seeking the removal of the product from the market. Others calling for restrictions, however, may not have such drastic outcomes as their central objective. In many cases, reluctance by industry to label may in fact be a result of the lack of clarity over the intended outcomes.

The third lesson relates to the questioning of the technological foundations for the new products. This is typically used to challenge the technological platform by raising moral concerns over the underlying patents. Opponents claimed that the patents used in margarine production were evil and represented a threat to public order. In many contemporary debates the act of patenting continues to be a source of considerable contention. This is certainly the case with the patenting of living organisms, which is a central pillar of the biotechnology industry.

Similar debates over intellectual property rights have raged in the field of software and have resulted in the open-source moment. In this case, however, the concern has been more about inclusion than about the morality of the inventions. Patent debates often express concern over technological exclusion, given the nature of intellectual property as a tool for conferring exclusive rights to inventors. Intellectual property rights confer on the owners the ability to alter the stream of benefits through new businesses or business models. In this regard, social anxieties associated with intellectual property rights are usually legitimate. But seeking to restrict intellectual property protection is probably not the best way to promote technological inclusion.

The fourth lesson relates to the dual role of public education in technological controversies. In the first instance, the dairy industry used a wide range of tools—including false advertising—to reach the public. It sought to show the potential risks of margarine. Some of the information was derived from studies that were designed to project a negative view of margarine. Policymakers can be easily pushed by public opinion and lobbying to make decisions on the basis of studies designed to achieve specific political objectives.

On the other hand, margarine advocates tried to counter the information through public education and advertising. The ability to communicate to the public and shape messages became an important aspect of the debate. The communication would extend to the highest levels of government, often seeking to take advantage of public sentiments on economic matters. The portrayal of margarine as a low-cost food helped to bolster its political appeal. The messaging to support both sides took many forms, the most interesting being the use of cartoons aimed at capturing public imagination. A key message for policymakers from this debate was the importance of monitoring the popular press. Today policymakers have an even harder task because of the diversity of media and the existence of diverse epistemic communities that share and advocate specific positions.

The fifth important lesson from the debate is coevolution between technological innovation and institutional change. The creation of lobby groups for the dairy industry predated margarine. But the entry of the product in the market shaped their agenda and public posture. Preexisting organizations often repurpose their missions in light of new technological developments. The margarine industry, on the hand, had to create its own support mechanisms at the state and national levels. These organizations would become the locus for advocating for the nascent sector through public education and lobbying. The tensions between the two industries were expressed through the missions of these organizations.

The last policy lesson from the debate is scientific uncertainty. Policymakers need to create regulatory mechanisms that are open to adjustment in light of new information. For a period, some consumers believed that margarine was healthier than butter. But as new information on the health impact of trans fat emerged, regulators adjusted their safety assessment methods. The way regulators handle scientific uncertainty is a critical aspect of trust in public institutions. The debate between butter and margarine still lingers, but the focus of food safety has shifted to specific ingredients of concern such as trans fat, not whole products.

5

Gaining Traction

Farm Mechanization

If you risk nothing, then you risk everything.

GEENA DAVIS

As shown in the last chapter, the tensions surrounding margarine were marked by efforts to curtail or eliminate the product from the market. Much of the negative campaign focused on segregating the product and giving it a unique identity that helped consumers to identify it and reject it.

The mechanization of American agriculture through the introduction of tractors took a different form. This chapter shows how the incumbent sources of animal power sought instead to find a way to coexist with the emerging mechanization revolution.

The story of the mechanization of rural America was transformational in the true sense of the word. Nearly half of the US population lived in rural areas in the early twentieth century. Rural America was dominated by small, diversified farms employing nearly half of the country's workforce and supporting nearly twenty-two million work animals. Today the agricultural sector is concentrated in sparsely populated rural areas on "large, specialized . . . highly productive and mechanized farms [that] employ a tiny share of U.S. workers and use five million tractors in place of the horses and mules of earlier days."[1]

According to a classic study by Alan L. Olmstead and Paul W. Rhode, this transformation was "a gigantic Schumpeterian confrontation as the defenders of entrenched methods appealed to popular sentiments and tried to capture legal and political institutions to forestall the process of creative destruction."[2] Sensing that they were swimming against the tide, however, they sought accommodation and coexistence. This chapter examines how the champions of the two sources of power advocated their positions. Essentially, a new technology with great potential for improvement was pitted against an incumbent source of farm power that had reached its biological capability. The competition between horses and tractors was marked by considerable uncertainty as the two initially performed different functions. This led to debates that focused on coexistence rather than on the exclusion of the new technology. Technological improvement, engineering skills, and diversification of tractor functions eventually rendered horses redundant.

The Lay of the Land

American farm mechanization, especially the introduction of tractors, was truly a transformation in ways that are akin to Schumpeter's characterization of the impact of railroads in transportation. Before mechanization, farming was primarily for subsistence, as most small farmers did not possess the capital and resources to farm commercially. During the antebellum years, farmers typically used basic tools such as axes and plows pulled by oxen and donkeys. Adoption of new farming technology was slow, even for simple methods such as the revolving horse rake.[3] Human labor was the main source of agricultural energy, so technologies were crafted to suit the patterns of household economies. One of the commonly used implements was the cast-iron plow. The plow was a mix of metal and wood that was pulled by horses or donkeys. It was an improvement from earlier, more provincial models. Even so, the wooden moldboard would often weaken and rupture due to the thickness of some soils. The cast-iron plow allowed a farmer to cultivate roughly one acre a day.[4] In addition, a plow named the prairie breaker, which was primarily aimed at cutting the dense soil of the prairie region, became popular. Heavy when compared to other plows, the prairie breaker could cut through tough soil but required intense physical exertion and only increased productivity by two acres per day.

To improve the efficiency of the laborious plowing, tilling, and planting techniques, several innovators began to develop alternative tools. In 1837, John Deere expanded on the work of another Illinois blacksmith, John Lane, to create a plow using highly polished wrought iron moldboards and steel shares. Steel was stronger and could cut through more types of soil. Take-up of Deere's steel plow was slow initially, and it was not until the late 1850s when farmers began to buy the new tool en masse. Steel was expensive, and typically only more affluent farmers could afford to buy the Deere plow. It was around the time of the Civil War when Deere's steel plow took hold in much of the Midwest region. By 1857, Deere was producing ten thousand plows annually.[5]

Deere was not the only farming innovator who changed agriculture's output efficiency and introduced the use of animal farm labor. Additional developments such as Cyrus McCormick's reaper enabled farmers to harvest upwards of twelve acres of grain per day. Innovations such as the reaper, however, were mostly pertinent to the Midwest and were of little use for non-grain growers. For the most part, advances in farm implements during this period were regionally exclusive, and farmers benefited little from their development.

With the onset of the Civil War and the ensuing political and social upheaval, farming in America underwent significant changes. The Civil War prompted the first agricultural revolution, transitioning from hand labor to horse labor.[6] With the surging demand for agricultural products and shortage of labor due to the draft, farmers were called upon to adopt practices that would foster productivity. Deere's steel plow and McCormick's reaper facilitated greater animal use and enabled farmers to produce more in a shorter period of time.

The value of grain, corn, and other farm products soared during the war, and advances in technology assisted northern farmers to meet the nation's demands. By the final years of the conflict the South's economy was in ruins and the North had optimized its diversified crop system. In many ways the war and the resulting loss of slave labor encouraged innovative farming methods and farm mechanization.

The late nineteenth and early twentieth centuries produced noteworthy changes in agriculture but are often considered to be periods of evolution rather than revolution. It was the Civil War period that ushered in new developments, while the years following the war generated slower progress. One notable development during the post–Civil War period was the steam-traction engine. Although the engine improved production and eased the workload of some farmers, steam-traction engines were not ubiquitous. Even at the peak of production, many farmers could not afford them. In the steam-traction engine's case, the new technology was less convenient than traditional farming methods.

Perhaps the steam-traction engine's major significance was the way it helped condition society to accept farm mechanization. Steam engines helped to make commercial farming possible and "inducted the farmer into a mechanical and corporate world."[7] Steam engines also paved the way for gasoline tractors. The production and adoption of the steam engine, though modest, helped to inspire future technological and engineering developments.

Harnessing New Technology

The inventor John Froelich created the first gasoline-powered tractor in 1892. During the first decade of the new century, a number of companies surfaced to promote their versions of the tractor. The competition encouraged greater innovation. By 1906, eleven major companies were producing tractors. The Hart-Parr Company was the first to take major steps toward commercial tractor production at the turn of the century. Following in its footsteps, International Harvester recognized the lucrative market in gasoline-powered tractors and by 1911 became the leading producer in America.

The number of tractor-producing companies boomed, but the proportion of farmers who bought their product remained small. The number of tractors sold was a small fraction of the number of farms. Manufacturers had not enticed mainstream farmers, who remained tied to draft power, to purchase their products. The tractor market was soon flooded. The boom years for the tractor industry during the early twentieth century ended.

It is notable that the rapid growth in the use of the gas tractor did not occur because it was superior to the horse. There were simply large tracts of unbroken prairie land that were being opened up in the West without a sufficient number of horses to do the work. Businesses, however, did not consider the tractor to be a good investment. The tractor did not operate as smoothly as the horse; maintenance often cost more than the purchase price; and its size and weight made it impractical for the small farm. Some felt that the manufacturing companies had brought the tractor to the market prematurely.

For all those who felt uneasy over the introduction of gasoline-powered tractors, there were others, such as members of the press, who were excited. Many influential journalists and their newspapers championed the development of the tractor and encouraged further advances to increase its popularity. The press viewed the gasoline-powered tractor as an asset for both the agricultural industry and the economy in general. Journalists viewed tractors as the next step in the inevitable process of farm mechanization and encouraged the public to recognize the benefits of technological development.

In the years following the tractor boom-bust period, the press's positive coverage helped stimulate new designs and versions of the gasoline-powered tractor. Primarily, companies such as

International Harvester wanted to produce a smaller, lighter, and less expensive machine. In the years preceding and during World War I, companies experimented with smaller, more efficient tractors. With the ensuing loss of labor and animals due to the war, tractors entered into the first phase of mass production.

Some of the final obstacles to tractor use were broken down once the machine became more reliable and versatile, but company malfeasance threatened to erode consumer trust irrevocably. By 1917 significant improvements had transformed the gasoline-powered tractor from a massive, cumbersome machine into a more manageable one. The number of tractors increased from 549,000 to 782,000 between 1925 and 1928, and by 1932 there were more than a million tractors on farms.[8] Even with the considerable surge in tractor production, farmers continued to weigh the costs and benefits of adoption. Before the 1925 boom there was heightened mistrust of the tractor industry. During the war, tractor companies took advantage of farmers by promoting and selling faulty tractors.

In the middle to late nineteenth century, the agricultural industry became chaotic. Prices plummeted, demand fell, and a plethora of small and unwieldy manufacturing companies lost business. "By 1920 the lack of standardized models, the failure of tractor firms and the resulting evaporation of dealerships and repairman, the economic depression in agriculture, and Henry Ford's dumping of one hundred thousand cheap Fordsons on the market strained what little credibility the tractor industry ever had."[9] From its inception in 1892 the gasoline tractor faced periods of success and failure. The tractor continued to try to meet the needs of average farmers, but was often met with apprehension.

Debating Power

The introduction of more versatile tractors set mechanization on a collision course with animal power. In 1924 International Harvest introduced the Farmall, "the first all-purpose, reliable, well-designed tractor on the market."[10] The Farmall could not only plow, but it also helped farmers with cultivation and planting as well. The versatility of the horse was being gradually but ominously reflected in the design of new tractors. Technological diversity would provide engineers and innovators with what evolution had built into biological diversity.

The introduction of the Farmall came as part of an incremental introduction of new tractor designs. "The Bull (1913) was the first small and agile tractor, Henry Ford's popular Fordson (1917) was the first mass-produced entry, and the revolutionary McCormick-Deering Farmall (1924) was the first general purpose tractor capable of cultivating row crops. The Farmall was one of the first to incorporate a power takeoff, which enabled it to transfer power directly to implements under tow."[11] Technological diversity, engineering skills, and internal improvements in the specific tractor played key roles not only in maximizing wealth but also in fostering rapid adoption. The adoption was therefore a result of coevolutionary changes in the agricultural sector.[12]

The year of the Farmall's introduction coincided with the onset of the great debate between advocates of tractors and horse champions. The two sides argued from different perspectives representing divergent socioeconomic worldviews. Tractor advocates, infused with a sense of technological optimism, appeared to promote the wholesale replacement of horses. Horse champions, however, took a different approach. Their flag-bearer was Wayne Dinsmore, executive secretary of the Horse Association of America (HAA). He appealed to the "complexity of farm operations, dearth of reliable, comparative information, and the popularity of horses among many engineers."[13] The HAA issued leaflets that presented farm animals as superior to tractors. One leaflet claimed, for example: "A mule is the only fool proof tractor ever built."[14]

The HAA used "slippery slope" arguments to deter its members from adopting the tractor. One of its newsletters asserted: "We believe all tractors are bad, only some are worse than others. When it comes down to actual dollars and cents, we believe that any farmer who disposes of his horses and intends to do all his farm work with tractors, will eventually 'hit the rocks,' and that he is only working for the man who sells the tractors, for as soon as he had made enough wheat or other farm products to pay for his tractor, it will be necessary for him to purchase another."[15] Indeed, there was some element of truth in this statement, given the rapid rate at which new tractors were being developed.

By the early 1920s tractors accounted for nearly 85 percent of the plowing in Illinois, Indiana, and Ohio. But the tractor could not yet perform many other farm tasks. In 1921 an Illinois agricultural bulletin noted the tractor's downfalls, stating that it could not engage in "mowing hay, plating and husking corn, hauling manure, threshing, hauling, raking, tedding, and putting hay into barn or stack, and picking up corn after binder, among other operations."[16]

The HAA was established in 1919 as one of America's early prominent lobbying organizations. Its stated mission was to "aid and encourage the breeding, raising, and use of horses and mules."[17] More broadly, it was created to "champion the cause of livestock dealers, saddle manufacturers, farriers, wagon and carriage makers, hay and grain dealers, teamsters, farmers, breeders, and other business interests that had a financial or emotional interest in horses and mules."[18]

Horses dominated the farm in the early 1900s and fueled an economic industry of their own. One-quarter of America's cropland was used just to grow feed for animals that worked on farms.[19] They were part of an economic system that extended beyond the farm. Draft animals consumed an estimated "68 percent of the nation's oat crop, 45 percent of the hay crop, 25 percent of the rye crop, and 24 percent of its corn crop. If draft animals disappeared, veterinarians, harness makers, farriers, and other parts of the vast support network would be affected as well. All this meant that a complex universe of traditions, occupations, and even knowledge would fade and disappear if the tractor forces had their way."[20] In a typical Schumpeterian scenario, the "old would be replaced by the new . . . but to horse advocates, the new structure supporting a petroleum-based agricultural system would be less human and its benefits would accrue to a much smaller number of people, especially on the local level."[21]

The HAA was therefore not just waging a war to stall the adoption of the tractor, but it was championing a moral cause to preserve a way of life. There were genuine concerns that the adoption of the tractor would render farmers dependent on urban supplies of expertise, spare parts, fuel, and other inputs that were previously available on the farm. Horses could reproduce themselves, whereas tractors depreciated. This became a potent argument against the technology.[22]

The goal of building a national lobbying organization was reinforced at the 1919 Farm Power Conference in Chicago, where the threat of the tractor industry became obvious.[23] Sounding an alarm over the technology, the HAA's president, Fred M. Williams, wrote that "the extravagant use of motor transportation in this country has passed far beyond the point of sanity and unless something is done to curtail this needless waste the ultimate result cannot be other than disastrous for the future welfare of the nation."[24]

From the outset, the HAA faced counterattacks. Soon after its establishment, the *Chilton Tractor Journal* noted that even with its "national campaign of anti-tractor propaganda . . . [it] cannot expect to stem the rising tide of tractor business even to the slightest degree."[25] The journal urged those "dealing in horses and mules, hay and harnesses, to get into the tractor business while it is yet young and full of opportunity."[26]

Representing the economic interests of those tied to the horse industry, the HAA organized an extensive grass-roots campaign to preserve the horse in the American economy. In contrast to other advocacy groups, the HAA did not call for the complete abandonment of the automobile and tractor, but rather sought a healthy and fair coexistence between horses and technology.

The HAA put forward a wide range of arguments to press the case for coexistence, which tractor advocates may have viewed as a tactic to stall the adoption of the new technology. The HAA bemoaned the inability of the US Department of Agriculture to "compel farmers to put horses or mules in place of trucks and tractors as they wear out."[27] Such a move would have guaranteed a market for farm animals and presumably would have provided a form of insurance against mechanical failure. But the proposal ignored that the tractor was in its early stages of development, and accordingly the tractor had greater potential for improvement than the horse.

There were, however, more radical voices that wanted the tractor to be exterminated. A Texas doctor, for example, wrote to President Franklin Roosevelt calling for all tractors and trucks to be destroyed. A farmer from Nebraska thought that the solution to the depression was to abolish tractor manufacturing. Another farmer from Ohio proposed a tax on tractors punitive enough to dissuade people from making purchases.[28]

The HAA, however, struck a less inflammatory tone. It argued that horses were already doing what the tractor promised to do and so there was no need to replace them. It argued that horsepower in tractors was fixed in the engine and therefore lacked flexibility. In other words, farmers could not adjust the scale of horsepower to suit the task that was being performed. Horses were modular and could be increased or reduced on the basis of need. Furthermore, a nonperforming horse could easily be replaced.

Horses were well proven, whereas tractors were unreliable and required maintenance that was not readily available to the farmer. Such lack of repair and maintenance capacity led to greater support for horses. As one farmer reportedly said, "I tried a tractor, but . . . I lost more time hauling my mechanical power out of mud holes than I gained from its use, ten times over."[29] The HAA also funded studies and testimonials demonstrating that horses were better suited for hauling heavy loads over short distances to persuade business owners not to switch to delivery trucks. On the other hand, proponents argued that although horses might be better equipped for the transport of heavy loads for shorter periods of time,[30] tractors could work longer hours and at a faster pace than their natural counterparts.

The HAA underwent a campaign to sway public opinion in favor of the horse to counter the growing perception that animals were becoming obsolete. The HAA approached its lobbying movement from three angles, employing tools such as a short film series, radio broadcasts, direct mailings, film ads, and a national tour by the executive secretary. It addressed the advantages of horses in military, urban, and rural environments.

The military was also worried about the decline in horse numbers and trained horsemen. Both General John Pershing and Major General George Patton advocated for the need to maintain a cavalry. In 1930 Patton forcefully argued that armored vehicles would never be able to replace horses.[31] The HAA built on the voices of military leaders and framed the decline in horses as a national security threat, arguing that draft animals were needed by the military for transportation, artillery, and reconnaissance in modern warfare.[32]

In urban areas, the HAA focused on the economic and legal issues surrounding the use of horses. It advocated against antihorse legislation put forth by local and state officials. For example, a "battle for the streets" emerged with cars, horses, and streetcars all vying for space on the road. The HAA staunchly opposed any measures that would inhibit the free movement of horses on city streets, fighting instead for parking restrictions for automobiles. Whereas those in the automobile industry argued that horses were a major cause of gridlock in city streets, the HAA asserted that parked automobiles were the primary source of congestion. In turn, the solution was not to eliminate horses from the roads but to prohibit parking in certain areas to free up traffic lanes.

The HAA was successful in Pittsburgh, Boston, and Los Angeles, which enacted parking restrictions for automobiles.[33] The lobbying organization also printed material citing the environmental and health risks of increased automobile use. Referencing scientific studies, it claimed that horse manure hardly posed a threat to the environment and human health when compared to automobile emissions. By printing such findings in mass-produced publications, while simultaneously engaging in a nationwide speaking tour, representatives from the HAA successfully disseminated information to the American public.

To promote the role of the horse in agriculture, the HAA targeted farmers, breeders, bankers, and researchers. The association focused on the relationship between increased tractor use and the reality of overproduction. It asserted that it was in the farmer's best financial interest, if he did not already own a tractor, to continue to work with horses. Breeders were encouraged by the HAA not only to continue breeding horses but to breed larger animals so that they could compete with tractors. In fact, the average weight for one animal increased from 1,203 pounds to 1,304 pounds from 1917 to 1943. The HAA pushed more research to maximize individual or team horse performance. It even formed the Animal Motors Committee in the American Society for Agricultural Engineers so it could influence academic research. Finally, to counter criticism of horse inefficiency compared to the tractor, the HAA established a number of thorough educational packages and lessons instructing farmers on how to better care for their horses.

In a 1921 public relations stunt in Fargo, North Dakota, the Tractor Department of the National Implement and Vehicle Association hosted a competition. Horses and tractors competed to prepare a ten-acre seedbed. They were judged on speed and quality.[34] The HAA declined to participate partly because of uncertainty over the outcome. It did not end well for the horses. Temperatures rose to 100 degrees Fahrenheit in Fargo that June, and five horses died as a result of the competition.[35]

The warring sides took advantage of every opportunity to high-light weaknesses in their opponent, but the jabs in turn led to improvements for both camps. The HAA pointed to the mechanical problems associated with tractors, which later inspired further engineering work. The tractor lobby seized on disease outbreaks among horses to dramatize their limitations. For example, when sleeping sickness (encephalomyelitis) broke out among horses in the late 1980s, tractor promoters made misleading claims that up to 40 percent of animals had died. The association responded to the alarm with direct mail, radio, and press releases. But it also started to encourage its members to pay more attention to good animal care and nutrition.[36]

The association put pressure on land-grant universities to allocate resources and efforts to studying the benefits of horses on the family farm.[37] Because the majority of farmers in America did not own tractors during the early twentieth century, the HAA believed that agricultural research stations should adjust their research accordingly. For a time, the HAA successfully swayed the agenda of a handful of research centers at land-grant universities.

Organizations with a stake in the automobile and tractor industries initially reacted to the advocacy of the HAA with a sense of sarcasm and overconfidence. Prominent tractor magazines likened the HAA's campaign to a temporary, backward-thinking movement that would soon dissipate. Any organization seeking to maintain a place for horses in the economy was, from their perspective, doomed from the beginning.

By 1945, even the HAA was admitting defeat. Its publications slowly shifted from case studies to articles on the recreational use of horses. Internal combustion engines ultimately triumphed over horses largely because of their universal applicability and the emergence of more powerful supportive institutions. The HAA's failure to protect the horse's place in the American economy, however, was not a result of any one rival lobbying movement. There was the sense that as technological and engineering developments emerged in cities, on farms, and in the military, the need for animal labor lessened. As the number of horses in these areas decreased, more Americans began to use horses for recreation.[38] As described above, the HAA engaged in an impressive public advocacy movement on behalf of those with a vested interest in the horse. Although its goals did not materialize, the work of the HAA serves as an example of how activists mobilize support on behalf of an incumbent industry or technology.

Analogous to the experience of the Horse Association of America is *California Agrarian Action Project v. The Regents of the University of California*. Presented to the Superior Court of California in 1979, this lawsuit exemplifies many of the same characteristics of the HAA's efforts decades earlier. Similar in aim, the cases differ, however, in use of tactics. The HAA undertook an advocacy and grassroots campaign, while the individuals in the latter used the court system to reach their goals. The transition in America from lobbying outside the judicial system to using the courts as a means to achieve a policy preference raises valuable questions about the success or failure of opposition movements and the role of the courts in general.

The California Rural Legal Assistance (CRLA) filed a suit on behalf of nineteen individual farmers and the nonprofit California Agrarian Action Project (CAAP) against the University of California (UC). CRLA claimed that the school's agricultural research program harmed the small farmer and that the university violated the spirit of the Hatch Act. The trial court reached a decision in 1987, ruling in favor of CAAP, and then the appellate court reversed this decision in 1989.

Passed in 1887, the Hatch Act created agricultural experimentation stations based out of universities that were funded by the federal government. The impetus behind its proposal and passage was to raise education and awareness of advances within agriculture to foster superior products and greater efficiency. The nonprofit CAAP, under the auspices of the CRLA, claimed that the majority of the funding and efforts by UC worked against the initial purpose of this act. CRLA claimed that UC overemphasized research on mechanization and agricultural technology, thus helping agricultural businesses at the expense of the family farm and the consumer. Specifically, the organization stated that UC's research displaced farmworkers, eliminated small farms, harmed consumers, impaired the quality of rural life, and impeded collective bargaining.[39] It asserted that in response to these grievances more resources should be applied to enhance the quality of life for small-scale farmers in California.

This case sheds light on the sensitivity of mechanization, as well as on the extent to which parties will go to protect their interests. The legal action taken by the CRLA raises meaningful issues regarding the academic freedom of research institutions and differences in interpretation of the law. Although mechanization impacted all areas of agricultural production, this case focuses primarily on the mechanization of the tomato harvester developed by UC researchers. Before the development of the tomato harvester, forty-four people worked to harvest tomatoes; the majority of these workers were illegal immigrants. By 1984 there were only eight thousand laborers involved in this process, and their main duty was to ride the harvesting machines.[40] When we examine these numbers, it appears as though there was clear labor displacement as a result of the mechanical harvester. Studies have shown that although jobs were lost in the tomato industry, demand in California grew for other labor-intensive produce. In this sense the loss of employment in one area was offset by demand in another, which became an argument used against the CRLA's assertion that mechanization endangered livelihoods of most farmers. Similarly, additional jobs were created in irrigation and factory work.

The debate over the mechanical tomato harvester is an example of the tension between farmers seeking to preserve their jobs and researchers wanting to create time- and labor-saving machines. The initial court decision of 1987 ruled in favor of the plaintiff and required UC to take steps to ensure that a specific amount of its federal funds be allocated to issues pertaining to the family farm.

In May 1989, however, UC won its appeal, as the court stated that it did not violate the stipulations in the Hatch Act. The court ruled that the Hatch Act did not clearly enumerate which farming constituencies should benefit from the federal funding. Its goals were to "aid in acquiring and diffusing among the people of the United States useful and practical information on subjects connected with agriculture, and to promote scientific investigation and experiment respecting the principles and applications of agricultural science." The court based its decision on both its interpretation of the legislation and precedent. Some viewed this reversal as a blow to the rural workforce, while others believed it defended academic freedom and safeguarded continuing technological and engineering improvements.

In a number of ways the CRLA trial can be viewed as an extension of the earlier HAA movement. Both advocated for more equitable policies, for horses and for small farmers, and both were forced to confront the presence of emerging and institutionalized technologies.

Technological uncertainty is also associated with moments of resilience in established industries, as illustrated by the campaign to protect horsepower in the face of mechanical power.[41] The introduction of mechanical power on the roads and on the farm threatened those who depended on horses for their livelihoods. Furthermore, it challenged the conventional view that farmers should be able to grow their own power to use on the farm.

Plowing New Ground

Given the fervent debate over farm mechanization and attempts to secure a niche for horses, it is necessary to discuss how this phenomenon eventually became institutionalized within society. As with most technological innovations, there is a process by which the technology is either embraced or rejected. With the invention of the gasoline-powered engine in 1892 and the subsequent commercial production of tractors in the early twentieth century, a new era in agriculture began. So did a new era of farm legislation and lobbying activities that sought to influence public opinion and agricultural business.

The passage of the Hatch Act enabled universities to focus on agricultural research that could then be circulated among farmers. Agricultural magazines and newspapers were established, and farmers obtained information about developments at the land-grant colleges through these publications. In addition, some universities created agricultural institutes that provided knowledge and scientific education to farmers; regardless of whether farmers immediately accepted new practices, the publications and institutes provided an institutional framework for the advancement of farm technologies and related engineering skills.

Two additional pieces of legislation—the Smith-Lever Act of 1914 and the Smith-Hughes Act of 1917—helped to normalize agricultural technologies and innovative thinking. The Hatch Act called for experimentation stations at universities, whereas both the Smith-Lever and Smith-Hughes acts sought to extend the work of the land-grant colleges to family farms and local communities. Usually through means of publication, these measures were geared at disseminating newly acquired knowledge to rural America.[42]

The Smith-Hughes Act provided federal funding to encourage high school programs to teach students about emerging farming technologies and engineering skills. These legislative measures coincided with the evolution of the tractor and helped the American people become more knowledgeable about mechanization. Agricultural legislation and institutions devoted to research and education helped to reinforce the importance of technology and engineering and served as a foundation for subsequent innovations.

As the tractor became widely adopted, farming legislation shifted focus to control prices and overproduction. The land-grant colleges and agricultural institutes continued to experiment and explore new farming methods, but the major concern was how to deal with growing surpluses that were forcing many farmers into poverty. President Franklin Roosevelt's Agricultural Assistance Act of 1933 sought to alleviate the hardship farmers faced from price depreciation and overproduction, and legislation followed.

As farmers and agricultural organizations lobbied on behalf of rural America, the mainstream public remained relatively quiet. Some argue that this lack of empathy is part of the reason that policymakers never passed legislation regulating the rate of mechanization. Furthermore, without the rallying of public sentiment it was difficult to create a coherent policy that balanced the needs of the farmer with the realities of capitalism. An overarching antimechanization policy never materialized on the federal level.

The role of the federal government, especially the US Department of Agriculture (USDA), remains one of the most puzzling aspects of the controversy. The USDA was created the same year as the land-grant system, so it owes much of its heritage to the resolve of the federal government to promote technological innovation. Its staff, however, held views as diverse as the society from which they originated. In efforts to maintain a level of impartiality, the USDA generally avoided taking sides on the issue, partly because both sides of the debate lobbied it for support. On many occasions statements by USDA officials would be distorted or misrepresented in popular communication to support the views of partisan interests.

Over time, the agency sought to avoid making any statement that could be misrepresented. In the earlier days, its secretary, Henry Wallace, stated in a confidential letter to Wayne Dinsmore: "If I stay here much longer I shall be suspicious of everybody and everything. I am beginning to understand why so many people in government seem afraid to open their mouths."[43]

Wallace opted not to choose sides in the tractor-horse debate. He said, "Both the horse and mechanical power have places on the farm, and will find their places, whatever may be said or done by the zealous, and perhaps at times over-zealous, parties of either."[44]

Wallace's choice to avoid intervening in the debate established an independent role for the USDA. The government organization initiated studies to inform debate rather than take sides—despite the professed mission of the agency. The need to monitor trends and provide status reports was poignantly stated in Wallace's letter to H. C. Taylor, then chief of the Bureau of Agricultural Economics: "Twenty years ago the power on the farm was furnished by horses and windmills. The horses were fed on stuff grown on the farm and this did not require an outlay of cash. Wind was free. All we had to do was to stick a wheel up in the air and harvest it. Now a large part of the power is furnished through engines. We have to pay cash for gasoline and for repairs. Grain formerly eaten by horses is now sold. Have we any way of measuring the effect of this change?"[45]

The change for which Wallace sought evidence could not be provided by simple calculations of how many horses needed to be part of a "Big Hitch" to compete with the latest tractor design, which was relatively easy to determine.[46] Wallace's question could only be addressed through a system-wide review of the effects of long-term technological and economic transformation in the agriculture industry.[47] Wallace never really got the answer he was looking for, but the triumph of the tractor over farm animals made it possible for research using counterfactual analysis to provide persuasive figures on the impact of the technology.[48] In hindsight, the widespread adoption of tractors was an expression of the changing times and the Schumpeterian sweep of innovation. It came with economic benefits even though its impact transformed the existing socioeconomic order.

The deliberation over farm mechanization continues today and is not restricted to one geographic location. Countries throughout the world are confronted with the task of trying to balance the economic benefits of mechanization with negative social consequences. In an expanding world economy, nations seek to maintain competitiveness. Many times this edge derives from innovation and acceptance of change. According to the Economic Research Service of the Department of Agriculture 41 percent of America's workforce in 1900 was employed in agriculture. By 1945 this decreased to 16 percent, with agriculture comprising 6.8 percent of the nation's GDP. In 2000, only 1.9 percent of America's workforce worked in agriculture, and in 2002 agriculture amounted to just 0.7 percent of total GDP.[49]

These statistics speak to the changes felt in the agriculture industry in terms of both the number of workers and its place in the American economy. With the rise of labor-saving technologies, worker displacement is as understandable as it is sobering. Mechanization displaced thousands of farmers and permanently altered rural America. At the same time, it increased America's competitiveness in the global economy. Whether the benefits of global competitiveness helped to mitigate local impacts remains in doubt. It is precisely this uncertainty in the wider distribution of benefits that leads to public concern over new technologies.

Conclusions

Tension over farm mechanization has been one of the most protracted battles over new technologies. As in the case of coffee, the farm mechanization debate is a global issue. It provides a diversity of lessons that are mirrored in contemporary technological controversies. Although economic factors played an important role in the debate, its roots ran deeper. The controversy, whose echoes are heard in other parts of the world today, was largely about widespread geographical and cultural transformation.[50] Agricultural production involves a wide range of life skills that shape the identity of communities. Agriculture is not just an economic activity, but also a way life.[51] This adds to the intensity of debates on new technologies that seek to transform the farming system.

A change in agricultural production technologies not only has economic implications, but also changes people's identities by transforming how they produce food. Social routines associated with food production and consumption are among the most conserved cultural practices. The struggle against farm mechanization continued to be a major feature of social movements over the last century. Debates over large-scale technological transformation are not just about shifts in the distribution of economic benefits and risks; they are also about the loss of cultural identity. Policymakers seeking to find solutions to such controversies have to look beyond the scope of conventional economic analysis.

The second lesson relates to the overwhelming influence that technological improvements had on the debate. Though early tractors were clumsy and appeared to be technically inferior to horses, they had greater scope for technical improvement. At first proponents of horsepower could not envisage any challenge arising from tractors. The inability to envisage rapid improvements in emerging technologies is an important barrier to realistic decisions among policymakers. The popular assumption is that technological innovation is slow and risky, and its impacts are uncertain. This tends to lead to support for incumbent technologies.

Policymakers are generally skeptical about emerging technologies. There are good reasons for this. Most new technologies do not advance beyond their prototype stages. Others perish in the early phases of their development. Time and time again policymakers are taken by surprise when technological controversies emerge. This is largely because they fail to foresee the impact of rapid or exponential technological advancement in new technologies. One of the consequences of such improvement in tractors was a shift among opponents from seeking outright prohibition to exploring opportunities in niche markets for horses. In the end the versatility of tractors and the emergence of a wide range of institutional and educational support systems led to the widespread adoption of tractors.

The third lesson relates to the role of government. The USDA was a nascent organization at the time of the debate and spent a considerable part of its time avoiding taking sides. However, it played an important role in monitoring technical advances and providing performance data. This positioned the agency as a broker, although it was under constant pressure to support either of the competing farming methods. The government, at least in its public pronouncements, bided its time until tractors had become the predominant source of power. This was necessary given the political nature of the debate and the influence of the farming community on local, state, and federal politics.

There are many other functions that the government performed that helped to entrench farm mechanization, such as a commitment to the modernization of agriculture. This was achieved in part through a wide range of educational programs. But probably the most profound influence came from the creation of land-grant colleges that trained a new cadre of farmers and agricultural entrepreneurs who sought to advance farm mechanization. It has been argued that land-grant colleges became purveyors of farm mechanization. They were a key locus for interactions between government, industry, academia, and farmers in exploring new technological opportunities. But in many cases the same colleges would also become forums for questioning the impact of new farming methods. Tensions between the two farming systems would indeed find their way into classrooms just as much as they permeated the public space.

The fourth lesson concerns the wider impacts of the two technological platforms on the economy. Horses were linked to their own supply chain. However, this was not as extensive as the supply chain of tractors, which included parts, sales representatives, maintenance services, and the associated fuel activities. At first this network may have appeared as a burden on farmers who otherwise would have been content with horses, which were able to reproduce themselves. But the extensive supply chain associated with tractors would provide a large network of supporters for the new technology. It is the same logic that led to the triumph of the automobile and other complex technological systems.

Not only did early concerns over farm mechanization provide important rhetorical tools for challenging new technologies, but many of the key players also trace their roots to the earlier struggles.[52] The topics may have changed, but the tactics have not. Farmers' organizations around the world continue to generate global empathy and play crucial roles in rallying concern over new agricultural technologies. They have also been effective in aligning their concerns with ecological considerations and thereby amplifying their influence. The story of farm mechanization has already been played out in various forms at different times in the industrial sector. Its key features and the lessons outlined above will continue to be part of the discourse over many technological systems to come. The horse may have given way to the tractor, but technological succession in other fields will continue to replay the same arguments as society seeks to find a new measure of stability between innovation and incumbency.[53]

6

Charged Arguments

Electricity

Fooling around with alternating current is just a waste of time.
Nobody will use it, ever.

THOMAS EDISON

The idea of technological coexistence has at least two dimensions. The last chapter illustrated the competition between two radically different technological regimes—horses and tractors—where the unfolding power of a new technology forced the proponents of the incumbent to delay being displaced by new market entrants. This chapter will illustrate a second dimension—that is, tensions between the proponents of Thomas Edison's direct current (DC) and the champions of George Westinghouse's competing alternating current (AC).[1] It's a story of the fight over who would control the electrification of the United States and the world, played out in the engineering arguments between DC and AC. In this case, Edison sought to delay the widespread adoption of DC until he was able to divest his investments from sections of the electricity market that were likely to be taken over by the new technology. His strategy was to relocate his investments to other activities rather than try to stop the spread of AC technology.

Thomas Edison electrified the Western world. He improved the incandescent light bulb that could burn consistently over many hours using DC. His light bulb is one of the greatest inventions of the last century.[2] It was so novel that he hosted a street lighting party, which attracted visitors by train. While the bulb he created initially was a symbol of modernization and innovation, it too eventually faced extinction. The global phaseout of the incandescent bulb and its replacement by new lighting systems such as light emitting diodes (LEDs) is another sign of technological transition. But the incandescent bulb's extinction marks an important stage in global perception of human creativity, engineering capabilities, and innovation.

This chapter examines the tactics Edison and his supporters used to slow down the adoption of AC. More specifically, the chapter analyzes how Edison and his supporters deployed stigmatization to spark public objection to AC and to protect their investments and patent in DC-related technologies. Examining the battle of the currents serves as a way to gain a deeper understanding of how stigmatization is used to suppress innovation and the associated institutional responses.[3]

New Light

Entrepreneurship is often associated with technological discontinuities driven by novelty and associated emergence of new economic properties.[4] The discontinuities, especially when championed by new entrepreneurs, pose great challenges to incumbent industries. Edison was a technological pioneer. He utilized the existing DC technology, which dates back to the 1830s, to create a light bulb and lighting system to power entire cities. His light bulb was not the first, it was just the best at the time. The first commercial lighting systems predate 1860 and the first generators date back to the 1830s.[5] Edison's brilliance lay in his ability to use existing technology to develop a product better than what existed using the DC system. His innovation too, however, was eventually outpaced by better technology.

George Westinghouse was an engineer and serial entrepreneur. He's credited with spearheading the use of AC in electrification, a move that pitted him against Edison. Faced with the superior AC technology commercialized by Westinghouse in the late 1800s,

Edison displayed remarkable capabilities in seeking to slow down the competition so he could divest from parts of the sector.

The standoff between Edison's DC and Westinghouse's AC occurred in a truly capitalist setting where competition was "an intense, intimate, transitory, invisible relationship created between players by their visible relations with others."[6] Mirroring this definition in many ways was the relationship between Thomas Edison and George Westinghouse. Their relationship was characterized by heated rivalry and, at some points, personal animosity. The battle between direct and alternating current was waged between Edison and Westinghouse and electric companies, and was often played within the public arena. The height of the dispute occurred between 1888 and 1895 and consisted of a series of public smears, personal attacks, and sensationalist propaganda.

The history of lighting is marked by a series of technological transitions from the use of oil to gas and finally to electricity. Competing economic interests and public concern about the newness of the invention always accompanied the technological changes. Each phase had unique technological and institutional arrangements. "In the early days [of New York and Brooklyn, the citizens who] went about the streets after dark, carried their own lanterns with them."[7] In 1697 the provision of street lighting became a civic duty in New York with the requirement that "every 7 householders should unite to pay the expense of lighting a candle in a lantern, suspended on a pole from the window of every seventh house on nights when there was no moon."[8]

Public-funded street oil lamps were introduced in New York in 1762 and continued until the introduction of gas lamps in 1823. The shift from oil to gas was associated with the emergence of new corporations with exclusive rights to light specific areas. The New York Gas Light Company was established in 1823 with initial capital outlay of $100,000 and given a thirty-year exclusive privilege to lay gas pipes in the area south of Grand Street. In 1830 the Manhattan Gas Light Company was formed with initial capital of

$500,000 to operate north of Grand Street. The number of gas-related firms grew as demand rose and later consolidated into fewer firms. This in turn drove down the price of gas and lighting.

Initially, however, the adoption of gas lighting in households was slow, as "many householders and landlords protested . . . for fear of explosions, and continued to use oil lamps and wax candles by preference."[9] Over time, gas became the main source of centralized lighting. Its rise to dominance was associated with its own tensions that provided important lessons for Edison.

Street lighting encountered early opposition in Europe. In 1819 a German newspaper published an article stating, "God had decreed that darkness should follow light, and mortals had no right to turn night into day."[10] The article claimed artificial light imposed an unnecessary tax on the people; caused health problems; led to people staying out late and therefore catching colds; removed the fear of darkness, leading to crime; and made robbers bold. Furthermore, the lights undermined patriotism as night public festivals undermined the value of public functions. Opponents claimed that artificial lighting made horses shy and ostensibly reduced their value in battle.

The public displayed distrust of the gas industry in the United States as well after claims surfaced that the industry mixed gas with air to increase volume and pumped air through the mains to make the meter run and the index to register. The use of larger gas pipes was seen as a ploy to increase gas consumption, and firms were accused of increasing pressure at night to make the meters run faster. The sale of larger burners was seen by some of the public as a way to sell more gas and not as a way to provide more light. Others believed that the gas companies simply defrauded consumers by making up the numbers on their bills. Still others thought that gas would flow back into the pipes after being registered in the meter, thereby leading to double billing. People also believed that larger pipes meant higher gas pressure, which in turn increased unnecessary consumption.[11] There were many other legitimate concerns related to the safety of gas lightning that became the subject of greater public interest. In the end, however, gas triumphed over oil but would later face its own competition challenge from electricity.

The transition from gas lamps to electricity was a subject of considerable debate and popular interest as well. Electricity fueled brighter lights. Writing in 1878, Robert Louis Stevenson acknowledged in *A Plea for Gas Lamps* the benefits of lighting. He said, "Cities given, the problem was to light them." Then he proceeded with an indictment of electricity in Paris, saying the "urban star now shines out nightly, horrible, unearthly, obnoxious to the human eye; a lamp for a nightmare! Such a light as this should shine only on murders and public crime, or along the corridors of lunatic asylums, a horror to heighten horror. . . .To look at it only once is to fall in love with gas, which gives a warm domestic radiance fit to eat by."

Optimism greeted the arrival of electricity in New York. "Edison's Newest Marvel. Sending Cheap Light, Heat, and Power by Electricity," read a headline from the September 16, 1878, *New York Sun*.[12] The acclaimed inventor, Thomas Edison, was embarking on yet another journey: the creation of an efficient electric lighting system. Although Edison did not invent the original light bulb, he strove to establish a system by which sustainable light could be transferred from generators to American homes and businesses. His incandescent light faced a number of obstacles, notably the existence of the powerful gas-lighting industry. With the help of his talented team of assistants, financial backing from investors, and his laboratories at Menlo Park, New Jersey, Edison intended to create a viable alternative to gas lighting.

Invented by William Murdoch in the early nineteenth century in Great Britain, gas lighting transformed the nature of business and access to knowledge. In the words of one gas-lighting historian, "It banished the darkness in many people's homes—not only the darkness of the night, but the darkness of ignorance."[13] Businesses were able to increase productivity by operating longer, and people had more opportunity to read novels and newspapers and expand their intellectual horizons.

Providing an alternative to candles and oil lamps, the invention and popularization of gas lighting extended from Europe to the United States. The first gaslight company was established in Baltimore, Maryland, in 1816, and by the 1820s a number of American cities were lighting their streets with gas. The gas industry soon became culturally and politically entrenched within society. In New York, where Edison would later test his first electrical lighting system, the gas industry was particularly important to the political machinery of Tammany Hall. Controlling most aspects of municipal life in New York, Tammany Hall had a vested interest in the continued success of gas lighting: Tammany provided political and financial support to the gas companies, while it received tax revenues and other kickbacks from their profits. Tammany was part of the network of players, each of which acted in its own self-interest while unanimously agreeing on the importance of gas lighting. Gas lighting had become normalized and embedded within society, and it was with this understanding that Edison proceeded to introduce his concept of electric light.[14]

A savvy innovator, Edison felt confident that he could create a system of lighting that would transcend that of the incumbent gas system. He began his work with the incandescent light bulb in earnest, following an encounter with a man named William Wallace. This 1878 meeting, in which Wallace revealed to Edison his electric-powered dynamo, inspired Edison to create his own superior version of light. Recognizing the flaws of the Wallace dynamo, such as its need for subdivided light, Edison began sketching ideas for an improved system.[15]

Within a week, Edison created an incandescent light bulb that produced a clear, bright light. Gaining confidence, he invited visitors to his workshop at Menlo Park to witness his electric light. He also spent this time acquiring legal advice and securing a group of wealthy investors, including J. P. Morgan, to finance his experiments. Edison's early bulb was plagued with problems of practicality, namely that most lamps could only operate for a limited amount of time. Edison's early incandescent bulb only stayed lit for one to two hours.

In response to this problem Edison tried to create a high-resistance light bulb by running a low current through thin copper wires. His team at Menlo Park also realized the importance of finding a resistant and durable filament that would not burn inside the glass bulb. Edison was certain that if he could overcome these technical challenges, then his electric light would be a success.

As noted, gas lighting was entrenched within society, and Edison was forced to confront New York's political machinery when attempting to reach his goal of illuminating the offices of Wall Street. Modeling his electric distribution system after that of the gas industry, Edison needed permits from city authorities to bury his wires underground. In hopes to sway city leadership, Edison and his lawyers hosted a gathering at Menlo Park where those who were either apathetic or skeptical could witness Edison's seemingly threatening innovation.

Neither Edison nor the New York aldermen were ecstatic about the meeting prospects. Accounts of the meeting show that the officials proposed that Edison pay a $1,000 tax per mile of wire he buried underground within the city borders. As the gas companies were not faced with such an outlandish tax, Edison was eventually able to negotiate a lower rate. Although no sweeping generalizations can be made based on this incident, it speaks to the level of concern from politicians with a vested interest in gas lighting. By the end of the meeting the tone was significantly lighter, as Edison provided the New York alderman with a hearty meal in a room lit with his incandescent light.

Edison and his team continued to work on their design, in addition to assessing both the political and economic environment in which his innovation would be presented. The team succeeded in creating an incandescent bulb, and then moved on to create generators, dynamos, and modes of distribution. By February 1881, Edison left his New Jersey laboratory for New York, where he prepared to fulfill his 1878 promise to illuminate Wall Street. More self-assured than ever, Edison stated, "My work here is done, my light is perfected. I'm now going into the practical production of it."[16]

In September 1882 work was completed at the Pearl Street station, where Edison's light was generated, and J. P. Morgan's house was illuminated. This early light was not without flaws. Issues included the loudness of the generators, random electrocution, and fire, all of which created a level of skepticism. Edison's DC system, was, though, the first attempt at the practical application of incandescent light.

While deeply engaged in creating and honing his electric light, Edison also contemplated how to introduce his system to the public. Aware of the potential concern his new technology would create among the public, he sought to ground aspects of its design in already existing technologies. He presented his lighting system's novel benefits while also showing its similarities to the gas system to boost societal support for his invention. To further allay anxiety, Edison had notices posted in homes that read: "Do not attempt to light with match. Simply turn key on wall by the door." It added, "The use of Electricity for lighting is in no way harmful to health, nor does it affect the soundness of sleep." Initially, electric lighting was more expensive than gas, but it was also safer, generated less ambient heat, produced fewer pollutants, and was more convenient to use.

The gas industry responded to Edison's light with technological improvements of its own that included inverted incandescent light and artificial pressure, which brought temporary relief to gas investors. These and other improvements prompted the inventor Charles William Siemens to risk the prediction: "I venture to think that gas lighting will hold its own as the poor man's friend, and the time is not far distant when both rich and poor will largely resort to gas as the most convenient, the cleanest, and the cheapest of fuels."[17] This prediction followed diversification of the use of gas for heating.

Edison's development of electric light was a robust design. His innovation was an improvement over gas lighting, and it left room for future expansion and adaptation. Indeed, "Edison's strategy and its success suggest that innovators may similarly foster the adoption of their ideas by designing the concrete details of their embodiment to embed them within—rather than distinguish them from—the established social system they seek to change, creating a robust design."[18]

Edison spent long hours studying the mechanisms behind gas production, distribution, and the associated social and economic factors. He also undertook extensive cost analysis, comparing his electric light to that of gas, and concluded that lighting by electricity was the economically sound choice. In the weeks following his meeting with Wallace and the ensuing inspiration to create incandescent light, "The image of the central gashouse and its distributing system, of gas mains running to smaller branch pipes and leading into many dwelling places, had flashed into his mind."[19]

Although Edison clearly intended to displace the incumbent gas industry, he was conscious of the social aspects of adoption and the need to have his electric light appear as an extension of the embedded institution. Although many great minds before Edison had worked with electricity, Edison was able to translate his concept of light into a practical innovation that investors and consumers alike could appreciate. The middle to late 1880s witnessed an increase in the use of electric light among businesses, but also saw the emergence of a number of energetic competitors that would question the utility of Edison's electrical system.

Sparking Conflict

In neighboring Pittsburgh, an engineer with an observant eye was closely following Edison's work. George Westinghouse decided to enter the field of electricity. Westinghouse was not new to the world of innovation. He resided in the nation's industrial hub and made his inventing debut in the railroad industry. He quickly learned the importance of patents and the need to protect ideas. His relations with the ruthless Pittsburgh railroad industry helped to mold him into an astute businessman and negotiator.

Westinghouse first created air brakes for railroad cars and electrical signals for railroads. These early inventions helped make railway travel safer. Certain scholars argue Westinghouse's focus on the utility and economic success of his inventions contrasted with Edison's creation of novelties.[20] While Edison was clearly concerned about his earning potential and had a desire to create successful inventions, he also devoted time to developing novelty items.

Edison and Westinghouse also differed in regard to patents. Westinghouse was willing to purchase other inventors' patents if he believed they would enhance his own work. Edison, on the other hand, was not known to make such transactions. Edison wanted patents only for his own designs. Both individuals possessed unique characteristics that distinguished them from one another and shaped the battle of the currents that was to come.

Having been exposed to electricity in his work with railroad signals, Westinghouse recognized its potential and the impact its universal adoption could have on society. He entered into the market believing that "the future foretold an insatiable demand for small direct current central stations serving mile-square areas and individual isolated plants," unlike the large central stations espoused by Edison.[21] Interestingly, as Edison mirrored certain aspects of the gas industry when developing his incandescent light, Westinghouse mirrored the already established direct current system. In 1884 he hired the great mind William Stanley, who had patented a DC dynamo as well as a carbonized silk filament light bulb.

Westinghouse experienced his "electrical epiphany" in 1885 while reading an article on AC in a British electrical journal. Immediately thereafter, he called one of his employees to meet with the inventors of the AC system to gain a better understanding of its workings. Lucien Gaulard and John Gibbs had been testing their system for a number of years when, at the request of Westinghouse, they sent a version of their machine to Pittsburgh for his review. At this time there were no American-made transformers similar to the Gaulard-Gibbs machine. After Westinghouse imported their machine and saw how it worked, he decided to purchase the patent to use the AC system in America. He paid $50,000 for the patent. Westinghouse envisioned a large market for the AC system.

One big and expensive problem to the DC system was its inability to travel long distances. For instance, the loud and cumbersome generator that lit J. P. Morgan's house in 1882 was powered by a system located within close proximity to his home. While DC functioned with Edison's preferred low voltage, AC operated with both high and low voltages (thus the "alternating" current). The Gaulard-Gibbs transformer allowed electricity to be transmitted over longer distances at a higher voltage, which it then converted to a lower voltage before entering into a home or business. DC, however, could only be delivered at short distances of less than a mile, so power plants had to be located in the middle of population centers, and more expensive copper wires were needed to connect consumers to the plant.

AC helped to increase access to electricity in America and afforded average people the opportunity to electrify their homes. AC provided more flexibility and fewer restrictions because of its ability to travel at high voltages for longer distances. This aspect of AC was logistically and economically beneficial and "promised to revolutionize electric lighting by so reducing the necessary cost as to put small towns substantially on an equal footing with large ones as to public illumination."[22] The idea of AC fascinated Westinghouse. After receiving the converter, Westinghouse and his team of engineers began testing AC in Pittsburgh. There they worked on an AC dynamo, additional transformers, and hundreds of lamps.

The following fall they tested their system, and after moving the lamps and converters to a different location, Westinghouse and his team turned on the AC dynamo. The experiment succeeded, and the dynamos located at Westinghouse Electric Company transmitted power to the lamps miles away. The dynamo "was operated first to supply one thousand volts and afterward two thousand," and the "lamps fed from this current were kept burning continuously for a fortnight."[23]

Meanwhile, Westinghouse sent Reginald Belfield and William Stanley to the small town of Great Barrington, Massachusetts, to work on creating more AC transformers. Westinghouse discovered that by arranging the transformers in a parallel fashion they produced higher voltages. He assigned Belfield and Stanley the task of constructing transformers in parallel to illuminate the streets of the rural Massachusetts town.

Much to the dismay of the Westinghouse Electric Company, Edison displayed his own electric light with his DC in Great Barrington, before Stanley and Belfield had a chance to implement their new AC dynamos. The people of Great Barrington were impressed with Edison's light. One week later, in March 1886, Stanley powered up his generators and transformers and successfully lit both the interior and exterior of a store using AC.

In the following weeks, Westinghouse connected a number of other buildings throughout the main street of the town. The success of the transmission of power in Pittsburgh, coupled with the smaller-scale exhibit in Great Barrington, set the stage for Westinghouse to begin commercially producing AC. He decided to introduce his system in Buffalo, New York. The first customer was the Adam, Meldrum & Anderson marketplace, along the city's waterfront.

The public was impressed. Reports from the time describe a scene where "the well-dressed crowds streamed up and down the four floors to ooh and aah over the lights, exclaiming how akin it was to pure sunlight, how truly you could see the colors of the Indian shawls and the weave of the draperies."[24] Westinghouse's first commercial illumination took place on the eve of Thanksgiving, and its positive response emboldened the Pittsburgh inventor to enter into full-scale production.

Edison and the DC advocates grew increasingly alarmed with Westinghouse's development and introduction of the AC system. Initially, however, Edison did not feel threatened by Westinghouse because he truly believed that AC was dangerous and could never fully come to fruition. Edison wrote to one of his associates, "None of Westinghouse's plans worry me in the least; the only thing that disturbs me is that Westinghouse is a great man for flooding the country with agents and travelers. He is ubiquitous and will form numerous companies before he knows anything about it."[25]

While some of his critics suggested that Edison possessed an aggressive, vengeful side, others asserted that Edison's sincere concern for the development of electricity fueled his challenge to AC.[26] He felt that AC would create intractable problems for those involved with electricity. Not only would AC take society by a surprise, its dangerous high voltage could result in accidents that would turn public opinion as well as state and federal legislation against the development of electricity. These concerns were justified.

Interestingly, Edison was introduced to AC in the early 1880s and was familiar with the Gaulard-Gibbs transformer. He had even sent members of his own staff to Europe to research the AC system, but was later unmoved by their report. Edison maintained his opinion that low voltage was more appropriate for electrical transmission. As AC gained popularity, however, Edison felt a growing personal rivalry with Westinghouse.

The Westinghouse Electric Company experienced record growth during the late nineteenth century, and the demand for AC among businesses throughout the states continued to increase. With key developments in AC such as the valve and meter, the DC producers realized they faced a formidable rival. Swaying public opinion was the primary way DC advocates could protect their interests. Public sentiment surrounding AC was mixed, and many felt uneasy about its high voltages and potential hazards.

The negative publicity surrounding Westinghouse and AC was exacerbated by Edison and other producers of DC, who were determined that AC should not succeed. The public idolized Edison and viewed him as a well-intentioned "wizard." The press also adored him, as Edison was at all times poised to make a public statement and often amused them with his wit and candor. Westinghouse preferred to stay out of the limelight and was often considered rather dull. Newspapers, magazines, and journals were the primary methods of communication during this period. The battle of the currents predominantly took place in letters and articles and involved well-respected newspapers.

The battle of the currents continued to escalate and receive publicity. Edison, while remaining behind the scenes, mounted a rather successful public campaign against his arch-rival Westinghouse and his AC system. As competition strengthened, Edison was forced to issue a pamphlet warning the public against the risks of adopting AC. He devoted much of the writing to claims that Westinghouse had pirated his ideas, thus trying to discredit him as an inventor. The first battles between Edison and Westinghouse were on patent claims.

Westinghouse responded by pointing to the superiority of AC. In a response published in the *North American Review*, he described Edison's central plant as "regarded by the majority of competent electrical engineers as in many respects radically defective; so defective, in fact, that, unless the use of alternative currents can be prohibited, it seems destined to be wholly supplanted by the more scientific and in all respects (so far as concerns the users or occupants of buildings) far safer inductive system."[27]

Westinghouse also pointed out that Edison's own troops were breaking ranks. He noted that the manager of the Detroit Edison Station had successfully introduced a resolution at the annual meeting of Edison Illuminating Companies calling on the parent company to offer "a flexible method of enlarging the territory which can be profitably served from their stations for domestic lighting by *higher pressures* and consequently *less outlay of copper* than that involved by the three-way system."[28]

By then Edison and many proponents of DC were starting to realize the rapid rate of AC current adoption. "Rather than vainly seeking to block the further development of the ... competitive electricity supply technology and so preserve a monopoly of the field for his DC system, Edison ... sees the juggernaut of a competitive technical system bearing down upon his own immediate economic interests with a swiftness he has not anticipated."[29] The undeniable economic and practical advantages of AC would force Edison and his supporters to employ extreme methods aimed at demonizing the technology in the hope of slowing down its adoption, thereby giving him room to recover his investments. Their approach took a rather gruesome turn.

The Devil Is in the Details

Marketing campaigns have shown that the public tends to stigmatize and thus avoid technologies, places, or products it sees as being dangerous or as posing health risks. Stigmatization is often associated with fear and potential fatality in situations that are involuntary and beyond individual control.[30] A key aspect of technological stigma is the association of a product with detrimental changes in consumer behavior arising from negative imagery, descriptors, or word associations. Each side in the fight between the DC and the AC camps made use of social fear on behalf of its own corner.

The battle of the currents during the final decades of the nineteenth century had ominous implications for convicted criminals facing capital punishment. As a result of both this battle and the rivalries between Westinghouse and Edison, electricity was soon associated with one of the penal code's most severe mechanisms for execution, the electric chair. Those with a vested interest in the DC system sought to elicit anger and fear toward AC among the public, and lobbied for anti-AC legislation with the motive of having "firmly fixed in the public mind through capital punishment by electrocution the association of alternating current with death."[31] Thus began the darkest chapters in the story of the competition between direct and alternating currents.

Spearheading the anti-AC campaign was Harold P. Brown. An obscure electrician, Brown made his debut into public affairs with the publication of his letter to the editor in the prominent *New York Evening Post*. His June 5, 1888, letter berated the producers of AC for caring more about their finances than public safety and referred to AC as "damnable."[32] He argued that the only reason to use AC was to save on copper wire costs: "That is, the public must submit to *constant danger from sudden death* in order that a corporation may pay a little larger dividend."[33] He warned that using AC was "as dangerous as a burning candle in a powder factory" and said a continuous current "such as is used by the Edison Company for incandescent lights, is perfectly safe."[34]

Westinghouse supporters responded by saying the attacks on AC were aimed at hurting the proponents of the technology rather than protecting public health. Some offered counterclaims that DC of the same tension was in fact more dangerous than AC. One electrician even suggested that AC could be life-saving. He claimed that when a person is felled by a lethal DC shock, "The passage of an alternating current through the body has been very efficacious in restoring life."[35] The electrician offered no support for the superstition, whereas Brown pointed out that damage to the human body was caused by the steady succession of shocks.

According to his letter, the fatal current had contributed to numerous accidental deaths and injuries, which DC could have prevented. He called for the regulation of AC so that its voltage would be reduced to less than three hundred volts. This would then strip the system of its comparative advantage, in turn enabling the DC system to once again dominate the market. Brown's letter provoked an impassioned response on behalf of prominent electrical engineers, businessman, and scientists. This letter, coupled with its response, sparked the most vitriolic battle between currents yet.

On July 16, 1888, those opposing Brown's position gathered to discuss how best to respond to his claims. They questioned everything from Brown's competence to his integrity and asserted that with the proper insulation and transformer, AC was extremely safe. To preserve his image and reputation, and in preparation for his public response to these criticisms, Brown undertook a series of experiments with both the AC and DC systems. He conducted these experiments with the assistance of Edison and his extensive laboratory in New Jersey.

Roughly two weeks after his critics gathered in response to his *Evening Post* article, Brown prepared to validate his claims with a demonstration revealing the danger of AC. Using a dog as his subject, Brown connected electrodes to its spinal cord and brain. He sent 300, 400, 500, 700, and finally 1,000 volts through the dog using DC.[36] Even after this torturous process, and as the dog's convulsing body and howls caused an uneasiness to spread throughout the hall, the dog was not dead. Brown then sent 300 volts of AC through the dog's body, which instantly killed it.

Although Brown felt his first public experiment was a success, many in the audience were thoroughly disturbed by its gruesome nature. Others believed that it failed to prove that AC was more dangerous, because the successive DC voltages had already seriously weakened the dog. To temper these concerns, Brown conducted several more experiments throughout the following days using only AC. These experiments proved successful, but as Brown gloated in his victory, he was unaware of the serious implications it would have for the status of capital punishment in New York.

At this point in the American justice system, hanging was the most common method of execution. In some instances hangings were public events, where families would travel long distances to witness an execution. Although there was a level of entertainment associated with public hangings, many people considered them to be brutal punishments. In theory, hangings were intended to break the person's neck. In actuality, however, this method resulted in strangulation rather than broken necks, which often lasted for a number of minutes, leading some to believe that hangings were cruel and unusual punishment. The search for a more humane and ethical punishment commenced during the height of the battle of the currents, and the state of New York was the first to adopt a new method.

New York state senator Daniel H. MacMillan, a vocal advocate of the death penalty, proposed a measure in the legislature calling for an independent commission to investigate alternative methods of capital punishment. According to some, MacMillan's proposal was aimed at countering those wanting to abolish the death penalty; if it became more humane, then there would be less of a need to prohibit it. New York governor David Hill approved the measure, and MacMillan chose the members of the newly established Death Commission. He chose his longtime friend and proponent of electricity, Dr. A. P. Southwick, who had observed Brown's experiments with animals, attorney Matthew Hale, and humanitarian Elbridge Gerry.[37]

In addition to a historical analysis of torture and the death penalty, the commission surveyed prominent legal and medical minds, seeking their opinions on the matter of electrocution. While the commission deliberated, it elicited the opinion of Edison, whom many considered the expert on all matters of electricity. Edison declined Southwick's initial request to offer technical advice, saying that he did not support the death penalty. But Southwick made another plea to which Edison responded in a letter: "The best appliance in this connection is to my mind one which will perform the work is the shortest space of time, and inflict the least amount of suffering upon its victim. This I believe can be accomplished by the use of electricity and the most suitable apparatus for the purpose is that class of dynamo-electric machine which employs intermittent currents."[38]

Elihu Thomson of Thomson-Houston, another electrical company competing with Westinghouse, also recommended AC as the most humane method of electrocution.[39] Basing their recommendation on their personal preferences as well as on the survey results, in which 43 percent favored electricity over 40 percent in favor of retaining the gallows, the commission proposed that electricity become the new mode of execution. "The bill that created the electric chair became law not because of the efforts of Southwick or the Gerry Commission but as a byproduct of one of the greatest rivalries in the history of American technology between Thomas A. Edison and George Westinghouse Jr."[40]

Upon the commission's recommendation to the New York legislature, the Medico-Legal Society of New York was assigned the task of determining the design of the electric chair. It hired Brown, along with Dr. Frederick Petersen, to assess the electrical and medical aspects of electrocution. Using Edison's laboratory and resources, the two men experimented with larger animals such as horses and calves to determine the appropriate voltages of electricity needed to quickly and painlessly terminate life. On December 12, 1888, they submitted the report to the Medico-Legal Society, which adopted it with minimal protest.[41] Their report specifically called for the usage of AC, as it was determined to be the most lethal.

At this point Westinghouse delivered his first public response to the crippling campaign against AC. In a letter in the *New York Times*, Westinghouse asserted that Brown's work was both unsubstantiated and motivated by the financial concerns of the Edison Electric Company. He went on to note that the benefits of the AC system were incontrovertible and that the proponents of the inferior DC system were using the capital punishment case as a rather macabre publicity scheme. In response to his piece in the *New York Times*, Brown invited Westinghouse to participate in a duel by electricity; each man would take his respective current and the first to cry out in pain would lose. Westinghouse rejected the unusual invitation and continued to maintain AC's practicality and benefits.

Meanwhile, the New York legislature passed the electrocution bill. It would be used for the first time in August 1890 on convicted murderer William Kemmler, who settled an argument with his lover using an ax. After his appeal failed, the prison issued a statement purported to be from Kemmler saying: "I am ready to die by electricity. I am guilty and I must be punished. . . . I am glad I am not going to be hung. I think it is much better to die by electricity than it is to be hung. It will not give me pain. I am glad that Mr. Durston is going to turn the switch. He is firm and strong. If a weak man did it, I might be afraid.. . . . I have never been so happy in life as I have been here."[42]

Brown was placed in charge of developing the electric chair, and one of his key challenges was obtaining a Westinghouse AC dynamo. Westinghouse went to great lengths to prevent this. Working on a deadline, Brown was faced with a dilemma, and as usual solicited the help of his friend Edison. He also went to Elihu Thomson, another Westinghouse rival, for assistance. After negotiations with a Boston associate, Thomson was able to secure a Westinghouse dynamo, and Brown continued to develop the mechanism by which Kemmler would be executed.

At this stage, it seemed as though Brown and Edison were making great strides in their efforts to discredit the AC system by associating it with the death penalty. Just weeks after Kemmler's imprisonment, however, attorney W. Bourke Cockran issued a writ of habeas corpus, challenging the convict's death sentence.[43] Although there are differing opinions as to whether Westinghouse paid the renowned attorney's fees, it is clear that Westinghouse Electric Company would have directly benefited if Cockran won his appeal.

Basing his case on the grounds that electrocution was cruel and unusual punishment, and thus in violation of the Constitution, Cockran attempted to show that those advocating electrocution lacked the skill sets necessary to confirm it was painless.[44] He questioned Brown's credentials as an electrical engineer as well as the relevance of Brown's experiments with animals when determining whether electrocution would be appropriate for humans. It seemed as though the case was progressing in Cockran's favor, until Edison testified. Revered in the community, Edison's testimony proved influential in the outcome of the case.

As reported in the *Albany Journal*, "At last an expert that knows something concerning electricity. Mr. Edison is probably the best informed man in America, if not in the world, regarding electrical currents and their destructive powers."[45] Although the testimony of Edison was not the only factor contributing to the decision to uphold Kemmler's death sentence, it helped to further the connection between alternating current and death.

After this legal defeat, Westinghouse took steps to take the case to a higher court, but his efforts were of no avail. Kemmler was executed on August 6, 1890.[46] Accounts of his execution vary. After the first currents ran through his body, witnesses assumed he had passed away, and Dr. Southwick, member of the Death Commission, exclaimed, "There is the culmination of ten year's work and study. We live in a higher civilization from this day!"[47] Soon after, witnesses realized that Kemmler was still alive and the current was once again administered. As the smell of burned flesh and hair permeated the room, observers stood with their mouths agape. The first legal electrocution made national headlines, and its aftermath provoked heated debate over the role of electricity in public life.

Edison's efforts to stigmatize AC occurred at a time of great panic about the safety of overhead wires in New York. The popular press widely echoed his warnings regarding the dangers of AC. For example, the *Tribune* wrote, "Mr. Edison has . . . declared that any metallic object—a doorknob, a railing, a gas fixture, the most common and necessary appliance of life—might at any moment become the medium of death."[48]

Edison was not convinced that burying the wires would reduce their dangers. He believed that "burying them would result only in the transfer of deaths to man-holes, houses, stores, and offices, through the agency of the telephone, the low-pressure system, and the apparatus of the high-tension current itself."[49] Despite his warning, Edison said he had "no intention, and I am sure none will accuse me, of being an alarmist."[50] His motives, however, were clear: "My personal desire would be to prohibit entirely the use of alternating currents. They are as unnecessary as they are dangerous."[51]

To reinforce the stigmatization of AC, Edison's lawyer proposed to the editor of *American Notes and Queries* that "as Westinghouse's dynamo is going to be used for the purpose of executing criminals, why not give him the benefit of this fact in the minds of the public, and speak hereafter of a criminal as being 'westinghoused,' or as being condemned to be 'westinghoused,' or to use the noun, we would say that such a man was condemned *to the westinghouse*. It will be a subtle compliment to the public services of this distinguished man"[52] In the meantime, the *World* combined "electro" and "execution" to give the world the word "electrocution" in 1889.

Attempts by electric journals to dismiss the scares had little impact on public opinion, which was swayed by regular reports, accidents, and the constant sight of overhead wires. The increase in electric wiring was associated with a rise in accidental electrocutions. There were many cases of defective insulation, and attempts to force utilities to improve the situation made little headway. Numerous attempts made by New York City authorities to require power and telegraph companies to relocate their overhead wires into conduits failed. "As a result of this neglect, the number of electrical accidents increased dramatically. Between May 1887 and September 1889, seventeen New Yorkers were killed by electric current."[53]

Public concern was heightened in October 1889 when a Western Union lineman named John E. H. Feeks was electrocuted in a gruesome accident in New York. His "body hung tangled up in the wires, smoking and sparking, for forty-five minutes until his fellow linesmen could cut him down."[54] The street swelled with spectators and hundreds of others watched from their windows as his body was lowered. For days New Yorkers lined up and donated up to $2,000 to his pregnant widow in a tin box attached to the pole.

Following the incident, building owners took the matter into their own hands, cutting wires hanging over their houses. As reported by the *World*, terrified people threw out their telephones, "as if the little wires which connect them went straight to the river of death."[55] The press published strong editorials castigating electric companies for caring more about profit than about human life. Writing in the *New York Tribune*, Howard Crosby said the wires were "a fearful source of death, and a constant menace to the lives of our fellow-citizens. It would be far better for us to go back to the gaslights than thus to risk precious lives. The companies who make their fortunes by the electric lights seem to have no regard for aught but their purses."[56]

Legal battles and outrage paralyzed the city for two months, after which point the Department of Public Works started to cut down unsafe wires. Over a million feet of wires were cut, "about one-quarter of the total amount of overhead wire, was removed. As a result, the arc electric lighting companies turned off their current, plunging fifty-six miles of streets into darkness."[57] Gaslights made a slow return, which created other problems such as concern over safety at night.

The *Tribune* complained that "the existing situation as regards the lighting of this city at night cannot be maintained long without great loss, discomfort and discontent. Already merchants are complaining, perhaps with some present inconsistency, of the adverse conditions under which they are compelled to do business, and certainly the streets are gloomy, if not unsafe."[58] The city had to increase police presence in some areas to deal with robberies.

The elimination of overhead wires favored Edison's electric company, which had all its wires underground, although it did not provide street lighting. Ironically, Edison had to contend with the temporary return of an old technology that he had sought to replace. But public opinion continued to demand safe access to electricity and strong regulation of corporate activities. The *New York Times*, for example, wrote, "We are not going permanently to put up with the inferior light of gas and oil simply because the corporations have been selfish and our public servants ignorant, inefficient, or corrupt. New Yorkers feared the new electrical technology, yet could not abandon it. To their surprise, they discovered urban life had become dependent on electric light."[59]

Slowly private enterprises started to replace faulty wires and to comply with the regulations requiring underground wiring. In a way, the panic forced Edison's competitors to adopt the same strategy he had used by emulating gas pipes. The difference was that this time they were being compelled by the law and the public panic that he himself had contributed to. The wire panic also played a significant role in New York politics and the demand for greater municipal control over corporate activities.

Blazing the Path

The development of electricity ushered in a period of technological innovation, where inspired inventors, businessmen, and companies competed for dominance. The rivalry between Thomas Edison and George Westinghouse embodies the spirit of the age and is relevant to the discussion of both institutional and individual reactions to change.

Interestingly, even with the tireless work of Edison, Westinghouse, and many other champions, electricity did not fully displace the gas industry until the twentieth century. As one scholar notes, "Indeed, gas light remained the principal source of illumination for most Americans until after World War I."[60] Although many economic historians focus on the emergence and advancement of electricity during the late nineteenth century, the gas industry also advanced. Some argue that the eventual dominance of electricity was not inevitable—that if popular opinion among investors and technical experts had been in favor of gas lighting, then the outcome could have been different.

Nevertheless, the introduction of electricity marks an important episode in American history. The battle of the currents contributes to the discussion of social tensions over technological development, as it offers insight into the motives and actions of those either challenging or embracing change. Edison was sensitive to the importance of gaining social acceptance for his incandescent light. To do this, he designed his innovation in a way that resembled gas lighting. While eventually seeking to displace the incumbent gas industry, Edison was pragmatic in his approach; he first sought to highlight the benefits of his lighting system while noting its similarities to gas.

As an inventor with a great entrepreneurial spirit, Edison realized that to maximize profit and encourage public acceptance of his incandescent lighting system, he would need to align himself strategically with certain aspects of the gas industry. While Edison outwardly embraced innovation and technological development, he felt deeply threatened by those seeking to displace his own inventions. As evidenced in the battle of the currents and the culminating debate over electrocution, Edison challenged technological development when it affected his personal reputation and economic fortunes. It was not his intent to stop the adoption of AC technology, which he knew was superior to his approach given the needs of the time. His strategy was to buy time so that he could divest his investments from sections of the power sectors and pursue alternative business opportunities.

Conclusions

Much of the tension over innovation is associated with technological competition within the same regime of power supply. Technological competition turned a leader in innovation into a cunning user of extreme tactics designed to slow down the adoption of competing systems. Edison's main reason for challenging the new technology was to buy time so he could exit the market. He achieved this goal and moved to marketing other technologies, "including making movies and records, milling iron ore and cement, and developing an alkaline storage battery for electric automobiles."[61] His financiers took control of part of his business and merged it with the AC-based firm Thomson-Houston in 1892, to create the General Electric Corporation.[62]

Edison's early work reveals great mastery in aligning this innovation with existing institutional arrangements. But when faced with technological competition, he resorted to extreme measures intended to stigmatize the new technology by associating it with execution of felons. Public panic regarding an electric accident played a key role in both shaping perceptions about the risks of AC and giving Edison additional ammunition. There are several lessons from this controversy that can inform contemporary debates on technological competition.

The first lesson comes from Edison's deep understanding of how technology and institutions coevolve to form integral systems. He learned this from seeking to introduce DC current in a market dominated by gas lighting. He designed his new system to look like the gas industry he was competing with. By doing so he was able to attract the gas interests to invest in his system despite the fact that it was based on a competing source of lighting. By adopting this approach, Edison was able to adopt a strategy that sought to include those who were likely to be displaced by his innovation. This approach stands in sharp contrast with contemporary appeals to technological disruptions that focus more on displacing incumbent players rather than on accommodating them. The term "disruptive innovation" has lost its original technical meaning as formulated by Christensen and is now generally refers to destruction of incumbent industries. This may bring a certain level of pride to innovators, but it can also heighten social tensions.

Edison's emulation approach helped to reduce the tensions between his innovation and incumbent players. Edison described his goal as "to effect exact imitation of all done by gas, so as to replace lighting by gas by lighting by electricity."[63] He sought to adapt his technology to the prevailing culture, and by so doing he reduced the potential for backlash. But by making this cultural decision that included the ability to turn off individual lights without affecting the rest of the system—just as was the case with gas lamps—Edison's innovation was constrained by real-world technical parameters. Indeed, "Electric engineers, if their devices are to work in the real world, have to adopt the concept of resistance, voltage, current and power, plus the demands of Ohm's and Joule's laws, as absolute representation of that world."[64] Edison's strategy for market entry and his deliberate efforts to include incumbent players demonstrated his knowledge of the fact that social forces shaped the evolution and adoption of new technologies.[65]

A central message in his approach is the importance of seeking to integrate new technologies in existing cultural contexts. The more a new technology augments an existing system, the more likely it is to be accommodated. Technological mimicry is not just a ploy to confuse consumers but an essential strategy that benefits from familiarity. Such mimicry may at times involve branding efforts that reinforce the perception of continuity in tradition. Edison thus chose to work with the system rather than seek to displace it. It is this deep knowledge of the political dynamics of technological succession that would make him a formidable force in his battle with Westinghouse.

The second important lesson lies in the extreme methods that Edison used to challenge AC. The most important aspect of Edison's strategy was his desire to buy time so he could exit part of the electric supply market. He initially responded by using patent claims to stem Westinghouse's expansion. He tried disparaging both Westinghouse and his business model. He accused him of lacking technical knowledge of the industries he was creating. Such tactics are not unusual in contemporary technological debates. In fact, firms sometimes ask their partners to sign nondisparagement contracts. When it became clear that these methods were not working, Edison would mount the most vicious demonization of AC by playing upon popular safety concerns pertaining to electricity. His team's efforts to have executioners use AC and to call the act "westinghousing" was a way to eponymously stigmatize the technology. Edison had mastery of the political lay of the field and knew how to stage the kinds of spectacles that would instill fear of AC in the mind of the public. Not many technological controversies go to such extremes.

The third lesson arising from these clashes is that technological superiority often becomes the final arbiter. In this case, AC was in many respects superior to DC. In the early stages the two systems were being applied in different geographical locations, so they could coexist in different market niches. Edison was aware that in the end his systems could not compete with AC, so he preferred to make a phased exit. The essential message for policymakers is to explore ways by which they can choose technological options that offer greater versatility. This can be achieved through consumer preferences. The phenomenon of technological lock-in, however, can easily exclude superior technologies from the market.

The fourth policy lesson relates to the role of standards in creating markets for new products.[66] The competition between the two power systems was essentially a clash between two competing technical standards, defined broadly as a requirement or norm for the electric power system.[67] Such conflicts can be averted through deliberations in standards-setting organizations that can establish technical or uniform engineering criteria, methods, processes, and practices pertaining to the proper functions of the electric power system. Standards are not simply technical criteria for engineering systems, but also embody the deeper socioeconomic interests of the participating parties. In fact, standards are usually the foundation under which industries acquire dominant roles in the market and define path dependence. Policymakers have an important role in defining these standards so that they provide a balance between technical feasibility, business interests and consumer protection, and wider ethical consideration.[68]

Technological superiority played a key role in determining the outcome of the debate. The final policy lesson from the controversy lies in the interactions between technological innovation and political governance. In this case, political connection between the power supplies and political representatives make it difficult to implement safety regulations. The power suppliers had become too dominant to be regulated, and as a result laws were simply not being implemented. One of the outcomes of the controversy was greater scrutiny of the role of monopolies in responding to safety concerns. It inspired new ways of thinking about municipal control of corporate activities that included greater citizen engagement. Such reforms were necessary because of the imbalance in the distribution of risks and benefits. Cases of accidental electrocution heightened the dangers of the innovation. The situation was compounded by the fact that a few firms reaped most of the benefits, while the risks were more widely distributed. Technological innovation in this regard stimulated complementary adjustments in the political arena.

Echoes of the debate can be heard today in world energy markets, which are experiencing major ecological challenges. The push for renewable energy and conservation has generated debates that mirror some aspects of the tensions over electrification as illustrated by attempts to introduce smart grid systems to promote energy conservation. The tensions revolve around issues such as privacy, security, pricing, and access to energy.[69] Much of the debate is about the health impacts of non-ionizing electromagnetic radiation and parallels earlier debates related to cell phone towers.

For example, the advocacy group Stop Smart Meters says that because of the installation of smart meters, "bills are skyrocketing, health effects and safety violations are being reported, and privacy in our homes is being violated." It cautions that "children, pregnant women, seniors, those with immune deficiencies, medical conditions, pacemakers, and implants are particularly at risk." According to the organization, the risks extend to animals and plants. Newspaper reports of the health effects of smart meters include headaches, interrupted sleep, dizziness, agitation, fatigue, skin rashes, ringing in the ears, leg cramps, and forgetfulness. But underlying these concerns are larger issues related to the inclusion of the public in control of utilities.[70]

The DC-AC debate appears to have been settled. However, new power supply systems such as solar photovoltaics and more efficient appliances are creating growing market niches for DC. It is unlikely that DC will become a serious competitor with AC, but the emerging trends suggest rising interest in diverse power supply systems. The appeal of decentralized DC supply systems will continue to be blunted by the established AC power regimes around the world.

7

Cool Reception

Mechanical Refrigeration

Test fast, fail fast, adjust fast.

TOM PETERS

Modern urban life in much of the world would be inconceivable without mechanical refrigeration. In fact, many of the routines associated with urban life are intertwined with the capacity to keep a wide range of products cold. Before the development of mechanical refrigeration, many people relied on natural ice as the main source of cooling for food and drinks. Mechanical refrigeration dramatically impacted the ice industry and triggered long debates on the safety of food and the mechanical refrigerators themselves. These concerns overshadowed the underlying socioeconomic concerns and became the subject of scrutiny.

A century ago a series of fires swept through New York City cold-storage warehouses. In response, the New York Board of Fire Underwriters pressured the city's Bureau of Fire Prevention to establish new safety regulations for cold-storage warehouses and ice plants. These events unfolded nearly a decade after the formation of the American Society of Refrigerating Engineers in New York. The city adopted new regulations that marked a turning point in the relationships between technical advancement, safety consciousness, and society in general in the evolution of the refrigeration industry.[1]

The last chapter showed the extent to which relationships between industry and government can impede safety improvements of emerging technologies. This chapter examines how expert advice was used to foster the technical improvements that made it possible for mechanical refrigeration to overcome objections from the natural ice industry. It underscores the importance of creating new institutions to advance emerging technologies. This coevolutionary approach helps to provide the technical basis and public forums needed to respond to new challenges using expert knowledge. The development of new technologies also equips society with the expertise needed to manage their risks. This is particularly important in situations where the risks of new technologies may be defined largely in the interest of those seeking to maintain incumbent products and not meeting societal needs at large.

Cracking a New Market

The story of refrigeration illustrates the controversies associated with changing the method of production, as opposed to the product itself as envisaged in Schumpeter's taxonomy of innovation. Ice was once a luxury. Before 1830, the American elite used ice to cool their beverages and create frozen delicacies, while food was preserved primarily through salting, spicing, pickling, smoking, and dehydration by the sun. Many Americans understood that cold conditions extended the life of food and prevented rotting— fishermen noticed their catch lasted longer in the winter—but the general public did not incorporate refrigeration into daily kitchen habits until after the nineteenth century, when it became technically feasible.

There was limited use of refrigeration prior to 1830. Farmers would transport their products by night to take advantage of the cooler temperatures, and ice-packed fish were occasionally shipped domestically.[2] Infrequently, fishermen and farmers would display the day's wares on ice, but by and large butcher sales took place in the early hours of the morning before preservation became necessary, and fish were kept alive until sold. Around 1830, taverns, hotels, and restaurants began to use icehouses and refrigerators on a limited basis to preserve food. Thomas Moore invented an oval cedar tub insulated with rabbit fur and a sheet metal butter container surrounded on four sides by ice. The ice necessary to fill Moore's refrigerator and larger icehouses was often prohibitively expensive.

The ice trade was a profitable industry in the nineteenth century, and many men became incredibly wealthy from the trade. Frederic Tudor, one of the first men to enter the ice-trading industry, wrote a letter to Senator Harrison Gray Otis describing ice as an important luxury because of the inhospitable summers and tepid water.[3] Tudor aspired to fulfill his childhood dream of becoming "inevitably and unavoidably" rich, and he saw trading ice as a way to do that.[4]

This opportunity came when another Boston merchant, Samuel Austin, approached Tudor with a business proposal. Ships from India emptied their goods in Boston but had to be loaded with ballast on the way back. The idea was to fill the ships with ice for sale to the British in Bombay, Madras, and Calcutta. On September 13, 1833, Tudor loaded the *Tuscany* with one hundred tons of naturally harvested ice to be shipped to Calcutta, the headquarters of the British East India Company. This was the first time ice was shipped overseas. The ship set sail in May and arrived in Calcutta after losing fifty-five tons of ice from melting. The arrival of ice piqued local residents' curiosity, who asked what tree ice grew on, how it was cultivated, and whether it grew in the country of origin or whether it was a transshipment from elsewhere. The voyage resulted in the British establishing the East India Ice Company. Despite the novelty of the ice, an 1836 article in *Mechanics Magazine* said, "The sale has not, we believe, been so rapid as might have been expected."

The only competition to Tudor's ice in India at the time was "Hughli" ice, a muddy slurry of crushed ice taken from the Hughli Plain River. Tudor undercut the cost of Hughli ice by half, and sold the ice as neatly cut two-foot by three-foot pristine ice blocks.

The blocks were in stark contrast to the dirty slush ice from the river. "I will not talk of nectar or Elysium," one Calcutta historian explained, "but I will say that if there be a luxury here, it is this. . . . A block of pure ice weighing 2 maunds."[5] Eventually, the British Royal Navy started to use the ice to cool gun turrets.

Ice prices remained exorbitant in the early half of the nineteenth century because harvesting methods were in their infancy. Individual farmers used axes and saws to hack out irregular blocks of ice that melted awkwardly and inefficiently when used to store food. Harvesting was often done speedily and erratically for fear that a sudden thaw would destroy an entire ice crop. The workforce was made up of off-season labor.

As the ice trade expanded within the American South and to some foreign ports, the industry developed more sophisticated harvesting methods. Around 1850, Nathaniel J. Wyeth developed a horse-drawn ice cutter to harvest uniform blocks of ice. The blocks were delivered to storage using a steam-powered continuous chain. Layers of sawdust prevented the blocks from freezing together. The method enabled six hundred tons of ice to be harvested in a single hour.[6]

The ice could generate temperatures around 35 degrees Fahrenheit, and it was mixed with salt to achieve colder temperatures. A certain amount of heat was created during the mixing of ice and salt that created a liquid, and its latent heat was removed from the mixture itself, resulting in a colder temperature. This discovery was applied to natural ice cooling, including those involving refrigerators, cold-storage houses, and refrigerated railroad cars. The concept of proper air circulation was also important in the development of this industry.

Improvements in natural ice preservation advanced processing and shipping in the food industry. As demand for a diversified diet including unsalted meats and fresh produce grew, however, it became clear that more efficient refrigeration was necessary. Bulky and highly perishable natural ice, despite

Wyeth's improved harvesting and transport methods, was often too expensive to ship to the South. Frequently, warmer winters in the North decreased the harvest and worsened this problem. Even with cold winters in the North, natural ice posed a challenge across several industries.

Ice was bulky and caused moisture in the air, making it an imperfect solution to many industries' refrigeration needs. Beer brewers shelved huge quantities of ice above the stored beer, necessitating heavy, expensive construction. Additionally, the air that natural ice created was often too moist and caused fungi growth during the fermentation process, which infected the beer.[7]

The meat industry paid premium prices to ensure that there was enough natural ice to meet its large demand. Natural ice would often take up half the space in a meatpacking plant.[8] Similar to the brewing industry, the ice made the air too moist. The dairy industry suffered many of the same problems. Moreover, dairy producers valued cleanliness, but natural ice often contained dirt and vegetation.[9]

The introduction of mechanical refrigeration was about to emerge as a solution to the problems for commercial food and beverage production.

The Cold War

Global demand for a more dependable and cheaper method of refrigeration, particularly after 1850, spurred scientists to advance the usefulness of refrigerants. Great Britain led the way in driving better cold-storage capabilities to preserve meat during ocean transportation. Great Britain had a growing urban population, and the country needed to ship and store larger quantities of perishable food to meet the needs of its new urban dwellers. Another big pressure point was the US brewing industry, largely based in the South. The brewing industry needed a lot of ice, but the ice came from the North, an unsustainable transport system.

The first major step toward mechanical refrigeration came in 1755. William Cullen, a Scottish physician, chemist, agriculturalist, and prominent professor at the Edinburgh Medical School, discovered a way to artificially create temperatures low enough to form ice. He found that he could lower the pressure on water stored in a closed container using an air pump. At very low temperatures the water either evaporated violently or steadily boiled at a low temperature. The heat needed to transform water from a liquid state to vapor came from the water itself. Substantial heat was absorbed and part of the remaining water turned to ice.[10]

More scientists joined the search for a method to refrigerate and soon discovered two chemicals that achieved the goal of creating ice. Scientists found that adding a second substance to water, particularly one that had a high affinity for water vapor such as sulfuric acid, accelerated the freezing process. Other experiments took place using rubber from India to test perpetual vaporization and condensation of a volatile liquid.[11] Researchers eventually found that both ammonia and carbon dioxide could be liquefied. Ammonia compression machines were adopted more widely in the United States for refrigeration, while Europe preferred carbon dioxide.

With advances in chemical refrigeration came the advent of the mechanically refrigerated warehouse. The vast urban areas that housed thousands of people isolated from agriculture centers fueled the demand for the technology. To achieve cold storage in a large space, chilled brine was sent through pipes in the warehouse. In other cases a refrigerant such as ammonia itself was allowed to evaporate in the pipes.

The road to widespread acceptance and integration of commercial and domestic refrigeration was bumpy. In the early nineteenth century, before efficient ice-harvesting methods evolved, ice was simply too expensive for extensive cooling use, particularly within the home. Even later, cheaper methods were developed, but the public didn't understand the mechanics of air circulation well enough to properly cool a refrigeration unit. As a result, many people had dusty, moldy, smelly units, where food flavors mixed. The industry did not evolve quickly because the public accepted these inadequate models as the status quo, and in many cases the use of ice blocks continued. Dr. John Gorrie obtained a US patent for his air-cooled refrigerator in 1851 and attempted to market the invention in New Orleans without success.[12]

War eventually created the catalyst for change. The Civil War may have divided the American North and South over the issue of slavery and states' rights, but Lincoln's proclamation to "prevent entrance and exit of vessels" from Southern ports also prevented Boston ice from reaching the Confederacy.[13] The blockade cut the number of ships entering Southern ports by two-thirds. The disruption was bad news for both the suppliers, who lost a significant share of the ice market, and the consumers, who had grown accustomed to having ice at their disposal. Southerners were forced to accept an alternative. Ferdinand Carré's ammonia-water refrigeration machines were soon covertly shipped into Texas and Louisiana. As more homes in the South began to use the machines, the manufacturers gradually improved the technology. But throughout the rest of the United States, where access to New England's abundant ice supplies continued, the manufactured ice and artificial refrigeration industry could not compete with the natural ice industry.[14]

The manufactured ice industry in the South boomed as the Civil War raged on. In 1889, Texas had fifty-three ice-manufacturing plants.[15] In fact, almost all successful ice manufacturers based in the States came from areas that had been cut off by the Union blockade from the rest of the country.

The rest of the United States continued to favor natural ice for some time. The new manufactured ice models were prone to gas and oil leaks and explosions, defects that stopped the artificial ice industry from encroaching on the natural ice industry in the rest of the United States. Additionally, natural ice was cheaper than the new technology. In fact, the natural ice industry survived longer than it otherwise likely would have because of its extremely low price point compared to the new artificial icemakers.

Things began to shift for natural icemakers when winters grew warmer and water pollution sparked public health and safety concerns. Philadelphia-based companies sold natural ice cut from the Schuylkill River and its tributaries, which became more and more polluted by refuse from slaughterhouses and breweries. Many people assumed at the time that freezing polluted water was safe because "germs trapped in ice froze to death."[16] Even the health department claimed that any "impurities" would escape when the ice was harvested. Industrial consumers such as grocers and taverns used the dirtiest ice, while other private consumers were willing to pay more for cleaner ice from ponds and streams.

Eventually an outbreak of typhoid fever in the 1880s turned public perception against natural ice after researchers proved that "typhoid germs could survive freezing . . . [and that] some bacteria did live long enough to infect people, particularly with a shorter cold chain and the development of a market for ice during the winter months."[17]

Pollution challenged the claim that natural ice was completely "pure." For example, ice from Walden Pond in Massachusetts and the Schuylkill River differed noticeably in color, taste, and amount of sediment remaining in a cup of ice water. Nevertheless, the merchants argued in a pamphlet distributed to consumers that "natural ice is stored in ice houses from three to twelve or even twenty weeks before it is consumed. . . . Twelve weeks storage makes ice practically sterile."

"Natural ice is always more than 90 percent purer than the water on which it forms," claimed the pamphlet, adding that "chemists have proved this." Although these "scientific" claims about purity are typical of the arguments that the natural ice industry used and would use in future campaigns, the fact that this defensive brochure exists is indicative of the beginning of the end of the natural ice industry. Indeed, the pamphlet openly acknowledges that

"manufactured ice and refrigeration have made gigantic encroach-
ments in a field which twenty, yes, fifteen years ago you falsely
imagined you monopolized." Although the industry remained in
business because harvesting natural ice was simply cheaper than
any mechanical or artificial form of refrigeration at the time, the
realization that natural ice afforded consumers less control over its
quality and cleanliness sparked a search for something better.

Faced with competition from manufactured ice, purveyors of
natural ice fought back. They harvested the ice more efficiently
using improved field and basin saws powered by gasoline engines.
They introduced more sophisticated elevators in ice-storage houses.

The ice industry also launched an advertising campaign to
defend their "old way." The advertising campaign capitalized on
the main problems associated with mechanical and artificial
refrigeration—safety and usability for the common consumer—
and contrasted them with the naturalness of harvested ice. "Simple,
saving, pure and cold / I work without being told," read a poem
titled "To Ice!"[18] Mary E. Pennington, director of the Household
Refrigeration Bureau, produced thirteen pamphlets, ranging from
The Romance of Ice to *Desserts Frozen with Ice and Salt* that, among
other praises, heralded ice as the "guardian and caretaker" of children's fresh milk. The industry also emphasized the purity of ice as
opposed to the dangerous chemical mystery of ammonia, claiming
that "just as falling snow purifies the atmosphere . . . so melting
ICE purifies air in the refrigerator."[19]

Both the artificial refrigeration and the natural ice industries
targeted the housewife in their campaigns to sway public opinion.
Natural ice proponents said ice's "moist cold air" was a better preservative for fresh food than the dry air of the mechanical fridge, as
well as a potential filter for "possibly dangerous food odors."[20] This
angle especially played upon the housewife's newfound anxieties to
include fresh milk, fruits, and vegetables in their children's diets.

The artificial ice industry claimed their product was most practical for the "conscientious housewife." The sector received a big

plug from the interior decorating magazine *House Beautiful*. The publication predicted that while "we in our time buy our ice . . . our children will *not* buy ice. . . . They will refrigerate mechanically." The magazine article enumerated the electrical refrigerator's advantages, which included that "it costs less money than the housewife has been paying out year after year for ice and for food spoilage"; "it relieves the housewife of one of her most exacting responsibilities" (ordering ice from the ice man); and "with the dry air produced by electrical refrigeration the action of the bacteria does not begin in ordinary ice refrigerator at 38, nor at 44 degrees, but only after the temperature rises beyond that point."[21]

Despite artificial refrigeration's headway in gaining positive press, it was in many ways still unsafe. The cold-storage building fire at the 1893 Columbian Exposition in Chicago killed seventeen and injured nineteen. Chicago historian Josiah Seymour Currey recalled how firemen "were plunged into the seething mass of flames" in the building as "a horrified throng of thousands of spectators" looked on.[22]

An 1894 issue of *Ice and Refrigeration* cautioned that the number of explosions would increase with the number of ice-making and refrigeration plants. The same issue contains multiple letters from concerned refrigerator owners, asking questions about ammonia leaking into the water, leaks in the condenser, and ammonia gas cylinder malfunctions. In one year in Chicago, gas leaks from refrigerators led to ten deaths and thirty accidents.[23]

The refrigeration industry continued to insist that the mechanical refrigerator was safe and not to be blamed for explosions, but the American people disagreed. Another article in *Ice and Refrigeration* observed that "whenever an accident occurs in an ice plant, the newspapers immediately attribute it to an ammonia explosion,"[24] highlighting the public's distrust of the now high-profile dangers linked to ammonia.

The industry refused to consider alternative designs that did not carry the risks of explosions from ammonia compression. In fact, the industry, in denial about the risks, used a variety of methods such as insurance pooling to avoid making the necessary technical adaption. Concerns increased over time, especially as consumers perceived that they were being exposed to fatal risks while manufacturers reaped the profits. But many in the industry continued to deny or doubt that ammonia could explode. An 1890 company pamphlet touted ammonia's "great stability, its non-inflammability and non-explosiveness."[25]

The industry argued that focus should not be on ammonia but on that which caused the accident in the first place. Most of the users did not have sufficient technical expertise to determine the level of risk to which they were exposed. But as technical knowledge about refrigeration increased, so did safety consciousness. In 1914 Massachusetts adopted safety regulations for refrigerators. A 1915 fire in New York led to the adoption of tougher regulations that were emulated in other states. These included emergency pipes to prevent ammonia buildup in the machine room. "The ordinance also banned open flames, arc lights, and direct openings to the boiler room in any area containing ammonia-refrigeration equipment. Eventually, thirty other large cities and several states passed similar measures."[26]

One of the outcomes of the Chicago fire was the creation of a safety certification organization, the Underwriters Laboratories (UL), in 1894 by William Henry Merrill. The twenty-five-year-old Boston-based electrical engineer went to Chicago to investigate the fire. He saw the potential to develop safety standard tests as well as design safety equipment to identify hazards. In 1903 UL published its first safety standard, regarding "Tin Clad Fire Doors." Its UL mark was introduced in 1905 on a fire extinguisher.[27]

As the mechanical ice industry grappled with safety concerns, the natural ice industry faced other forms of competition. Too many dealers had entered an already saturated market. Salesmen with refrigerating machinery, hawking their low operating costs, often brought ice-works to areas that did not need another dealer.

The same held true for freelance dealers. Some industries, such as breweries and ice cream manufacturers, sold ice as a byproduct and were able to easily undercut regular manufacturers.[28] As a result, price-cutting was rampant, and the industry floundered.

Several regions took steps to address the issue. Trade associations brought industry members together to discuss ideas. In some regions—New York, Buffalo, Chicago—ice exchanges arose to address the need to regulate prices. Ice-cutting outfits consolidated. Some of the consolidation backfired, as in the case of the American Ice Company in New York. The company soon established a monopoly and eventually controlled New York City's ice supply. In May 1900, it doubled its prices.

Although American Ice stood out as an anomaly, the public widely felt it was being gouged. Press coverage used phrases such as "ice trust" to describe industry's various good-faith efforts to rectify the price-cutting situation. The public failed to understand the economics of the situation. Factors such as warmer winters, the high cost of distribution, and market flooding by small firms kept prices realistic. Nonetheless, widespread distrust of the ice industry created a favorable market for alternative refrigerants.

The distrust created on both sides of the ice argument also led to new forms of regulation and control. In the early days of refrigeration, cold storage was seen as a health menace.[29] Industry champions bemoaned the rise in negative attitudes toward refrigerated foods. "The people, quite generally, led by newspaper agitation, entertained the idea that cold-storage facilities were used to artificially control markets and increase prices; that foods were carried for long periods of time, and that the process was detrimental to the public health."[30] One response was to pass laws that sought to shorten the period warehouses could store food. The laws also required dealers to label foods with the date they had been put in cold storage.[31]

But as cities grew and as natural ice gradually became impractical and unhealthy, the need for better methods of storing perishable produce became greater. Yet critics alleged that food was kept in cold storage for so long that it became unwholesome and unpalatable.[32] In addition, information on how to store food properly was lacking in the early days of cold-storage warehouses, leading to deterioration in food quality. For example, eggs were not candled to determine which were sound before being preserved. The industry also made the mistake of accepting goods back into cold storage after they had thawed, leading to unsafe conditions and deterioration.

Furthermore, dealers often deceived consumers by thawing better grades of cold-storage items and marketing them as fresh, because consumers demanded fresh, out-of-season goods. The poorer grades of preserved food, as well as the poorer grades of some fresh food, were sold as "storage goods." Therefore, consumers who vehemently questioned cold storage ate these goods on a regular basis while believing them to be fresh. Refrigerated products earned the morbid label of "embalmed food." In international trade, countries seeking to protect local produce imposed tariffs on imported frozen beef.

A 1912 report by a Massachusetts commission to investigate cold storage cited the testimony of Junius T. Auerbach, who claimed that when he heard arguments that refrigeration could in fact improve the quality of food, he felt compelled to testify. He himself had been a victim of "ptomaine poisoning," which "specialists" had traced to chicken from a refrigeration warehouse. Ironically, he also declared that "all the specialists in the world couldn't make [him] believe that there isn't some change in the fiber of the food after it is frozen."[33] Auerbach's main quarrel with the cold-storage industry was that "the public ought to know whether an egg has been in storage a short time or a long time"—knowledge that would forestall deceptions of freshness as well as availability of (and therefore price of) food.

As methods improved, however, it became clear that there was little evidence to back up the claim that cold storage resulted in public health risks. Refrigerated warehouses provided a much more sanitary environment than a typical "butcher's icebox" or even a household refrigerator. As William Sedgwick of the Massachusetts Institute of Technology testified in the same report, cold storage was "one of the greatest aids to public health, in that it makes food more accessible and more abundant, and thus enables people to keep up their strength and avoid such diseases as scurvy."[34] The warehouses provided, for the most part, a safe and sanitary environment for preserved food. Eventually the United States Department of Agriculture (USDA) and other government agencies played a major role in informing customers of the innocuous, beneficial nature of warehouse cold storage by mechanical means.

The second charge against cold storage stemmed from general public anxiety over rising living costs, which reached a climax in 1909. Critics alleged that it caused an increase in food prices, which was based in part on the speculative nature of preserving food—that is, buying perishable food in times of surplus and selling in times of low supply. In the Massachusetts commission report, Auerbach accused the cold-storage industry of taking foodstuffs out of storage only "when the price meets their approval, or the supplies are so low they can get a higher price."[35] Economic pressures also provided checks on warehousing speculation. Storage, insurance, interest, and the risk of depreciation in food value all caused anxiety for the warehousemen.

Another charge against cold storage came from the warehousemen, who argued that cold storage caused a decline in prices. Cold storage led to greater uniformity in food prices, though it was not the only factor at work. Overall, the introduction of refrigeration "brought about a significant dampening of seasonal fluctuations . . . and a tightening of spatial price linkages," as has been demonstrated in the case of butter.[36] Moreover, "The adoption of refrigeration in the late-nineteenth-century United States increased dairy consumption by 1.7 percent and overall protein intake by 1.25 percent annually after the 1890s."[37] The public, however, needed an explanation for why food prices were increasing. By virtue of being a new factor in the economy, refrigeration became a target for the rising anger over higher food prices, and politicians resorted to manipulation.

In 1912, the Massachusetts Commission to Investigate the Subject of Cold Storage of Food deemed cold-storage food both safe and cost-beneficial for the consumer. Soon after that, the American Public Health Association issued a statement commending the industry for making varied and wholesome supplies available year round. This, along with the USDA's system of voluntary reports by warehousemen that provided the public with knowledge about the economic phases of individual commodities, helped to ameliorate public prejudice toward cold storage.[38] It is an interesting phenomenon, as Anderson notes, that public prejudice—by providing the impetus for investigation, legislation, and education involving cold storage—ultimately led to the industry's widespread acceptance.[39]

As cold storage grew in popularity, the natural ice industry launched an advertising campaign to compete with the artificial refrigeration industry. The advertising campaign intended to "create respect for and confidence in the ice industry," "to build a new stratum of ice businesses," "to increase the ice consumption of present consumers," "to promote ice as a refrigerant in competition with the small machine," and last, to "undertake scientific and practical research to show the value of ice as a refrigerant."[40]

Yet the ice industry was on the defensive, claiming that "[ice] is the natural way of chilling food," superior because it is "moist enough to retard the drying out of food." Still another advertisement promised that eating ice-chilled foods would help women "snap [their] fingers at avoirdupois" by adhering to a delicious diet of lettuce, olives, and celery, all kept fresh by natural ice. Wet ice, the industry repeatedly claimed, could preserve food's necessary moisture in a way that the dry refrigerator could not.

The Chicago-based meatpacking industry saw the benefits of refrigerated railway cars.[41] There were many ostensible advantages to shipping refrigerated meat as of 1880. Farmers gained the ability to market at the most profitable times of year and to slaughter livestock at their peak, and shipping only the useful parts of the dead animal saved money on freight. Animal byproducts could be shipped separately at more affordable rates.

The railroads, however, were initially skeptical of the refrigerated car technology, and moreover had a vested interest in transporting live pigs and cattle, with investments in docking and feeding stations. Until a compromise was reached, the railways charged a rate on dressed meat to yield the same return as shipping live animals.

Back east, the cosmopolitan slaughtering industry, fearful of losing capital, was also skeptical and did all it could to encourage public prejudice and fear regarding butchered meat shipped from afar. Many on the receiving end who made their living as butchers as well as handlers responded by refusing to distribute Chicago meat. They lobbied extensively for state and municipal measures against shipments of dressed meat.[42] Those in the dressed meat business responded by either opening their own branch houses for distribution back east, or by taking the local slaughterers into partnership. Antagonism dissipated over the next decade as dressed meat became more cost effective than shipments of livestock.

Leaving It to the Experts

Producing artificial ice involved considerable understanding of engineering principles. This meant that much of the discussion on advances was restricted to technical circles. In fact, engineers played a key role in the advancement of the field, especially between 1890 and 1917.

In addition to the use of ammonia and carbon dioxide as coolants, engineers focused on the "miniaturization" of refrigerators.

Early attempts to make smaller machines failed, but by 1917 "units with capacities ranging from one-fourth to three or four tons were used widely. They did not require highly skilled attention, but they were not automatic."[43] These small units had higher maintenance costs and so created new avenues for improvement to reduce cost. For example, brine was used to store the refrigerant, and internal combustion engines were employed where cheap steam was not available.

These improvements were associated with considerable technical diversity. By 1916, for example, over twenty-four different makes of household machines were available. Some of the European design concepts started to make inroads into the US market. For example, the "Audiffren," which used sulfur dioxide for compression, was designed in France but manufactured in the United States by General Electric. The diversity in models and subsequent improvements were shaped by a wide range of social factors.[44]

The emergence of new design concepts and the associated technical challenges had to meet the needs of diverse markets that called for greater exchange of technical information. In 1891 *Ice and Refrigeration*, the first periodical of the industry, was founded in Chicago. "Books appeared which made technical data available to engineers, cold-storage men, brewers, packers, and others. Not only the first periodicals, but the first books as well were of American origin."[45]

The need to collect and disseminate information led to the creation of trade and industry associations. In 1904, the American Society of Refrigerating Engineers was formed in New York to "promote the Arts and Sciences connected with Refrigerating Engineering."[46] Louis Block, president of the western chapter, gave this address at the first meeting: "We are no longer in our infancy. We have now grown to vigorous manhood and have arrived at a more conservative age; still, we are plunging ahead, making improvements, spreading out, and anyone who wants to keep up with the refrigerating industries must travel fast. We dare not stand still, and our aim will be in the future, as it has been in the past, to not only improve and simplify machinery and apparatus, but to make improvement in the line of cutting down the cost of refrigerating and ice making plants."[47] The trade associations and publications helped to bring to the industry the transparency that was needed to address public concerns but also promote greater standardization.

Science, technology, and engineering played an even more significant role in advancing refrigeration globally. The implications of the technology for international trade had become obvious. European countries, for example, saw the technology as a viable way to expand trade with their colonies. Numerous national congresses had been held to advance the field. In 1908 the First International Congress of Refrigeration was convened in Paris. The congress had one major objective: to create a centralized institution to help advance the field of refrigeration. It achieved this objective in 1909 with the creation of the International Association of Refrigeration (IAR), which is headquartered in Paris.

The IAR was restructured in 1920 and renamed the International Institute of Refrigeration.[48] This visionary institution is the only independent intergovernmental organization dealing with the science, technology, and engineering aspects of refrigeration. It promotes knowledge of all refrigeration fields, ranging from cryogenics to air conditioning, covering liquefied gas, the cold chain, refrigeration processes and equipment, refrigerants, and heat pumps. It addresses key issues such as energy efficiency and savings, health, food safety, global warming, and ozone depletion.

Its founding conference was a landmark event. "More than 5000 delegates from 42 countries around the world were gathered in Paris, at the Sorbonne, in order to discuss issues concerning the striking developments in the area of artificial cold."[49] The conference was driven by national committees but the discussions were divided into thematic issues covering "(1) low temperatures and their general effects, (2) refrigerating materials, (3) application of refrigeration to alimentation, (4) application of cold to other industries, (5) application of cold to commerce and transports, and (6) legislation." More fundamentally, it was a scientific, technical, and engineering conference. "Scientific and technical issues were intrinsically involved in all the aforesaid domains, especially in the definition of the measures and standards, the units and nomenclature used in the refrigeration industry."[50]

It is notable that the conference and the subsequent creation of the IAR were the result of intellectual leadership provided by two prominent scientists in the field, Heike Kamerlingh Onnes from the Netherlands and Charles-Édouard Guillaume from Switzerland. Both men would later receive Nobel Prizes in Physics (1913 and 1920 respectively). A combination of the rising significance of refrigeration and the intellectual force of its champions made it possible to convene "scientists, engineers, industrialists and businessmen for the resolution of some pressing problems emerging from the developing area of artificial cold."[51]

Political leaders played an equally important role in the preparation of the conference. The organizing committee was headed by André Lebon, who later became the president of the French IAR. He "was a successful businessman, a former minister of Commerce and the Colonies, professor at the very liberal École Libre des Sciences Politiques [now called Sciences Po], and later occupied key positions in some of the flagships of the French economy."[52] Other champions included Jean de Loverdo, a prominent Parisian engineer who had studied the role of refrigeration in agriculture.

The men managed to rally France's leading academic, administrative, and legislative institutions behind the conference and its aims. They exercised considerable influence and prevented Germany and Austria from challenging the creation of a centralized organization in favor of decentralized committees. In fact, the final outcome accommodated the two approaches without compromising the original focus on creating an institution to champion refrigeration.

The association was designed in such a way that it did not interfere with national activities. It aimed to centralize all relevant information; encourage industrial advancement; find the best solutions to scientific, technical, and industrial questions, as well as the best administrative measures concerning the transportation of perishable produce; collect information on legislative developments; popularize the science behind refrigeration; establish cooperation between the different national groups; and coordinate activities of its members.[53]

The founding years of the IAR were marked by expected tensions surrounding national and international activities. The centralization of information dissemination also demanded greater investment in translation. This was a major source of concern for German engineers, for example. Similarly, those such as Kamerlingh Onnes who expected the association to play a bigger role as a source of research funding grew increasingly frustrated. Despite these challenges, the association stands out as an important institutional innovation that sought to define the challenges of the industry by offering technical solutions while leaving social concerns to national associations and their members.

The refrigeration community found an institutional home in Europe, where it did not face challenges from the natural ice industry. Back in the United States, however, the two industries and their associations had to coexist, at least in the interim.[54]

Cooling Tensions

The convenience of having artificial refrigeration began to outweigh its dangers. The ice industry gained the support of mothers by recommending "fresh" milk and food for children. Simultaneously, the inconvenience of having an icebox rather than an artificial refrigerator was amplified by the mess, smell, and design. Of course, there were barriers: the size, noise, and cost of the early artificial refrigeration system were all prohibitive to its popularity in the typical American household.[55]

But with technological improvement and advancement in engineering techniques, refrigerated storage by mechanical means revolutionized numerous industries. Beginning around 1920, meatpackers became aware that removing animal heat from the carcass fairly immediately upon death was an important factor in preserving the meat. Improved warehouses with brine sprays were created—and butchery became a more complex process. Carcasses were moved to cooling rooms directly after slaughter. The cooling rooms helped control humidity levels while the meat awaited shipment or underwent the curing process. If necessary, the meat would be frozen later. This applied to meat byproducts as well. A multistep processing system helped meatpackers keep up with market fluctuation.

Air conditioning was developed, which regulated humidity in storage, therefore preventing both dehydration and mold. The industry depended heavily on the refrigerated railroad car, which led to the creation of monopolies as large Midwestern concerns took control of all steps of the refrigeration from slaughter to shipment. Later, the industry would begin to decentralize as refrigerated motor trucks came on the scene. With the new methods of processing and plastic-packaging the meat, smaller packer concerns became as efficient as larger ones.

Meanwhile, fruit and vegetable production skyrocketed during the early part of the twentieth century. Body icing was a major innovation in the shipping of produce. In 1930, a crusher-slinger was developed that would deposit snowlike crushed ice on all parts of a refrigerator car using a flexible hose. The USDA initiated a relentless series of product-specific tests to determine the optimal shipping conditions for individual kinds of fruits and vegetables. Regional specialization in produce prevailed.

Refrigerated car technology generally improved during this decade. In the case of produce, precooling began to take place in the cars—fans were installed in individual cars to circulate air over the produce until the natural force of air circulation (resulting from the high speeds of the train) took force. Also employed was a very efficient automated method of hosing down the vegetables with water cooled on contact with the crushed ice upon which they were resting.

Refrigerated ships carried produce for domestic trade through the Panama Canal. Many people also looked forward to air transport, which would both streamline the industry and account for major new costs. Many thought that, for the time, air transport would only potentially be useful in obtaining tropical and subtropical items.

After 1923, refrigerated storage spread to rural (produce production) areas. As Anderson notes, two innovations made this possible: "the perfection of the small commercial [refrigeration] machine and the extension of electrical facilities to rural areas."[56] There were many advantages to this movement in the industry— construction costs and land values were cheaper out in the country, and the farmer gained more leverage in deciding when and where to release his harvest to the market.

Those dealing in produce began experimenting with freezing around 1917. In 1931 the Department of Agriculture established its frozen pack laboratory in Seattle to investigate the steps to making quality frozen foods. Around 1945 a very successful method for freezing orange juice was developed and gained great public acceptance. The concentrate technique was extended to lemon, grapefruit, and grape juice. Canned produce items maintained their status during this stage, as they still held the advantage of storage at room temperature.

The advent of cold storage saw many agencies clamoring to influence its public perception, from committees formed by the warehouse owners themselves, to government agencies and politicians.

The USDA played a large role in disseminating information to the public and dissuading its fears regarding the supposed dangers of cold storage. In the early years of the twentieth century its studies revealed that "meats, poultry, butter, fish, eggs, etc." could be held in cold storage nine to twelve months "without an appreciable loss of flavor."[57] This could be done for even longer periods without losing nutritional value.

As mentioned above, research by the Department of Agriculture affirmed that cold storage generally contributed to a uniformity of prices. In response to the Committee on Cold Storage of the Warehousemen's Association's claim that Republicans promoted cold storage as a way to increase the cost of living in order to preserve high tariffs, the Senate established a committee to investigate living expenses. The committee eventually determined that limits should be set on the amount of time an item could be kept in cold storage—this, it determined, would help to stabilize prices.

Although legislation never took place on a national scale, states did pass laws regarding cold storage. Routine sanitary inspections took place in most areas, and most states required foods to be marked with the date they went into storage. The laws were slowly calibrated. Earlier legislation was overturned. These laws set short storage maximums that effectively eliminated the purpose of cold storage for some commodities altogether, while other laws concerning goods' re-entry into refrigeration obstructed legitimate warehouse-to-warehouse transfers.

The USDA played a major role in the success of refrigerated transport. After 1930 the agency, as Anderson notes, "was untiring in its efforts to improve the techniques of refrigerated rail transportation."[58] As a result of these improvements, regional specialization became a prominent aspect of the produce industry. In the beginnings of rail transport, the farmer's distance from his market was the cause of anxiety: "Quality confusion and misunderstanding were inevitable."[59] So were glutted markets.

However, the market-news network established by the USDA in 1913 and the rise of cooperative marketing associations eliminated this tension. The farmer could now bargain effectively with the buyer without ever meeting him face to face. The USDA also played a major role in recommending market standards and for a fee offered a federal inspection service. In 1943, the National Association of Refrigerated Warehouses established and endowed the Refrigeration Research Council to find new ways and varying applications of preserving produce. Around the same time, the USDA was highly invested in the US Horticultural Station at Beltsville, Maryland, where endless horticultural experiments took place surrounding the use of cold storage.

Conclusions

Socioeconomic concerns on the part of the natural ice industry drove some of the early debates on mechanical refrigeration. The main concerns in the industry, however, were more technical. By addressing these concerns, the artificial ice industry was able to respond to the challenges while meeting diverse market needs. The global diffusion of refrigeration can therefore be attributed largely to the responsiveness of the industry in addressing technical and engineering challenges. There are several lessons from the debate that can inform many of the contemporary technological debates.

The first major lesson from the case of refrigeration was the role of safety regulations in shaping technical responses to the industry. For example, to address the risks associated with ammonia explosions, in the 1930s the industry shifted to Freon, a family of stable and nonflammable chemicals known as chlorofluorocarbons (CFCs). Some industries promoted the use of Freon by invoking the fear of ammonia explosions. Freon would later be identified as a major source of the depletion of the ozone layer. This led to another round of product substitution, as many CFCs were banned or severely restricted under the 1987 Montreal Protocol on Substances that Deplete the Ozone Layer. It is notable that few international treaties focus on technical innovation as a way to promote environmental or human safety.

The focus of the regulations was not to stifle the industry but to advance safety. In this respect, safety became the standard against which technical improvements were based. Other technical criteria such as efficiency and convenience were equally important, but they were not driven by legislation as in the case of safety considerations. These engineering efforts contributed to scientific advancement just as much as new knowledge was used to improve engineering designs. The adoption of better technical practices was achieved through the creation of industry associations that used publications, conferences, and seminars to share information. Publications such as *Ice and Refrigeration* played an important role as vehicles for public education and technical advancement.

The case of refrigeration shows that, contrary to popular belief, regulation can serve as a stimulus for innovation. In this case, many of the advances that made it possible for consumers to access safe and regional mechanical refrigeration resulted from regulation and new standards.[60] The regulation of the industry, however, was informed by the need to strike a balance between technological advancement and safety promotion. Such an approach requires continuous interactions between government, industry, and academia. It also involves scientific advice, which was achieved in part through public hearings on the benefits and risks of the technology.

The second lesson was the creation of new institutions such as trade associations to support the industry. The most important development was the creation of the IAR. Prior to its establishment, there were many regional and national organizations in countries such as the United States, United Kingdom, Germany, France, and the Netherlands devoted to advancing refrigeration. As it became apparent, however, that these endeavors needed to be coordinated, the IAR was created.

The creation of the IAR was an important focus for advancing technological development. It afforded the scientific and engineering communities a nonpolitical platform through which to share technical information. It also helped to advance the field of scientific research in its own right independent of industrial benefits. The associated International Institute of Refrigeration was an important secretariat for managing the affairs of the refrigeration movement. Its creation was visionary and helped to show the degree of professional dedication to the advancement of the field. There are many emerging fields today that could benefit from such bodies.

This lesson may be relevant to addressing emerging technologies such as synthetic biology, artificial intelligence, robotics, and drones. It is not particularly necessary to create institutions for every emerging technology. However, it is important not to foreclose this option largely because of bureaucratic efficiency. Many of the existing institutions may not be well equipped to address emerging technologies or may require long periods of internal adjustment to accommodate the needs of new technologies. The common tendency is to define emerging technologies so they can fit existing regulatory practices. For example, there are efforts to advance and regulate synthetic biology as an extension of transgenic crops. This ignores the fact that synthetic biology is also based on the principles of engineering, which seek to control the kinds of uncertainties that led to the creation of the research and regulatory systems for transgenic crops. Some synthetic biology products may take on the risk profile of engineering rather than biological products. Given such regulator uncertainty, it may be necessary to at least entertain the possibility that synthetic biology might share common attributes with refrigeration, thereby requiring separate treatment. The same thinking may also apply to artificial intelligence and robotics.

The third lesson pertains to the familiar theme of the fear of loss. The natural ice industry grew out of remarkable entrepreneurial efforts that saw a seemingly local product reach markets as far away as India. It was a product that relied heavily on seasonal change and benefited from the surplus agricultural labor available off-season. This was its strength as a business model but also its subsequent undoing. Mechanical refrigeration freed the industry from reliance on seasonal changes. It promised decentralized cold storage for businesses and homes. Part of the perception of loss extended to debates over the wholesomeness of refrigerated products. But pollution of natural ice and the associated disease outbreaks would shake the image of the product and the appeal to purity. Policymakers not only have to deal with the technical aspects of new technologies, but they also have to confront more philosophical concerns about how the public perceives new products.

The fourth lesson is about the prospects for technical improvement in advancing a new industry. A wide range of technical difficulties marked the early stages of mechanical refrigeration. The industry focused technological improvements in ways that were akin to the development of farm mechanization. Considerable effort went into building scientific and engineering communities as well as associations that promoted knowledge sharing on advances in the industry. Policymakers could play more active roles in helping to create mechanisms for sharing information and setting technical standards. Similarly, research-oriented institutions could also advance knowledge in emerging technologies.

A contemporary example of the importance of technical advancement to enhance the competitiveness of new industries through initial niche applications is solar photovoltaics. The most significant photovoltaic advance involved the use thin-film cells, which contributed to the other overall annual market growth rate of 35–40 percent in recent years.[61] The growth of the industry has been associated with product and process innovation. In addition, governments around the world have come up with a wide range of incentives aimed at expanding the market and increasing its competitiveness with incumbent sources of electric power. Much of this global growth stemmed from new entrants such as China.[62]

The methods used to stimulate the solar photovoltaic industry included market subsidies that the United States saw as a way to contravene antidumping rules.[63]

Finally, there is the generally contentious issue of the role of government. As in the case of farm mechanization, the government played an important role as a source of technical information upon which other regulators as well as industry associations could base their decisions. In this respect, the government—mostly through the USDA—complemented the information generated by industry associations. Other ways by which the government provided information included public hearings convened by state and federal legislative bodies to examine the risks of the technology. This provided opportunities for technical submissions that would not have otherwise been available to the general public.

Facing the Music

Recorded Sound

Only those who will risk going too far can possibly find out how far it is possible to go.

T. S. ELIOT

In a 2003 interview in *Rolling Stone* Apple cofounder Steve Jobs said that the "subscription model of buying music is bankrupt. I think you could make available the Second Coming in a subscription model, and it might not be successful." In 2015 his prophecy was tested in an epic confrontation between Apple Music and the world-famous American singer, songwriter, and actress Taylor Swift.

To attract customers, Apple offered a three-month free subscription over which period artists would not be paid. "Three months is a long time to go unpaid, and it is unfair to ask anyone to work for nothing," Swift wrote in an open letter explaining why she would be withholding her popular album *1989* from the streaming service. "We don't ask you for free iPhones. Please don't ask us to provide you with our music for no compensation." Apple Music backed down in a major victory by an artist against the world's richest corporation.

The same concerns were expressed in the early history of recorded music, leading to a long history of confrontation between the industry and musicians. This chapter examines the case of the 1942 ban by the American Federation of Musicians (AFM) on recorded music in the United States as a result of the social tensions that new music-recording technology wrought. The ban was a result of union leaders work to protect their musician and engineer members, whose livelihood they believed was under threat from music-recording advances. In addition to outlining the dynamics surrounding the ban, the chapter reviews its wider implications, which include the creation of new music genres as well as the expansion of the recording industry. It is true that the recording industry eroded opportunities for traveling musicians, but recording also resulted in the diversification of the music industry.

For a Song

Schumpeter put considerable emphasis on the economic gains arising from innovation. He also understood, however, that the process of "creative destruction" caused considerable misery for those affected. He visualized large sections of society being crushed by the wheels of novelty.[1] One of the biggest fears people have when new technologies are introduced is becoming unemployed. This is often a genuine concern. New technologies tend to be more efficient and therefore require less manual labor. Or new technologies introduce business models that shift wealth to new and fewer hands. Such shifts are a source of considerable social tension across industries and generations. The shifts sometimes lead to calls by labor organizations to ban certain technologies.

Throughout the last century, the music industry developed under a wide range of technological successions. Its Schumpeterian "gales of creative destruction" were in most cases the source of new economic opportunities. But the waves of technological innovation also came with welfare costs. Previous chapters illustrated how new technologies can trigger considerable social anxiety because of their potential repercussions on individual's livelihoods.

Artists and engineers feared that changes to music-recording technology signaled the end of their economic livelihood. The union came to their rescue. In 1942, the most powerful union in the music industry, the American Federation of Musicians, brought music recording to a standstill with a ban on recorded music and caused severe economic losses for producers. All music recording stopped, and artists from around the world refused to engage with producers in the United States. The union wielded significant power in the 1942 ban, enflaming the social tensions caused by technological innovation and becoming a symbol of the fear incumbents feel when faced with industry change. The power awarded to the union in fights like the 1942 ban can be traced all the way back to the Luddite rebellion in England, one of the first examples where organized labor and technological innovation clashed. The Luddite protests occurred in the early nineteenth century when textile workers opposed the introduction of power looms, spinning frames, and stocking frames. The changes threated employment. Contrary to popular folklore, the Luddites were not against technological improvement but were defending their livelihoods. The Luddite rebellion was one of the first of many confrontations that unions and industry would have through history and innovation. The same threads of dissent and fear played out during the 1940s among musicians and their funders.

One of the legacies of the Luddite era was the creation of organized labor to defend the interests of its members and to protect them from losses arising from changes in management and production methods. Since then unions have negotiated extensively with employers using a variety of approaches. In many cases they have waged direct opposition to specific technologies. Technological developments and innovation alter both the social and the economic fabric of a region. Traditional modes of operation are challenged, and people are presented with alternative ways of living. The distribution, benefits, and risks of technological innovation are often fiercely debated, largely because of distributional uncertainties and the potential for erosion of assets such as human capital that are slow to replenish.

The music industry in America during the early and middle twentieth century is a perfect example of how the threats created by technological and engineering developments affected the lives of people involved in an industry. With the onset of recorded music, and in turn the emergence of the recording and radio industries, the life of the musical performer changed significantly.[2] Live music was historically viewed as something between an artisanship and a profession. It takes a long time to acquire musical skills, and much of the learning is done early in life. It is harder to build musical skills later in life, and therefore the propensity to seek job protection is quite high. In addition, many skills are highly specific and not readily transferable to other instruments or sectors of the economy.

Musicians today are afforded respect and admiration, but that wasn't always the case. At one time, musicians existed to amuse the public. Musicians were hired to play at weddings, funerals, parties, and other social events. They weren't social icons or role models. Many musicians would take other jobs to earn supplemental income, primarily working as carpenters, salesmen, or similar occupations. The musicians were employed by a system where employers would hire contractors who would in turn hire musicians. As a result, the rank-and-file musicians did not fully reap the economic benefits of their work. Competition "between contractors to secure the engagement from the employer tended to reduce the remuneration of the musician still further because the contractor has less money to distribute among the men."[3] The livelihoods of musicians during this era were characterized by heated competition and economic uncertainty. Labor unions soon became advocates for the struggling musician and sought to control competition and foster employment.

Musicians began to organize within their communities, and local unions sprang up in cities throughout America. For example, New York, Chicago, and Cincinnati established working standards and imposed regulations to enhance the quality of life for their members. In 1886, local union leaders convened in Cincinnati and created the National League of Musicians

(NLM). The NLM served as the foremost labor organization for musicians.[4]

As the years progressed the NLM grew in both numbers and authority. At one point the leader of the American Federation of Labor (AFL), created in 1886 as an alliance of craft unions, invited the NLM to join its organization. Leaders of the NLM opposed affiliation with the types of laborers in the AFL, and feared they could lose their authority if they agreed to run their organization under its auspices. In the end, division over whether to establish a relationship with AFL leader Samuel Gompers's organization divided the NLM, and in October 1896 the American Federation of Musicians (AFM) was established.[5] This union embraced its affiliation with the AFL, and from its inception tirelessly fought to increase the economic status of its members.

AFM's leaders were initially concerned with controlling competition outside the union boundaries. The union believed the key to increasing the economic strength of its members was to ensure there was a market for employment. According to the union, the two major threats were military bands and foreign musicians. On the whole, they represented cheap labor and as a result contributed to the unemployment of American musicians. Elements of both racism and nativism fueled opposition to foreign musicians. Union members even sought to invoke the Alien Contract Labor Law but were eventually rebuffed.[6]

The AFM also strongly opposed military bands and orchestras, whose musicians received payment from the military and were thus able to work for less. Union leaders negotiated with military administrators and eventually lobbied for a law to forbid military musicians from competing with civilian performers.

Musicians and their union faced both victories and defeats. The tumultuous nature of their industry, however, would only grow more chaotic as technological improvements began to change the nature of their profession and introduce a new element of commercialization and power bases.

Calling the Tune

The emergence of recorded music drastically changed the music landscape. Sound recording democratized music and made listening more convenient. But it threatened the employment of live musicians in America.

The breakthrough in sound recording came in 1877 when Thomas Edison created the phonograph. His work built upon Frenchman Leon Scott's phonautograph, invented in 1856.[7] The phonautograph could record sound, but the recordings were not reproducible. It was initially intended to record phone messages, but Edison and other inventors saw its potential to record other forms of sound. Throughout the late nineteenth century, a number of inventors worked toward creating a commercially viable phonograph. By 1900 phonographs were being duplicated and sold to American families, paving the way for the emergence of a major global music industry.[8]

The impact of machines on music itself had become a subject of considerable debate in the industry. When American avant-garde composer George Antheil's *Ballet Méchanique* premiered in Carnegie Hall in New York, newspaper headlines screamed: "Mountain of Noise out of an Antheil" and "Boos Greet Antheil Ballet of Machines." Antheil's work featured "ten pianos, a pianola, xylophones, electric bells, sirens, airplane-propellers and percussion."[9] Earlier attempts by Luigi Russolo, an Italian futurist painter and composer, to create a complete orchestra with newly invented noise machines did not go down well. When he put the instruments on stage in 1914, a huge crowd had "gathered, whistling, howling and throwing things even before the concert had started and it remained in great uproar throughout the performance."[10]

Early recording machines had many flaws, and the AFM sought to capitalize on the early stage problems of the new technology. The limitations enabled continued popularity of live performances. AFM president Joseph Weber noted that the phonograph helped musicians because it increased public awareness of music, which in turn had the potential to create jobs. At the 1926 AFM convention, Weber tried to reassure musicians: "There is absolutely nothing to fear from radio . . . radio will have the same result as the phonograph . . . it will ultimately increase the employment of musicians."[11]

Musical performers and their labor union did not perceive early recordings as a threat to their livelihoods because the recordings were mostly of poor quality. It was not long before musicians "began to wonder whether recordings of popular artists or songs would undermine the demand for live music. For a time, however, recorded music was too scratchy to pose a serious threat, even though it played in commercial places and offered a few performers a way to supplement their income."[12]

Additionally, during the early days of recording, radio stations preferred using live musicians on their programs. Sound from live performances was better quality, and stations at this time rarely used recordings. Broadcasters respected union demands for employment and decent wages, because the alterative use of recordings was even less attractive. They made efforts to employ orchestras, bands, and vocalists to perform on radio programs. There was relative balance between live music and technology in the early innovation stages. With increased improvements in electrical recording, however, this balance soon changed.

The rise of chain broadcasting changed the tide for musicians and the union on the radio. Affiliated stations began to use records and transcriptions to fill in the time between network broadcasts. Small radio stations that relied wholly on records started to spring up. Musicians were concerned. In 1930, the AFM lodged a futile complaint with the Federal Radio Commission to control or eliminate records on air. Concern increased with the invention of the jukebox around 1932. As the jukebox became popular, job losses followed. Throughout the thirties, many hotel, restaurant, and bar managers replaced live musician acts with coin-operated record machines because they were cheaper and didn't require interacting with demanding and unionized musicians.[13]

The introduction of recorded music also infiltrated the movie industry, although it had a bumpy start. Technological and engineering challenges bedeviled the early use of recording in movies. Warner Brothers was an early adopter. It used recorded sound to enhance its competitiveness, hoping it could grow small neighborhood cinemas to compete with the "opulent downtown movie palaces."[14]

The advent of recorded music not only changed the commercial landscape for musicians and the recording industries, but it transformed the nature of leisure and musical exposure for the American public. Before recordings, people had to leave their homes to listen to music. They usually attended live musical performances in groups. Recorded music changed the public's music listening experience and allowed people to seek out music as an individual activity and to explore a wider array of sounds.

Recordings gave music a sense of both tangibility and portability.[15] Because music was recorded and stored on a disc, and later cassette and CD, it became an object. People could share and borrow music, and they were able to collect it for posterity. Music also could travel. Unlike a live performance that occurred in a specific area of the country and was heard by a small group of people, recorded music had the ability to be shipped and disseminated to a larger population.

The tangibility and portability of recorded music also risked turning music into a commodity. There is a commercial aspect attached to music once it is tradable, and this was a major source of contention among the musicians and their union in the early and middle nineteenth century. The artist feared becoming alienated from the song and its relationship with the listener.

Some people also questioned the quality and morality of mass-produced music because recorded sound reduced the human interaction afforded by live music. Critics noted that a transportable music jeopardized its intrinsic qualities. Critics argued that much of the thought and feeling behind jazz stemmed from African American urban areas. They said jazz recordings removed music from its source, and as a result it lost its authenticity and meaning.

Recorded music introduced another element that didn't exist with live performance. Recorded music could be played repeatedly at will. As the musicologist Mark Katz wrote, the ability to play a song on repeat "is perhaps the most unbridgeable difference between live and recorded music."[16] A band can play the same song at every show, but it will be unable to play the song in the exact same way each time. The characteristic of repeatability changed the musical experience for both the musicians and the listeners. Listeners developed certain expectations of live performances, and they expected the recordings of these pieces to meet those standards. The ability to repeat elevated the role of the sound technician and made the musician subservient to technology and, by extension, to those who controlled the sound production.

An editorial in the *International Musician* in 1945 vividly captured this unique feature of music: "This peculiar circumstance, the record's reproducibility, obtains in no other craft or industry. A drinking cup does not multiply itself and render useless other drinking cups; a house does not become a village; a lump of coal does not father other lumps of coal. Labor in general stands in no danger of its commodities ruining both their makers and brother members of the craft. For each extra article entails extra work, and payment can be estimated accurately and paid directly to the worker. Only the musician suffers from the fecundity of his creations."[17]

As time progressed, live performances were judged on how they compared with the recorded versions. This was often detrimental to musicians as fewer people attended live shows. Musicians often felt pressure to record a perfect version of a song because they knew it would be mass-produced and repeatedly played. Musicians started to experience less freedom in the recording studio than they did on stage.

Technology has historically distinguished the way music is produced. In a live jazz concert a bass player can provide the audience with a ten-minute jam session but is unable to do so if making a record. Time and space limits on early discs precluded this liberalized performance style. Often, pieces would be separated into a number of discs leading to a lack of continuity. In addition to length, musicians had to take into account how the machinery recorded and absorbed their sound. Especially in the early days of recording, human voices as well as instruments were often distorted once recorded.

To prevent such distortion, it was up to the musician to alter the sound to accommodate the nascent recording technology. This spanned musical genres, and jazz musicians as well as orchestras almost molded their works around recording parameters. Many musicians were receptive to the limitations and benefits of technology and created their records accordingly. The recording limitations began to filter into stage performance. Musicians were restricted to three-minute songs in the recording studio and they soon kept their songs to that length on stage too.

Playing Second Fiddle

Technological unemployment is one of the most potent sources of innovation resistance. As the economic historian Joel Mokyr writes, "New knowledge displaces existing skills and threatens rents: technological change leads to substantial losses sustained by those who own specific assets dedicated to the existing technology."[18] If we apply this statement to music, it is evident that the surge of recording technologies led to job losses for live musicians. Musicians and leaders of the AFM were primarily concerned with lost profit as a result of being overtaken by the machine.

Musicians' fears grew as the power of the four major recording companies over musical recording and dissemination increased.

Columbia, RCA Victor, Decca, and later Capitol Records controlled the industry, and from the perspective of their critics transformed music from something artistic to a money-making enterprise. These companies earned large profits from record sales, while musicians slowly lost control of their creations. Existing copyright laws and practices, despite their long history of evolution and adaptation, failed to protect music creators.[19]

The loss of employment as a result of technological advances in the recording industry was coined "technological unemployment." Indeed, "The AFM contends that the unrestricted commercial use of records is detrimental to the employment of musicians. In this respect it has often referred to the problem of 'technological unemployment,' pointing to the unilateral reproducibility of the record and to the wide use that may be made of it."[20] With the mass production of records and their substitution for live performances, musicians became displaced and increasingly unemployed. AFM sought greater control and participation in the recording process and wanted to restrict the extent of commercial use of records.

James Caesar Petrillo was one of the most vocal union leaders seeking to regulate the recording industry. From his perspective, when musicians agreed to make records, they were putting themselves out of business. Based in Chicago as the city's local union leader, Petrillo tried to limit the number of times a radio station could play a record. In 1935 he "succeeded in obtaining an arrangement whereby all recordings were destroyed after being broadcast once. Subsequent playing of recordings was permitted only after the radio stations employed a 'stand-by' orchestra of live musicians equal in number to those making the record."[21]

Petrillo won nearly all his union battles in Chicago except one. He failed to unionize church organists. His wife is given credit for objecting, but taking on church organists may have been a tougher task even for the most determined unionists.[22] Prohibition resulted in the closure of thousands of saloons. The depression made things worse and the adoption of recorded sound in movie theaters added to unemployment among musicians. Petrillo worked relentlessly to promote the interests of his members, which in turn earned him many enemies. He once told the Chicago Park Board, "You feed the monkeys but you won't pay the musicians."[23]

At the AFM, Petrillo focused his efforts on increasing musicians' employment at radio stations, and he had some early success. In 1938, the AFM demanded that a fixed number of union musicians be employed at each of the major radio stations. Complying radio stations could transfer files and programs with each other, but they were not permitted to work with stations that did not employ union musicians. After heated negotiations, the major stations agreed to increase their musician payroll by $2 million.[24]

The union win was short-lived. The Department of Justice deemed such deals illegal, and as a result, the quota agreement terminated in 1940. Subsequent actions taken by the AFM included trying to restrict the use of records to the home. In the end this proved to be ineffectual because it was virtually impossible to fully regulate a commodity once it entered the market. Over time, musician unemployment steadily increased, and AFM leaders realized that drastic measures were needed to combat the recording-radio monopoly over music. Petrillo's strategy "included (in chronological order) the capture of soloists and conductors from another AFL union, the American Guild of Musical Artists (AGMA); the unionization of the Boston Symphony Orchestra; and, finally, the ban on all recordings."[25]

Petrillo offered vivid imagery of the impact of technology on musicians in numerous interviews. His typical argument was that nowhere else "in the mechanical age does the workman create the machine which destroys him, but that's what happens to the musician when he plays for a recording. The iceman didn't create the refrigerator, the coachman didn't build the automobile. But the musician plays his music into a recorder and a short time later the radio station manager . . . says, 'Sorry, Joe, we've got all your stuff on records, so we don't need you any more.' And Joe's out of a job."[26]

In June 1942, Petrillo announced that "after August 1, members of the AFM would not play or contract to make records, transcriptions, or other types of mechanical reproduction of music."[27] Following the AFM's lead, music unions in both Great Britain and Puerto Rico instated recording bans and ceased the shipment of records to America. Musicians felt that their needs were being ignored and that their livelihoods were being threatened by both big business and advancing technology.

The ban sent shock waves throughout the recording and broadcasting industries, as well as throughout the public. Radio was embedded in society in terms of both news and music. Many people were outraged that the union would issue a ban during the war, as music boosted morale in the midst of the conflict overseas. The US Department of War Information argued that a "recording ban was detrimental to the war effort by eventually causing small radio stations to fail (and thereby hurting the flow of vital information) and causing undue hardship for defense workers and military personnel who needed the recreation supplied by jukeboxes in restaurants and cafes."[28] In a poll taken soon after the ban, 73 percent of Americans called for legal action against the AFM, and Petrillo was portrayed as a musical dictator.[29]

The public thought the union had gone too far with its demands. For example, it required broadcasters to employ "platter turners" who spun and flipped records at scale wages. Politicians challenged Petrillo at a congressional hearing on why musicians were needed on the radio. He responded: "Because the record is made of music."[30] He argued that "if there is music on the record, then the man who puts the record on the machine should be a member of the musicians' union."[31] The industry capitalized on this public sentiment and, with the help of the press, thoroughly vilified Petrillo and the AFM in general. Drawing from the prevailing political climate, the press disparaged Petrillo as "Boss of US Music," "music czar," "tyrant," "Mussolini of Music," and "musical Hitler" and mocked his middle name by calling him "little Caesar."[32] He was the subject of numerous unfavorable cartoons. At one point the AFM headquarters in New York displayed over three hundred cartoons published between 1942 and 1949 unfavorable to Petrillo and the federation.[33]

Petrillo was vilified for fighting for what he believed in and for the contingent of suffering musicians whom he represented. He failed to build media or public support for his campaign. "None of the editorials discussed the impact of mechanization on the employment opportunities of musicians or even acknowledged that Petrillo was the democratically elected head of a union with 513 locals, all of which supported the recording ban."[34]

The federal government intervened in the 1942 ban. In 1943 the government called Petrillo to testify before the Senate Committee on Interstate Commerce. Petrillo used this hearing as a forum where he could communicate his concerns and the reasoning behind the ban. In responding to the committee's questions, Petrillo stressed that the ban was the result of the control and exploitation of the music industry by the broadcasting and recording companies. These businesses were increasing their profits, he noted, at the expense of hard-working musicians who were unable to compete with both commercial and technological advances. By the end of the hearing, Petrillo had eloquently made his case before the committee, but he agreed to establish a plan to end the recording ban.

The ban did not completely dismantle the recording industry, but it did hinder growth. Businesses anticipated the radical union measures, increased production, and created record stockpiles to use in the case of a ban. As a result, there were enough records to maintain productivity for a ban of up to six months. Additionally, radios hired musicians outside the AFM union membership to appear on their programs.

To end the dispute, the AFM presented the recording companies with a proposal to pay royalties to the AFM for each record made by union musicians. Prices would be set in accordance to the cost of each record. The union would use the royalties to create a Recording and Transcription Fund to support unemployed musicians.

The fund was an important part of AFM. In the first three years following the agreement, the fund accumulated over $4.5 million. And two years after the ban ended, AFM published its "First Plan for the Expenditure of the Recording and Transcription Fund," which included a detailed set of rules outlining who was eligible to receive funds and a sample chart to show how funds would be allocated. The funds were used to support musicians and also yielded nineteen thousand free music concerts in schools, parks, and other public places.[35]

But not all the major players agreed to the terms of the agreement or made contributions. Decca Records was the first major company to agree to the terms of the union's proposition, along with many other small companies. Columbia, RCA Victor, and the transcription division of NBC continued to object. As a result, the strike continued despite involvement by the federal War Labor Bureau and President Roosevelt himself. Neither side was willing to capitulate. On October 4, 1944, President Roosevelt wrote to Petrillo: "In a country which loves democratic government and loves keen competition under the rules of the game, parties to a dispute should adhere to the decision of the Board even though one of the parties may consider the decision wrong. Therefore, in the interest of orderly government and in the interest of respecting the considered decision of the Board, I request your union to accept the directive orders of the National War Labor Board. What you regard as your loss will certainly be your country's gain."[36]

The congressional hearing played a key role in forging a negative view of Petrillo and the AFM, following the failure of the National War Labor Board and President Roosevelt's efforts to end the ban. An editorial in the *New York Times* on August 5, 1942, noted that Petrillo was "grossly mistaken, for example, when he assumes that if he forbids radio stations and restaurants from using records they will have to use orchestras and bands."[37] The editorial claimed that the impact of the ban would simply be less music. The *Nation*, on the other hand, said that because of advances in technology the measures taken by the AFM "would not restore the musician to his pre-jukebox position. Small-time musicians have become as obsolete as the Indian. James Caesar Petrillo, for all of his confident toughness, will not be able to erase that fact."[38]

As time progressed, the companies that had opposed the deal began to feel the economic impacts of the ban, and they signed the deal with the AFM. By November 1944, tensions momentarily subsided and the first national recording ban came to an end. In 1948 AFM embarked on another strike, this time arising from the outlawing of the Recording and Transcription Fund through the Taft-Hartley Labor Relations Act. The strike ended with a compromise that involved the crafting of new provisions that resulted in the Music Performance Trust Fund.

Jazzing Up the Industry

The 1942 ban was to a large extent just an episode in the long history of the technological evolution of music. It was a moment of political drama that morphed into two important trends. First, the immediate impact of the ban was closely associated with the emergence of new musical genres. The industry responded by encouraging new mutations, especially in jazz. The second development arose from technological diversity that resulted in the growth of new industries. On the whole, the musical industry was transformed in a way that offered little benefit to musicians, who continued to struggle to earn a living.

In the years preceding the recording ban, jazz underwent a transformation. Beginning in the late thirties and extending through the forties, the bebop style of jazz began to materialize. Challenging traditional notions of rhythm and improvisation, bebop employed "a more intricate rhythmic sensibility . . . arising not from the steady quarter-note dance beat but from contrasts and accents unfolding within mercurial streams of eighths and sixteenths."[39]

The main impetus behind the recording and broadcasting industries was to make a profit. Business executives wanted to produce records that would sell. The industry appealed to the popular culture of the day, basing record production on what the public wanted to hear. For the most part this included ballads, pop songs, and big band music. Major recording companies felt comfortable selling what they knew would garner a profit, and in turn they hesitated to liberally invest money and effort in jazz.

Jazz, in terms of recording, was adversely impacted by wartime shortages of material: "Unless record fans rise up in arms immediately, there will not be any more good jazz on discs except by accident. Retrenchment necessitated by the shortage of shellac has already caused recording executives to go conservative in the extreme, which means no more young bands, no more 'sleeper tunes,' and no initiative or experimentation. . . . All the companies are devoting themselves to tunes either on or slated for the hit parade."[40]

People of varying social class could either purchase records or listen to music on the radio. Along these lines, the 1942 recording ban emboldened smaller recording companies and shattered the elite control over the recording industry. Whereas the "Big Four"—RCA Victor, Columbia, Capitol Records, and Decca—historically had monopolized the industry, the ban enabled smaller companies to materialize.

Specifically, the 1943 deal Petrillo presented to the companies in order to end the ban hurt the recording monopoly. In the days following the ban only Decca capitulated and signed the deal with the AFM, while the other large companies refused to compromise. This offered an unprecedented opportunity for smaller recording companies to sign the deal with the AFM and to become active members of the recording market. During this time the demand for records had soared, and recording companies were starting up throughout the major cities in America.

In other words, "Anybody with twelve bucks and some spare time wants to go into the recording field."[41] While key recording companies, which had controlled most of the production before the ban, stood firm against Petrillo's deal, smaller companies took advantage of the surging market.

The increase and decentralization of the recording industry had positive implications for bebop and jazz in general. As major recording firms mainly focused upon producing music that would yield the greatest profit, the new companies were able to capitalize on the demand for records and focus on genres such as jazz.

The ban's impact upon innovation in jazz was significant. It created a base from which smaller, jazz-centered companies could flourish. Jazz continued to be a unique, and somewhat obscure, style of music for mainstream America. Even so, the increasing number of recordings entrenched jazz within society and afforded it the opportunity for innovative growth.

The aftermath of the ban also saw a significant shift in the character of bands. The era of the big band was coming to an end. Over the period of the strike, singers started to take center stage and were gradually becoming more visible than the rest of the band. This shift would later culminate in the present-day adulation of musical stars with the associated relegation of the band to a backstage support role. These changes were also accompanied by radical technological innovation across the full chain of musical activities.

The two strikes have a larger meaning than just opposing new technology. The "struggles need to be understood as organized moments of critical intervention and protest to the construction of a new, dominant economy of music production that would be based on recordings rather than the production of musical performances."[42] The challenge was not to "a specific technology or machine, but rather a particular technocultural assemblage that displaced musicians from directly controlling the production and reproduction of music. Writ large, these strikes were involved in a struggle over the terms, forms, and goals of popular musical production in the United States."[43]

It is not possible to attribute these changes solely to the actions of the unions. The inner dynamics of innovation in the industry transformed the social organization in the music industry in ways that challenged the power of the AFM. In the meantime, the recording industry matured and faced its own intellectual property challenges. A decade after the ban, the Recording Industry Association of America (RIAA) was created. Its original mission was to manage recording copyright fees and challenges, work with trade unions, and undertake research on the record industry and government regulations. The creation of the RIAA marked a significant transition in establishing a support organization for the recording industry. It represented recognition of recording music as a new feature of the economic landscape. Many of the challenges regarding technological unemployment and protection of incumbent interests that the AFM had to address were passed on to the RIAA but in a different age of rapid technological change.

Conclusions

Anxiety over technological unemployment played a key role in fueling concerns over recorded music. The fear of job displacement remains one of the most important sources of concern over new technologies. Although much of the anxiety is overstated, the threat of job dislocation is often real. What is often ignored, however, is that new technologies create new economic opportunities elsewhere. Technological succession has been an incessant feature of the digital world. The succession has swept away major industries but also created new ones. Compact discs, for example, have given way to other forms of media storage. This transition has also changed the nature of employment. The case of music recording provides a number of lessons for policymakers.

First, the benefits of sound recording on society cannot be assessed solely by the number of musicians that are directly employed by the industry. Sound recording has made it possible to diversify musical genres and make them accessible to the public.[44] The evolution of these genres was associated with a wide range of sound-recording technologies from using magnetic instruments to computers.[45] The benefits, however, also came with greater consolidation of the music and broadcasting industries.

But even more important, the sound-recording sector has been characterized by remarkable technological diversification and succession. The most profound example is the transition from tape recorders to DVDs to online downloading. The rise of new technologies has created subindustries and new branches of technological development. The introduction of the Sony Walkman portable cassette player in 1979 inspired a wide range of similar technologies, culminating in the iconic iPod released by Apple in 2001. A new generation of wearable technologies has since followed, most of them in fields that are unrelated to music.

The second lesson related to the extent to which technical advances have expanded the scope for creativity, which included synthesized music. Such developments were not necessarily a direct result of the ban but a general outcome of technological evolution. The main message in this case is that sound-recording technology revolutionized many aspects of the cultural landscape in ways that could not have been anticipated by focusing only on the impact of musicians. It would serve as a platform for new industries, many of which interacted with the music sector. In the end, sound recording helped to enhance the creative capabilities of society irrespective of its commercial implications.

The third lesson is about the role of legal conflicts in matters such as intellectual property, as embodied by the music file-sharing company Napster and its demise. At the turn of twenty-first century, Napster rose to prominence as a pioneering peer-to-peer file-sharing Internet service that enabled the sharing of audio music files for free. Soon after its creation Napster was sued for copyright violation.[46] In 2001, Napster shut down its operations to comply with a court injunction. It agreed to pay copyright holders and music creators $26 million for past unauthorized uses of music. It also paid $10 million in advance against future licensing royalties.

During the court proceedings Napster said it had developed software that could block the transfer of 99.4 percent of identified infringing material. The court rejected this proposal, prompting observers to argue that if 99.4 percent was not good enough, then the case was more about a war on file sharing than about copyright infringement. The suit concealed deeper concerns about Napster as a source of "destructive creation" of existing industries.[47] It merely appeared to shift value to new beneficiaries.[48] Napster heralded the end of the age of canned music: "It's just that the science of recording isn't as remote, mysterious, and awe-inspiring as it once was. Thanks to technology, the magic finally escaped from the can."[49] Part of the escape of the magic was the development of new technologies that allowed for musical creations that did not involve live musicians. Much of that capability is now embodied in basic computers and software, making it easier for people to create their own music without using any musical instruments. The technology has also empowered more people to become creators in ways that that were not possible before. These developments have also come with new norms of sharing creations that include the open-source movement.

The fourth lesson from the debate around technological innovation and music production is the importance of understanding responses from organized labor. In many cases what appears as positive "creative destruction" to one group is viewed by others as "destructive creation" without obvious benefits to society. Managing such technological transitions therefore requires a better understanding of their nature, distribution, and welfare implications. This is particularly important today given the global nature of technological innovation.

So far there are no effective international mechanisms for managing the welfare impacts of new technologies at the global level. Without such institutions, nations will continue to be tempted to find ways of protecting their industries from technological disruption. In this respect, tensions over new technologies will become increasingly global in nature. Welfare considerations such as technological inclusion will in turn become an even more important part of international trade negotiations. Currently, many of the trade disputes brought before the World Trade Organization carry deeper concerns about the welfare implications of technological innovation.

The final lesson concerns how bans or restrictions can serve as a source of stimuli for the diversification of technologies and their associated creations. Efforts to ban recorded music led to temporary benefits for the union, but they also resulted in attempts to find alternative outlets for musicians. The industry reorganized itself in new ways so as to beat the ban. The recording technology itself served as a platform to expand human creativity. It helped to extend the capabilities of some actors by allowing music to be more widely distributed. This trend would create its own challenges associated with the concentration of the industry.

The relationship between artists and technology continues to evolve. The Taylor Swift case shows how successful artists can influence corporate strategies by withholding their music from being marketed through new business arrangements. This is partly because the same technology that threatens some musicians has also been a source of power and influence for the successful ones. It is notable that Swift sought to represent the interests of the less influential artists, thereby playing nearly the same role that unions have played in the past. Music is so fundamental to human existence that it will continue to be a source of new tensions as new technologies and business models unfold.

9

Taking Root

Transgenic Crops

I can't understand why people are frightened of new ideas.
I'm frightened of the old ones.

JOHN CAGE

The transition toward sustainable agriculture that is good both for the environment and for human health remains one of the world's most pressing challenges.[1] Mass agriculture–based food production currently relies heavily on insecticides to kill bugs and other pests that can destroy large crops of fruits and vegetables. The use of insecticides has been the subject of extensive international environmental campaigns.

Amid these concerns scientists added new genetic engineering tools that could help to control pests with minimal use of insecticides. The techniques involve inserting genes in crops that allow them to produce their own insecticides. This technology opened up opportunities to increase food production while reducing the impact of chemical use. It reflected the emerging environmental vision set out by Rachel Carson in her classic environmental book, *Silent Spring*. She viewed the available technology as a "truly extraordinary variety of alternatives to the chemical control of insects. . . . Some are already in use and have achieved brilliant success. Others are in the stage of laboratory testing. Still others are little more than ideas in the minds of imaginative scientists, waiting for the opportunity to put them to the test."[2] She noted that these were "*biological* solutions, based on understanding of the living organisms they seek to control, and of the whole fabric of life to which these organisms belong."[3]

One of the pioneers of genetic engineering, Marc Van Montagu of Belgium, aptly captured both the scientific enthusiasm and the frustration arising from nearly two decades of use of pest-resistant genetically modified crops: "I remain overawed by how far and how rapidly we progressed with our knowledge of the molecular basis of plant growth, development, stress resistance, flowering, and ecological adaptation, thanks to the gene engineering technology. I am impressed, but also frustrated by the difficulties of applying this knowledge to improve crops and globally develop a sustainable and improved high-yielding agriculture."[4]

The chapter uses the case of trade conflicts between Europe and the United States together with other leading grain exporters to illustrate the tensions between the new technology and incumbent agricultural systems. Unlike other cases in this book, the controversy over transgenic crops occurred in the context of a globalizing trading system governed through the World Trade Organization (WTO) and took on international dimensions from the outset. For this reason, governments sought to resolve their difference through diplomatic negotiations under the auspices of the United Nations.

Deep Roots

The case of transgenic crops reflects Schumpeter's contention that the process of technological innovation proceeds in leaps. But more importantly, it is associated with considerable uncertainty about the benefits and risks. The uncertainties shaped the framing of the debate in ways that amplified future risks of transgenic crops. Essentially, the regulations were based on the probability of harm and not evidence of it. The potential of harm (hazard) was over time presented to the general public as probability of the harm occurring.[5] New regulations governing the technology assumed that the identified hazards could have catastrophic consequences for the environment, farmers in developing countries, and human health. It was only through familiarity with the technology and the accumulation of evidence that it became possible to reevaluate the premises of the original formulation of international biosafety rules.[6] This chapter is not intended to replay the debate and take sides, but to outline the dynamics of the controversy as evidence unfolded to identify its lessons for other technological controversies.

The advent of pest-resistant transgenic crops provides a partial solution to the challenge of economically growing large amounts of food for a rising world population while also minimizing the use of external supplements. One application involves inserting in crops a gene from the common soil bacterium *Bacillus thuringiensis* (Bt), which enables the crops to produce Bt toxins that kill certain pests.[7] This transgenic technique is now widely used as a substitute for chemical control of certain pests. It builds off of decades of nontransgenic use of Bt by organic farmers, for whom it is an approved pesticide.

The technology was developed at a time of heightened concern over the ecological and human health effects of pesticides. Civil society organizations in various parts of the world campaigned against the use of chemical pesticides. Developers considered transgenic crops that used Bt toxins to control pests to be a potential solution to the environmental concerns. But the commercial release of Bt crops was met with widespread opposition by some governments, environmental groups, consumer organizations, and academics around the world. The opposition continued despite widely documented economic, health, and environmental benefits.[8]

Transgenic crops have radically transformed a large part of global agriculture in a span of two decades filled with controversies associated with the process. The ability to express genes from one species in another plant was successfully demonstrated more than thirty years ago by Belgian and American scientists.[9] Even though the potential agricultural applications were evident, the transformational nature of the technology was not obvious. But as scientists and policymakers started to reflect on the implications of a platform technology with broad applications, the economic ramifications became apparent.[10]

Concerns over global food security, coupled with rising food prices, heightened the search for technologies needed to enable farming to meet the needs of a growing population. Over time the need to address the emerging challenges of climate change and resource conservation also added to the impetus for agricultural innovation. The impediments to attaining global food security are numerous and varying and will require as many different techniques and technologies as can be brought to bear on the various challenges. The introduction of fertilizers and pesticides was in itself an innovation that transformed food production and commercial farming. Agrochemicals and the associated enterprises over time became an integral part of modern farming systems. Around the introduction of agrochemicals grew a powerful business industry. Efforts to shift new farming systems away from pesticide use must contend with the wider sociotechnical inertia in agricultural systems.

There are three major types of pesticides: herbicides, insecticides, and fungicides.[11] Pesticides are used in nearly all types of agriculture in varying quantities. The introduction of pesticides in agriculture led to increased crop output and productivity. These pesticides also have a wide range of health and environmental side effects if not properly used.

The twentieth century witnessed the gradual emergence of chemical pesticides as the dominant pest control strategy.[12] This was mainly because of their efficacy and convenience of use. They were also aggressively promoted through new alliances that included research institutes, government ministries, and private enterprises. They benefited considerably from a new worldview that put considerable faith in the role of science and technology in addressing agricultural challenges. The pervasiveness of chemically dependent agricultural systems shaped institutional structures. From the training of farmers to the establishment of market and policy infrastructure, institutions evolved to serve the needs of conventional agriculture dominated by pesticide use.

The agricultural system was adapted to rely on pesticides. This occurred because farmers, extension services, agricultural policies, and agricultural research systems depend on and support the use of pesticides. This makes the parties involved resistant to change, making it difficult for new technologies to gain a foothold. For example, the slow adoption of disease-resistant wheat cultivars in Belgium was not a result of poor technical characteristics but of resistance at all levels of the food chain, from farmers to input suppliers to policymakers.[13] Dominant wheat systems were organized around a system that favored the use of chemical inputs, and the incumbents made it difficult for new entrants and new technology, such as disease-resistant wheat cultivars, to disrupt the food-growing practices in place. Private stakeholders could influence crop protection practices in three ways: an internal bias in supply companies in favor of agrochemicals rather than seed sales; a bias toward agrochemical applications among supplier salespeople; and low priority attached to breeding for disease and pest resistance in seed companies.[14]

Public agricultural and extension services influence farmers' choices of agricultural technology and practices. Applied scientific and policy research tends to concentrate on the incumbent cropping systems as effort is put into improving current systems rather than replacing them. Public agricultural extension officers are influenced by their own perceptions of the power of existing technologies when advising farmers and policymakers. Government regulations also tend to reinforce existing agricultural practices by imposing higher safety requirements on new technologies.

At a political level, incumbent agricultural systems are reinforced by agricultural support programs. Farm subsidies are among the most powerful economic and political tools used by interested parties to entrench incumbent practices, as illustrated by European agriculture. The European Common Agricultural Policy (CAP), created in 1962, is an example of continuity and inertia driven by powerful economic and political forces. For example, "Article 39 of the Treaty of Rome contains commitments to and objectives for the support of agriculture. This set the agenda for the Stresa conference of 1958 and strongly conditioned subsequent negotiations about establishing the CAP. In particular, the ambition to raise agricultural productivity and support technological progress heavily influenced the choice of high prices as the principal instrument of support."[15]

The timing of the emergence of transgenic technology is an important part of the debate around its safe use. The collapse of the Soviet Union opened the door for the enlargement of the European Union to include former Eastern European nations. This not only signaled potentially large new markets for American produce, but also offered opportunities to extend European agricultural trade into the region. Agricultural produce was a large part of the potential contribution of Eastern European countries, as well as Greece, to the European common market. Free-market competition arising from cheaper agricultural produce from the United States directly threatened Europe's aspirations of enlarging its economic and geopolitical footprint further east. Viewed differently, globalization threatened the political identity of Europe. These political conditions selected for cautious preferential economic liberalization without the full exposure of the new countries to global competitiveness or competition among European countries.[16]

Over the twentieth century, Europe emerged as the world's leading chemical powerhouse. The chemical firms built their competitiveness around their distinctive core competencies in chemistry. As a result, they were highly stable and defined by their core technology profiles. Their interest in new technologies focused in areas where they had market power and prior technological strength. Their research and development programs also focused on reinforcing their areas of product specialization.[17] Firms that led in pesticide production tended to pursue research in the same area.

One of the consequences of building on existing technology legacies was the slow rate of new product development among European chemical firms. It was expected that the new products would be linked to their core chemical and allied platforms. To compete effectively in the new field of biotechnology, European firms needed to acquire knowledge in biology. But "their internal technological cultures and their external linkages had been based on chemistry. The change demanded required grafting a new culture onto well-established internal traditions and establishing new links and roots in the biological sciences."[18]

The strategy ensured market dominance by European firms in a variety of agrochemical fields. But it also made them more susceptible to disruptions arising from new competitive products from novel technology platforms such as recombinant DNA technologies. Given the difficulties of branching out into new technologies such as genetic engineering, European firms were late to adopt the technique, even though it was originally demonstrated in Europe (Belgium). When they did, they opted to invest in American small, dedicated biotechnology firms (DBFs) with the hope that over time they could acquire the knowledge and integrate them into their European operations. They did this in two main ways. First, they relied on using R & D outposts in North America "to link into the US academic base, often using such linkages explicitly as a means of teaching home-based researchers."[19] Second, they relied on their research contracts with American DBFs as an indirect way to benefit from American market dynamism and the associated research. This also offered the firms ways to hedge bets and test the robustness of the technology before adopting it. The successful linkages "were often later consummated through acquisition."[20]

This was indeed a risky strategy whose success depended on the ability of the European firms to transfer the knowledge back home. Therefore, being close to the leading edge of research in US universities and in contact with the DBFs who advanced the technology mattered.[21]

Debugging the Farm

The introduction of transgenic crops coincided with an intensifying social movement against pesticides. Popular concern over the health and environmental effects of insecticides led to interest in benign insecticides. The resurrected use of the *Bacillus thuringiensis* bacterium as a more benign biological insecticide emerged even before Rachel Carson's *Silent Spring* popularized the ecological fears around insecticides. The insecticidal properties of Bt were known long before the bacterium itself was identified. It has been suggested that Bt spores may have been used in ancient Egypt. In 1901 the bacterium was isolated by the Japanese biologist Shigetane Ishiwatari while studying silkworm wilt disease. He called it *Bacillus sotto*. A decade later Ernst Berliner isolated the bacterium "from a diseased Mediterranean flour moth (*Ephestia kuehniella*) in the German province of Thuringia, and it was named *Bacillus thuringiensis*."[22]

The first use of Bt as a microbial biopesticide against a moth larvae occurred in 1938. The biopesticide was commercially available before World War II for use by vegetable farmers to control caterpillar infestations. Its ability to target a few select species and leave beneficial organisms such as ladybirds and lacewings unharmed enhanced its popularity. After World War II synthetic chemistry became the most dominant source of new pesticides. But as pests developed resistance and the rate of discovery of new chemical compounds declined, scientists started to look at biopesticides for pest control solutions.

Topical applications of Bt are of limited value, as the protein degrades quickly upon exposure to sunlight and moisture. Before World War II pesticides were not used so widely as after, and afterward it took a while for pest resistance to synthetic chemicals to suggest the need for additional modes of action. Bt was favored primarily because it was a different, and more specific, mode of action. It was not because it was a biological or, necessarily, less toxic product. Newer formulations also mitigated its degradation by light and moisture.

Bt toxins generally lost their effectiveness through degradation within a few days, thus requiring frequent spraying. In the 1960s, scientists started to explore ways of identifying and selecting the specific proteins responsible for pest control. The transfer of Bt protein genes into the crops themselves offered a solution. "In transgenic crops, Bt toxin is continuously produced and is protected from the elements. It therefore retains its ability to kill pests during the entire growing season. Moreover, the toxin is generally expressed in every part of the plant, including internal tissues that are difficult to protect with topically applied pesticides."[23]

Starting in the early 1990s a number of private firms entered the Bt market to capitalize on the public's pesticide fears and the renewed focus on the potential Bt offered to kill crop-destroying pests more safely. The first Bt-focused private firms paved the way for boosting the biopesticide industry. It cost up to $40 million to develop a pesticide derived through synthetic chemistry, compared to $5 million for a biopesticide, based on biochemistry. The process to bring a new synthetic pesticide to market took up to twelve years instead of three for a biopesticide.

A number of leading agricultural firms moved into the Bt market, including Abbot Laboratories, American Cyanamid, BASF, Caffaro, Ecogen, DeKalb, ICI, Mycogen, NovoNordisk, Rohm and Haas, and Sandoz. They focused on four main subspecies: *B. aizawai, B. israelensis, B. kurstaki,* and *B. tenebrionis,* all of which contain related proteins with effects specific to particular groups of lepidopteran or coleopteran pests. By early 1992 up to fifty-seven crops covering over two million acres were being treated with Bt in the United States. The rise in the popularity of Bt coincided with increased environmental awareness and the call to shift production methods toward biological and organic processes.

At the same time that Bt's use grew, so did the concept of organic farming as another supposed means of reducing reliance on applications of synthetic pesticides. Contrary to popular belief, organic production allows the use of a long list of approved substances, including many "natural" pesticides, some of considerable toxicity. These include fungicides derived from sulfur and copper. Organic farming also uses approved oil-based pesticides. The now-discontinued rotenone pesticide was considered safe because it was derived from plants. But research showed that it caused in rats symptoms similar to those associated with Parkinson's disease. Organic farmers prefer a more holistic integrated pest management strategy,[24] including crop rotation and labor-intensive crop husbandry. The divergent approaches helped to pave the way for the clashes that would follow when transgenic crops using Bt genes were introduced, especially in the United States in the new millennium.

Transgenic crop development was made possible by the scientific community's better understanding of genes in general. Genetic transformation offered direct access to vast pools of useful genes previously unavailable to plant breeders. Genetic engineering allowed for simultaneous use of several desirable genes in a single event. Applied transgenic research, like conventional crop breeding, aims to selectively alter, add, or remove a specific trait to address productivity constraints. It also offers the possibility to introduce desirable traits from closely related plants without including unwanted genes.

The first transgenic plants with Bt genes were developed in 1985 by the Belgian firm Plant Genetic Systems. The first Bt-containing crops were commercialized in 1996. Today, genes conferring resistance to insect pests have been inserted into several plants, including corn, cotton, potatoes, tobacco, rice, broccoli, lettuce, walnuts, apples, alfalfa, and soybeans. The cry-type toxins from Bt are effective against the crop-destroying pests cotton bollworm, corn earworm, European corn borer, and rice stem borers. The toxins kill pests by disrupting the permeability of cell membranes in the pests' digestive tract, causing the insects to stop eating and die.

The early success of Bt cotton led four major cotton-growing countries quickly to adopt it: the United States, China, India, and Argentina. By 2001, Bt cotton was grown commercially in the United States, Australia, and a few developing countries. India officially approved Bt cotton for sale in 2002. By 2014, Bt cotton accounted for 96 percent of total cotton production in the United States. Results from a study in 2010 showed the adoption of Bt cotton in China increased farmers' incomes and reduced chemical use.[25] The latest data in 2014 shows farmers' income rose by more than $16.2 billion from 1997 to 2013 and increased $1.6 billion in 2013 alone.[26]

The most significant event in the adoption process was the emergence of Monsanto as a world leader in transgenic technology. In contrast to the incremental strategy adopted by European chemical firms, US-based Monsanto adopted a more radical approach by first reinventing itself as a life science company with internal expertise in the field. It supplemented this through "(i) the use of external sources of knowledge from a systematic search (which helps the firms not to be locked in a narrow network but to fully benefit from the flexibility of networks); and (ii) the strong coherence and integration capacity of the internal research organization."[27]

Monsanto's strategy involved cooperation with a research laboratory at Washington University in St. Louis that "resulted both in the application for a major patent—which opened a main avenue for the commercialization of plant biotechnology—and in the publication of a number of scientific papers. The patent (applied for in October 1985) was a major breakthrough in plant biotechnology since it proved that plants could acquire resistance to [the tobacco mosaic virus] by the expression of the coat protein gene of that particular virus."[28] The transformation of Monsanto was supported by a wide range of agreements with life science organizations.[29]

These developments occurred during a period of intense technological competition where emerging platform technologies were viewed largely in the context of national strategies in a global marketplace. The rise of microelectronics and the emergence of new Asian economic actors had heightened US policy concerns over national support for emerging technologies. The US Congressional Office of Technology Assessment (OTA) noted in the early 1990s that though nascent, the emerging science was being credited for having "revolutionized the way scientists view living matter and has resulted in research and development (R&D) that may lead to the commercialization of products that can dramatically improve human and animal health, the food supply, and the quality of the environment."[30]

The OTA stressed biotechnology's national character and global significance: "Developed primarily in U.S. laboratories, many applications of biotechnology are now viewed by companies and governments throughout the world as essential for economic growth in several different, seemingly disparate industries."[31] European countries were fully aware of this potential and were also searching for strategies that would enable them to harness the technology for global competitiveness.[32]

The outcome of this industrial reorganization contributed to the emergence of large global biotechnology firms such as Monsanto, DuPont, and Syngenta through consolidation in the seed industry and the concentration of technological power in the hands of a few large firms.[33] The dominance of a few firms would later become a concern among certain civil society groups. The concerns included the perceived loss of autonomy among researchers through closer university-industry cooperation. This close cooperation is credited with promoting the competitiveness of the US biotechnology industry. But it also came with concerns over conflict of interest and the associated public distrust of biotechnology researchers in universities.[34] The growing dominance of the private sector in plant breeding also created considerable concern over the ability of developing countries to gain access to biotechnology.[35] The perception of corporate control of biotechnology as constructed by opponents persisted and became a major obstacle to the adoption of biotechnology irrespective of whether the research was being done by the public or private sector.[36]

It is important to note, however, that these firms adopted different corporate approaches to technology development. Whereas Monsanto shifted focus away from its chemical, feed, and other platforms, and eventually shed them to concentrate on genetics, the other major corporations were much slower to add biotechnologies to their portfolios. Monsanto would therefore stand out as the symbol of the agricultural biotechnology revolution. It positioned itself to reap most of the benefits but also to incur much of the public wrath and demonization.

Questioning Science

Regulatory uncertainties plagued genetic engineering from the beginning, but the scientific community self-regulated those concerns in many instances, understanding the potential dangers genetic engineering posed to the public and to science. Genetic engineering's transformative power was evident from the time the gene-cloning technique was developed in 1973 by Herbert Boyer and Stanley Cohen. Two years later, participants at the 1975 Asilomar Conference on Recombinant DNA called for a voluntary moratorium on genetic engineering to allow the National Institutes of Health to develop safety guidelines for what some feared might be risky experiments. By being proactive, the scientific community took responsibility for designing safety guidelines that were themselves guided by the best available scientific knowledge and principles. The scientists set in motion what would become a science-based risk assessment and management system that was applied to subsequent stages in the development of genetic engineering.

In 1984 the US White House Office of Science and Technology Policy proposed the adoption of a Coordinated Framework for Regulation of Biotechnology.[37] The framework was adopted in 1986 as a federal policy on products derived from biotechnology. The focus of the policy was to ensure safety without creating new burdens for the fledgling industry. The policy was based on three principles. First, it focused on the products of genetic modification and not the process itself. Second, its approach was based on verifiable scientific risks. Finally, it defined genetically modified products as being parallel to other products, which allowed them to be regulated under existing laws. Matters pertaining to food safety were assigned to the Food and Drug Administration (FDA), while those relating to the environment fell under the Environmental Protection Agency (EPA). The US Department of Agriculture was put in charge of regulating the agricultural aspects of transgenic crops.

Another landmark in the development of science-based regulatory principles occurred in 1987 when the US National Academy of Sciences (NAS) set guidelines for introducing transgenic organisms into the environment. A committee established to provide advice on this issue reached two fundamental conclusions. First, it found no evidence that "unique hazards exist either in the use of R-DNA techniques or in the transfer of genes between unrelated organisms."[38] Second, "The risks associated with the introduction of R-DNA-engineered organisms are the same in kind as those associated with the introduction into the environment of unmodified organisms and organisms modified by other genetic techniques."[39] That same year, NAS provided separate advice on the strategic importance of agricultural biotechnology global competitiveness.[40]

A 1989 NAS study on field testing of transgenic crops reinforced the science-based risk assessment approach.[41]

The emergent science-based regulatory system had three important elements. First, it established a regime under which transgenic products were considered on the basis of the characteristics of the product and not on the process by which they were developed. Second, the regulatory system adopted a case-by-case approach where the risks of each transgenic organism were assessed based on the type of modification done, the organism in which the genes were inserted, and the environment into which the organism was to be introduced. Third, by adopting the hazard identification and risk assessment, data-based approach, existing regulatory agencies dealing with human health effects, agricultural effects, and environmental impacts were deemed to have sufficient existing regulatory authority and needed no new laws specifically focused on recombinant DNA technologies and their products. The parallel development of technological advancement and regulatory structures put the United States ahead of other nations and facilitated the development and commercial release of transgenic crops.

The United States sought to internationalize a science-based regulatory approach through the Organization for Economic Cooperation and Development and through United Nations agencies such as the World Health Organization (WHO) and the Food and Agriculture Organization. The science-based regulatory principles were consistent with international trading rules under the General Agreement on Tariffs and Trade and its successor, the World Trade Organization.

The debate over agricultural biotechnology has focused on international trade in transgenic foods. Attempts to resolve the differences through the UN Convention on Biological Diversity (CBD) dealt largely with environmental aspects of living modified organisms. Ironically, the discussions over biotechnology in the late 1990s focused on its potential to address the needs of developing countries. Governments negotiated and signed the CBD, which included provisions on the potential role of biotechnology in development. But not all countries supported the provision. Agenda 21, adopted at the Earth Summit in Rio in 1992, focused extensively on the beneficial potential of biotechnology in agriculture for developing countries.

The CBD paved the way for new negotiations that resulted in the adoption on January 20, 2000, of the Cartagena Protocol on Biosafety to the Convention on Biological Diversity. The central doctrine of the Cartagena Protocol is the "precautionary approach" that empowers governments to restrict the release of products into the environment if they feel biodiversity might be threatened even if no conclusive evidence exists that they are harmful. One of the key features of the approach is that it reverses the burden of proof and places it on those generating the technology by calling on them to perform the logical impossibility of proving a negative.[42]

The Cartagena Protocol reveals its precautionary approach in Article 1: "In accordance with the precautionary approach contained in Principle 15 of the Rio Declaration on Environment and Development, the objective of this protocol is to contribute to ensuring an adequate level of protection in the field of the safe transfer, handling and use of living modified organisms resulting from modern biotechnology that may have adverse effects on the conservation and sustainable use of biological diversity, taking also into account risks to human health, and specifically focusing on transboundary movements."[43]

In a clear reversal of science-based risk assessment, the protocol states in Article 10(6): "Lack of scientific certainty due to insufficient relevant scientific information and knowledge regarding the extent of the potential adverse effects of a living modified organism on the conservation and sustainable use of biological diversity in the Party of import, taking also into account risks to human health, shall not prevent that Party from taking a decision, as appropriate, with regard to the import of the living modified organism in question . . . in order to avoid or minimize such potential adverse effects."[44]

This provision became the first de facto articulation of the precautionary approach in international law. It empowered countries to arbitrarily prohibit imports, request additional information, and extend the time period for decisionmaking on genetically modified products. Public concern, irrespective of validity, was sufficient to trigger a ban in many countries.[45] Similarly, many countries adopted stringent measures that restricted transgenic research, field trials, and commercial release. Many of the laws and regulations against transgenic foods continue to have negative implications on local researchers who study agricultural genetics.

While transgenic crops have the potential to greatly increase crop and livestock productivity as well as improve nutrition, a backlash against transgenic foods created a difficult political atmosphere under which stringent regulations have been developed. Much of the inspiration for restrictive regulation comes from the Cartagena Protocol.[46]

Around the time the CBD was being developed, five European Union members—Denmark, Greece, France, Italy, and Luxembourg—formally declared in June 1999 their intent to suspend authorization of transgenic products until rules of labeling and traceability were in place. This decision followed a series of food-related incidents such as "mad cow disease" in the UK and dioxin-contaminated animal feed in Belgium. These events undermined confidence in regulatory systems in Europe and raised concerns in other countries. Previous food safety incidents tended to shape public perceptions over new scares.[47] In essence, psychological factors and campaigns by opponents shaped public reactions to the transgenic foods.[48] Much of this was happening in the early phases of economic globalization, whose risks and benefits were uncertain and open to question, including the very moral foundations of economic systems.[49]

Two important diplomatic developments followed the moratorium. First, the EU used its influence to persuade its trading partners to adopt similar regulatory procedures that embodied the precautionary principle. Second, the United States, Canada, and Argentina took the matter to the WTO for settlement in 2003.[50] Under the circumstances, many African countries opted for a more precautionary approach partly because they had stronger trade relations with the EU and were therefore subject to diplomatic pressure. Their links with the United States were largely through food aid programs.[51] In 2006, the WTO issued its final report on the dispute. Its findings were largely based on procedural issues and did not resolve the role of the "precautionary principle" in WTO law.[52]

Many developing countries started passing strict biosafety regulations even before the protocol was adopted. This was a sign of the political momentum to find ways to curtail the adoption of transgenic crops. The EU, which served as a role model for developing countries, adopted a three-pronged approach: it sought to develop specific regulations, reinterpret the precautionary principle, and create a European Union Food Safety Agency. In 2003, the EU adopted stringent regulations concerning authorization procedures, labeling, and traceability of the sources of food components. It extended the precautionary principle from environmental protection to consumer and health protection. New provisions in the 2003 regulations explicitly included the principle of "consumer choice" via mandatory labeling and traceability; a formalization of the distinction between risk assessment, risk management, and risk communication; and public participation in risk communication.

The roots of challenge to transgenic technology run deep in African regulatory cultures.[53] For example, even after developing a transgenic potato resistant to insect damage, Egypt refused to approve it for commercial use partly because of fear that it could lose its European export market. Eventually, a number of African countries stopped accepting unmilled transgenic maize from the

United States as food aid. A severe drought in 2001 and 2002 left fifteen million Africans with severe food shortages in southern Africa, yet countries such as Zimbabwe and Zambia turned down shipments of transgenic corn, fearing the kernels would be planted instead of eaten.

One of the most widely followed controversies surrounding Bt crops was the claim in a 1999 paper by Cornell University scientists that the Bt protein could kill monarch butterflies.[54] The paper generated massive public concern and led to demonstrations against transgenic crops. To settle the debate, key stakeholders from government, industry, academia, and civil society produced six studies that were published in the *Proceedings of the National Academy of Sciences* in 2001. The papers showed the widely used Bt corn pollen could not harm monarch butterfly larvae in concentrations that the pest (i.e., the European corn borer larvae) would be exposed to in the fields.[55] They also showed that another Bt product from Syngenta had higher toxin concentration though its application was quite limited. The publication of the studies was expedited and their data published despite objections by some scientists.[56]

While some parts of society fought against the use of food derived from crops improved through biotechnology, the cotton industry was an exception and embraced the technology. Cotton was the target of 25 percent of worldwide insecticide use until the early 1990s because of the crop's vulnerability to pest attacks.[57] Bt cotton became the technology of choice for farmers because it increased profit and yield while reducing pesticide and management costs.[58] Countries such as China took an early lead in adopting the technology and have continued to benefit from reduced use of pesticides in cotton.[59]

In addition to the legislative restrictions, cultivation bans, and cumbersome approval procedures, transgenic technology became a target of vandalism. The "vast majority of destroyed academic or governmental experiments were field evaluations designed to assess the safety of GMOs."[60] The alleged "corporate control" of the seed sector is viewed by some as a major threat to global agriculture,[61] but most of the vandalism has been directed at transgenic research, "including experiments dedicated to risk assessment."[62] One of the most important outcomes of the attacks was a delay in the availability of research results that could have helped regulators to evaluate the safety of products intended for commercial release.

One of the arguments used against transgenic technology research was that it lacked sufficient transparency and as a result it was not being done in a democratic manner. These concerns resulted in the adoption of procedures that required public disclosure of research projects and their location, which is part of a complex array of bureaucratic approval requirements.[63] This information was used by vandals to target research sites. The "openness (imposed by law) has not been accompanied by adequate measures from the political authorities to prevent acts of vandalism that are facilitated by this openness."[64] In fact, it is the political use of transparency that raises concerns over calls for labeling of transgenic products. Some of those who call for labeling are interested in getting the information needed to discriminate against a product based on prejudice. Court decisions to ban cultivation of transgenic crops were used by vandals to justify their actions. Much of this was fueled by a variety of misconceptions about risks that shifted the focus of regulation from products to production processes.[65]

Negative public reaction, coupled with cumbersome government regulation, has over time increased the cost of conducting transgenic research. In Switzerland, for example, "For every Euro spent on research, an additional 78 cents were spent on security, an additional 31 cents on biosafety, and an additional 17 cents on government regulatory supervision. Hence the total additional spending due to government regulation and public opposition was around 1.26 Euros for every Euro spent on the research per se."[66]

Adding to the costs, the Swiss government responded to vandalism in 2012 by agreeing to establish a protected field site at an annual cost of €600,000 over the 2014–2017 period. The site is located on three hectares of federal land and enables researchers to conduct experiments without worrying about additional security costs and vandalism.[67] Vandalism, like prohibition, may have delayed the technology, but to a large extent it appears to be driving it offshore. If the original demand for transparency was democratic governance, it appears that the nondemocratic methods used have only succeeded in undermining the very principle of transparency.

Gaining Ground

Despite opposition, Bt technology adoption has continued at a rapid rate, while insecticide use has declined. The initial concerns by opponents that the technology would only be used in industrialized countries have been overturned by evidence of rapid adoption in developing countries. The absence of systematic information to assess the contributions and impact of transgenic crops provided considerable space for a variety of unverified claims about the technology.

The creation of the International Service for the Acquisition of Agri-biotech Applications (ISAAA) has over time played a key role in information on trends in the adoption of transgenic crops. The ISAAA was created in 1992 as a not-for-profit international organization to share biotechnology's benefits with resource-poor farmers in developing countries. It is supported by both private and public sector donors including Bayer, Monsanto, the US Agency for International Development, the US Department of Agriculture, and the US Grains Council. In addition, it also gets support from two banks—Fondazione Bussolera in Italy and Ibercaja in Spain.

In addition to seeking the transfer of technology, the ISAAA has been an important source of data on trends in the adoption of transgenic crops. It has dispensed information mainly through the *ISAAA Briefs*, of which the most notable is its flagship annual report, *Global Status of Commercialized Biotech/GM Crops*. The brief is authored by ISAAA founder Dr. Clive James. It first appeared in 1996. In the absence of other sources of information on adoption trends, the annual brief has emerged as an authoritative reference document. The briefs now serve as a source of data for scholarly publications in peer-reviewed journals. The ISAAA operates on a moderate annual budget of $2–$2.5 million that is negligible compared to the financial outlays of various organizations opposed to the adoption of transgenic crops.

The outreach of ISAAA is expanding considerably. The 2014 annual brief recorded 30,769 downloads in the first ninety days. The ISAAA website clocks nearly four thousand visitors a day. The briefs also serve as reference documents for a series of seminars hosted by the organization around the world. In 2014 over thirty such seminars were conducted in Africa, Asia, and Latin America. The ISAAA also issues a free weekly electronic *Crop Biotech Update* newsletter that reaches nearly twenty thousand subscribers in 175 countries. In addition, the ISAAA website hosts an online global database of approved transgenic crops. The ISAAA's operations include the Global Network of Biotechnology Information Centres in twenty countries.

Critics have challenged the reports, citing methodological issues, connections with industry, and lack of independent validation or peer review. Those who rely on ISAAA data—for example the PG Economics research group in London—to undertake deeper analysis of the impact of transgenic crops are subjected to the same criticisms. Despite these concerns, the briefs remain a major source of information and play a critical role in reducing uncertainty over adoption rates.

The ISAAA and other sources have helped offer a basis upon which to discuss broad trends in the adoption of transgenic crops. But current uses of the technology are still concentrated in major crops such as cotton and corn. As technological familiarity spreads, developing countries will likely begin to adapt the technology as a means of addressing their own unique pest issues. In addition, developing countries will also start to undertake their own research that will add to the repertoire of Bt techniques available.

China was an early adopter of Bt technology and has witnessed many benefits. The reduced use of insecticides and increased use of Bt technology conferred health benefits to farmers in China by reducing exposure to harmful pesticides that had made many farmers ill.[68] India followed suit, broadening the use of the technology to include more small-scale farmers. Researchers showed that "Bt cotton has reduced pesticide applications by 50 percent, with the largest reductions of 70 percent occurring in the most toxic types of chemicals . . . models confirm that Bt has notably reduced the incidence of acute pesticide poisoning among cotton growers. These effects have become more pronounced with increasing technology adoption rates. Bt cotton now helps to avoid several million cases of pesticide poisoning in India every year, which also entails sizeable health cost savings."[69]

A study in India concludes that "Bt cotton now helps to avoid at least 2.4 million cases of pesticide poisoning every year, which is equivalent to a health cost saving of 14 million US$. These are lower-bound estimates of the health benefits, because they neglect the positive spillovers that Bt cotton entails. Alternative estimates suggest that Bt cotton may avoid up to 9 million poisoning incidences per year, which translates into a health cost saving of 51 million US$. In any case, the positive health externalities are sizeable."[70]

Many of the benefits of Bt technology were anticipated. But other unexpected benefits emerged. The National Research Council forecast in 2010 that Bt technology when used effectively would reduce the need to use insecticides.[71] There have been other positive unintended consequences, such as the area-wide suppression of pests among neighboring farmers who grow conventional crops. Take the case of the United States in 2009, when Bt corn was planted on over 22.2 million hectares, accounting for 63 percent of the US crop. Applying statistical analysis of per capita growth rate estimates, researchers found "that areawide suppression of the primary pest *Ostrinia nubilalis* (European corn borer) is associated with Bt maize use."[72] Furthermore, cumulative "benefits over 14 years are an estimated $3.2 billion for maize growers in Illinois, Minnesota, and Wisconsin, with more than $2.4 billion of this total accruing to non-Bt maize growers. Comparable estimates for Iowa and Nebraska are $3.6 billion in total, with $1.9 billion for non-Bt maize growers."[73] Moreover, other studies have shown that the benefits of suppressing pests also extended to nearby non-Bt crops.[74] In some regions of the United States the crops have been so effective at suppressing the European corn borer that it has become economical for farmers to switch to less expensive non-Bt corn with minimum threat of the pest.[75]

These findings raise important issues regarding risk assessment and turn the application of the precautionary principle on its head. Such large benefits arising from unintended impacts of Bt technology reinforce the importance of basing decisions on an evolving generation of evidence rather than on dogma. It would appear that with such potential large gains, the adoption of a new technology serves to reduce agricultural uncertainty. These findings also suggest that farmers who choose to create buffer zones of refuge with noncrop plants still have the benefit of the technology without having to adopt it.

As the political disputes created by opposition campaigns raged, the United States continued to apply its science-based risk management practices. In 2001, the EPA "completed a comprehensive reassessment of the time-limited registrations for all existing *Bt* corn and cotton. As part of the assessment the agency decided to extend the registrations with additional terms and conditions, including requiring confirmatory data to ensure protection of nontarget organisms and lack of accumulation of *Bt* proteins in soils, measures to limit gene flow from *Bt* cotton to wild (or weedy) relatives, and a strengthened [insect resistance management] program, especially in regard to compliance."[76]

Recent reviews of the literature have examined the effects on biodiversity of nontarget species such as birds, snakes, nontarget arthropods, and soil macro- and microfauna. The studies showed little or no evidence of negative effects of Bt crops. Although two reviews reported negative impacts on nontarget arthropods, these studies were criticized "mainly for the statistical methods and the generalizations between crops expressing Bt proteins (commercialized), proteinase inhibitors (only a transgenic cotton line SGK321 present in the Chinese market) and lectins (not commercialized)."[77] In fact, some of the emerging evidence is showing the contribution of Bt technology to the biological control of pests.[78]

One of the lingering concerns about the technology is the risk of insects developing resistance to Bt technology.[79] Indeed, "Reduced efficacy of Bt crops caused by field-evolved resistance has been reported now for some populations of 5 of 13 major pest species."[80] But much of the discussion ignores evidence that resistance to Bt predates the introduction of transgenic crops.[81] What is needed is a long-term view of managing the use of the technology irrespective of the method of its generation.[82] The challenge lies in finding ways to delay the development of pest resistance to Bt given the inevitability of mutations.[83] A recent study suggests that though natural refuges delay resistance, they are not as effective as an equal area of non-Bt cotton refuges. It recommends that switching to "Bt cotton producing two or more toxins and integrating other control tactics could slow further increases in resistance."[84] The question of resistance management is not an issue of product or environmental safety, nor is it an issue unique to biotech crops. In fact, it is an issue of product lifetime or obsolescence, which has historically been left to markets to manage. In imposing refugia requirements on registrants, the EPA has chosen to construe Bt proteins as public goods to be managed by government regulators. This is unprecedented, and largely unremarked upon.

Conclusions

One of the promises of technological innovation in agriculture, including transgenic crops, was to expand opportunities to transition toward sustainable agriculture. Bt technology offered great prospects for reducing the use of potentially harmful chemicals against which health and environmental advocates have long campaigned. Paradoxically, the same groups found themselves ferociously challenging the new technology. Furthermore, some sovereign states that saw themselves as being environmental champions also found themselves at odds with the new technology.

To resolve this paradox one has to look beyond scientific uncertainty and explore the underlying lessons. The general clichés of ignorant opposition to new technology have generally not yielded helpful insights into one of the most complex public controversies of the new millennium.

The unfolding of evidence on the impact of transgenic crops was accompanied by new questions over whether there was sufficient consensus on the safety of the products. The first decade of the commercialization of transgenic crops was dominated by claims and legislation that relied heavily on characterizing hazards as if they were actual risks. Studies carried out by scientific academies such as the National Academy of Sciences provided overviews of the balance of evidence that reinforced the assessments that transgenic crops carried the same risk profile as their conventional counterparts.

Drawing from the language used by the Intergovernmental Panel on Climate Change, supporters of the technology started to argue that there was scientific consensus on the safety of the products. Opponents countered this view with declarations that there was no consensus. One of the critical differences in the claims was an apparent false balance between those using assessment of existing evidence and those relying on single studies. The latter group pointed to reported cases of risks to stress that there was no scientific consensus on safety. In this case the real issue was not the results of actual studies but the way the evidence was being handled to reach certain conclusions. False balance is reinforced by the press, which often treats opinion on a scientific study as carrying the same weight as the study itself. By doing so the press inadvertently works against scientific consensus and ends up misleading the public.

The controversy also reveals that transgenic crops were used as a proxy for other issues that have little to do with the safety of the products. For example, opponents have cited issues such as corporate control of the global food system, intellectual property over living forms, globalization of markets, and American market dominance as primary sources of concern. These issues deserve discussion in their own right. However, opposition to transgenic technology is often the cover for the debate. One of the consequences of this lack of transparency in structure of the debate is the inability to find a common ground because of unspoken motives.

Six major lessons arise from this case. First, the main sources of concern lie in the benefits that the challenging forces derive from incumbency at two fundamental levels. The first is inertia of the sociotechnical structure in which agrochemicals play a decisive role. Second, the path dependence of major corporate actors on one knowledge platform limited the scope for innovation. As a result, these firms could not compete in new knowledge arenas such as plant biotechnology. These factors, compounded by the existence of agricultural policies that support incumbent farming methods, made the challenge to transgenic technology almost inevitable.

From the outset the implications of transgenic crops for incumbent agricultural systems raised issues of trust in the technology. This is partly because transgenic crops emerged at a time when critical markets such as Europe were undergoing internal political change. This was also a period when the European public lost trust in the food safety system following a series of major food scares. Policymakers need to be cognizant of how a wide range of factors can converge to provide sections of the population with the ammunition needed to challenge new technologies.

The second lesson is the global nature of the controversy. Unlike other examples of concern over innovation, the transgenic controversy has two unique attributes. Transgenic technology was the first major innovation to emerge when the global trading system was expanding under the WTO. The process of European enlargement and economic integration added to the complexity of the debate. New EU entrants were largely agricultural economies with limited capacity to withstand intense innovation-driven competition. What was at stake here was not traditional protectionism but interest in lowering risks to the European enlargement agenda. To some extent African countries shared similar sentiments. Their economies were dependent on exports to Europe, and as a result they were susceptible to diplomatic pressures from importers of their products. The challenge to transgenic crops in the United States, however, was largely driven by the rapidly expanding organic farming industry.

The third lesson is the use of preemptive regulations. African countries were among the first to enact laws that were more stringent than agreed in international standards. Their actions may have relegated many of these countries to the backwaters of innovation in agricultural biotechnology. They had nothing to lose by maintaining the status quo at the height of the debate. In fact, many Asian countries took this position. But by choosing to own a large part of the challenge, they may have preempted their own future role in the biotechnology revolution. Europe, on the hand, has the knowledge base to chart a new path or redefine the biotechnology debate as an economic rather than environmental issue. It can create a new path, while many African countries will be forced to contend with the consequences of this application of the precautionary principle.

A related preemptive regulation issue was the decision of US organic farmers to define their products to exclude transgenic material. This decision has created considerable tension between organic farmers and producers of conventional foods, mostly fueled by adversarial marketing techniques that seek to demonize transgenic crops. Efforts to promote coexistence between the two groups did not enjoy the support of a major faction of the organic farming movement, which continues to seek mandatory labeling laws initially at the state level and then at the federal level. They pursued a strategy similar to that adopted by the dairy industry in its challenge to margarine.

The accumulation of evidence that contradicts the original justification for biosafety laws provides a fourth important lesson. It is important to make clear distinctions between hazards and risks. It is necessary to find a legal framework for addressing hazards. But such a framework should not take the form of rigid laws whose adoption needs to be guided by evidence of harm. More flexible standards that allow continuous assessment of emerging safety issues related to a new product are another way to address hazards. This approach would allow for evidence-based regulation.

The fifth lesson relates to those countries that have actually adopted transgenic crops. In these countries the new products served real needs for which there are no viable alternatives. Efforts to use chemicals to control corn or cotton pests have begun to plateau. Transgenic traits offer a superior way of controlling the pests. Moreover, the new methods also reduce the use of harmful insecticides and therefore confer environmental and human health benefits. It is this technological superiority that largely accounts for the rapid adoption rate of Bt crops.

This point is important when viewed in the context of the balance between risks and benefits. The perception of the risks of transgenic crops was first expressed largely in the form of scientific uncertainty. However, concerns over corporate control and the need to protect local farming systems were also major sources of tension. There were other elements related to perceptions of exclusion. African countries, for example, were concerned about technological exclusion and resented the thought of being relegated to being importers rather than producers of new technologies. A more viable policy response in such situations would be to focus on international technology and business partnerships.

The last lesson relates to the systemic nature of the adoption of transgenic crops. This lesson has two aspects. In the case of European and African countries, the perception was that the crops were likely to have far-reaching implications for the overall agricultural systems. Indeed, the uncertainties associated with systemic changes seemed to call for caution. The other aspect of the systemic nature of the technology—the level of development of agricultural systems—is discernible in adopting countries. Most of the countries that have adopted transgenic crops also had functioning agricultural systems in which the new traits could be embedded. This is true of North America, South Africa, and Asia. Africa, on the other hand, could hardly move to adopt the crops partly because of its weak agricultural systems and political support to small-scale farmers and partly because of susceptibility to European diplomatic influence.

The importance of system-wide technology development is underscored by the case of Bt cotton in Burkina Faso. In 2015 the country began phasing out transgenic cotton production because of compromised fiber quality.[85] The development was used as a reason for Africa not to pursue transgenic cotton adoption. There are two important lessons from the experience. First, there is no effective way to determine the viability of the technology except through its use. Second, the experience reinforces the case for strengthening domestic biotechnology research to ensure that new varieties can meet expected quality standards irrespective of whether they are transgenic or not. This is a case where the problem is too little agricultural research. Burkina Faso was long aware of this challenge and took the initiative to set up a regional cotton research university.[83] The way forward is strengthening such initiatives and not retreating from technological innovation.

Second-generation biotechnology now enables stacking traits and transferring one or more specific genes into exact locations in recipient plant genomes. These traits include the ability to increase photosynthetic and nitrogen and phosphate use efficiency. Other traits increase tolerance to aluminum and salinity. Advances in synthetic biology could significantly simplify plant-breeding methods. The methods "confer multiple traits (herbicide, insect, disease, stress resistance, and nutritional enhancement)."[86]

As the genomes of more plants are sequenced, and as new gene-editing techniques become more accessible, it will become much easier to enhance desirable traits in crops, such as sweetness, pest resistance, and disease resistance. Such crops would not contain transgenic material.[88] These advances are calling into question existing regulatory practices that are based on concerns over transgenic modifications. Already Argentina, the EU, the United States, Australia, New Zealand, and other countries are considering new regulations for genetically edited crops.[89] Another important policy shift was the European Union's decision in 2015 to allow member states to decide on the adoption of transgenic crops.

Advances in RNA interference (RNAi), for example, offer powerful tools for advancing agriculture without the use of transgenic material. Gene-editing or precision-breeding techniques "[have] been employed successfully to bring about modifications of several desired traits in different plants. These modifications include nutritional improvements, reduced content of food allergens and toxic compounds, enhanced defence against biotic and abiotic stresses, alteration in morphology, crafting male sterility, enhanced secondary metabolite synthesis and seedless plant varieties."[90]

Gene-editing techniques are especially important because they do not use the more demonized aspects of genetic modification. They rely on "tweaking" or editing plant DNA. Gene editing allows synthetic biologists to delete sequences of unwanted DNA and edit or adjust existing DNA to enhance certain endogenous traits. Furthermore, scientists have developed ways to address one aspect of the uncertainty surrounding genetically modified organisms—specifically, how to prevent them from escaping into nature, which is a major concern of genetic modification critics. The new technique involves altering the genetic code, making them dependent on an artificial amino acid, without which the bacteria die. This essentially amounts to inserting a "built-in self-destruct mechanism into bacteria."[91] The study focused on *E. coli*, but the technique could eventually be applied to other organisms.

On the other hand, another example of the power of gene editing lies in the development of new tools such as Clustered Regularly Interspaced Short Palindromic Repeats (CRISPR), which allows scientists to alter a cell's DNA with an utmost degree of precision. What makes it especially unique is its ability to spread the edited trait through wild populations via a process called "gene drives."[92] The process is hardly new: in nature, "certain genes 'drive' themselves through populations by increasing the odds that they will be inherited."[93] In this case the goal would be to spread the modified trait through nature using gene-editing techniques.

The human health, environmental, and agricultural applications for this technology are vast. Gene drives, for example, represent another method of vector control for malaria. Mosquitoes could be altered either to promote male sterility, thereby reducing the population over several generations, or to suppress the malaria transmission gene. Gene drives could also be used to help reverse ecological degradation by limiting invasive species and eliminating the need for pesticides. In all cases, each intervention must be evaluated on an individual basis to assess the benefits and consequences.

The need for more inclusive assessments is illustrated by the outbreak of the Zika virus, which was linked to the spread of microcephaly in Brazil. The outbreak followed the release of genetically modified *Aedes aegypti* (not using gene drives) to control dengue. In early 2016 the World Health Organization declared the Zika-related microcephaly and neurological abnormalities a public health emergency of international proportion. Amid the global concern, opponents of genetic engineering raised unsubstantiated fears that the spread of Zika and the associated health impacts may have been caused by the genetically modified mosquitos. They called for a halt on further release of genetically modified mosquitos.[94] Oxitec, the UK-based firm responsible for the genetically modified mosquito, attempted to quell the concerns by calling them conspiracy theories and appealing for more collaboration to control the spread of dengue and Zika. Such a call is unlikely to be heeded by opponents of the technology. But it underscores the importance of inclusive approaches and judicious public policies when introducing transformative technologies. If not handled responsibly, such episodes can quickly undermine the use of a new technology even in situations where it may be one of the best options available.

The potential use of these techniques in health, the environment, and agriculture is likely to be influenced by ethical concerns over both the editing of the human genome[95] and the externalities of altering wild populations. The case for the coevolution of technology and social institutions is evident in these examples and will continue to feature in future debates regarding genetic technologies.

What started as a trade dispute between the European Union and the United States over transgenic crops has morphed into a major technological divide between nations. The shift in trade alliances is associated with technological drift from Europe to the United States and emerging economies. The 2015 bid for the Swiss-based Syngenta for $43 billion by China's state-owned ChemChina marks a new phase in the realignment of economic forces behind agricultural technology, including genetic technologies. This global reorganization of agricultural technology will come with its own controversies whose future form remains uncertain.

Swimming against the Current

AquAdvantage Salmon

Leave the beaten track occasionally and dive into the woods. You will be certain to find something that you have never seen before.
ALEXANDER GRAHAM BELL

Providing sufficient protein to a growing world population remains one of the most pressing global food challenges. The increased demand for protein has threatened the sustainability of fish resources through ecosystem degradation, climate change, and overfishing. Maritime governments and multilateral organizations have responded to these threats by focusing on policy that will conserve marine resources. Traditionally that has been accomplished through regulation and fishing limits. Despite the efforts, new pressures on marine ecosystems are mounting. It is projected that there will be more plastic waste than fish in world oceans by 2050.[1]

Business has responded to the decline in natural fish stocks by investing in fish farming. The dramatic increase in global fish output from farms has been achieved mainly through conventional fish-breeding programs analogous to practices in other kinds of livestock. Fish farming too has its own environmental problems and economic challenges. Fish farming generates pollution, and the profit margins are tight. Fish farming alone hasn't solved the fish and protein needs of a growing population.

A third outlet has emerged to tackle the fish problem: genetic modification. In the mid-1990s, the Massachusetts-based firm AquaBounty Technologies entered the fish scene with a genetically engineered salmon (*Salmo salar*) that can mature in half the time of a regular fish. Nearly twenty years after AquaBounty Technologies first applied to the US Food and Drug Administration (FDA) for approval to sell its AquAdvantage salmon, the company finally received government approval in November 2015. The approval made AquAdvantage the first transgenic animal to be approved by FDA for human consumption.[2] Although the transgenic fish had passed all the human health and environmental safety assessments required by the FDA by 2009, even with the approval in 2015, the AquAdvantage salmon cannot be commercially consumed for at least another six years.

This is a story about a technological response to the state of world fisheries. It is also a story of the struggles of an American entrepreneur, Elliot Entis, who set out to commercialize a transgenic salmon that had the potential to change the fish industry.[3] As outlined by Schumpeter, innovation is the product of the efforts of entrepreneurs. It is entrepreneurs who, as result, come in direct contact with social reactions to their creation. This chapter explores the challenges that entrepreneurs face when championing a platform technology that paves the way for a new field of innovation. It traces the technological, social, and political dynamics of two decades of efforts by AquaBounty Technologies to seek government approval to commercialize the first transgenic animal for food purposes. The intensity of the debate reflects many of the economic and psychological factors associated with other products. The approval of the fish opened the door for other transgenic animals for human consumption. The platform nature of the technology not only raised concerns across a broad range of sectors beyond fisheries, but also inspired greater caution on the part of regulatory agencies.

Taking Stock

Fish are a significant part of the global diet, accounting for nearly one-sixth of the animal protein consumed worldwide. But the fish industry faces significant challenges that threaten future supplies. Fish production has risen 3.2 percent a year over the last five decades. In 2010, capture fisheries and aquaculture farms provided nearly 148 million tons of fish valued at US$217.5 billion. At the same time, wild fish supplies are dwindling. The United Nations Food and Agriculture Organization projects that another 14 million tons of fish per year will be needed to satisfy global demand in 2020. Almost all of this additional demand will come from developing countries and emerging economies. China, with its increasingly wealthy middle class, will account for over half of the global increase in demand for fish by 2020.[4]

Fishing, the last major frontier where humans still hunt for the food, is in deep trouble. Nearly 86 percent of the fish consumed globally come from habitats that are overfished. Government subsidies to the fishing industry, estimated globally at US$18.5 billion for developing countries and another US$8.8 billion for industrialized nations, has enabled fleets to travel further out to sea, leaving almost no body of water untouched by fishing nets.[5] Excessive and unregulated fishing threatens marine ecosystems around the world. Fish and their natural habitats are under additional strain by coastal developments, pollution, the introduction of invasive species, and climate change. The loss of biodiversity is considered the greatest threat to marine ecosystems today.[6] Some researchers predict that all currently fished seafood will be extinct by 2048 if current levels of wild-catch fishing continue.

In addition to the decline in stocks, a large proportion of the seafood produced is wasted. It is estimated that up to 47 percent of edible seafood support over the 2009–2013 period was wasted in the United States. The "greatest portions of this loss occurred at the level of consumers (in and out of home) (51–63% loss attributed to consumption), bycatch discarded by commercial fisheries (16–32%), and in distribution and retail operations (13–16%)."[7] The waste underscores the importance of broadening the opportunities for improving the management of fisheries resources, in addition to increasing production.

An industry of fish farms called aquaculture emerged to meet demand and supplement wild fish. Aquaculture developed after many governments decided to promote alternative forms of fish production to reduce the demand for wild fish. Aquaculture transformed fisherman into fish farmers. Aquaculture started in coastal areas separated from the open water by nets or in artificial or natural ponds on land. Between 2008 and 2010 alone, the share of farmed fish in global production rose from 38 percent to 45 percent, making it the fastest-growing agricultural sector worldwide.[8] China, the world's biggest aquaculture producer, generates over 60 percent of the world's farmed fish. The advantage of aquaculture over wild-catch fishing is that it does not draw on natural fish stocks.

The phenomenal fish farm expansion came with its own set of economic and environmental problems. Farming fish in ponds or in separated areas of the sea is significantly more expensive than catching wild fish because facilities need to be built, maintained, and monitored. Fish eggs need to be purchased. The costs for fishmeal and antibiotics, to prevent the spread of disease in the tanks, are high. There are also concerns over the sustainability of fish-farming practices because of the rising cost of energy. There is the added concern that farmed fish can escape and spread disease. On top of all that, fish farms produce significant amounts of effluent discharges that leak into the environment.

To sustain current global levels of fish consumption, current aquaculture production will have to triple over the next thirty years. This is a daunting challenge given the cost of farming and the environmental damage it causes.[9] Against this backdrop, Elliot Entis learned that a simple change in one fish gene had the power to transform aquaculture by making fish grow faster while consuming fewer resources in the process.

Riding the Biotechnology Wave

Entis was raised around fish. His father owned a business that sold seafood to restaurants in Boston, Massachusetts. He swore that he'd never enter the fish business himself. He went to Harvard College and studied international relations, then received a master's degree from the University of California, Berkeley, in 1971. He held government positions and founded a research firm in Washington, DC, that he ran for many years. He started a family. Eventually he felt frustrated because he became convinced that in Washington too frequently you were rewarded for your worst work and punished for your best. "There was always the desire to connect your work to a measurable benefit for someone else—something tangible and measurable. Something as simple as food. In that I was not alone. Dinner conversations with friends frequently gave way to the frustrations of working on policy issues that somehow did not bear fruit, whether tangible or symbolic." His father convinced him to come home and join the family business. Then one Sunday morning back in Boston, an article in the *New York Times* set Entis off on an entrepreneurial journey to try to sell the first genetically engineered fish.

Entis read about a protein discovered initially by scientists in Woods Hole, Massachusetts, but studied further by scientists in California and Canada. The protein, naturally produced by marine life in the coldest Arctic and Antarctic waters, protected life against damage from the extreme cold. It was named the "antifreeze protein." The protein became the source of a simple transformation that would allow salmon and other fish to grow to their full normal size quickly and with fewer feed requirements. His initial thought was the protein could preserve fish freshness year round. He contacted the researcher, who was traveling through Cambridge, and they met for a beer. Their partnership soon evolved to using the antifreeze protein to preserve human organs. With colleagues he helped to found A/F Protein in 1992 to do just that. Shortly after the founding of the company, one of the researchers mentioned offhandedly that research showed that since the antifreeze gene produced protein year round, it could also be used to turn on the growth hormone in salmon year round, resulting in salmon that could grow twice as fast. Salmon generally produce growth hormone only in the summer. A portion of the antifreeze gene (the "promoter" or "on button") could be linked to the salmon growth hormone gene and reinserted in a salmon. The result was an all-fish product with hormones and proteins normally found in all salmon. In fact, with the change, the salmon did not produce antifreeze protein, nor an excess of its own growth hormone. The change gave the fish a more consistent supply of the hormone and allowed it to use the hormone more efficiently. In 2000 AquaBounty Technologies was spun off of A/F Protein with the mission to promote transgenic fish, starting with salmon.[10]

With the researchers in Toronto, Entis licensed the new fish technology. He believed the project would be welcomed by industry. It could cut in half the time to grow a fish. That was good for fish and environmental sustainability. Fish farmers could grow more fish with less resource input.[11] Plus, the work to develop the AquAdvantage salmon was being carried out against a worsening state of world fisheries. Indeed, Entis had the ability to get a lot of people behind him. In 2006, he raised US$37.6 million in an initial public offering for the firm. Despite investor interest, AquaBounty Technologies soon faced public resistance and government hesitation.

The story of world fisheries mirrors that of agriculture. Fishing—a form of aquatic and marine hunting—has over the decades been in decline, while fish farming or aquaculture has been on the rise. As in agriculture, fish farming has been accompanied by increasing application of science and technology. Much of this initially relied on selective breeding aimed at adapting fish to different locations. As in agriculture, the ability to transfer genes across species to confer new traits became appealing to fisheries research. Transgenic methods enabled the farmers to confer traits such as growth enhancement, freeze resistance, cold tolerance, disease resistance, sterility, metabolic modification, and production of pharmacological proteins onto the fish.[12] All of this sped up the rate of fish production and output. The AquAdvantage salmon developed by AquaBounty Technologies contains a salmon-growth gene from the Chinook ("king") salmon (*Oncorhynchus tshawytscha*) and a short DNA sequence (promoter) from the ocean pout (*Zoarces americanus*) that enables the fish gene to produce growth hormone year round.[13] This enabled the fish to reach maturity in eighteen months instead of thirty-six months while using 25 percent less feed. The fish is materially equivalent to regular Atlantic salmon.[14]

The development of the transgenic salmon occurred against a background of rising concerns over the potential ecological impacts of transgenic fish in general. The concern that received the most attention by the media was the "Trojan gene hypothesis" advanced in 1999 in an article in the *Proceedings of the National Academy of Sciences*.[15] The Trojan gene hypothesis surmised that fast-growing transgenic male fish could selectively breed and pass on the growth hormone gene to wild species. The hypothesis assumed the transgenic fish would disproportionately attract and mate with females because of their larger size, beating out their wild competitors. The concern was that the offspring would be less fit to survive. Computer models demonstrated that the result would be an ever decreasing wild population of salmon, with each generation smaller than the previous one, and that extinction within forty-two generations was a possibility.

Since the initial submission of AquaBounty's application to the FDA for its fish—AquAdvantage salmon—various scientific studies and impact assessments of the transgenic salmon provided evidence that the risks associated with AquAdvantage salmon are minimal. AquaBounty Technologies' transgenic salmon is equivalent to regular Atlantic salmon with respect to nutritional requirements, growth properties, and disease resistance and meets the legal definition of an Atlantic salmon.[16] Both AquAdvantage salmon and conventional salmon have been shown to have the same amount of growth hormone circulating in their bodies. However, AquAdvantage salmon uses the growth hormone more efficiently because the gene switch causes it to be produced closer to the liver.

Transgenic salmon are not only cheaper and faster to produce, but their dietary requirements make them more environmentally sustainable than regular wild and farmed salmon.[17] The salmon grows well on a diet of some plant-based protein, whereas regular salmon primarily feed on other fish and are typically raised on a diet with significant amounts of fishmeal, which is made from other fish in an energy-intensive and expensive process.[18]

Following FDA approval, AquaBounty Technologies plans to grow triploid (three set of similar or homologous chromosomes) all-female AquAdvantage salmon in land-based freshwater tanks at an FDA-inspected aquaculture facility in Panama, from which escape to the oceans is virtually impossible. From there fish would be shipped to market. If the company wanted to grow the fish at other land-based facilities, they would need to obtain FDA approval for those additional production sites. To address the concerns around the risks of interbreeding with wild Atlantic salmon species (Atlantic salmon are unable to interbreed with Pacific salmon [*Oncorhynchus*] species), AquaBounty says it would situate land-based tank facilities only in land areas where the surrounding oceans would not support their survival in the unlikely event of escapees.

Regulatory Process and Adaptation

AquaBounty Technologies, like most firms, hoped for a faster approval process. But government regulators tread the regulatory path for transgenic animals slowly and carefully. The concern was that the approval would generate new pressures for approving a wide range of transgenic animals in research and development and whose fate awaited demonstration of a functioning regulatory system for transgenic food animals. AquaBounty Technologies did not only test the public perception of transgenic food but also forced government regulation to play catch-up with science.

Since the FDA's formation in 1906, the agency has overseen the evaluative and legislative processes of new technologies in food, human and animal drugs, and cosmetics. The FDA was the main agency involved in establishing the regulatory processes for transgenic crops in the 1970s. No other US agency has more extensive experience and expertise in the evaluation and regulatory oversight of new food and drug technologies.[19]

However, when AquaBounty Technologies first approached the FDA with its application for the approval of AquAdvantage salmon in 1995, the FDA did not have a designated regulatory process for transgenic animals. It had to rely on the Coordinated Framework for the Regulation of Biotechnology used for regulating crops.[20] The agencies responsible for implementing the principles outlined in the framework as they apply to transgenic salmon are the FDA and the Environmental Protection Agency (EPA). Nonetheless, the lack of a specifically designated regulatory process for transgenic animals was a major source of controversy and criticism in the debate surrounding the salmon.[21] AquAdvantage salmon was not the only transgenic animal product that has been submitted to the FDA, but it was the one to fight the longest for approval.

Regulation responded to new technologies such as AquaBounty's salmon by placing transgenic animals in the United States under the remit of a new animal drug provision of the FDA's Food, Drug, and Cosmetic Act (FD&C). The approval processes for transgenic animals and plants differ in two ways. First, transgenic animals are approved and regulated mainly by the FDA, whereas transgenic plants that are genetically engineered for pest resistance are regulated by several agencies such as the US Department of Agriculture

(USDA), the FDA, and the EPA under a coordinated framework. All other transgenic plants are regulated by at least two agencies. Transgenic animals need to have the FDA's premarket approval prior to commercialization. Transgenic plants, however, are regulated based on voluntary premarket consultations.[22]

A second difference between the regulatory processes for transgenic animals and plants relates to the transparency of the approval process. For transgenic plants, all relevant approval documents, such as the USDA's environmental impact assessment of the plant, are made publicly available, although some information may be deleted from public copies to protect intellectual property rights. On the other hand, the FDA keeps all preapproval documents for "new animal drugs," including transgenic animals, confidential unless the sponsor of the animal wishes to make the information public. A summary of the relevant documents has to be released once the transgenic animal is approved for both animals and plants.

When AquaBounty Technologies first applied for regulatory approval, the FDA had not yet decided which regulatory path transgenic animals would follow and gave AquaBounty the choice between following either the New Animal Drug Application (NADA) or the Food Additive Application regulatory path.[23] AquaBounty Technologies chose to submit a NADA instead of a Food Additive Application because NADA was more rigorous and ended with a concrete approval or disapproval. In the AquAdvantage salmon case, independent studies were conducted to verify that the salmon develop normally, that they perform as claimed by the developers, and that the genetically engineered traits of the salmon are stably inherited over multiple generations. In 2010, all of these data were presented to the Veterinary Medicine Advisory Committee at a public meeting in Washington, DC. Additionally, the company made all of the regulatory data and studies available to the public on a website. In 2012 the FDA issued the "finding of no significant impact," declaring the AquAdvantage salmon safe for human consumption, for the environment, and for the concerned animals.

The 2010 finding was followed by a public comment period. During the comment period, public and private stakeholders expressed their opinions and concerns in writing and at public hearings for the FDA's consideration as the agency prepared to make its final ruling on whether or not to approve the product in question. The public comment period for transgenic salmon was the longest that FDA regulatory processes had seen to date, as it was extended repeatedly since the FDA began holding public hearings in 2010.

These extensions and delays were requested by opponents of the salmon, who felt that the FDA's scientific assessments of the human health and environmental impacts of the salmon had not been sufficiently thorough and transparent.[24] The FDA responded positively to opponents' requests for extensions because the regulatory process for transgenic animals in the NADA path—though scientifically thorough—was only established as the FDA began to consider AquaBounty's application.

One of the most problematic issues of the current regulatory process for transgenic animals under the NADA is that it lacks a clear timeline for when decisions by the different regulatory bodies have to be made. Another criticism of the current process was that it lacked specific provisions regarding environmental risks associated with transgenic organisms. Similarly, public acceptance of the regulatory process could potentially be increased if it contained scientific benchmarks to distinguish acceptable and unacceptable levels of change from regular to transgenic animals.

The FDA does have extensive expertise. It consults a number of national and international experts on transgenic technology and considers all concerns voiced during the public comment period before regulatory decisions are made. In the case of transgenic salmon, multiple public hearings allowed for direct exchange between AquaBounty and both supporters and critics of the technology. The FDA consulted with all the relevant US environmental agencies regarding its conclusion that transgenic salmon do not present an environmental hazard. All of these agencies explicitly endorsed this conclusion.[25]

Although the FDA is responsible for the assessment of human, animal, and environmental health impacts of transgenic animals, it does not have established mechanisms to deal with the social and ethical issues surrounding genetic engineering. Additionally, the scientific assessments required by the current FDA regulatory process for transgenic animals are heavily focused on the potential risks, but do not pay sufficient attention to the benefits of the new technology over existing products.

There are two issues with the FDA approach to transgenic animals. First, if the process for producing the technology changes without changing the product (such as the phenotype of the transgenic organism), a new risk assessment becomes necessary even though there is no substantial difference in the product. Second, the evaluation of process-based risks fails to compare the risks and benefits associated with the new product to those of existing production systems, even though it is precisely this difference that should form the basis of a regulatory decision on new technologies.[26] This distorts public perceptions of the hazards of animal biotechnology. People have a general tendency to maintain the status quo in the face of uncertainty. Because people fear causing greater harm through taking action than through doing nothing, they are reluctant to act when facing risks. Thus, they tend to underestimate the risks of inaction and to overweigh the risks of action.[27]

At the same time, people take greater risks than they should when it comes to avoiding potential losses, because potential losses loom larger than potential gains.[28] Critics of transgenic salmon overemphasized the potential risks of taking action—approving transgenic salmon—to capitalize on people's overly strong aversion to the potential losses associated with such action. Yet the risks associated with inaction regarding prevailing salmon-fishing and salmon-farming practices were considerable. While natural fish stocks are in distress because of overfishing, current aquaculture practices are far from risk free. Many experts on technological innovation and regulation argued that the review and regulatory decisionmaking processes around the AquAdvantage salmon had been among the most thorough and transparent to date.[29] The FDA regulatory approval process for transgenic animals could have been more effective if it considered both potential risks and benefits of the new technology in comparison to existing technologies and based its decision on such a balanced account.[30]

As Entis reflected on his experience with the regulatory process, he said the FDA process felt like it got tangled up with broader politics in the country and the bigger public debate on organic and natural foods. He noted it wasn't ready for transgenic animal products. Eventually the multiple studies and scientific conclusions of the FDA in favor of AquAdvantage salmon had not been strong enough in the face of political and public opposition to transgenic animals, he added. He also said he missed some warning signs that the process wasn't going to be as smooth as he initially thought. "I was so excited about the possibility," he recollected. He obviously underestimated the reaction of people who held different views on his product.

Troubled Waters

Elliot Entis said one of the most important lessons he learned as an entrepreneur in the transgenic products space was to never stop talking to people who do not like you.[31] AquaBounty Technologies had many supporters, but it also had many critics. The drama over transgenic salmon was set between two major trends that were vividly captured by the Center for Food Safety (CFS), a leading opponent of AquAdvantage salmon's approval. In a 2013 pamphlet summing up its stand, the CFS acknowledged that marine ecosystems and the dependent fisheries were at a crossroads because of "decades of over-fishing, pollution, agricultural runoff, and deficient management."[32] The organization said the development of genetically engineered fish was the next chapter in the development of industrial aquaculture, but the CFS believed AquAdvantage salmon were a source of new "threats to food safety, the environment, the economic wellbeing of fishermen, animal welfare, and the international marketplace."[33] The solution, according to CFS, "is to bring our wild salmon populations—and the ecosystems they depend upon—back to sustainability."[34] This is a legitimate objective but not a strong argument against alternative approaches to fish production. The situation is analogous to agriculture. It is important and urgent to reduce the ecological impacts of agriculture, but this is not an argument against practices such as hydroponics and urban rooftop farming.

The position outlined by CFS had been a popular rallying cry in the campaign against transgenic fish in general. Ahead of FDA hearings on the AquAdvantage salmon in 2010, CFS together with other civil society organizations mounted public protests against the product. The organizations included the Food & Water Watch, Friends of the Earth, Organic Consumers Association, Food Democracy Now, and CREDO Action. A notable inclusion in the campaign was the CEO of the ice cream producer Ben & Jerry's. The firm, which operates in over thirty countries around the world, had already taken an earlier decision not to use antifreeze technology in its products despite the fact that its parent firm, the Anglo-Dutch Unilever conglomerate, had developed the technology for food use.

The groups directed their protests at both the FDA and the White House. They argued that the FDA had kept them in the dark regarding the regulatory process and so their last recourse was to petition the president of the United States. The protesters questioned the firm's sterility assurances and claimed that there was a chance some of the fish could be fertile and if they escaped would breed with wild populations. They also questioned the validity of the safety studies undertaken by AquaBounty Technologies.

Subsequent efforts by the opponents, which included Consumers Union, involved pressuring groceries across the United States to pledge not to carry the transgenic fish in the event that it was approved. As of 2015 some of the major firms that agreed not to sell the fish included: Aldi, Giant Eagle, H-E-B, Hy-Vee, Kroger, Meijer, Target, Trader Joe's, Safeway, and Whole Foods. They represented nearly nine thousand stores in the United States. The focus of the campaign is to deny AquAdvantage salmon access to existing distribution outlets in the event that it is approved.

Economic interests lay at the heart of much of the political resistance against the commercialization of transgenic salmon. In 2011, Rep. Don Young (R-Alaska) and Rep. Lynn Woolsey (D-California) proposed an amendment to the FDA appropriations bill that suggested ending funding for the FDA if it were to approve AquAdvantage salmon. The amendment was voted on by fewer than 10 of the 435 members of the chamber while the remaining representatives were at a congressional barbeque sponsored by the White House. Entis said that "Young . . . gamed the system to get this amendment passed."[35]

Many supporters of AquAdvantage salmon agreed with this view. The goal of Representative Young and the Alaskan delegation pursued seems to have been the protection of the Alaskan wild salmon industry, which contributes 78,500 jobs and an estimated US$5.8 billion each year to the Alaskan economy.[36] Their concern was that if AquAdvantage salmon were to enter the market and increase the supply of salmon, US salmon prices could drop and reduce profits for Alaskan salmon producers. In a 2012 interview with the *Washington Post* Representative Young said, "You keep those damn fish out of my waters. . . . If I can keep this up long enough, I can break that company," referring to AquaBounty Technologies, and "I admit that's what I'm trying to do."[37] The resolute tone of the statement was reminiscent of the early opponents of margarine.

It should be noted, however, that Alaskan wild salmon was being sold in a price-premium market. Most farmed salmon, including AquAdvantage salmon, is intended for a lower-price segment of the market, so they would not directly compete with most Alaskan wild-catch salmon. Margaret Hamburg, the FDA commissioner, received multiple letters from US senators challenging the approval process for transgenic salmon. They asked the agency to stop its approval process for the salmon altogether. Again, underlying these calls were economic concerns rather than scientific evidence.[38]

Even though President Obama promised in 2009 that his administration would "embrace science and technology" as drivers of economic growth, the president's ability to follow through with this statement was limited. When the FDA issued a 2012 draft environmental assessment stating that "the approval of AquAdvantage Salmon ... will not jeopardize the continued existence of the United States populations of the threatened or endangered Atlantic salmon, or result in destruction or adverse modification of their critical habitat,"[39] AquaBounty Technologies hoped that its transgenic salmon would soon be granted approval. However, the statement was issued at a time when President Obama struggled with record low popularity ratings running up to the presidential elections. Nearly 54 percent of Americans thought that Obama was doing a poor job, and Mitt Romney had emerged as a strong candidate from the Republican primaries. Observers thought that Obama's success in the election would depend on getting broad support that included environmentalists. His office did not want to inflame the sensitivities of environmentalists by approving the fish.[40]

The food industry operates on extremely small profit margins and is therefore particularly conscious about the risks it takes with regard to the types of products and production processes it chooses to sell. Food producers fear that they might lose even a few percent of their customer base to a competitor if they agree to sell a new product such as transgenic salmon, where the customer response is uncertain. Because of these small profit margins, losing even a fraction of their customer base could be detrimental to food producers.[41] Announcements by the US grocery chains Whole Foods and Trader Joe's that they would not sell transgenic salmon regardless of regulatory approval reflect this economic reality.

Such cautious reactions by the food industry had been especially pronounced in Europe, where influential green parties, a general sense of suspicion against US initiatives, and lower trust in the government's ability to accurately assess the safety of food products had contributed to widespread challenge of transgenic foods. Salmon producers in Norway and the UK, who controlled most of the world market for salmon, were particularly afraid of the potential consumer backlash against transgenic fish.

Since overfishing and the pollution of water resources had become global problems, the fishing industry had come under pressure from environmental organizations regarding the sustainability of current production processes. Understandably, salmon producers and fish farmers in general were reluctant to exacerbate the public adversity they face through adopting transgenic technology as a production process that could intensify public concern over their activities.

Additionally, the salmon-farming industry was relatively young compared to the wild-catch industry. Consumers of farmed salmon could easily switch over to nonfarmed fish if transgenic technology was to become common in fish farming and consumers reacted as negatively as producers expect. This explained why salmon-farming industry associations in the United States, Canada, Chile, and Norway expressed grave reservations about transgenic salmon. Some announced that they would wait to take a position until the FDA grants approval for the salmon. In many ways, it was producers' fear of consumers' fear—rather than actual consumer behavior—that presented a major obstacle to the commercial adoption of transgenic salmon technology.[42] Special interest groups, on the other hand, continued to claim that AquAdvantage salmon represented a threat to the environment. They demonized it as "Frankenfish" and misrepresented the fish as capable of growing to twice the size of conventional salmon. Their misleading claims helped feed general suspicions driven by economic interests.

While the opponents of AquAdvantage salmon managed to delay its regulatory approval for nearly two decades, its supporters continued to gain ground. Former member of Congress Barney Frank was one of many concerned politicians and wrote a letter to the FDA, urging the agency to "treat AquaBounty Technologies as [it] would any other product from the standpoint of the technical review."[43]

In November 2012, over fifty academics from leading research universities across the United States and investors from a variety of industries—including the seafood sector—sent a letter to President Obama to urge the FDA to move forward with the decision on AquAdvantage salmon. They expressed concern over the slow and opaque process surrounding the approval process for the transgenic salmon: "The inexplicable regulatory bottleneck that has been encountered by the AquAdvantage salmon suggests that the FDA's science-based regulatory review process for the products of animal biotechnology has no predictable timeline and is holding up the development of an industry that promotes economic growth, innovation, competitiveness, and job creation in the United States."[44] The signatories worried that biotechnology developers might commercialize their products outside of the United States if the regulatory process was not streamlined and freed from political obstruction by special interest groups.

In a broadening of their challenge, opponents questioned the claim that the fish indeed grows twice as fast its conventional counterparts. This claim was an important selling point for AquaBounty Technologies, especially to potential investors. In 2015 Food & Water Watch asked the US Securities Exchange Commission (SEC) to reject the registration filings of the company to join the NASDAQ stock exchange. It said that its claims on the growth rate of fish are misleading. The letter requested SEC to compel AquaBounty Technologies to revise its registration document to update investors on new scientific findings that the fish did not grow as fast as had been claimed. In addition, the organization also wanted AquaBounty Technologies to state that the fish experienced unique diseases. The intent of the communication was to raise doubts among investors on the viability of the technology and the company.

These challenges were mounted in the context of growing efforts on various fronts to seek the labeling of transgenic foods. Alaska had passed a law requiring the labeling of transgenic salmon. This prompted other organizations to seek the adoption of legislation that would prevent states from adopting labeling laws. On the whole, the controversy over transgenic salmon was largely influenced by the wider context set by debates over transgenic crops. Through all of the debate, Entis said, he has sought to engage with as many people as possible. He garnered a reputation for being diplomatic. He said as an entrepreneur it was important to remember that the protechnology message did not get out as much, and that the critics were often louder. "The idea is to raise questions in people's minds. Some will change their minds," he said.[45]

Entis thought the technology would be "wildly used" in the future. He stopped predicting how, though. Since then, he has focused his energies on a new project, using the antifreeze protein in a cosmetics line called LIFTLAB Skin Regeneration. The cosmetic line uses the protein to help with skin regeneration by increasing the amount of protein the skin produces. He has turned his entrepreneurial energy and the lessons he learned from championing a new platform technology to other purposes.

Entis was adamant that he would still go through the regulatory process with his salmon if he had a second chance. He said he would have invested more time seeking broad support from different political groups and the various stages of the food chain.

Conclusions

The two decades of debate over transgenic salmon demonstrated the challenges that future technologies are likely to face, especially if they are based on novel platforms that are likely to pave the way for a new generation of products. The concerns are generally compounded by the lack of familiarity with the product among regulators and the public in general. Transgenic salmon experienced negative reactions not only from politicians with vested economic interests but also directly from the salmon-farming community and food industries. In addition to economic consideration, uncertainty over the safety of the product to human health and the environment could not be easily allayed using scientific evidence generated by the developers of the technology. The potential for transgenic fish to survive in nature continues to remain a matter of scientific uncertainty.[46]

The timing of its development coincided with opposition to transgenic crops. As a result, many of the arguments used against genetic engineering in agriculture could be easily applied to the product. But unlike agriculture, where transgenic technologies were adopted by farmers, it proved difficult from the outset to interest fish farmers in considering the technology. Many of them were already facing criticisms from environmental and consumer groups and did not want to be associated with a new technology that could also compound public concern over their products.

Ironically, it is the appeal to familiarity that led US regulatory authorities to avoid creating new systems for approving transgenic animals. Future efforts to solve the world's grand challenges will require the deployment of new species of technologies systems. These technologies will face challenges similar to those that have blocked transgenic salmon, especially when introduced in economic sectors that are already stressed by preexisting pressures such as rising production costs and mounting ecological concerns.

The case of transgenic salmon offers a number of important lessons for policymakers managing controversies surrounding new product species. First, the history of the product and the associated tensions are a clear result of conflicts with incumbent fishing and fish-farming systems. But that is only part of the story. The second aspect of the tensions relates to the fact that transgenic salmon is a pioneering product whose commercial release would pave the way for other transgenic products whose risk profiles are yet to be studied. Herein lies a dilemma for policymakers. On the one hand, they would like to maintain global leadership and approve the product. On the other hand, they need assurances that the new product does not open the door for others that might pose new risks. The outcome has therefore been a highly cautious approach. The costs associated with this slow regulatory approach would prohibit most entrepreneurs from advancing novel product categories.

Second, the future of transgenic salmon in the United States still depends on whether it can also be grown locally. This will determine whether the country can maintain its role as a global leader in agricultural biotechnology. This entails offering innovators a reliable, predictable, and science-based approval process and a constructive public debate based on scientific facts. If the US government moves to review and update a rigorous and efficient approval process for future animal biotechnology products, it would define model regulatory standards and best practices for the rest of the world.

Losing the leading position in the biotechnology sector to countries that place a lower value on environmental and human health safety standards and that do not have thorough regulatory oversight processes in place could have severe implications for the safety of biotechnology applications. As the world leader in biotechnology research, innovation, and commercialization, the United States could set an example in the regulation of biotechnology innovations to ensure that society derives the highest possible benefit from these technologies in the safest possible way. The public needs nonpartisan information about the scientific facts, benefits, and potential risks associated with transgenic animals, as well as the rigor of the regulatory approval process.

Third, the regulatory approval process for transgenic animals needs to be made more reliable and predictable. This could be done through the introduction of a clear decision timeline and milestones as well as a fixed number of days for public comment. Moreover, responsibilities of the different regulatory agencies in the assessment and decisionmaking processes need to be clearly defined. The required assessments and studies need to be strictly science-based, known to applicants ahead of time, and focused on the safety of the end product rather than on the nature of the production process. To this end, the regulatory agencies need to collaborate with research institutions and private developers of biotechnology to define uniform standards for the health and environmental safety of transgenic animals.[47]

Fourth, policymakers need to be conscious of the staying power of initial responses to a new product. One of the persistent concerns over transgenic salmon is the so-called Trojan gene hypothesis that the fish could interbreed with wild relatives and lead to the collapse of wild salmon populations. The original authors of the hypothesis have on numerous occasions said that their model does not apply to the transgenic salmon in question. This has not prevented opponents from using the claim against the fish. In this case the early narrative has become the basis for defining the risks of transgenic salmon, and its opponents continue to make the claim. The general message from the case is the difficulty of putting early myths about new products to rest. Such myths linger on despite protestation. This is mainly because they fit well in the broader narrative. There have been other examples that include numerous statements against transgenic crops.

In the final analysis, global problems will require international solutions, and the sooner these lessons are learned, the easier it will be to reduce the tensions between innovation and incumbency. The possibility that the fish might be grown in another country and exported to the United States may appear to address some of the environmental concerns. However, it has done little to win over its opponents. Their activities to pressure supermarkets to not stock the fish illustrate their commitment to delaying the sale of the fish. Other measures against the fish include calls for labeling despite the absence of any information that the fish carries risks that are different from those addressed by existing fish-marking methods.

Growing the fish in the United States will continue to be challenged. In early 2016, Senator Lisa Murkowski (R-AK) showed what lay ahead for the fish. After a select Senate committee confirmed Robert M. Califf as the new FDA Administrator, she vowed to block his candidacy in the full Senate as a result of the approval of transgenic salmon. The debate surrounding Califf's nomination mainly centered on his connections with the pharmaceutical industry. Murkowski, however, represents a state with an interest in salmon production. She said that "when it comes to the F.D.A., the one thing that is really important is what is going on with fish."[48] The socioeconomic origins of opposition to the transgenic fish cannot be allayed by safety arguments alone.

Oiling the Wheels of Novelty

No intelligent idea can gain general acceptance unless some stupidity is mixed in with it.

FERNANDO PESSOA

As the cases in this book have shown, new technologies often generate social tensions as well as threaten to transform the existing socioeconomic fabric. This Schumpeterian process of incessant refreshing that is essential for economic renewal is also a source of public controversy. The tensions take many forms that include prohibitions, trade restrictions, demonization, and delayed market approvals. In many cases regulatory interventions help to reduce the sources of public concern and facilitate the adoption of new technologies.

The cases in this book offer many lessons for contemporary public policy challenges. The world is entering a new age that is dominated by three major trends. First, there is growing awareness of grand challenges such as the need to foster economic growth, protect the environment, and improve governance. Second, these challenges are now recognized as both being global in nature and requiring concerted international action. Third, technological innovation as an expression of human ingenuity will play an even greater role in the search for solutions to the global grand challenges requiring large-scale transitions.[1] "Our generation has inherited more opportunities to transform the world than any other. That's a cause for optimism, but only if we're mindful of our choices."[2]

Cautionary voices on the risks of rapid technological advancement are becoming louder. Take the case of robots. The conventional view regarding the introduction of robots tends to assume incremental patterns with limited disruptions. It is often argued that robots are being recruited to fill skill gaps. In this respect, robots are therefore not displacing workers but merely reassigning them to other tasks. This line of reasoning has led to the view that robots are more likely to replace mundane tasks while humans will retain their role in more creative tasks. It is argued, for example, that "economies like the UK and US where creative occupations make up a large proportionate of the workforce may be better placed than others to resist the employment fallouts from future advances in computerization."[3]

Others, however, argue that the pace of automation, adoption of robotics, and advances in artificial intelligence will have far-reaching implications for the economy irrespective of the nature of the tasks being performed. This view is guided by the understanding that perhaps technological advancement has reached a point where it is displacing more jobs than it can create. As a result, it is threatening the very fabric of society by creating disparities and unemployment. The outlook for employment and prosperity is gloomy. "If, however, we can fully leverage advancing technology as a solution—while recognizing and adapting to its implications for employment and distribution of income—then the outcome is far more likely to be optimistic."[4]

Conspicuous societal problems will coexist with scientific and technological abundance. The inability of society to harness the available technology to address the challenges could lead to disenchantment with the scientific enterprise itself. Moreover, those who associate certain business models with the worsening of the human condition are likely to increase their demands for curtailing technological innovation.

Resolving this dilemma will require, at the very minimum, a worldview of the future that visualizes exponential technological advancement, appreciates perceptions of loss in complex socioeconomic systems, and develops more appropriate approaches for supporting informed decisionmaking. This chapter concludes with a more detailed examination of the implications of technological controversies for governance.

Leading Forward: Executive Action

One of the primary functions of leadership is to chart new paths for society. This is often done under conditions of uncertainty. Leadership, as Schumpeter put it, is a form of entrepreneurship exercised in the public arena. This is especially so when fostering the creation of new economic combinations also rearranges the distribution of the benefits and risks arising from innovation. Actions such as Pope Clement VIII's decision to declare coffee a Christian beverage are entrepreneurial in character because they help to add new combinations to the economy. Such acts of leadership are not restricted to executive branches of government. The 1980 landmark *Diamond v. Chakrabarty* case in the United States played a decisive role in the emergence of the biotechnology industry by making it possible to patent inventions arising from living forms. In many other cases legislative branches play an equally vital leadership role in making it possible for new industries to emerge. The reverse also happens quite often when leadership suppresses innovation and sides with incumbent industries.

Deliberative decisionmaking is an important aspect of democratic governance. The process helps society to identify areas of common interest and learn how to share risks and benefits. But there is no guarantee that the appeal to activities such as public consultation will result in the best interest of society. It is doubtful, for example, that the deliberative process that led to severe restriction on the cultivation of transgenic crops in various countries was beneficial to those nations. Indeed, many of them are revisiting their decisions in light of new challenges or evidence.

There are many moments in the history of new technologies when decisions need to be taken by those in executive offices who control large amounts of political capital. Deliberation and advice set the stage for such executive actions, but they cannot substitute for the exercise of executive authority. It takes considerable political courage to promote innovation. For example, the risks associated with adopting the Green Revolution in India were clear from the outset. But it took the political courage of the minister for food and agriculture, Chidambaran Subramaniam, to push forward with what was clearly a risky agricultural gamble. His actions were guided by a different calculation. He was more concerned with the risks of doing nothing than the side effects of adopting the Green Revolution. In fact, many of the concerns expressed about the Green Revolution turned out to be justified. His interest, however, was in increasing agricultural yields. It was an act of political courage that paid off with regard to the objectives he set out to achieve.

As national and global challenges mount, so too will the demand for decisive leaders to champion the application of new technologies. There are two examples that offer diverse needs for leadership. The first is the field of energy transitions. A variety of concerns such as climate change and international security call into question the continued use of fossil fuels. Much of this debate has occurred under the auspices of the United Nations Framework Convention on Climate Change. Reaching agreement on climate presupposes the existence of sovereign champions willing to promote the adoption of renewable energy technologies and other climate mitigation measures. The rise in the adoption of solar and wind energy technologies has been associated with considerable opposition from a diversity of social groups, including lobby groups representing the fossil fuel industry. Strong entrepreneurial leadership could play a significant role in shaping the transition toward sustainability through support for specific technologies.

Similarly, leadership is needed to help address the expected impacts of some of the emerging technologies. Three examples stand out. The first is the case of automation. Concerns over the implications of automation—and more specifically the use of robots—are not new. The general understanding has been that such advances create more jobs than they replace. Under this scenario it is possible to increase productivity gains through automation while retraining workers to undertake new tasks. But because of the exponential growth in knowledge and engineering capabilities, it is not certain that the classical view of the impact of automation still holds true in practice. It is possible that job destruction is likely to occur faster than society can design the appropriate responses to retrain workers or redesign educational systems. In many areas of automation or artificial intelligence, it will become increasingly difficult to distinguish between humans and technology. The convergence will make the popular dichotomy irrelevant.[5] Decisive leadership is needed under such circumstances to help balance the benefits and risks of automation.

One key policy measure is ensuring that people can have access to the kind of education and skill development opportunities that enable them to be productive members of society. An inclusive economy comprises "mature technologies that operate on a large scale, creating jobs and profits. It includes developing technologies that provide opportunities for future jobs and profits."[6] Achieving such inclusion will require novel government interventions, institutional reforms, and new management strategies that are yet to be conceived. The alternative could lead to the spread of political unrest and resentment toward technological innovation.

The second area where decisive leadership is needed is in the field of synthetic biology, especially given the dramatic drop in gene-editing costs. These techniques offer immense opportunities to address a wide range of medical, agricultural, and environmental problems. However, the same techniques also pose new ethical, economic, and ecological challenges at scales that society has not experienced before. Take the potential use of "gene drive" to confer sterility or other traits in malaria-carrying mosquitoes. The technology could have a significant impact on reducing malaria. But the ecological consequences of suppressing species from existing ecosystems are little understood. In fact, they are only fully knowable after the fact. It will take decisive leadership to balance between potentially extraordinary benefits and the risk of catastrophic consequences.

The final example that demonstrates a need for decisive leadership at the national and international levels involves the technological transformation of medicine and healthcare. Rapid scientific and technological advances are providing a wide range of low-cost technologies for diagnosis, drug delivery, therapeutics, and other medical applications. Information and communications technologies, for example, are already transforming healthcare and offering opportunities for global applications, including in emerging nations. In fact, in many cases emerging nations can leapfrog into new applications without having to follow the same pathways pioneered by industrialized nations.[7] But existing medical practices and regulatory practices are not adapting fast enough to embrace the new technologies. There is a clear case for decisive leadership to bring new healthcare practices to these countries, enabling them to benefit from emerging technologies.

As global challenges mount and technological opportunities expand, leadership will need to take on a different character. It cannot be reactive and wait until the course of action is obvious. In many cases waiting to see how events unfold could compound the challenges. It is therefore important that decisions are guided by ethical values that reflect the demand for inclusive innovation, better use of scientific and technological advice, continuous adjustments in social institutions, and greater public understanding of science and technology. The rest of this chapter addresses these issues in greater detail.

Take My Advice: Science, Technology, and Innovation

The next frontier of leadership will focus largely on how society is prepared to respond not only to global grand challenges but also to new social problems generated by technological advancement and engineering applications. Leaders will need to be more adaptive, flexible, and open to continuous learning. They will be called upon increasingly to take decisions in the face of uncertainty and amid controversy. They may weigh the circumstances and err on the side of caution and wait for the evidence to unfold. But such actions may result in forgoing important technological opportunities. Such a world calls for entrepreneurial leaders who are capable of using the available knowledge to assess the situation, take informed executive action in a timely manner, and continue to monitor technological advances and their impacts.

In fact, technological controversies are often resolved with executive intervention, as evidenced by the executive decisions to reverse religious edicts against coffee in the medieval Middle East. The decision to approve the first commercial release of transgenic products in the United States was finally made by the Office of the President.

Europe, on the other hand, was unable to make much headway despite the appointment of a chief scientific adviser to the Commission of the European Union. After four years of experimentation, the position was abolished in 2014. Opponents of the position pointed to the fact that the incumbent in the position sought to overturn the scientific consensus upon which the EU regulatory system was founded. They argued for more options for scientific advice and saw the position as a barrier for effective guidance. Political pressure on scientific advisory bodies is not unique. In the United States, for example, legislators pushed for a 2014 bill to prevent the US Environmental Protection Agency from using its own scientific advice.

Leaders who think technological matters should be handled by experts may not be fully cognizant of the extent to which innovation is interwoven with politics. This is true at all levels of economic development. Emerging economies have to make complex decisions related to the impact of infrastructure projects in the same way that advanced countries grapple with social concerns in new fields such as nanotechnology, robotics, unmanned aerial vehicles, synthetic biology, artificial intelligence, and additive manufacturing (3D printing).[8]

Much of the public debate is intended to influence government policy on science, technology, and engineering. In this regard, the capacity of governments to assess the available information and use it for decisionmaking is an essential element of the debate. Political leadership on innovation and the existence of requisite institutions of science and technology advice are an essential aspect of economic governance. Such institutions need to embody democratic practices such as transparency and citizen participation that accommodate diverse sources of expertise.[9]

Science, technology, and engineering are practiced in increasingly informed and democratic societies. "Citizens, stakeholders, patients and users all have their own views, opinions, and knowledge of ... society with its science and technology. Democratic governance of ... cultures requires that these forms of knowledge and experience are recognized and allowed to play a role, together with specific ... expertise of scientists and engineers."[10] Such participation also needs to be managed through institutions whose procedural integrity reflects democratic practices and fosters trust in light of the uncertainty associated with innovation.[11] It is not just the quality of advice that matters, but the nature of the structure of procedures used to obtain such advice despite variations in conditions under which they have evolved.[12] Scientific advisory institutions are therefore largely custodians of procedures and managers of scientific assessments. Their role includes determining when advice is needed.

There are at least three structured ways by which decisionmakers receive scientific and engineering advice. The first involves convened or ad hoc advice provided as recommendations from workshops, conferences, and seminars. This is by far the most common method of generating advice and probably the least effective. In most cases it serves more to educate the public than as a source of systematic advice. Advice is also provided by internal organs of various public institutions. Government departments may have standing scientific committees that serve this function. Third, advice can come from independent bodies such as scientific, engineering, and medical academies. Many of these bodies are national, but at least one international assessment body, the Intergovernmental Panel on Climate Change, has acquired global recognition.[13]

Not all scientific and engineering academies are designed to provide systematic advice. There are two traditions of such institutions. The first type of academies, mostly in Europe and its former colonies, are largely honorific and focus on recognizing lifelong achievements. They may be called upon from time to time to give advice, but this is not their primary function. Their contributions to policy debates tend to be limited by their mandates and focus on recognizing excellence. The United States, on the other hand, has evolved since the Civil War days a new class of academies that combine both the recognition of excellence and a robust system of providing independent policy advice to government.[14]

Scientific, engineering, and medical academies can generate sound advice when requested. But their effectiveness depends on the existence of complementary advisory institutions in executive offices. The existence of chief scientific advisers in offices of presidents and prime ministers as well as in key ministries is an essential part of the ecology of advice. It is notable, for example, that sixteen African countries have national scientific academies and yet as of 2015 no single African president has an office of science and technology advice. Under the circumstances the advice of the academies would fall on deaf ears.

Much of the public debate over technology is intended to influence government policy on specific issues. Political leadership on technology and the existence of requisite institutions of science and technology advice are an essential aspect of the governance of new technologies. This advice will be insufficient, however, unless governments view science and technology as integral to the development process. In this regard, enhancing the capacity of leadership to address science and technology issues will contribute to the effective management of public debates over new technologies in general and biotechnology in particular.

One of the key themes that future generations will have to face involves how to manage uncertainty. Finding solutions to global challenges will involve more risk-taking, experimentation, and a commitment to open futures. Past worldviews that seek to mitigate risks by suppressing innovation as pursued in some circles under the negative interpretation of the "precautionary principle" will need to give way to new approaches.[15] A positive application of precaution should lead to taking action when faced with a challenge, not avoiding it.[16] Otherwise doing nothing could lead to greater risks. In fact, a precautionary view would require early positive action. The biggest risk that society faces by adopting approaches that suppress innovation is that they amplify the activities of those who want to preserve the status quo by silencing those arguing for a more open future.

Advisory institutions will need to be vigilant and help leaders manage the tensions between innovation and incumbency. Doing so will require broadening the regulatory scope for framing the uncertainty of risk. So far there are dominant doctrines that are used by regulatory agencies. The first is proof of harm, as used by the United States in approving transgenic crops. Under this system the burden of proof lies with those bringing forward evidence of harm. An alternative framework relying on the precautionary principle reverses the burden of proof and places it on producers and regulators. Broadening the framework would include the use of precaution through evidence. Such an approach would also take into account the emergence of new regulatory challenges arising from complex interactions between actors.

This approach "views the formal and informal decisions made about appropriate levels of exposure to risk as products of complex interactions of opinions, positions and interpretations of facts held by various stakeholders in regulatory frameworks."[17]

The precaution-through-evidence approach provides a framework for continuous governance beyond initial stages of approval. Implementing the approach could include temporary or limited approvals of new products while providing opportunities for consultation and interaction among stakeholders. In fact, variants of this approach are used in time-bound approvals where the products have to be reauthorized. The essential element of the approach is to place stronger emphasis on postcommercialization monitoring and consultation.

The process of technological innovation and the associated engineering activities will need to take into account some of the fundamental drivers of social discontent. At least two come to mind. First, issues of social inclusion need to be reflected in the design of new technologies. Innovation or business models that do not reflect the demand for social and economic inclusion will continue to be challenged. Science, technology, and engineering education as well as the associated arts will need to be strengthened at all levels. This is essential for the emergence of more open and democratic societies. Advisory institutions will need to guide leaders on how to foster more creative and democratic cultures. Second, concerns over the environment in particular and sustainability in general will dominate future debates over the role of science, technology, and engineering in society. In this respect, public policies will need to grapple with how to leverage the power of science, technology, and engineering to foster sustainability.[18] Engineers, technologists, and entrepreneurs will increasingly be called upon to design products that reflect the demands of open sustainability futures.[19]

Fortunately, advances in the sciences are helping humanity learn more about how nature functions and how it can serve as a source of heuristics for ecological design. The challenge for advisory bodies is how to leverage the curiosity of scientists, the design competence of engineering, and the societal acumen of entrepreneurs to reshape the future in an ecological image.[20] It is not the absence of new technologies that stands in the way of solving global problems, but the success of the previous sociotechnical fabric from which today's cultures are woven. Advisory organizations will need to identify pathways that help to integrate new ideas into new systems while managing the potential political fallout. The wheel of novelty must be reinvented continuously in light of contemporary realities.

Much of the subject matter in this book is not the focus of academic research. Science and technology studies only make passing references to the topic. Similarly, social studies of technology pay occasional attention to resistance to innovation. Most marketing studies view the topic as adoption failures. The popular dismissal of resistance to innovation as futile acts of neo-Luddites undermined the close scrutiny of drama surrounding cultural evolution. Given the significance of the tensions between innovation and incumbency, the time has come to develop this field as a distinctive area of scholarly endeavor, especially in technology universities. The results of such coordinated research efforts will help to inform policymaking and public engagement on technological controversies. At the very least this book has sought to map the contours of such research programs.

We Are in It Together: Inclusive Innovation

Many of the global technological controversies over issues such as access to medicine, transgenic crops, or clean energy are manifestations of divergent views over inclusive innovation. The underlying technologies are viewed by large corporations as products to be sold in globally competitive markets. Emerging nations, on the other hand, may view them as generic technologies that provide new platforms for local innovation. For example, when transgenic cotton seed was introduced in India's Gujarat State, it was quickly adopted by local farmers who used it to upgrade their cultivars with the new pest-resistance traits. For the farmers the seed was seen as a platform for further innovation. For Monsanto, however, this may have been seen as lost revenue from product sales.[21]

The distinction between products and platforms makes it harder to maintain strict demarcations between those who oppose and those who support new technologies. Advocates of inclusive innovation are more likely to engage directly with technology-generating firms. Those with a narrow product view tend to focus on defining the political discourse in zero-sum terms. The two groups are informed by different objectives and a different understanding of the nature of the technology in question. Those countries that viewed microelectronics as a platform for innovation were able to harness the technology and build new industrial polices to spur innovation in the sector. Those that viewed it as a set of products were focused on protecting existing industries and hardly benefited from the revolution. A similar scenario is unfolding with regard to the differences in the patterns of adoption of transgenic crops in South America and Asia on the one hand and Africa on the other.

New controversial technologies are likely to enjoy more local support where the business models include provisions for inclusive innovation. This may entail greater involvement of public sector institutions to provide training in the emerging fields, creation of joint ventures, equitable management of intellectual property rights, segmentation of markets to enable the technology to be used for noncompetitive products, and improvement of the policy environment to support long-term technology partnerships. Fundamentally, building local capabilities and fostering public engagement in technology development are critical elements of inclusive innovation. In most cases, opposition to new technology arises from a sense of exclusion. It is about understanding the subtle distinctions between technology as products and technology as platforms for generating new solutions that may not be the priority of the sales departments of foreign firms.[22] It is not a surprise, though, that the absence of inclusive strategies leads to intense debates over questions of justice, equity, corporate control and challenges to intellectual property system. The lessons learned from controversies over agricultural and pharmaceutical technologies should help in crafting more inclusive strategies for emerging technologies such as gene editing, artificial intelligence, robotics and drones. The case for inclusive innovation is even more urgent and income disparities around the world become increasingly associated with technological innovation and business models that do not necessarily create new value but transfer existing value to new owners.[23]

Joseph Schumpeter left the world a vivid image of the sweeping impact of new technologies. He showed ambivalence about the long-term consequences of innovation on human welfare. He considered a review of the social benefits of entrepreneurship to be "so complex and perhaps even hopeless that I beg to excuse myself from entering into it."[24] In chapter 7 of his classic *Theory of Economic Development*, Schumpeter foretold the suffering that befalls sections of society whose economic services become obsolete. "Even the pain which these losses cause, have their function in the faster removal of the outdated, in the incentive towards activity. But those people who participate in the drama themselves, and those who are close to them, have a different point of view. . .. They cannot close their ears to the cries of those about to be crushed, when the wheels of the new era roll over them."[25]

Schumpeter paints a grim picture of the fate of those enterprises that are swept aside by the wheel of innovation. "Through generations, the people in question live a poorer . . . life with ever more bleak hopelessness. Slowly, they lose the moral and intellectual level, the more so, the darker the economic prospects around them are becoming. Their firms become poorer and poorer, tumble even into ever more unfavourable situations, become breeding ground for social grievances and fall into the hands of ever more despicable public persuaders."[26]

With this observation Schumpeter laid out quite clearly the extent to which innovation creates the conditions for its own challenge. The transformative nature of emerging fields such as robotics, 3D printing, and artificial intelligence raises the specter of technological unemployment that echoes the early debates over recorded music. There are new concerns over the extent to which much of today's technological innovation creates new value or simply shifts it to new owners. Such larger societal anxieties are part of renewed concern over inequity and its potential political ramifications.

The concerns over innovation are not limited to specific technological introductions but to their wider societal implication, as illustrated by the long delay in the adoption of the printing press for religious texts in Ottoman lands. What appears on the surface as conservatism or irrational rejection of new ideas may represent a deeper logic of societal stability woven around moral values, sources of legitimacy, and economic interests. Under such conditions the objections to new technologies must be sought in the wider social system and not just in the rhetorical tools used by opponents.

The fear of loss is one of the most fundamental drivers of concern over new technologies. In most cases decisions about new products are driven by perceptions of potential loss to individuals, communities, nations, and regions. The clashes are usually not about actual loss because of their vicarious nature. They are often shaped by visions of the future based on historical and contemporary trends. For example, it is remarkable that two major technologies—transgenic crops and the mobile phone—emerged at the same time but were managed quite differently in the United States and Europe. Transgenic crops appeared to threaten European incumbent agriculture. Mobile phones, on the other hand, seemed to align with the forces of economic and political integration.

As a result, the adoption of mobile phones in the United States was relatively slow but did not face the kinds of challenges that transgenic crops faced in Europe.[27] Africa followed the European path, with even more rapid adoption of mobile phones, but more stringent laws against transgenic crops. One of the most fundamental features of these adoption patterns was the perception of the distribution of risks and benefits and the extent to which emerging technologies reinforced or threatened popular aspirations for inclusion (whether it was the less advantaged communities in Africa or Eastern European nations seeking to decouple their economies from Russia).

In most cases, public perceptions are formed based on hazards, not on actual risks. This is often expressed through postponement, rejection, or opposition to new products or ideas.[28] There are many manifestations of such fear, but economic ones are among the most enduring. For example, in 2015 California recently proposed a law—Senate Bill 1298—that would require driverless cars to have a licensed driver present and capable of taking over if needed.[29] This necessitates the presence of a steering wheel—a major drawback for Google's cars that "famously do not include a steering wheel or pedals for human operation."[30] The bill was introduced despite the fact that driverless cars demonstrated the potential for a greater safety record than human-driven cars. The bill seemed to have been inspired by economic rather than safety concerns. It is reminiscent of the Red Flag Acts enacted in the UK in the 1860s–1890s. The intent of the laws was to regulate vehicles on public roads in the name of public safety. The laws severely restricted the speed at which vehicles could travel and required a man with a red flag to walk ahead of any vehicle connected to two or more cars. The Red Flag Act was a disincentive to investing in faster automobiles. Germany, which dispensed with restriction, was able to build faster cars and related transportation infrastructure. A similar scenario is feasible with markets without incumbent automobile industries and infrastructure leapfrogging into the driverless age for a diversity of land, air, and water vehicles. Crewless boats, for example, could become new modes of transportation in remote waterways around the world. In both cases, the intent was to stall the adoption of the new technology, mostly due to its economic ramifications. The safety record of driverless cars will likely wreck the car insurance industry. The technology also poses new challenges for policing due to uncertainties over the locus of liability.

Even though the basic concerns regarding radical innovations are economic, additional fuel is provided by intellectual and socio-psychological factors. Challenges to coffee were not always direct but often clothed in other concerns depending on contemporary social and political factors. In England, for example, the coffee-house was a new institution that promoted freedom of speech during a period of considerable political uncertainty.

While economic arguments fueled negative reactions to coffee, the government used security concerns to put down coffeehouses. Therefore, the combined economic and security concerns defined the place of coffee in English society, not any one of these factors operating independently. Scratching the surface of intellectual and psychological arguments does not automatically uncover the deeper socioeconomic forces that drive challenges to new technologies. Explanations for this can be found more easily in societal interactions and less in direct causation.

The debates often reflect the tension between the transformational nature of new technologies and inertia or path dependency in the prevailing social and economic order. Over time, technologies coevolve with social institutions to form a complex cultural fabric woven together by a wide range of economic interests.[31] Overcoming path dependency requires recognition of opportunities in open systems for the generation of new paths.[32] New ideas start in hospitable niches from which they spread to other sections of society. Those niches are often created by waves of entrepreneurial efforts whose success is never guaranteed in advance. In many cases such niches are likely to flourish where they do not compete with incumbent practices. This demands greater innovative efforts under more uncertain conditions.

In some cases, inclusive innovation and coexistence of products is a strategy for reducing social tension and market conflicts, especially where competing products have wider economic benefits. For example, in 1714, "Eleven coffeemakers joined to form a trade association, and the coffee trade in Vienna came of age. As coffee grew in popularity, a bitter contention arose between the coffee-boilers guild and distillers guild. In 1750 Maria Theresa finally settled the quarrel by forcing the coffee-boilers to sell alcohol as well as coffee and the tavern keepers to sell coffee as well as alcohol, a measure that unified the two guilds."[33] Now that the two guilds could bear the costs and benefits of both products, it became possible for the government to tax alcohol, which helped increase coffee sales. In other words, technological inclusion is critical to dealing with perceptions of loss arising from new technologies.

The steady adoption of coffee and its emergence as a global commodity was largely driven by the superiority of the beverage. But equally important was the transformational nature of the product. Not only did the adoption of coffee create new values and social norms, but its impact influenced lasting structural changes such as the design of urban and rural areas and the associated pattern of social interaction.[34] Coffeehouses created novel institutions that played new roles in society and wielded their own political power.[35] Coffee adoption helped create new industries and stimulated the expansion of trade in complementary sectors such as aluminum.[36] These changes extend to the wider global value chains created through the cultivation, production, process, distribution, and marketing of coffee and coffee products.

The need for inclusive approaches is also reflected in strategies that are aimed at slowing down the adoption of a technology rather than seeking to extinguish it. Several examples come to mind. Edison's initial efforts to stall the adoption of alternating current aimed to give him time to relocate his investments to other activities. He could see the grand wheel of innovation rolling in his direction. Similarly, the Horse Association of America was largely interested in creating a niche for animal power, not necessarily stopping the march of tractors.

The same can be said about sections of the opposition to transgenic crops concerned with preserving its market share. But more fundamental concerns about inclusion are at work. Many of those who question transgenic crops in Africa do not oppose the technology. They are more concerned about the risks of technological exclusion. They are mostly interested in having access to new technologies and applying them to address their own problems. Their perceived rejection of imported technology conceals their desire to acquire the same techniques but use them differently. Paradoxically, the intensity of their challenge to the technology may in fact be an expression of their interest in the technology, not in its rejection. The tensions are often rooted in the view that not all innovations are good, as illustrated by concerns over the welfare impacts of novelty.[37] There is ample evidence from the financial sector that underscores the fact that quite often innovation can indeed constitute "destructive creation."[38]

Even seemingly modest technical improvements in agriculture, for example, represent control of uncertainty and in turn become a source of political power and influence. "Behind the production of a head of lettuce are many seemingly mundane technical decisions like how crops are fertilized or how bugs are controlled, but these same details form the basis for an industry: they make a structure that grows crops but also produces power."[39] It is through deliberation that one can at least identify and shape opportunities for inclusion.[40]

While businesses may adopt such approaches that call for coexistence, movements often include factions that are bent on the extermination of the technology itself. It is usually these vocal voices that in the end tend to define the nature of the debate, invoking an equally strong response from advocates of new technologies.[41] In many cases, the flow of hostility goes both ways. Early dialogue, consultation, and accommodation are therefore essential in promoting technological coexistence. Intensive public risk dialogue makes it possible to understand the full implications of technological options.[42] Efforts that are initiated too late end up worsening the conflict and result in drastic measures such as Edison's macabre electrocution of live animals or the efforts by the American Federation of Musicians to ban recording of music.

More benign acts of technological intolerance arise from the perception that some people will be excluded from international trade. This is particularly pertinent in international trade arrangements where the winner takes all. The rise of transgenic crops in the United States and the prospects of preempting European latecomers heightened tensions between the two markets. Differences in rates and types of technological innovation may lead to perceptions of market loss, which results in efforts by lobbying groups to erect trade barriers. An example of this was trade barriers imposed against Japanese cars in the United States.[43] More inclusive international trade therefore can help to reduce tensions between innovation and incumbency. This view suggests that new technologies may coexist with incumbent products for a period. This may provide opportunities for technological latecomers to invest in emerging technologies rather than seek to reduce the adoption of new technologies. Reducing barriers to innovation may thus play a key role in helping latecomer economies or industries to become players in the market.[44]

Much of the controversy over new technologies occurs when new products challenge incumbent ones. Inclusive innovation in this respect involves negotiating the risks associated with the available technological options. Another way by which innovation fosters inclusion is where it addresses unmet needs. For example, the rapid adoption of mobile phones was facilitated by the fact that they serve new unmet needs and help to spread the benefits of technological innovation. So even if they generate tensions with traditional banking systems, they still gained support because they brought banking to people who had been excluded.[45] Advances in fields such as drug delivery and tissue engineering are already addressing medical challenges that could not be met using existing technologies.

Like in mobile communication, these advances serve as new platforms for a wide range of medical applications and associated industries. The emerging field of nanotechnology, which involves systems on the order of one-thousandth the thickness of human hair, is expanding the possibilities of creating new applications that do not compete with existing practices. This is mainly because the small size and the enormous surface area to volume ratio "create uniquely advantageous abilities to enter cells, release drugs slowly over time, modulate small-molecule payload toxic effects, and in some cases, amplify a signal that depends on surface contacts."[46] These properties create great prospects for new medical applications in therapeutics, diagnostics, and imaging.

Technological inclusion could also occur as emerging technologies start to replace previous applications and shift power to users. Healthcare represents a major opportunity for new technologies to do for medicine what mobile phones did for communication. One way by which technology is changing the healthcare landscape is through patient participation in medical data management. "Patients are generating their own data on their own devices. Already any individual can take unlimited blood pressure or blood glucose measurements, or even do their own electrocardiogram (ECG) via their smartphone. The data are immediately analyzed, graphed, displayed on the screen, updated with new measurements, stored and, at the discretion of the individual, shared."[47] The range of technologies that will contribute to this transformation is expanding dramatically as a result of exponential growth in scientific advancement. Digital medicine has an even greater potential of taking root in regions of the world, such as sub-Saharan Africa, that have limited access to healthcare.[48] Such regions could become the source of new medical applications that would otherwise be obstructed by incumbent interests in industrialized countries. This could follow the patterns of mobile money transfer and banking that first emerged in Africa before they spread to industrialized countries through the process of reverse innovation.[49]

The emergence of new fields such as the Internet of Things, 3D printing, digital learning, and open-source movements provide collaborative opportunities for inclusive innovation.[50] Collaborating innovation changes the way productive systems are organized. However, this does not automatically lead to inclusive innovation. Existing policy frameworks need to "be modified to allow for particular features of inclusive innovation, including the nature of innovations required, the actors involved and their interrelations, the type of learning they undertake, and the institutional environment in which they operate. Four system domains must be effective if inclusive innovation is to succeed: the product, its retailing and support, the micro-enterprises that provide these demand-side services, and the wider context."[51] It is not sufficient that policies are inclusive; their formulation and the design of new technologies also need to include potential beneficiaries.[52]

In the final analysis, policymakers will have to invest in managing change, especially where investments in new technologies are needed. Policymakers seeking to support radical technologies must appreciate the challenges of getting support from project managers. In many cases, "Managers with restrictive mental models will adopt up to five disruptive innovation rejection strategies: rewarding incrementalism; ignoring the positive aspects of disruptive innovation; focusing on historical perceptions of success; creating perceptions of success with high effort; and holding beliefs in the face of disconfirming information."[53] Addressing these sources of reluctance to allocate resources to disruptive technologies requires a more holistic understanding of the innovation process, including lessons from discontinued or unsupported technological opportunities that became the foundation for new businesses elsewhere.[54]

Playing Catch-Up: Institutional Adaptation

Laws are among the most explicit expressions of social institutions. The case of margarine shows how laws were used to seek to curtail the adoption of the product. Similar measures were adopted to control the spread of coffee in Germany. Similarly, regulations slowed down the acceptance of mechanical refrigeration. Recent decades have seen an increase in the adoption of international treaties that seek to either curtail or promote the adoption of new technologies. In fact, globalization has heightened the importance of science and technology diplomacy.

Two examples illustrate this point. In efforts to reduce the depletion of the ozone layer, governments adopted the 1987 Montreal Protocol on Ozone Depleting Substances. In a series of amendments, the protocol sought to balance restrictions on the production of certain ozone-depleting substances with the promotion of technology to produce alternatives. In contrast, the Cartagena Protocol on Biosafety to the Convention on Biological Diversity created a regime that sought to restrict the use of transgenic crops without necessarily offering viable alternatives. The Cartagena Protocol became a source of national legislation seeking to slow down the adoption of transgenic crops. It aimed to effect internationally what margarine and refrigeration laws tried to achieve in the United States.

Institutional factors play an important role in the framing of public discourse as a way to rally support and create social movements.[55] A central feature of the tactics is to appeal to a variety of democratic principles to advance political objectives. In effect, these are political movements whose activities are not necessarily related to the objectives that they espouse. For example, some of the organizations that challenge transgenic crops claim that they are doing so to protect biological diversity. But many of them can hardly prove that their actions will achieve their stated goals. They often attack the very technologies that might benefit biological diversity. In effect, such organizations are simply using biological diversity to promote other political goals.

Similarly, proponents of new technologies tend to appeal to popular sentiments about improvements in health and the environment, but usually their technologies are in the early stages of their development. Under such situations conflicts tend to rage on the basis of hypothetical claims rather than on the basis of evidence. It is usually evidence or the disappearance of protagonists that tends to settle the debate.

Labeling of products offers interesting insights into the nature of the tensions. Consumers have the right to know what is contained in the products that they purchase. In fact, regulatory bodies around the world have set criteria for determining the various forms of labels. These include changes in the nutritional composition of food, presence of additives, or known sources of allergy. There are varying labeling doctrines, but the most common is to focus on products rather than the processes by which they were produced. Many of the controversies surrounding labeling of new products arise from the gap between advocates' stated objectives and their actual political motives. The public may have seen demands to label margarine as an act of consumer protection, but beneath the surface, there were often unstated protectionist objectives.

What may appear as a legitimate appeal for the right to know may in fact be driven by an effort to brand a product so it can be rejected by consumers for protectionist reasons. It is for this reason that many firms remain intransigent against labeling even when it appears that it would meet the democratic standard of the right to know. Under such circumstances, it is not easy to distinguish between claims that are motivated by the right to know and the desire to brand for political purposes, given that many of those seeking political outcomes often come dressed as advocates of public interest.

One of the features of the tensions is the extension of regulatory principles from one product to another through the use of legislative analogy. One of the examples of such regime stretching can be witnessed in the field of synthetic biology, a confluence of engineering, biology, and physics. This emerging field involves the application of engineering principles to biology. The convergence of this field raises regulatory uncertainties. It is not clear whether the risk profile of the products of synthetic biology should be governed by safety measures developed for engineering or biotechnology products. The obvious approach would be to assess the risks of each application on its own merit. For example, new applications with potentially large-scale ecological ramifications such as gene drives may warrant greater scrutiny and public consultation than more benign editing of genomes in crops that are already in widespread use.[56]

Some of the concerned groups, however, have sought to apply the principles developed for transgenic crops under the Cartagena Protocol to synthetic biology. They see the field as an extension of genetic engineering and want it to be regulated as such. This type of regime stretching is not new. Opponents of coffee in the medieval Middle East sought to restrict the beverage by drawing parallels with alcohol, whose use had already been banned.

Technological advances in genetic engineering and synthetic biology are forcing governments to rethink the way they regulate new products. Responding in ways that radically differ, some governments are using emerging information to review their regulatory practices. Indeed, in 2014 researchers in the UK started to call for such legislative reforms. Such reform will continue to play an important role in innovation management for two main reasons.

First, the introduction of new technologies will in many cases require a coevolutionary process that involves the development of new regulatory principles and practices.[57] This is illustrated by the long history of finding ways to regulate novel product categories such as transgenic salmon without having to create new regulatory regimes. Approval of new products under such systems requires incremental change in existing regulation, a process that presupposes institutional flexibility and legislative learning. Second, creating space for new technologies may involve repealing old laws. This was done in the case of margarine and will need to be done with transgenic products in many countries. Given the important role that legislation plays in establishing social order, countries with adaptive legislative systems will be in a better position to foster coevolution between technology and social institutions as part of a broader governance agenda.[58] This will require the same level of scientific literacy in judicial systems as will be demanded of legislative and executive branches of government, as well as in the general public. It will not involve turning lawyers into scientists and engineers, but it will require a deeper appreciation of the coevolution and the two-way interactions between technology and society.

On the whole, it is necessary to ensure that "regulations have strong empirical foundations, both through careful analysis in advance and through retrospective review of what works and what does not."[59] This calls into question the tendency for regulators to operate cautiously when confronted with emerging technologies. With the held evidence, regulators "can use experimental rules, regulatory sunsets, or rulemaking deadlines to calibrate their approach to novel technologies or business practices."[60] The point is to provide a framework for informed decisionmaking and rulemaking. Equally important is the role of science and technology advice in ensuring that the law can adequately reflect the characteristics of emerging technologies.

An example of the tensions is the rise of additive manufacturing, or 3D printing, which is advancing faster than the law can catch up.[61] One of the main legal challenges is the potential convergence of digital information and physical objects.[62] Proposals to reduce technological tensions could include exempting digital information used in 3D printing from copyright infringement.[63] What may appear on the surface as being intellectual property concerns may in fact reflect deeper tensions between technological innovation and incumbency.

Inclusive innovation is not just about symbolic efforts to foster wider societal participation. It entails a deeper understanding of the deeper sources of exclusion or injustice that shape the social responses to innovation. One of the most significant sources of tensions over new technologies is gender disparities. The potential impact of new agricultural technologies on rural women, for example, has inspired long-standing social movements against new technologies around the world. Gender-related backlash against seemingly beneficial technologies is widely recorded in history. Its relevance, however, still escapes most technology analysts.

The invention of the infant incubator in France in 1880 serves as a good illustration. The original device, developed by Dr. Stéphane Tarnier, was initially based on the assumption that the role of the mother was simply to provide warmth to the infant. The backlash against the technology resulted in a redesign that put the mother at the center of the nursing process with the doctor acting as supervisor.[64]

Gender is an important aspect of the organization of society. But there are many other factors such as age, income, social mobility, educational attainment, and marginalization of communities that need to be properly understood and acknowledged as key factors in innovation. In the final analysis, new technologies are most likely to amplify social disparities. Perceptions of such disparities are sufficient to create anxieties about new technologies.

Learning Cultures: Public Education

Technological controversies tend to focus on the physical and more evident aspects of the application. For example, objections to wind energy and mobile phones focused on the turbines and cell towers respectively. The obvious response to such objections is to offer engineering solutions that either reduce the visibility of the turbines or make the cell towers mimic trees and blend into the landscape. These engineering responses are usually inadequate unless they are accompanied by deep efforts in public education.[65]

Many public education programs fail because they assume that the root cause of social concern over new technology is ignorance. To the contrary, it is quite common to find that concerns over new technologies come from well-informed and educated sections of the population. This has been the case with transgenic crops as well as vaccination. Educational programs that focused on the instrumental function of countering ignorance have in some cases only ended up alienating the public. Public education should therefore have higher aims of enhancing the legitimacy and quality of risk assessment processes.[66] Ultimately, the goal should be to manage risk perception and foster trust.[67] Such efforts need to be science-based and may include working with national regulators in institutionalizing trust. This was done in the case of irradiated food in response to opponents who sought to associate the technology with the horrors of nuclear bombs. In this case, "Food irradiation activists initiated wholesomeness studies to generate data in order to prove the safety of food, in an attempt to establish a science-based trust regime."[68]

It is much harder, however, to rebuild public trust when it has been undermined by accidents or disease outbreaks. Usually the loss of trust is not just in the product and the firms involved but in the associated system, which includes regulatory authorities. Rebuilding trust under such circumstances may require new negotiations to stabilize the different elements, which include production, control, and identity of the brand. Such efforts much be carried out with total transparency. This was shown to work in Norway in 1987 when children were infected by salmonella after eating chocolate produced by Nidar, a Trondheim-based confectionary firm. In this case rebuilding trust "required each of the different elements that constituted the brand (the trust in production, the trust in the control systems and the trust in its identity) to be negotiated and stabilized anew."[69]

Debates over new technology are part of a long history of social discourse over new products. Claims about the promise of new technology are at times greeted with skepticism, vilification, or outright opposition—often dominated by slander, innuendo, scare tactics, conspiracy theories, and misinformation. The assumption that new technologies carry unknown risks guides much of the debate. This is often amplified to levels that overshadow the dangers of known risks. For example, a large number of pesticides used in agriculture carry known risks. The focus tends to be on the unintended risks of new products rather than on unintended benefits. Another characteristic of the debate is the assumption that adopting new technologies comes with new risks, while doing nothing is risk free. As a result, most communication efforts do not include the risks of inaction.

Historical antecedents play key roles in technological polemics. They provide heuristics and analogies for structuring debates about new technologies. Products that have been previously banned or restricted are often used as templates by groups seeking to ban new ones. Efforts to draw analogies between wine and coffee or between chemical pollution and gene flow provide an example of this. Considerable creativity goes into using such logical fallacies and demonization. In fact, much of the debate over new products is a clash of fallacies, often associated with a lack of interest in acknowledging them. In the heat of the moment most people do not normally point out logical fallacies. Their focus is usually to score political points, not to reason or provide evidence. The end tends to justify the rhetorical means.

Examples include "Satan's Drink," "Junior Alcohol,"[70] "Embalmed Food," "Bull Butter," "Genetic Pollution," "Frankenfoods," "Frankenfish," and the "Devil's Instrument," as the telephone was derided when first introduced in Sweden. In most cases mainstream communication hardly panders to sloganeering.[71] Some terms such as "Frankenfoods," however, have become an enduring feature of the debate over transgenic crops. The overall purpose, though, is to generate negative perceptions of the technology and its advocates. This effort is accompanied by the slander of products, abject misinformation, and personal attacks or character assassinations of those whom the critics associate with new technologies.

Demonizing innovation is often associated with campaigns to romanticize past products and practices. Indeed, the Schumpeterian process of creative destruction entails the sweeping away of the new. These efforts use nostalgia to amplify a communal sense of loss, often captured by the cliché, "the good old days." The apocalyptic horrors that are often attributed to the present are cultural memories of "the bad old days."[72] Opponents of innovation hark back to traditions as if traditions themselves were not inventions at some point in the past.[73] The point here is not to denigrate traditions but to note that romanticizing the past is used as a political tool to undermine the acceptance of the new. The demonization creates a temporal dichotomy that makes it difficult to expand technological options by blending the old and the new.[74] The idea of technology blending adds credence to the importance of inclusive innovation. Champions of new technologies ought to be equally sensitive to the socioeconomic implications of their creations by appealing more to inclusive innovation.

The attacks also extend to instances where scientific evidence is denigrated or dismissed as biased or masterminded by corporate interests. Proponents, on the other hand, tend to overstate the benefit of new products and understate their risks. Granted, issues of conflict of interest shape public perceptions, and the shift from public to private sector research support has undermined public trust in transgenic crops, renewable energy, and other emerging technologies.

Public trust is an important element in the management of uncertainty and risk.[75] Trust involves relying on another agent or person to act in one's interest.[76] It entails the ability to share in both the benefits and the risks of social interactions and is essential in even the most basic of market-based activities.[77] It is not possible to know in advance all the attributes of a product being sold, so for the market to work there has to be a suspension of judgment and reliance on trust. Trust is not just an act of faith but is guaranteed by social institutions such as social norms, ethnic loyalty, or regulatory bodies. Trust helps to reduce the tendency for fear-mongering, often in the form of rumor, because of the prospects of shared risks and benefits.

Rumor is often the mode of transmission of negative perceptions. One such example is the risk of mobile phone sparks. As a result, mobile phone use at petrol stations was restricted in parts of the United States.[78] Upon further investigation, it turned out that the sparks were originating from the body static of drivers reentering their vehicles while refueling, and mobile phones were mere scapegoats.[79] Many of these rumors are extreme. Coffee, for example, was extensively rumored to cause sterility. In 2003 rumors started spreading in the Philippines that men who stood in a field of transgenic crops would turn gay. A decade later the rumor spread in Uganda that transgenic crops contained pig genes. Such rumors were intended to fan religious hostilities. But some of the rumors were grounded in truth, as was the case following the introduction of nylon stockings in the United States in the 1940s and their evident displacement of silk. Rumors spread that women "were already getting cancer of the legs."[80] It turned out that some of the dyes used for the stockings caused allergic reactions. It was also reported, without verification, that a woman walked through the exhaust of a bus and discovered that "the fumes had taken the nylon hose right off her legs."[81]

Disputes associated with new products under such uncertain circumstances are often resolved through protracted debates without clear criteria for the triumph of either side. In many cases resolution is achieved through an appeal to higher authorities, a route that is also pursued by incumbents to suppress new technologies. This could take the form of judicial rulings or even edicts by leaders. But in some cases conflicts have been resolved through compromise that reflects the sharing of risks and benefits.

It is notable that critics of new technology often define the rules of the debate in two fundamental ways. First, they have managed to create the impression that the onus for demonstrating safety lies with advocates of the technology. In other words, new technology products are considered unsafe until proven otherwise. Second, critics have been effective in framing the debate in environmental, human health, and ethical terms, thereby masking the underlying international trade considerations. By doing so, they manage to rally a much wider constituency of activists who are genuinely concerned about environmental protection, consumer safety, and ethical social values.

There is a general view that concerted efforts to promote public debate will improve communication and lead to the acceptance of new products. This may be the case in some situations, but generally the concerns are largely material and cannot be resolved through public debate alone. This is mainly because the root causes of the debate lie in the socioeconomic implications of the technology and not mere rhetorical considerations. It is possible that public debates only help to clarify or amplify points of divergence and do little to address fundamental economic and trade issues.

Much of the debate on the role of technology is based on hypothetical claims, with no real products in the hands of producers or consumers. Under such circumstances, communication and dialogue are not enough until there is a practical reference point. In other words, rebutting the claim of critics is not as important as presenting the benefits of real products in the marketplace. This can be best achieved through collaborative efforts among local scientists, engineers, entrepreneurs, policymakers, and civil society organizations. Under such collective approaches, much of the outcome depends on shared beliefs rather than on scientific evidence per se.[82]

Addressing the issue of science and technology communication requires an improved understanding of the changing ecology of communication and the risks of poor communication.[83] While critics tend to use a diverse array of social movements to advance their cause, advocates have focused on the use of centralized institutions, whose impact is largely negligible in the modern communication ecology. But creating the necessary diversity requires a broadening of the base of social movements that champion the role of science and technology in human welfare.

Members of the scientific and engineering community often communicate in ways that alienate the general public. The first and most common aspect of this is the use of jargon. This is a common feature of most professions. Learning how to communicate to the general public is an important aspect of reducing distrust. Scientists and engineers often appeal to a certain level of heroism that may inadvertently reduce their ability to engender trust in new technologies.

There is the cautionary tale from the early history of the aviation industry, when the image of the "intrepid birdman" only helped spread the fear of flying. The problem was serious enough that "a medical doctor . . . invoked Darwin's theory of evolution in claiming that pilots were descended from birds whereas the vast majority of humankind descended from fish and therefore would never be able to pilot a plane."[84] The industry survived by engaging women pilots, whose presence communicated ease of flight and safety. But this would cause its own tensions, as women ended up being relegated to support roles after the public gained confidence in the industry.

The key message here is that scientists and engineers may be implicitly undermining their own trust with the public by making it look like it takes a special kind of person to do what they are doing. If this is the case, then the general public may perceive that there are risks in new technologies that are not being communicated to them. The issue is less about educating the public than about members of the scientific and engineering community seeking to connect with others so scientists and engineers can be viewed as part of society and not as unique individuals whose feats are beyond popular understanding.

The traditional view that science is based on immutable facts that can be passed on from an authority to the general public is being challenged by approaches that demand greater participation in decisionmaking. In other words, scientific information is being subjected to democratic practices. The debates push the frontiers of public discourse on technical matters. On the one hand, society is being forced to address issues that are inherently technical, and on the other, the scientific community is under pressure to accept nontechnical matters as valid inputs for decisionmaking. The scientific, technological, and engineering communities will not only need to demonstrate a clear sense of leadership but also adapt their communication methods to suit the growing complexity and diverse needs of science.

Much of today's science and technology communication focuses on highlighting the nature of the breakthroughs, with little attention given to the implications of emerging technologies for society at large. Whenever this is done, it follows a standard press release template that usually refers to some potential benefit. There is usually little assessment of the implications of existing industrial practices. It is quite common that new technologies are used to address the risks associated with earlier technologies. Bioremediation is an example of a new technology used to clean up pollution caused by earlier technologies. Also, the invention of lithography made it easier to address many of the aesthetic and cost concerns raised regarding using typography to print books in Arabic. Science and technology communication that specifically helps the public to visualize the potential benefits of new technologies relative to existing ones would go a long way toward fostering more informed deliberations on the benefits and risks of emerging technologies. To some extent, this approach presupposes the existence of a capability to undertake timely science and technology assessments. But such assessments would have little impact in shifting public perceptions after they have become part of the public narrative. For example, evidence about the safety record of nuclear reactors and their potential impact on reducing energy-related deaths has had little impact in shifting public perceptions.[85] Such assessments, including the determination of their possible effectiveness, could be undertaken by schools or think tanks devoted to science, technology, and innovation policy studies. The perceived independence of such studies is critical to their effectiveness as sources of credible information.

In the final analysis, it is the range of useful technological products available to humanity that will settle the debates. This view requires a different approach in dealing with skepticism by shifting from adversarial responses to collective learning. In many cases advocates of new technologies tend to focus too much attention on specific sources of challenge. Efforts aimed at getting skeptics to change their minds to support new technologies may appear strategic. They often fail to appreciate, however, that skeptics usually represent a small section of the population. The more active among them often spend their time trying to sway the opinions of the larger majority that may not have formed an opinion on the new technology. Focusing solely on the skeptics often takes away the energy and time needed to promote collective learning among the rest of the population. The point is not to ignore sources of skepticism but to appreciate how the seemingly silent majority might in the end determine the fate of new technologies. In this respect, a learning approach that focuses on inclusion may in fact be a more important strategy than an adversarial one.

Conclusion

Discernible paradoxes will mark the future of the global community. Its challenges will grow just as its scientific, technological, and engineering capabilities will expand. In time, the same technologies that foster creativity and innovation also become the sources of cultural inertia. The ability to harness the power of technology and engineering to solve social problems must be accompanied by complementary adaptations in social institutions. These advances will in turn demand the emergence of more scientifically and technologically enlightened societies guided by democratic principles in the social, political, and cultural arenas.

Cultural history around the world has shown that human beings aspire to more than just basic existence. "We need challenge, we need meaning, we need purpose, we need alignment with nature. Where technology separates us from these it brings a type of death. But when it enhances these, it affirms life. It affirms our humanness."[86] It is this affirmation of the human spirit of adventure, purpose, continuous improvement, and mastery that will define the champions of human well-being.

The tensions between innovation and incumbency will not go away, however enlightened and deep our analysis may be. Society is accustomed to allocating a greater index of risk to innovation than incumbency. In an increasingly complex and uncertain world, the risks of doing nothing may outweigh the risks of innovating. In the final analysis, technology, economy, and the wider society coevolve as a whole. Neither the proponents nor opponents of emerging technologies can be uprooted without unraveling and weaving an entirely new socioeconomic fabric. Old design patterns are usually not a good predictor of what comes next. Keeping the future open and experimenting in an inclusive and transparent way is more rewarding than imposing the dictum of old patterns.

As Albert A. Bartlett, professor of physics at the University of Colorado (Boulder) aptly put it, "The greatest shortcoming of the human race is our inability to understand the exponential function." I hope future policymakers will pay greater attention to the disjuncture between rapid technological innovation and the slow pace of institutional adjustment. A better understanding of this complex phenomenon will help bring clarity to the tensions between innovation and incumbency.

Notes

Introduction

1. I got early inspiration for this book and its title from Joel Mokyr, "Innovation and Its Enemies: The Economic and Political Roots of Technological Inertia," in Mancur Olson and Satu Kähköhnen, eds., *A Not-so-Dismal Science: A Broader View of Economies and Societies* (New York: Oxford University Press, 2000).

2. Joseph A. Schumpeter, *The Theory of Economic Development* (Cambridge, MA: Harvard University Press, 1934), 87.

3. Schumpeter, *Theory of Economic Development*, 87.

4. Schumpeter, *Theory of Economic Development*, 84.

5. For an excellent analysis of resistance to innovation for marketing and organizational behavior perspectives, see Oreg Shaul and Jacob Goldenberg, *Resistance to Innovation: Its Sources and Manifestation* (Chicago: University of Chicago Press, 2015).

6. James Wei, *Great Inventions That Changed the World* (Hoboken, NJ: John Wiley, 2012), stands in sharp contrast with Julie Halls, *Inventions That Didn't Change the World* (London: Thames & Hudson, 2014).

7. Adam Burgess, *Cellular Phones, Public Fears, and a Culture of Precaution* (Cambridge: Cambridge University Press, 2004), 2.

8. The essence of technology and its relationship with humanity have been a subject of extensive philosophical exploration. See, for example, Martin Heidegger, *The Question Concerning Technology and Other Essays*, trans. William Lovitt (New York: Harper and Row, 1977); Michael E. Zimmerman, *Heidegger's Confrontation with Modernity: Technology, Politics, and Art* (Bloomington: Indiana University Press, 1990).

9. Ulrich Dolata, *The Transformative Capacity of New Technologies: A Theory of Sociotechnical Change* (London: Routledge, 2013).

10. John Grin, Jan Rotmans, and Johan Schot, *Transitions to Sustainable Development: New Directions in the Study of Long Term Transformative Change* (New York: Routledge, 2010); and Pamela Matson, William C. Clark, and Krister Andersson, *Pursuing Sustainability: A Guide to the Science and Practice* (Princeton, NJ: Princeton University Press, 2016).

11. For a Darwinian view of innovation, see George Basalla, *The Evolution of Technology* (Cambridge: Cambridge University Press, 1988).

12. David Ropeik, *How Risky Is It, Really? Why Our Fears Don't Always Match the Facts* (New York: McGraw-Hill, 2010).

13. Brian E. Wynne, "Public Engagement as Means of Restoring Trust in Science: Hitting the Notes, but Missing the Music?," *Community Genetics* 9, no. 3 (2006): 211–220.

14. Paul B. Thompson, "Need and Safety: The Nuclear Power Debate," *Environmental Ethics* 6, no. 1 (1984): 57–69. Dual-use concerns are also a major area of concern in relation to emerging technologies. See, for example, Jonathan B. Tucker, *Innovation, Dual Use, and Security: Managing the Risks of Emerging Biological and Chemical Technologies* (Cambridge, MA: MIT Press, 2012).

15. Such studies include Iain Gately, *Tobacco: A Cultural History of How an Exotic Plant Seduced Civilization* (London: Simon & Schuster, 2001); David Kinkela, *DDT and the American Century: Global Health, Environmental Politics, and the Pesticide That Changed the World* (Chapel Hill: University of North Carolina Press, 2011); Steve Maguire and Cynthia Hardy, "Discourse and Deinstitutionalization: The Decline of DDT," *Academy of Management Journal* 52, no. 1 (2009): 148–178; Peter Stegmaier, Stefan Kuhlmann, and Vincent R. Visser, "The Discontinuation of Sociotechnical Systems as a Governance Problem," in *The Governance of Sociotechnical Systems: Explaining Change*, ed. Susana Borrás and Jakob Edler (Cheltenham, UK: Edward Elgar, 2014), 111–131.

16. Naomi Oreskes and Erik M. Conway, *Merchants of Doubt: How a Handful of Scientists Obscured the Truth on Issues from Tobacco Smoke to Global Warming* (New York: Bloomsbury, 2010). For a related study on the harassment and defamation of scientists seeking to bring research to bear on justice, see Alice Dreger, *Galileo's Middle Finger: Heretics, Activists, and the Search for Justice in Science* (New York: Penguin, 2015).

17. See, for example, Michael W. Bauer, Andrew Jordan, Christoffer Green-Pedersen, and Adrienne Héritier, *Dismantling Public*

Policy: Preferences, Strategies, and Effects (Oxford: Oxford University Press, 2012); Stegmaier, Kuhlmann, and Visser, "Discontinuation."

Chapter 1

1. Eyal Ert and Ido Erev, "On the Descriptive Value of Loss Aversion in Decisions under Risk: Six Clarifications," *Judgment and Decision Making* 8, no. 3 (2013): 214–235.

2. National Academy of Engineering, *Grand Challenges for Engineering* (Washington, DC: NAE, 2008).

3. Graeme Laurie, Shawn Harmon, and Fabiana Arzuaga, "Foresighting Futures: Law, New Technologies, and the Challenges of Regulating for Uncertainty," *Law, Innovation and Technology* 4, no. 1 (2012): 1–33.

4. Ray Kurzweil, *The Singularity Is Near: When Humans Transcend Biology* (New York: Penguin, 2005).

5. "The overall collection of technologies bootstraps itself upward from the few to the many and from the simple to the complex. We can say that technology creates itself out of itself." W. Brian Arthur, *The Nature of Technology: What It Is and How It Evolves* (New York: Free Press, 2009), 21.

6. Dezhi Chen and Richard Li-Hua, "Modes of Technological Leapfrogging: Five Case Studies from China," *Journal of Engineering and Technology Management* 28, nos. 1–2 (2011): 93–108.

7. See, for example, Eric J. Topol, *The Creative Destruction of Medicine: How the Digital Revolution Will Create Better Health Care* (New York: Basic Books, 2013).

8. Nicholas G. Carr, *The Glass Cage: Automation and Us* (New York: Norton, 2014), 232.

9. Nathan Rosenberg, "Why Technology Forecasts Often Fail," *Futurist* 29, no. 4 (1995): 16–21.

10. Rachel Carson, *Silent Spring* (Boston: Houghton Mifflin, 1962).

11. Gary E. Merchant, Blake Atkinson, David Banko, Joshua Bromley, Edith Cseke, Evan Feldstein, Devin Garcia, et al., "Big Issues for Small Stuff: Nanotechnology Regulation and Risk Management," *Jurimetrics* 52, no. 3 (2012): 243–277.

12. Thomas Esper, "The Replacement of the Longbow by Firearms in the English Army," *Technology and Culture* 6, no. 3 (1965): 390.

13. Esper, "Replacement of the Longbow," 392.

14. Esper, "Replacement of the Longbow," 392–393.

15. Lynn T. White, *Medieval Technology and Social Change* (Oxford: Oxford University Press, 1962), 28.

16. Joseph A. Schumpeter, *The Theory of Economic Development* (Cambridge, MA: Harvard University Press, 1934), 66.

17. Richard Swedberg, "Rebuilding Schumpeter's Theory of Entrepreneurship," in *Marshall and Schumpeter on Evolution: Economic Sociology and Capitalist Development*, ed. Yuichi Shionoya and Tamotsu Nishizawa (Cheltenham, UK: Edward Elgar, 2007), 188–203.

18. Joseph A. Schumpeter, *Capitalism, Socialism and Democracy* (New York: HarperCollins, 2008), 82.

19. Hugo Reinert and Erik S. Reinert, "Creative Destruction in Economics: Nietzsche, Sombart and Schumpeter," in *Friedrich Nietzsche: Economy and Society*, ed. Jürgen G. Backhaus and Wolfgang Drechsler (Boston: Kluwer, 2005), 55–85.

20. See Esben S. Andersen, "Railroadization as Schumpeter's Standard Case: An Evolutionary-Ecological Account," *Industry and Innovation* 9, nos. 1–2 (2002): 41–78.

21. Schumpeter, *Capitalism, Socialism and Democracy*, 82.

22. Schumpeter, *Capitalism, Socialism and Democracy*, 83.

23. Norman Clark and Calestous Juma, *Long-Run Economics: An Evolutionary Approach to Economic Growth* (New York: Bloomsbury, 2014).

24. Joseph A. Schumpeter, *Business Cycles: A Theoretical, Historical and Statistical Analysis of the Capitalist Process*, vol. 1 (New York: McGraw Hill, 1939), 73.

25. Schumpeter, *Business Cycles*, 73.

26. Schumpeter, *Business Cycles*, 73.

27. Dan Yu and Chang Chieh Hang, "A Reflective Review of Disruptive Innovation Theory," *International Journal of Management Reviews* 12 (2010): 435–452.

28. Clayton M. Christensen, *The Innovator's Dilemma: When New Technologies Cause Great Firms to Fail* (New York: HarperCollins, 2010), xv.

29. Christensen, *The Innovator's Dilemma*, xv.

30. Constantinos Markides, "Disruptive Innovation: In Need of Better Theory," *Journal of Product Innovation Management* 23 (2006): 19–25.

31. Gerard J. Tellis, "Disruptive Technology or Visionary Leadership?," *Journal of Product Innovation Management* 23 (2006): 34–38.

32. Rebecca M. Henderson and Kim B. Clark, "Architectural Innovation: The Reconfiguration of Existing Product Technologies and the Failure of Established Firms," *Administrative Science Quarterly* 35 (1990): 9–30.

33. Michael L. Tushman and Philip Anderson, "Technological Discontinuities and Organizational Environments," *Administrative Science Quarterly* 31 (1986): 439–466.

34. Philip Anderson and Michael L. Tushman, "Technological Disconti- nuities and Dominant Designs: A Cyclical Model of Technological Change," *Administrative Science Quarterly* 35, no. 4 (1990): 604. For an attempt to stan- dardize the nomenclature for the concept of dominant design, see Johann Peter Murmann and Koen Frenken, "Toward a Systematic Framework for Research on Dominant Designs, Technological Innovations, and Industrial Change," *Research Policy* 35, no. 7 (2006): 925–952.

35. Erwin Danneels, "Disruptive Technology Reconsidered: A Critique and Research Agenda," *Journal of Product Innovation Management* 21 (2004): 246–258; Steven Keppler and Kenneth L. Simons, "Technological Extinctions of Industrial Firms: An Inquiry into Their Nature and Causes," *Industrial and Corporate Change* 6, no. 2 (1997): 379–460.

36. Constantinos Markides and Paul A. Geroski, *Fast Second: How Smart Companies Bypass Radical Innovation to Enter and Dominate New Markets* (San Francisco: Jossey-Bass, 2005).

37. Susana Borrás and Jakob Edler, "Introduction," in *The Governance of Socio-Technical Systems: Explaining Change*, ed. Susana Borrás and Jakob Edler (Cheltenham, UK: Edward Elgar, 2014), 11; originally in italics.

38. Joshua Gans, *The Disruption Dilemma* (Cambridge, MA: MIT Press, 2016).

39. Charles Edquist and Björn Johnson, "Institutions and Organisations in Systems of Innovation," in *Systems of Innovation: Technologies, Institutions and Organizations*, ed. Charles Edquist (London: Pinter; Washington, DC: Cassell Academic, 1997), 51–55.

40. Paul A. David, "Clio and the Economics of QWERTY," *American Economic Review* 75, no. 2 (1985): 332–337; Paul A. David, "Why Are Institutions the 'Carriers of History'? Path Dependence and the Evolution of Conventions, Organizations and Institutions," *Structural Change and Economic Dynamics* 5, no. 2 (1994): 205–220; W. Brian

Arthur, *Increasing Returns and Path Dependence in the Economy* (Ann Arbor: University of Michigan Press, 1994).

41. Paul Pierson, "Increasing Returns, Path Dependence, and the Study of Politics," *American Political Science Review* 94, no. 2 (2000): 251–267.

42. Arthur, *Nature of Technology*, chap. 3.

43. Arthur, *Nature of Technology*, 23.

44. Arthur, *Nature of Technology*, 28 (emphasis in original).

45. Arthur, *Nature of Technology*.

46. Stefaan Blancke, Frank Van Breusegem, Geert De Jaeger, Johan Braeckman, and Marc Van Montagu, "Fatal Attraction: The Intuitive Appeal of GMO Opposition," *Trends in Plant Science* 20, no. 7 (2015): 414–418.

47. Arne Öhman and Susan Mineka, "Fears, Phobias and Preparedness: Toward an Evolved Module of Fear and Fear Learning," *Psychological Review* 108, no. 3 (2001): 483–522.

48. Valerie Curtis, Michéal de Barra, and Robert Aunger, "Disgust as an Adaptive System for Disease Avoidance Behaviour," *Philosophical Transactions of the Royal Society B* 366 (2011): 389–401.

49. Joshua M. Tybur, Debra Lieberman, Robert Kurzban, and Peter DeScioli, "Disgust: Evolved Function and Structure," *Psychological Review* 120, no. 1 (2013): 65–84.

50. Blancke et al., "Fatal Attraction," 416.

51. Mary Douglas, *Purity and Danger: An Analysis of the Concept of Pollution and Taboo* (London: Routledge, 1966).

52. James H. Young, *Pure Foods: Securing the Federal Food and Drug Act of 1906* (Princeton, NJ: Princeton University Press, 1989); Gabriella M. Petrick, "'Purity as Life': H.J. Heinz, Religious Sentiment, and the Beginning of the Industrial Diet," *History and Technology* 27, no. 1 (2011): 37–64.

53. Martijntje Smits, "Taming of Monsters: The Cultural Domestication of New Technology," *Technology in Society* 28, no. 4 (2006): 489–504.

54. Adam J. Berinsky, "Rumors and Healthcare Reform: Experiments in Political Misinformation," *British Journal of Political Science*, published online June 19, 2015, doi: http://dx.doi.org/10.1017/S0007123415000186.

55. Maarten Boudry, Stefaan Blancke, and Masimo Pigliucci, "What Makes Weird Beliefs Thrive? The Epidemiology of Pseudoscience," *Philosophical Psychology* 28, no. 8 (2014): 1177–1198.

56. Katrina Navickas, "Luddism, Incendiarism and the Defence of Rural 'Task-Scapes' in 1812," *Northern History* 48, no. 1 (2011): 59–73.

57. Adrian Randall, *Before the Luddites: Custom, Community and Machinery in the English Woollen Industry, 1776–1809* (Cambridge: Cambridge University Press, 1991).

58. Adrian Randall and Andres Charlesworth, eds., *Moral Economy and Popular Protest: Crowds, Conflict, and Authority* (New York: St. Martin's Press, 1999).

59. See, for example, the implications of innovation of naval doctrine: Haico te Kulve and Wim A. Smit, "Novel Naval Technologies: Sustaining or Disrupting Naval Doctrine," *Technological Forecasting and Social Change* 77, no. 7 (2010): 999–1013.

60. Elting E. Morison, *Men, Machines, and Modern Times* (Cambridge, MA: MIT Press, 1966): 17–44.

61. Eric Hobsbawm, "The Machine Breakers," *Past and Present* 1, no. 1 (1952): 59.

62. Hobsbawm, "The Machine Breakers," 60.

63. Hobsbawm, "The Machine Breakers," 65.

64. Adrian Randall, "The 'Lessons' of Luddism," *Endeavour* 22, no. 4 (1998): 152–155.

65. See, for example, Martin W. Bauer, ed., *Resistance to New Technology: Nuclear Power, Information Technology and Biotechnology* (Cambridge: Cambridge University Press, 1995).

66. Schumpeter, *Theory of Economic Development*, 58.

67. Schumpeter, *Theory of Economic Development*, 64 n. 1.

68. For a review of the role of innovation in sustainability, see Jochen Markard, Rob Raven, and Bernhard Truffer, "Sustainability Transitions: An Emerging Field of Research and Its Prospects," *Research Policy* 41, no. 6 (2012): 955–967; Staffan Jacobsson and Anna Bergek, "Innovation System Analyses and Sustainability Transitions: Contributions and Suggestions for Research," *Environmental Innovation and Societal Transitions* 1, no. 1 (2011): 41–57; Adrian Smith, Jan-Peter Voß, and John Grin, "Innovation Studies and Sustainability

Transitions: The Allure of the Multi-level Perspective and Its Challenges," *Research Policy* 39, no. 4 (2010): 435–448; and Xiaolan Fu and Jing Zhang, "Technology Transfer, Indigenous Innovation and Leapfrogging in Green Technology: The Solar-PV Industry in China and India," *Journal of Chinese Economic and Business Studies* 9, no. 4 (2011): 329–347.

69. The same dynamics apply to the process of scientific discoveries: Simon S. Duncan, "The Isolation of Scientific Discovery: Indifference and Resistance to a New Idea," *Science Studies* 4, no. 2 (1974): 109–134.

70. Joel Mokyr, "Technological Inertia in Economic History," *Journal of Economic History* 52, no. 2 (1992): 327.

71. Charles Seife, *Zero: The Biography of a Dangerous Idea* (New York: Penguin, 2000): 6.

72. Alfred North Whitehead, *An Introduction to Mathematics* (New York: Henry Holt, 1911), 63.

73. Mokyr, "Technological Inertia," 328.

74. Mokyr, "Technological Inertia," 329.

75. Mokyr, "Technological Inertia," 330 n. 17. An extension of this view clarifies the relationship between guilds and market size: "For small markets, firm profits are insufficient to cover the fixed cost of adopting the new technology, and hence, specialized workers have no reason to form guilds; for intermediate sized markets, firm profits are large enough to cover the higher fixed costs, but not large enough to defeat workers' resistance, and so workers form guilds and block adoption; and for large markets, these profits are sufficiently large to overcome worker resistance and so guilds disband and the more productive technology diffuses throughout the economy." Klaus Desmet and Stephen L. Parente, "Resistance to Technology Adoption: The Rise and Decline of Guilds," *Review of Economic Dynamics* 17 (2013): 437–458.

76. See, for example, Rachel Schurman and William A. Munro, *Fighting for the Future of Food: Activists versus Agribusiness in the Struggle over Biotechnology* (Minneapolis: University of Minnesota Press, 2010).

77. Mokyr, "Technological Inertia," 332.

78. Bruce J. Hunt, "'Practice vs. Theory': The British Electrical Debate, 1880–1891," *ISIS* 74, no. 3 (1983): 235–283.

79. A. D. Farr, "Early Opposition to Obstetric Anaesthesia," *Anaesthesia* 35 (1980): 902.

80. Rachel Meyer and Sukumar P. Desai, "Accepting Pain over Comfort: Resistance to the Use of Anesthesia in the Mid-19th Century," *Journal of Anesthesia History* 1, no. 4 (October 2015): 115–121. For a similar discussion over blood pressure instruments, see Hughes Evans, "Losing Touch: The Controversy over the Introduction of Blood Pressure Instruments into Medicine," *Technology and Culture* 34, no. 4 (October 1993): 784–807.

81. Mokyr, "Technological Inertia," 332–336.

82. Joseph LaDou, Barry Castleman, Arthur Frank, Michael Gochfeld, Morris Greenberg, James Huff, Tushar Kant Joshi, et al., "The Case for a Global Ban on Asbestos," *Environmental Health Perspectives* 118, no. 7 (2010): 897–901.

83. Patrick Bond, "Emissions Trading, New Enclosures and Eco-social Contestation," *Antipode* 44, no. 3 (2012): 684–701.

84. John S. Daniel, Susan Solomon, Todd J. Sanford, Mack McFarland, Jan S. Fuglestvedt, and Pierre Friedlingstein, "Limitations of Single-Basket Trading: Lessons from the Montreal Protocol for Climate Policy," *Climatic Change* 111, no. 2 (2012): 241–248.

85. Amitai Etzioni, "The Great Drone Debate," *Military Review* 93, no. 2 (2013): 2–13.

86. Thomas R. Wellock, *Preserving the Nation: The Conservation and Environmental Movements, 1870–2000* (Wheeling, IL: Harlan Davidson, 2007).

87. Max H. Bazerman and Don Moore, *Judgment in Managerial Decision Making* (New York: Wiley, 2008).

88. Charles Duhigg, *The Power of Habit: Why We Do What We Do in Life and Business* (New York: Random House, 2012).

89. Jagdish N. Sheth, "Psychology of Innovation Resistance: The Less Developed Concept (LDC) in Diffusion Research," in *Research in Marketing*, vol. 4, ed. Jagdish N. Sheth (Greenwich, CT: JAI Press, 1981), 273–282.

90. Sheth, "Psychology of Innovation Resistance."

91. Daniel Kahneman and Amos Tversky, "Prospect Theory: An Analysis of Decision under Risk," *Econometrica* 47, no. 2 (1979): 263–292.

92. For a more detailed explanation, see Daniel Kahneman and Amos Tversky, "Choices, Frames, and Values," *American Psychologist* 39, no. 4 (1984): 341–350; and Daniel Kahneman, *Thinking, Fast and Slow* (New York: Farrar, Straus and Giroux, 2011).

93. Bazerman and Moore, *Judgment*.

94. William Samuelson and Richard Zeckhauser, "Status Quo Bias in Decision Making," *Journal of Risk and Uncertainty* 1 (1988): 7–59.

95. Bazerman and Moore, *Judgment*.

96. Ilans Ritov and Jonathan Baron, "Reluctance to Vaccinate: Omission Bias and Ambiguity," *Journal of Behavioral Decision Making* 3 (1990): 263–277.

97. Ritov and Baron, "Reluctance to Vaccinate"; Daniel Kahneman and Dale T. Miller, "Norm Theory: Comparing Reality to Its Alternatives," *Psychological Review* 93, no. 2 (1986): 136–153.

98. Ritov and Baron, "Reluctance to Vaccinate."

99. Nidhi Gupta, Arnout Fischer, and Lynn Frewer, "Socio-psychological Determinants of Public Acceptance of Technologies: A Review," *Public Understanding of Science* 22 (2012): 817–831.

100. Hee-Dong Yang and Youngjin Yoo, "It's All about Attitude: Revisiting the Technology Acceptance Model," *Decision Support Systems* 38, no. 1 (2003): 19–31.

101. Kahneman and Tversky, "Prospect Theory."

102. Jennifer L. Dunn, "The Politics of Empathy: Social Movements and Victim Repertoires," *Sociological Focus* 37, no. 3 (2004): 237.

103. Nathan Rosenberg, "The Direction of Technological Change: Inducement Mechanisms and Focusing Devices," *Economic Development and Cultural Change* 18, no. 1 (1969): 1–24.

104. "Gasoline-engine trucks succeeded not because they were better at doing what electric trucks were already doing (that is, displacing horses in urban areas) but because they offered the possibility of universal service, thereby creating an entirely new market." Gijs Mom and David A. Kirsch, "Technologies in Tension: Horses, Electric Trucks, and the Motorization of American Cities, 1900–1925," *Technology and Culture* 42, no. 3 (2001): 491–492.

105. Geoff Watts, "Turn On, Tune In, Stand Back," *New Scientist*, June 7, 2001, 50.

106. Succession is part of a large context of technological evolution as outlined by Michael B. Schiffer, *Studying Technological Change: A Behavioral Approach* (Salt Lake City: University of Utah Press, 2011).

107. Shane Greenstein, *How the Internet Became Commercial: Innovation, Privatization, and the Birth of a New Network* (Princeton, NJ: Princeton University Press, 2015).

108. Joel Mokyr, *The Gifts of Athena: Historical Origins of the Knowledge Economy* (Princeton, NJ: Princeton University Press, 2002), 257–258.

109. Tali Kristal, "The Capitalist Machine: Computerization, Workers' Power, and the Decline in Labor's Share within U.S. Industries," *American Sociological Review* 78, no. 3 (2013): 361–389.

110. Kjell Erik Lommerud, Frode Meland, and Odd Rune Straume, "Globalisation and Union Opposition to Technological Change," *Journal of International Economics* 68, no. 1 (2006): 1–23.

111. For a detailed history of Bell Labs, see Jon Gertner, *The Idea Factory: Bell Labs and the Great Age of American Innovation* (New York: Penguin, 2012).

112. Mark Clark, "Suppressing Innovation: Bell Laboratories and Magnetic Recording," *Technology and Culture* 34, no. 3 (1993): 534.

113. Clark, "Suppressing Innovation," 534.

114. Frank W. Geels, "Regime Resistance against Low-Carbon Transitions: Introducing Politics and Power into the Multi-Level Perspective," *Theory, Culture and Society* 31, no. 5 (2014): 21–40.

115. Similar dynamics of success are evident in the field of scientific research as illustrated in Thomas Kuhn, *The Structure of Scientific Revolutions* (Chicago: University of Chicago Press, 1962).

Chapter 2

1. Suzanne Bush, "Coffee Cleared in Chemical Court," *BBC News*, September 30, 2003.

2. Bush, "Coffee Cleared."

3. Joseph A. Schumpeter, *Business Cycles: A Theoretical, Historical and Statistical Analysis of the Capitalist Process*, vol. 1 (New York: McGraw Hill, 1939), 73.

4. Calestous Juma, *The Gene Hunters: Biotechnology and the Scramble for Seeds* (Princeton, NJ: Princeton University Press, 1989), 41.

5. Brian W. Beeley, "The Turkish Village Coffeehouse as a Social Institution," *Geographical Review* 60, no. 4 (1970): 475–493.

6. William H. Ukers, *All about Coffee* (New York: Tea and Coffee Trade Journal Company, 1922), 370.

7. Ukers, *All about Coffee*, 5.

8. Quoted in Jeffrey T. Schnapp, "The Romance of Caffeine and Aluminum," *Critical Inquiry* 28, no. 1 (2001): 249.

9. Lawrence E. Klein, "Coffeehouse Civility, 1660–1714: An Aspect of Post-courtly Culture in England," *Huntington Library Quarterly* 59, no. 1. (1996): 30–51.

10. Steven Pincus, "'Coffee Politicians Does Create': Coffeehouses and Restoration Political Culture," *Journal of Modern History* 67, no. 4. (December 1995): 807–834.

11. "The Sufis used coffee in the performance of their religious ceremonies, for they found that its wakeful properties incited them to mystical raptures during the performance of their lengthy and repetitive recantations." Markman Ellis, *The Coffee-House: A Cultural History* (London: Phoenix, 2004), 14.

12. Ralph S. Hattox, *Coffee and Coffeehouses: The Origins of a Social Beverage in the Medieval Near East* (Seattle: University of Washington Press, 1985), 33.

13. Edward Robinson, *The Early History of Coffee Houses in England* (London: Kegan, Paul, Trench, Trubner, 1893).

14. Bennett A. Weinberg and Bonnie K. Bealer, *The World of Caffeine: The Science and Culture of the World's Most Popular Drug* (London: Routledge, 2002), 14.

15. Hattox, *Coffee and Coffeehouses*, 119.

16. Hattox, *Coffee and Coffeehouses*, 56.

17. Hattox, *Coffee and Coffeehouses*, 56.

18. Hattox, *Coffee and Coffeehouses*, 56.

19. Rudi Matthee, "Coffee in Safavid Iran: Commerce and Consumption," *Journal of the Economic and Social History of the Orient* 37, no. 1 (1994): 27.

20. Weinberg and Bealer, *World of Caffeine*, 15.

21. Matthee, "Coffee in Safavid Iran," 29.

22. Ukers, *All about Coffee*, 547.

23. Mark Pendergast, *Uncommon Grounds: The History of Coffee and How It Transformed Our World*, rev. ed. (New York: Basic Books, 2010), 8.

24. Ukers, *All about Coffee*, 31.

25. Ukers, *All about Coffee*, 31.

26. Pendergast, *Uncommon Grounds*, 8.

27. Such visual allusions seeking to stigmatize were not uncommon. Potatoes were outlawed in Burgundy in the 1660s because it was thought that they caused leprosy, owing to similarities in appearance between the skins of sufferers and those of potatoes.

28 Weinberg and Bealer, *World of Caffeine*, 93.

29. Henry Hobhouse, *Seeds of Change: Five Plants That Transformed Mankind* (London: Sidgwick and Jackson, 1985), 93–137.

30. Denys M. Forrest, *Tea for the British: The Social and Economic History of a Famous Trade* (London: Chatto and Windus, 1973). Edmund Weller's poem *Of Tea, Recommended by Her Majesty* was written a year after Catherine's marriage, as part of the royal family's association with the promotion of tea consumption. The marriage brought some of Portugal's commercial interests in India under the purview of Britain.

31. Jacob later moved his business to London. See also Anthony Clayton, *London's Coffee Houses: A Stimulating Story* (London: Historical Publications, 2003).

32. Brian W. Cowan, *The Social Life of Coffee: The Emergence of the British Coffeehouse* (New Haven: Yale University Press, 2005), 92.

33. Weinberg and Bealer, *World of Caffeine*, 92.

34. Aytoun Ellis, *The Penny Universities: A History of the Coffee Houses* (London: Secker and Warburg, 1956).

35. Cowan, *Social Life of Coffee*, 95.

36. "The growth of coffee-houses has greatly hindered the sale of oats, malt, wheat, and other products. Our farmers are being ruined because they cannot sell their grain; and with them the landowners, because they cannot collect their rents." Ukers, *All about Coffee*, 64.

37. Ukers, *All about Coffee*, 72.

38. Robinson, *Coffee Houses in England*, 163.

39. "They come from it with nothing *moist* but their snotty Noses, nothing *stiffe* but their Joints, nor *standing* but their Ears: They pretend 'twill keep them *Waking*, but we find by scurvy Experience, they *sleep quietly* enough after it. A Betrothed *Queen* might trust her self a bed with one of them, without the nice Caution of a *Sword* between

them: nor can all the Art we use revive them from this Lethargy, so unfit they are for Action, that like young Train-band-men when called upon Duty, their *Amunition* is wanting; peradventure they *Present*, but cannot give *Fire*, or at least do but *flash in the pan*, instead of doing Execution." See http://www.staff.uni-giessen.de/gloning/tx/wom-pet.htm (italics in original).

40. A man's reply to the petition appeared in 1676, providing the medical, economic, and social benefits of coffee, and suggested that men might decide to migrate to other countries if women did not limit their attacks. The response, however, did not get as much visibility as the petition.

41. Robinson, *Coffee Houses in England*, 166. King Charles II had previously issued declarations aimed at protecting certain trades. For example, in 1660, he issued a proclamation urging his subjects to strictly observe Lent because it was good for the employment of fishermen.

42. Weinberg and Bealer, *World of Caffeine*, 160.

43. Robert Liberles, *Jews Welcome Coffee: Tradition and Innovation in Early Modern Germany* (Waltham, MA: Brandeis University Press, 2012), 133.

44. Liberles, *Jews Welcome Coffee*, 133.

45. "There are documents to show that throughout the fourteenth century the cargo of the vessels that set sail from Rostock, another of the Hansa ports, was chiefly beer. Their usual destination was Bruges; but the thievish Danes often plundered them in the Sound, and carried off the beer-casks in triumph to Copenhagen." H. E. Jacob, *Coffee: The Epic of Commodity* (New York: Viking Press, 1935), 54.

46. Jacob, *Coffee*, 54.

47. Ukers, *All about Coffee*, 46.

48. Ukers, *All about Coffee*, 47.

49. Marie Clark Nelson and Ingvar Svanberg, "Coffee in Sweden: A Question of Morality, Health, and Economy," *Food and Foodways* 5, no. 3 (1993): 239–254.

50. Mats Essemyr, "Prohibition and Diffusion: Coffee and Coffee Drinking in Sweden 1750–1970," in *Coffee in the Context of European Drinking Habits*, ed. Daniela Ball (Zurich: Johann Jacobs Museum, 1989), 87.

51. David Edgerton, *The Shock of the Old: Technology and Global History since 1900* (Oxford: Oxford University Press, 2007), 30.

52. Hattox, *Coffee and Coffeehouses*, 7.

53. Hattox, *Coffee and Coffeehouses*, 7.

54. Hattox, *Coffee and Coffeehouses*, 7.

55. Paul Slovic, ed., *The Feeling of Risk: New Perspectives on Risk Perception* (London: Earthscan, 2010).

56. Jennifer Smith Maguire and Dan Hu, "Not a Single Coffee Shop: Local, Global and Glocal Dimensions of the Consumption of Starbucks in China," *Social Identities* 19, no. 5 (2013): 670–684.

Chapter 3

1. F. A. al-Razzak, "The Kingdom of the Book: The History of Printing as an Agent of Change in Morocco between 1865 and 1912," PhD dissertation, Boston University, 1990, 224.

2. Emilie Savage-Smith, "Islam," in *The Cambridge History of Science*, vol. 4, ed. Roy Porter (Cambridge: Cambridge University Press, 2003), 656.

3. Fatma M. Göçek, *East Encounters West: France and the Ottoman Empire in the Eighteenth Century* (Oxford: Oxford University Press, 1987), 112.

4. Thomas F. Carter, "Islam as a Barrier to Printing," *Muslim World* 33, no. 2 (1943): 213.

5. Carter, "Islam as Barrier," 213.

6. Carter, "Islam as Barrier," 216.

7. Francis Robinson, "Technology and Religious Change: Islam and the Impact of Print," *Modern Asian Studies* 27, no. 1 (1943): 233.

8. Toby E. Huff, *Intellectual Curiosity and the Scientific Revolution: Global Perspectives* (Cambridge: Cambridge University Press, 2010), 129.

9. Jeremiah E. Dittmar, "Information Technology and Economic Change: The Impact of the Printing Press," *Quarterly Journal of Economics* 126, no. 3 (2011): 1133.

10. Dittmar, "Information Technology," 1133.

11. Savage-Smith, "Islam," 647–668.

12. Huff, *Intellectual Curiosity*, 130–131.

13. Robinson, "Technology and Religious Change," 232.

14. Salah al-Din al-Munajjid, "Women's Role in the Art of Calligraphy," in *The Book in the Islamic World: The Written Word and Communication in the Middle East*, ed. George N. Atiyeh (Albany: State University of New York Press, 1995), 147.

15. al-Munajjid, "Women's Role," 147.

16. al-Munajjid, "Women's Role," 147.

17. Robinson, "Technology and Religious Change," 234.

18. Constance E. Padwick, *Muslim Devotions: A Study of Prayer-Manuals in Common Use* (Oxford: Oneworld Publications, 1961), 119.

19. William A. Graham, *Beyond the Written Word: Oral Aspects of Scripture in the History of Religion* (New York: Cambridge University Press, 1987), 81.

20. William A. Graham, "Traditionalism in Islam: An Essay in Interpretation," *Journal of Interdisciplinary History* 23, no. 3 (1993): 511.

21. Robinson, "Technology and Religious Change," 235.

22. Franz Rosenthal, "'Of Making Many Books There Is No End': The Classical Muslim View," in Atiyeh, *Book in Islamic World*, 36.

23. Jared Rubin, "Printing and Protestants: An Empirical Test on the Role of Printing in the Reformation," *Review of Economics and Statistics* 96, no. 2 (2014): 271.

24. Dittmar, "Information Technology," 1133.

25. Elizabeth L. Eisenstein, *The Printing Revolution in Early Modern Europe*, 2nd ed. (Cambridge: Cambridge University Press, 2005).

26. Rubin, "Printing and Protestants," 271.

27. Dittmar, "Information Technology," 1141.

28. Adrian Johns, *The Nature of the Book: Print and Knowledge in the Making* (Chicago: University of Chicago Press, 1998).

29. U. Neddermeyer, "Why Were There No Riots of the Scribes?," *Gazette du livre médiéval* 31 (1997): 6.

30. Neddermeyer, "Why No Riots?," 6.

31. Lucien Febvre and Henri-Jean Martin, *The Coming of the Book: The Impact of Printing, 1450–1800*, trans. David Gerard, ed. Geoffrey Nowell-Smith and David Wootton (London: Verso, 1958), 288.

32. Rubin, "Printing and Protestants," 272.

33. Douglas Miller, *Armies of the German Peasants' War, 1524–26* (Oxford: Osprey Publishing, 2003).

34. Rubin, "Printing and Protestants," 273.

35. Febvre and Martin, *Coming of the Book*, 291.

36. Lewis W. Spitz, *The Protestant Reformation, 1517–1579* (New York: Harper & Row, 1985), 89.

37. Rubin, "Printing and Protestants," 272.

38. Febvre and Martin, *Coming of the Book*, 291.

39. Rubin, "Printing and Protestants," 273.

40. Rubin, "Printing and Protestants," 280–281.

41. Dittmar, "Information Technology," 1133.

42. Metin M. Coşgel, Thomas J. Miceli, and Jared Rubin, "The Political Economy of Mass Printing: Legitimacy and Technological Change in the Ottoman Empire," *Journal of Comparative Economics* 40, no. 3 (2012): 363.

43. Niyazi Berkes, *The Development of Secularism in Turkey* (New York: Routledge, 1998), 37–38.

44. Berkes, *Development of Secularism*, 40.

45. Berkes, *Development of Secularism*, 40.

46. Mohammed Ghaly, "The Interplay of Technology and Sacredness in Islam: Discussions of Muslim Scholars on Printing the Qur'an," *Studies in Law, Ethics, and Technology* 3, no. 2 (2009): 3.

47. Yasemin Gencer, "İbrahim Müteferrika and the Age of the Printed Manuscript," in *The Islamic Manuscript Tradition: Ten Centuries of Book Arts in Indiana University Collections*, ed. Christiane Gruber (Bloomington: Indiana University Press, 2009), 158.

48. Berkes, *Development of Secularism*, 40.

49. Michael W. Albin, "Early Arabic Printing: A Catalogue of Attitudes," *Manuscripts of the Middle East* 5 (1990–1991): 115.

50. Albin, "Early Arabic Printing," 115.

51. Savage-Smith, "Islam," 659.

52. Orlin Sabev, "The First Ottoman Turkish Printing Enterprise: Success or Failure?," in *Ottoman Tulips, Ottoman Coffee: Leisure and Lifestyle in the Eighteenth Century*, ed. Dana Sajdi (London: Taurus Academic Studies, 2007), 63–194.

53. Savage-Smith, "Islam," 657.

54. Robinson, "Technology and Religious Change," 233.

55. Muhsin Mahdi, "From the Manuscript Age to the Age of Printed Books," in Atiyeh, *Book in Islamic World*, 1.

56. Mahdi, "Manuscript Age," 1.

57. Mahdi, "Manuscript Age," 10–11.

58. Mahdi, "Manuscript Age," 11.

59. Mahdi, "Manuscript Age," 9–16.

60. Ghaly, "Interplay of Technology," 15.

61. Ghaly, "Interplay of Technology," 16.

62. Ghaly, "Interplay of Technology," 17.

63. Daron Acemoglu and James A. Robinson, *Why Nations Fail: The Origins of Power, Prosperity, and Poverty* (New York: Crown Publishing, 2012), 215.

64. Coşgel, Miceli, and Rubin, "Political Economy," 357.

65. Yakup Bektas, "The Sultan's Messenger: Cultural Constructions of Ottoman Telegraphy, 1847–1880," *Technology and Culture* 41, no. 4 (2000): 696.

66. Bektas, "Sultan's Messenger," 696.

67. Bektas, "Sultan's Messenger," 696.

68. Savage-Smith, "Islam," 658–659.

69. Merlyna Lim, "Clicks, Cabs and Coffee Houses: Social Media and Oppositional Movements in Egypt, 2004–2011," *Journal of Communication* 62, no. 2 (2012): 231–248.

70. Gencer, "İbrahim Müteferrika," 183.

Chapter 4

1. Bentley Glass, "Oleomargarine Territory," *Science*, n.s. 153, no. 3744 (1966): 1595–1596.

2. For a comprehensive analysis of the controversy, see David L. Seim, "The Butter-Margarine Controversy and 'Two Cultures' at Iowa State College," *Annals of Iowa* 67 (2008): 1–50.

3. Joseph A. Schumpeter, *The Theory of Economic Development* (Cambridge, MA: Harvard University Press, 1934), 86.

4. Geoffrey P. Miller, "Public Choice at the Dawn of the Special Interest State: The Story of Butter and Margarine," *California Law Review* 77, no. 1 (1989): 89.

5. Miller, "Public Choice," 90.

6. Richard A. Ball and J. Robert Lilly, "The Menace of Margarine: The Rise and Fall of a Social Problem," *Social Problems* 29, no. 5 (1982): 491.

7. Henry C. Bannard, "The Oleomargarine Law: A Study of Congressional Politics," *Political Science Quarterly* 2, no. 4 (1887): 549.

8. Bannard, "Oleomargarine Law," 549.

9. Miller, "Public Choice," 90–91.

10. Miller, "Public Choice," 91.

11. Ball and Lilly, "Menace of Margarine," 488–489.

12. Ball and Lilly, "Menace of Margarine," 489.

13. Ball and Lilly, "Menace of Margarine," 489.

14. J. H. van Stuyvenberg, "Aspects of Government Intervention," in *Margarine: An Economic, Social and Scientific History, 1869–1969*, ed. J. H. van Stuyvenberg (Liverpool: Liverpool University Press, 1969), 281–327.

15. Ball and Lilly, "Menace of Margarine," 491.

16. Ball and Lilly, "Menace of Margarine," 491.

17. W. T. Mickle, "Margarine Legislation," *Journal of Farm Economics* 23, no. 3 (1941): 568.

18. Ball and Lilly, "Menace of Margarine," 492.

19. Ball and Lilly, "Menace of Margarine," 492.

20. S. F. Riepma, *The Story of Margarine* (Washington, DC: Public Affairs Press, 1970), 5.

21. Ball and Lilly, "Menace of Margarine," 492.

22. It is particularly instructive that this debate was occurring when the "pure foods" crusade was in high gear: Lorine Goodwin, *The Pure Food, Drink, and Drug Crusaders, 1879–1914* (Jefferson, NC: McFarland, 1999).

23. Ball and Lilly, "Menace of Margarine," 492.

24. Katherine Snodgrass, *Margarine as a Butter Substitute* (Stanford, CA: Stanford University Press, 1930), 89–98; Riepma, *The Story of Margarine*, 85–107.

25. Mickle, "Margarine Legislation," 576.

26. Mickle, "Margarine Legislation," 570.

27. Miller, "Public Choice," 114–115.

28. Bannard, "Oleomargarine Law," 547–548.

29. Bannard, "Oleomargarine Law," 546.

30. Miller, "Public Choice," 125.

31. Miller, "Public Choice," 125–126.

32. Bannard, "Oleomargarine Law," 548.

33. Bannard, "Oleomargarine Law," 549.

34. Bannard, "Oleomargarine Law," 550.

35. Mickle, "Margarine Legislation," 571.

36. Mickle, "Margarine Legislation," 571.

37. Mickle, "Margarine Legislation," 571.

38. Mickle, "Margarine Legislation," 576.

39. Ruth Dupré, "'If It's Yellow, It Must Be Butter': Margarine Regulation in North America since 1886," *Journal of Economic History* 59, no. 2 (1999): 353.

40. J. S. Abbott, *False Advertising: An Exposé of the Propaganda against Margarine and the Margarine Industry* (Washington, DC: Institute of Margarine Manufacturers, 1928), 9.

41. Abbott, *False Advertising*, 13.

42. Abbott, *False Advertising*, 19.

43. Abbott, *False Advertising*, 5.

44. Abbott, *False Advertising*, 5.

45. Robert Ferber and George W. Ladd, "Trends in State Margarine Legislation," *Journal of Marketing* 24, no. 4 (1960): 65.

46. Ball and Lilly, "Menace of Margarine," 495.

47. William R. Pabst Jr., "Interstate Trade Barriers and State Oleomargarine Taxes," *Southern Economic Journal* 7, no. 4 (1941): 507.

48. L. D. Howell, "Internal Trade Barriers for Margarine," *Journal of Farm Economics* 25, no. 4 (1943): 802.

49. Pabst, "Interstate Trade Barriers," 509.

50. Howell, "Internal Trade Barriers," 803–804.

51. Howell, "Internal Trade Barriers," 804.

52. Dupré, "If It's Yellow," 356.

53. Dupré, "If It's Yellow," 356.

Chapter 5

1. Carolyn Dimitri, Anne Effland, and Neilson Conklin, *The 20th Century Transformation of US Agriculture and Farm Policy* (Washington, DC: United States Department of Agriculture, 2005).

2. Alan L. Olmstead and Paul W. Rhode, "The Agricultural Mechanization Controversy of the Interwar Years," *Agricultural History* 68, no. 3 (1994): 36.

3. Clarence H. Danhof, "Gathering the Grass," *Agricultural History* 30, no. 4 (1956): 169–173.

4. R. Douglas Hurt, *American Farm Tools: From Hand-Power to Steam-Power* (Manhattan, KS: Sunflower University Press, 1982), 133.

5. Wayne D. Rasmussen, "The Impact of Technological Change on American Agriculture, 1862–1962," *Journal of Economic History* 22, no. 4. (1962): 574.

6. Rasmussen, "Impact of Technological Change," 578; Wayne D. Rasmussen and Paul S. Stone, "Toward a Third Agricultural Revolution," *Proceedings from the Academy of Political Science* 34, no. 3 (1982): 174–185.

7. Robert C. Williams, *Fordson, Farmall, and Poppin' Johnny: A History of the Farm Tractor and Its Impact on America* (Urbana: University of Illinois Press, 1988), 11.

8. Williams, *Fordson*, 90.

9. Deborah Fitzgerald, *Every Farm a Factory: The Industrial Ideal in American Agriculture* (New Haven: Yale University Press, 2003), 97.

10. Fitzgerald, *Every Farm*, 97.

11. Alan L. Olmstead and Paul W. Rhode, *Creating Abundance: Biological Innovation and American Agricultural Development* (Cambridge: Cambridge University Press, 2008), 373.

12. Dinah Duffy Martini and Eugene Silberberg, "The Diffusion of Tractor Technology," *Journal of Economic History* 66, no. 2 (2006): 354–389.

13. Fitzgerald, *Every Farm*, 98.

14. George B. Ellenberg, "Debating Farm Power: Draft Animals, Tractors, and the United States Department of Agriculture," *Agricultural History* 74, no. 2 (2000): 553.

15. Ellenberg, "Debating Farm Power," 553.

16. Robert E. Ankli, "Horses vs. Tractors on the Corn Belt," *Agricultural History* 54, no. 1 (1980): 137.

17. Olmstead and Rhode, "Agricultural Mechanization Controversy," 39.

18. Olmstead, and Rhode, "Agricultural Mechanization Controversy," 39.

19. Olmstead and Rhode, "Agricultural Mechanization Controversy," 38.

20. Ellenberg, "Debating Farm Power," 553.

21. Ellenberg, "Debating Farm Power," 553.

22. Robert C. Williams, "Farm Technology and 'The Great Debate': The Rhetoric of Horse Lovers and Tractor Boosters, 1900–1945," in *At Home on the Range: Essays on the History of Western Social and Domestic Life*, ed. John R. Wunder (Westport, CT: Greenwood Press, 1985), 137–155.

23. Ellenberg, "Debating Farm Power," 547–548.

24. Ellenberg, "Debating Farm Power," 549.

25. Olmstead and Rhode, "Agricultural Mechanization Controversy," 45.

26. Olmstead and Rhode, "Agricultural Mechanization Controversy," 45–46.

27. Ellenberg, "Debating Farm Power," 563.

28. Ellenberg, "Debating Farm Power," 549.

29. Fitzgerald, *Every Farm*, 99.

30. Olmstead and Rhode, "Agricultural Mechanization Controversy," 41.

31. Randy Steffen, *The Horse Soldier* (Norman: University of Oklahoma Press, 1979).

32. Olmstead and Rhode, "Agricultural Mechanization Controversy," 51.

33. Olmstead and Rhode, "Agricultural Mechanization Controversy," 42.

34. Olmstead and Rhode, "Agricultural Mechanization Controversy," 47.

35. Olmstead and Rhode, "Agricultural Mechanization Controversy," 47.

36. Olmstead and Rhode, "Agricultural Mechanization Controversy," 48.

37. Olmstead and Rhode, "Agricultural Mechanization Controversy," 51.

38. Olmstead and Rhode, "Agricultural Mechanization Controversy," 52.

39. Philip L. Martin and Alan L. Olmstead, "The Agricultural Mechanization Controversy," *Science* 227, no. 4687 (1985): 601.

40. Martin and Olmstead, "The Agricultural Mechanization Controversy," 601.

41. Olmstead and Rhode, "Agricultural Mechanization Controversy," 35–53.

42. Hurt, *American Farm Tools*, 256; R. Douglas Hurt, *American Agriculture: A Brief History* (Ames: Iowa State University Press, 1994).

43. Ellenberg, "Debating Farm Power," 556.

44. Ellenberg, "Debating Farm Power," 556.

45. Ellenberg, "Debating Farm Power," 557.

46. For historical attempts to compare the two sources of power, see Naum Jansy, "Tractor versus Horse as a Source of Farm Power," *American Economic Review* 23, no. 4 (1935): 708–723.

47. For a similar discussion regarding the impact of railroads, see Robert W. Fogel, *Railroads and American Economic Growth: Essays in Econometric History* (Baltimore: Johns Hopkins Press, 1964).

48. Through the use of detailed counterfactual analysis, Richard Steckel and William White concluded that "mechanization in the production of farm products increased GDP by more than 8.0 percent, using 1954 as a base year." Richard Steckel and William White, *Engines of Growth: Farm Tractors and Twentieth-Century US Economic Welfare* (Cambridge, MA: National Bureau of Economic Research, 2012). See also Alan L. Olmstead and Paul W. Rhode, "Reshaping the Landscape: The Impact and Diffusion of the Tractor in American Agriculture, 1910–1960," *Journal of Economic History* 61, no. 3 (2001): 663–698.

49. Economic Research Service, *The 20th Century Transformation of US Agriculture and Farm Policy* (Washington, DC: United States Department of Agriculture, 2005).

50. See, for example, Ernesto Clar and Vicente Pinilla, "Path Dependence and the Modernization of Agriculture: A Case Study of Aragon, 1955–1985," *Rural History* 22, no. 2 (2011): 251–269.

51. William H. Friedland, "Engineering Social Change in Agriculture," *University of Dayton Review* 21, no. 1 (1991): 5–42.

52. Friedland, "Engineering Social Change," 25–42.

53. See, for example, Clar and Pinilla, "Path Dependence."

Chapter 6

1. AC and DC are two types of current used to conduct and transmit electrical energy. In other words, DC and AC form the basis of electricity through the flow of electrons. DC is electric current that is constant in value and flows in one direction. AC is electric current that reverses direction at regularly recurring intervals.

2. Thomas P. Hughes, *Networks of Power: Electrification in Western Society, 1880–1930* (Baltimore: Johns Hopkins University Press, 1983), 1.

3. For a detailed discussion of novelty and the associated indeterminacy as well as nonlinear jumps, see Joseph A. Schumpeter, "Development," *Journal of Economic Literature* 43, no. 1 (2005): 108–120.

4. Bruce G. Link and Jo C. Phelan, "Conceptualizing Stigma," *Annual Review of Sociology* 27 (2001): 363–385.

5. Michael B. Schiffer, *Power Struggles: Scientific Authority and the Creation of Practical Electricity before Edison* (Cambridge, MA: MIT Press, 2008), 1.

6. Richard Swedberg, *Explorations in Economic Sociology* (New York: Russell Sage Foundation), 97.

7. William P. Gerhard, *The American Practice of Gas Piping and Gas Lighting in Buildings* (New York: McGraw, 1908), 263.

8. Gerhard, *American Practice*, 263.

9. Gerhard, *American Practice*, 267.

10. Gerhard, *American Practice*, 2.

11. Gerhard, *American Practice*, 8–11.

12. Jill Jonnes, *Empires of Light: Edison, Tesla, Westinghouse, and the Race to Electrify the World* (New York: Random House, 2003), 55.

13. John C. Griffiths, *The Third Man: The Life and Times of William Murdoch, 1754–1839* (London: Andre Deutsch, 1992), 353.

14. "The actors that participated in the production and consumption of gas for lighting, as both individuals and organizations, had the makings of such an institutionalized field, extending from the coal manufacturers to the city-employed lamplighters, and including suppliers, customers, and investors alike." Andrew Hargadon and Yellowlees Douglas, "When Innovations Meet Institutions: Edison and the Design of Electric Light," *Administrative Science Quarterly* 46, no. 3 (2001): 485.

15. Jonnes, *Empires of Light*, 49.

16. Matthew Josephson, *Edison: A Biography* (New York: McGraw-Hill, 1959): 251.

17. Gerhard, *American Practice*, 271.

18. Hargadon and Douglas, "When Innovations Meet Institutions," 488.

19. Josephson, *Edison: A Biography*, 179.

20. Steven W. Usselman, "From Novelty to Utility: George Westinghouse and the Business of Innovation during the Age of Edison," *Business History Review* 66, no. 2 (1992): 254.

21. Jonnes, *Empires of Light*, 119.

22. Francis E. Leupp, *George Westinghouse: His Life and Achievements* (Boston: Little, Brown, 1918), 139–140.

23. Leupp, *George Westinghouse*, 139.

24. Jonnes, *Empires of Light*, 137.

25. Richard Moran, *Executioner's Current: Thomas Edison, George Westinghouse, and the Invention of the Electric Chair* (New York: Vintage Books, 2002), 53.

26. A. J. Millard, *Edison and the Business of Innovation* (Baltimore: Johns Hopkins University Press, 1993), 101.

27. Jonnes, *Empires of Light*, 202.

28. Jonnes, *Empires of Light*, 203.

29. Paul A. David, "Heroes, Herds and Hysteresis in Technological History: Thomas Edison and 'The Battle of the Systems' Reconsidered," *Industrial and Corporate Change* 1, no. 1 (1992): 171.

30. Robin Gregory, James Flynn, and Paul Slovic, "Technological Stigma," *American Scientist* 83, no. 3 (1995): 220–223; Erving Goffman, *Stigma* (Englewood Cliffs, NJ: Prentice-Hall, 1963).

31. Thomas P. Hughes, "Harold P. Brown and the Executioner's Current: An Incident in the AC-DC Controversy," *Business History Review* 32, no. 2 (1958): 145.

32. Hughes, "Harold P. Brown," 145.

33. Mark Essig, *Edison and the Electric Chair: A Story of Light and Death* (New York: Walker, 2003), 141.

34. Essig, *Edison and Electric Chair*, 141.

35. Essig, *Edison and Electric Chair*, 142.

36. Jonnes, *Empires of Light*, 172.

37. Craig Brandon, *The Electric Chair: An Unnatural American History* (London: McFarland, 1999), 52.

38. Essig, *Edison and Electric Chair*, 117.

39. Hughes, "Harold P. Brown," 151.

40. Brandon, *The Electric Chair*, 68.

41. Hughes, "Harold P. Brown," 152.

42. Jonnes, *Empires of Light*, 205.

43. Hughes, "Harold P. Brown," 159.

44. Hughes, "Harold P. Brown," 159.

45. Brandon, *The Electric Chair*, 25.

46. Jonnes, *Empires of Light*, 208.

47. Brandon, *The Electric Chair*, 177.

48. Essig, *Edison and Electric Chair*, 220.

49. Essig, *Edison and Electric Chair*, 220.

50. Essig, *Edison and Electric Chair*, 220.

51. Essig, *Edison and Electric Chair*, 220.

52. Essig, *Edison and Electric Chair*, 161.

53. Joseph P. Sullivan, "Fearing Electricity: Overhead Wire Panic in New York City," *Technology and Society Magazine* 14, no. 3 (1995): 9.

54. Sullivan, "Fearing Electricity," 11.

55. Essig, *Edison and Electric Chair*, 215.

56. Sullivan, "Fearing Electricity," 12.

57. Sullivan, "Fearing Electricity," 13.

58. Sullivan, "Fearing Electricity," 13.

59. Sullivan, "Fearing Electricity," 13.

60. Richard Swedberg, ed., *Explorations in Economic Sociology* (New York: Russell Sage, 1993), 235.

61. Schiffer, *Power Struggles*, 316.

62. Schiffer, *Power Struggles*, 315–316.

63. Frank L. Dyer and Thomas C. Martin, *Edison: His Life and Inventions* (New York: Harper, 1910), 264.

64. Walter G. Vincenti, "The Technical Shaping of Technology: Real-World Constraints and Technical Logic in Edison's Electrical Lighting System," *Social Studies of Science* 25, no. 3 (1996): 565.

65. For detailed discussions of the nontechnical shaping of technology, see Donald MacKenzie and Judy Wajcman, eds., *The Social Shaping of Technology: How the Refrigerator Got Its Hum* (Milton Keynes, UK: Open University Press, 1985); and Wiebe E. Bijker, Thomas P. Hughes, and Trevor J. Pinch, eds., *The Social Construction of Technological Systems: New Directions in the Sociology and History of Technology* (Cambridge, MA: MIT Press, 1987).

66. Susanne K. Schmidt and Raymund Werle, *Coordinating Technology: Studies in the International Standardization of Telecommunications* (Cambridge, MA: MIT Press, 2008).

67. Tom McNichol, *AC/DC: The Savage Tale of the First Standards War* (San Francisco: Jossey-Boss, 2006).

68. For a discussion of the complexities surrounding such issues, see Shelley McKellar, "Negotiating Risk: The Failed Development of Atomic Hearts in America, 1967–1977," *Technology and Culture* 54, no. 1 (2013): 1–39.

69. Timothy Kostyk and Joseph Herkert, "Societal Implications of the Emerging Smart Grid," *Communication of the ACM* 55, no. 11 (2012): 34–36.

70. David J. Hesse and Jonathan S. Coley, "Wireless Smart Meters and Public Acceptance: The Environment, Limited Choices, and Precautionary Politics," *Public Understanding of Science* 23, no. 6 (2014): 688–702.

Chapter 7

1. For a comprehensive review of the technical history of the industry, see Roger Thévenot, *A History of Refrigeration throughout the World*, trans. J. C. Fidler (Paris: International Institute of Refrigeration, 1979).

2. Oscar E. Anderson, *Refrigeration in America: A History of a New Technology and Its Impact* (Princeton, NJ: Princeton University Press), 8.

3. F. Tudor, *Ice House Diary*, August 12, 1805.

4. Gavin Weightman, *The Frozen-Water Trade: A True Story* (New York: Hyperion, 2003), 195.

5. Philip Chadwick Foster Smith, "Crystal Blocks of Yankee Candles," *Essex Institute Historical Collections*, 1961. http://www.iceharvestingusa.com/crystalblocks1.html.

6. Anderson, *Refrigeration in America*, 15.

7. Anderson, *Refrigeration in America*, 69.

8. Anderson, *Refrigeration in America*, 69.

9. Anderson, *Refrigeration in America*, 69.

10. Anderson, *Refrigeration in America*, 71.

11. Anderson, *Refrigeration in America*, 69.

12. Weightman, *The Frozen-Water Trade*, 214.

13. *Abraham Lincoln Proclamation*, no. 82, April 19, 1861.

14. Weightman, *The Frozen-Water Trade*, 224–225.

15. Susanne Freidberg, *Fresh: A Perishable History* (Cambridge, MA: Belknap Press of Harvard University Press, 2009), 25.

16. Jonathan Rees, *Refrigeration Nation: A History of Ice, Appliances, and Enterprise in America* (Baltimore: Johns Hopkins University Press, 2013), 55.

17. Rees, *Refrigeration Nation*, 63–64.

18. James Cullen, "To Ice!" *Ice and Refrigeration* 73 (1927): 162.

19. *Ice and Refrigeration* 73 (1927): 211–218, quoted in Freidberg, *Fresh*, 243

20. Lisa Mae Robinson, "Safeguarded by Your Refrigerator," in *Rethinking Home Economics: Women and the History of a Profession*, ed. Sarah Stage and Virginia B. Vincenti (Ithaca, NY: Cornell University Press, 1997), 60.

21. E. Whitehorne, "Household Refrigeration," *House Beautiful*, September 1921, 212–214.

22. J. Seymour Currey, *Chicago, Its History and Its Builders: A Century of Marvelous Growth* (Chicago: SJ Clarke, 1912), 67.

23. Joel I. Connolly, Thomas J. Claffy, and John J. Aeberly, "Difficulties Encountered in the Control of Mechanical Refrigeration," *American Journal of Public Health* 20, no. 3 (1930): 252–256.

24. *Ice and Refrigeration* 67 (October 1924): 239.

25. Jonathan Rees, "'I Did Not Know … Any Danger Was Attached': Safety Consciousness in the Early American Ice and Refrigeration Industries," *Technology and Culture* 46, no. 3 (2005): 546.

26. Rees, "I Did Not Know," 554.

27. It has since then built sixty-four laboratory, testing, and certification facilities supporting customers in 104 nations. In 2012 UL transformed itself from a nonprofit firm into a for-profit corporation. Its activities have expanded from its original electrical and fire safety base to cover a wider scope that includes environmental sustainability, safety and compliance education, hazardous material, water quality, food safety, and performance testing.

28. Anderson, *Refrigeration in America*, 115–116.

29. For a detailed review of the debate over refrigerated foods, see Susanne E. Freiberg, "The Triumph of the Egg," *Comparative Studies in Society and History* 50, no. 2 (2008): 400–423.

30. Frank Horne, "Some Aspects of Food Conservation by Refrigeration," *Annals of the American Academy of Political and Social Science* 50 (1913): 4; Lorian P. Jefferson, "Cold Storage," *American Political Science Review* 5, no. 4 (1911): 573–574.

31. Jefferson, "Cold Storage," 573–574.

32. Anderson, *Refrigeration in America*, 131.

33. Commonwealth of Massachusetts, *Report of the Commission to Investigate the Subject of the Cold Storage of Food and of Food Products Kept in Cold Storage* (Boston: Wright & Potter, January 1912), 269.

34. Commonwealth of Massachusetts, *Report of the Commission*, 272.

35. Commonwealth of Massachusetts, *Report of the Commission*, 269.

36. Barry K. Goodwin, Thomas Grennes, and Lee A. Craig, "Mechanical Refrigeration and the Integration of Perishable Commodity Markets," *Explorations in Economic History* 39, no. 2 (2002): 154–182.

37. Lee A. Craig, Barry K. Goodwin, and Thomas Grennes, "The Effect of Mechanical Refrigeration on Nutrition in the United States," *Social Science History* 28, no. 2 (2004): 325–336.

38. Anderson, *Refrigeration in America*, 140.

39. Anderson, *Refrigeration in America*, 141.

40. "The National Education and Goodwill Advertising Campaign for the Ice Industry," *Ice and Refrigeration* 72 (1927): 158–161.

41. Gary D. Libecap, "The Rise of the Chicago Packers and the Origins of Meat Inspection and Antitrust," *Economic Inquiry* 30, no. 2 (1992), 242–246.

42. Anderson, *Refrigeration in America*, 58.

43. Anderson, *Refrigeration in America*, 99–100.

44. Ruth S. Cowan, "How the Refrigerator Got Its Hum," in *The Social Shaping of Technology: How the Refrigerator Got Its Hum*, ed. Donald MacKenzie and Judy Wajcman (Milton Keynes, UK: Open University Press, 1985), 202–218. For a review of how gender roles later shaped the design of refrigerators, see Shelley Nickles, "'Preserving Women': Refrigerator Design as Social Process in the 1930s," *Technology and Culture* 43, no. 4 (2002): 693–727.

45. Anderson, *Refrigeration in America*, 101.

46. *Transactions of the American Society of Refrigerating Engineers*, vol. 5 (New York: American Society of Refrigerating Engineers, 1912).

47. *Transactions*, 31.

48. Dirk van Delft, "Facilitating Leiden's Cold: The International Association of Refrigeration and the Internationalisation of Heike Kamerlingh Onnes's Cryogenic Laboratory," *Centraurus* 49, no. 3 (2007): 230–240.

49. Faidra Papanelopoulou, "The International Association of Refrigeration through the Correspondence of Heike Kamerlingh Onnes and Charles-Édouard Guillaume, 1908–1914," *Annals of Science* 66, no. 3 (2009): 351.

50. Papanelopoulou, "International Association of Refrigeration," 351.

51. Papanelopoulou, "International Association of Refrigeration," 349.

52. Papanelopoulou, "International Association of Refrigeration," 349–350.

53. Papanelopoulou, "International Association of Refrigeration," 353.

54. Richard O. Cummings, *The American Ice Harvests: A Historical Study in Technology, 1800–1918* (Berkeley: University of California Press, 1949), 101.

55. Freidberg, *Fresh*, 111–112.

56 Anderson, *Refrigeration in America*, 238.

57. Anderson, *Refrigeration in America*, 132.

58. Anderson, *Refrigeration in America*, 252.

59. Anderson, *Refrigeration in America*, 254.

60. For an illustration of how incumbent industries can stand in the way of otherwise important technical improvements that enhance public safety, see R. John Brockmann, *Exploding Steamboats, Senate Debates, and Technical Reports: The Convergence of Technology, Politics and Rhetoric in the Steamboat Bill of 1838* (Amityville, NY: Baywood, 2002).

61. T. M. Razykov, C. S. Ferekides, D. Morel, E. Stefanakos, H. S. Ullal, and H. M. Upadhyaya, "Solar Photovoltaic Electricity: Current Status and Future Prospects," *Solar Energy* 85, no. 8 (2011): 1580–1608.

62. Kelly S. Gallagher, *The Globalization of Clean Energy Technology: Lessons from China* (Cambridge, MA: MIT Press, 2014).

63. Jon Deutch and Edward Steinfeld, *A Duel in the Sun: The Solar Photovoltaics Technology Conflict between China and the United States* (Cambridge, MA: Massachusetts Institute of Technology, 2013). For an analysis of China's industrial subsidies policies and practices, see Usha C. Haley and George T. Haley, *Subsidies to Chinese Industry: State Capitalism, Business Strategy, and Trade Policy* (Oxford: Oxford University Press, 2013).

Chapter 8

1. Christian Schubert, "How to Evaluate Creative Destruction: Reconstructing Schumpeter's Appproach," *Cambridge Journal of Economics* 37, no. 2 (2013): 227–250.

2. David Morton, *Off the Record: The Technology and Culture of Sound Recording in America* (New Brunswick, NJ: Rutgers University Press, 2000).

3. Robert D. Leiter, *The Musicians and Petrillo* (New York: Bookman Associates, 1953), 12.

4. James P. Kraft, *Stage to Studio: Musicians and the Sound Revolution, 1890–1950* (Baltimore: Johns Hopkins University Press, 1996), 21.

5. Kraft, *Stage to Studio*, 24.

6. George Seltzer, *Music Matters: The Performer and the American Federation of Musicians* (London: Scarecrow Press, 1989), 16.

7. David Morton, *Sound Recording: The Story of a Technology* (Baltimore: Johns Hopkins University Press, 2004), 2–5.

8. David Suisman, *Selling Sounds: The Commercial Revolution in American Music* (Cambridge, MA: Harvard University Press, 2009).

9. Karin Bijsterveld, "A Servile Imitation: Disputes about Machines in Music, 1910–1930," in *Music and Technology in the Twentieth Century,* ed. Hans-Joachim Braun (Baltimore: John Hopkins University Press, 2002), 121.

10. Bijsterveld, "A Servile Imitation," 121.

11. Anders S. Lunde, "The American Federation of Musicians and the Recording Ban," *Public Opinion Quarterly* 12, no. 1 (1948): 46–47.

12. Kraft, *Stage to Studio*, 62.

13. Tim Anderson, "'Buried under the Fecundity of His Own Creations': Reconsidering the Recording Bans of the American Federation of Musicians, 1942–1944 and 1948," *American Music* 22, no. 2 (2004): 235.

14. Elizabeth Fones-Wolf, "Sound Comes to the Movies: The Philadelphia Musicians' Struggle against Recorded Music," *Pennsylvania Magazine of History and Biography* 118, nos. 1–2 (1994): 14.

15. Mark Katz, *Capturing Sound: How Technology Has Changed Music* (Berkeley: University of California Press, 2004), 9.

16. Katz, *Capturing Sound*, 24.

17. Anderson, "Buried under the Fecundity," 246.

18. Joel Mokyr, *The Gifts of Athena: Historical Origins of the Knowledge Economy* (Princeton, NJ: Princeton University Press), 277–278.

19. Randal C. Picker, "From Edison to the Broadcast Flag: Mechanisms of Consent and Refusal and the Propertization of Copyright," *University of Chicago Law Review* 70, no. 1 (2003): 281–296.

20. Lunde, "American Federation of Musicians," 49.

21. Lunde, "American Federation of Musicians," 47.

22. Seltzer, *Music Matters*, 30.

23. Seltzer, *Music Matters*, 31.

24. Leiter, *The Musicians and Petrillo*, 69.

25. Seltzer, *Music Matters*, 33–34.

26. Seltzer, *Music Matters*, 41.

27. Leiter, *The Musicians and Petrillo*, 132.

28. Seltzer, *Music Matters*, 40.

29. Leiter, *The Musicians and Petrillo*, 134.

30. Marina Peterson, "Sound Work: Music as Labor and the 1940s Recording Bans of the American Federation of Musicians," *Anthropological Quarterly* 86, no. 3 (2013): 795.

31. Peterson, "Sound Work," 795.

32. Peterson, "Sound Work," 791–823; Seltzer, *Music Matters*, 41.

33. Seltzer, *Music Matters*, 279.

34. Kraft, *Stage to Studio*, 140.

35. Anderson, "Buried under the Fecundity," 246.

36 "FDR Telegram to Petrillo," *Broadcasting and Broadcast Advertising* 27, no. 15 (October 1944): 11.

37. Anderson, "Buried under the Fecundity," 239.

38. Anderson, "Buried under the Fecundity," 239.

39. Scott DeVeaux, "Bebop and the Recording Industry: The 1942 Recording Ban Reconsidered," *Journal of the American Musicological Society* 41, no. 1 (1988): 129.

40. DeVeaux, "Bebop," 146.

41. DeVeaux, "Bebop," 148.

42. Anderson, "Buried under the Fecundity," 232.

43. Anderson, "Buried under the Fecundity," 232.

44. M. William Krasilovsky and Sidney Schemel, *The Business of Music: The Definitive Guide to the Music Industry*, 10th ed. (New York: Watson Guptill, 2007).

45. Andre Millard, "Tape Recording and Music Making," in Braun, *Music and Technology*, 158–167.

46. Lisa M. Zepeda, "A&M Records, Inc. v. Napster, Inc.," *Technology Law Journal* 17, no. 1 (2002): 71–90.

47. David E. Cavazos and Dara Szyliowicz, "How Industry Associations Suppress Threatening Innovation: The Case of the US Recording Industry," *Technology Analysis and Strategic Management* 23, no. 5 (2011): 473–487.

48. Stan J. Liebowitz, "File Sharing: Creative Destruction or Just Plain Destruction?," *Journal of Law and Economics* 49, no. 1 (2006): 1–28.

49. Mark Coleman, *Playback: From the Victrola to MP3, 100 Years of Music, Machines, and Money* (Cambridge, MA: Da Capo Press, 2005), 208.

Chapter 9

1. My work on agricultural biotechnology for Africa dates to the mid-1980s. My first major publication on the subject in 1989 was titled *The Gene Hunters: Biotechnology and the Scramble for Seeds*. This was nearly seven years before the first commercial release of the transgenic crops in North America. During 1995–1998 I served as the first permanent Executive Secretary of the Secretariat of the UN Convention on Biological Diversity. The focus of my work has been on identifying technologies that could contribute to sustainable development in Africa. I have advocated policies that seek to reduce the negative consequences of new technologies while maximizing their impacts. A fuller account of my views is available in *The New Harvest: Agricultural Innovation in Africa* funded by the Bill and Melinda Gates Foundation. No funding from the Foundation was used to support the preparation of this chapter or any part of this book.

2. Rachel Carson, *Silent Spring* (New York: Houghton Mifflin, 1962), 278.

3. Carson, *Silent Spring*, 278.

4. Marc Van Montagu, "It Is a Long Way to GM Agriculture," *Annual Review of Plant Biology* 62 (2011): 1.

5. David Ropeik, *Risk: A Practical Guide for Deciding What's Really Safe and What's Really Dangerous in the World Around You* (New York: Mariner, 2002).

6. The hazard-based approach is explicit in the Cartagena Protocol on Biosafety of the Convention on Biological Diversity. Its preamble states that the parties to the protocol are aware of "the rapid expansion of modern biotechnology and the growing public concern over its potential adverse effects on biological diversity, taking also into account risks to human health." Secretariat of the Convention on Biological Diversity, Cartagena Protocol on Biosafety to the Convention on Biological Diversity (Montreal: Secretariat of the Convention on Biological Diversity, 2000). 2.

7. There is considerable confusion over the use of terms such as "genetically modified organisms" (GMOs). In effect, all plant-breeding practices that confirm to crops new traits are forms of genetic modification. Popular objections have been focused on "transgenic crops" that are modified using genes from other species, though opposition

is also being extended to crops that are bred using gene-editing techniques that do not involve transferring traits across species.

8. Drew L. Kershen, "Health and Food Safety: The Benefits of Bt-Corn," *Food and Drug Law Journal* 61, no. 2 (2006): 197–235; Matin Qaim, "Benefits of Genetically Modified Crops for the Poor: Household Income, Nutrition, and Health," *New Biotechnology* 27, no. 5 (2010): 552–557; A. M. Mannion and Stephen Morse, "Biotechnology in Agriculture: Agronomic and Environmental Considerations and Reflections Based on 15 Years of GM Crops," *Progress in Physical Geography* 36, no. 6 (2012): 747–763; Graham Brookes and Peter Barfoot, "Global Income and Production Impacts of Using GM Crop Technology 1996–2013," *GM Crops and Food* 6, no. 1 (2015): 13–46; and Matin Qaim, *Genetically Modified Crops and Agricultural Development* (New York: Palgrave Macmillan, 2016).

9. N. Van Larebeke, C. Genetello, J. Schell, R. A. Schilperoort, A. K. Hermans, J. P. Hernalsteens, and M. Van Montagu, "Acquisition of Tumour-Inducing Ability by Non-oncogenic Agrobacteria as a Result of Plasmid Transfer," *Nature* 255 (1975): 742–743; M. D. Chilton, M. H. Drummond, D. J. Merio, D. Sciaky, A. L. Montoya, M. P. Gordon, and E. W. Nester, "Stable Incorporation of Plasmid DNA into Higher Plant Cells: The Molecular Basis of Crown Gall Tumorigenesis," *Cell* 11, no. 2 (1977): 263–271; R. Fraley, S. G. Rogers, R. B. Horsch, P. R. Sanders, J. S. Flick, S. P. Adams, M. L. Bittner, et al., "Expression of Bacterial Genes in Plant Cells," *Proceedings of the National Academy of Sciences* 80, no. 15 (1983): 4803–4807.

10. Organisation for Economic Cooperation and Development (OECD), *Biotechnology: Economic and Wider Impacts* (Paris: OECD, 1989); and Henk Hobbelink, *Biotechnology and the Future of World Agriculture* (London: Zed, 1991).

11. The term pesticide includes: antimicrobials, animal repellents, avicides, bactericides, disinfectants, fungicides, herbicides, insect growth regulators, insecticides, molluscicides, nematicides, piscicides, predacides, rodenticides, sanitizers, and termiticides.

12. Gaëtan Vanloqueren and Philippe V. Baret, "Analysis: Why Are Ecological, Low-Input, Multi-resistant Wheat Cultivars Slow to Develop Commercially? A Belgian Agricultural 'Lock-In' Case Study," *Ecological Economics* 66, nos. 2–3 (2008): 436–446.

13. Vanloqueren and Baret, "Analysis."

14. Vanloqueren and Baret, "Analysis."

15. Adrian Kay, "Path Dependency and the CAP," *Journal of European Public Policy* 10, no. 3 (2003): 441.

16. Kym Anderson and Rod Tyres, "Implications of EU Expansion for Agricultural Policies, Trade and Welfare," in *Expanding Membership of the European Union*, ed. Richard E. Baldwin, Pertti Haapararanta, and Jaakko Kiander (Cambridge: Cambridge University Press, 1995), 209–239; Richard E. Baldwin, Joseph F. Francois, and Richard Portes, "The Costs and Benefits of Eastern Enlargement: The Impact on the EU and Central Europe," *Economic Policy* 12, no. 24 (1997): 125–176.

17. Pari Patel and Keith Pavitt, "The Technological Competencies of the World's Largest Firms: Complex and Path-Dependent, but Not Much Variety," *Research Policy* 26, no. 2 (1997): 141.

18. Margaret Sharp, "The Science of Nations: European Multinationals and American Biotechnology," *International Journal of Biotechnology* 1, no. 1 (1999): 146.

19. Sharp, "Science of Nations," 146.

20. Sharp, "Science of Nations," 146.

21. "Failure to keep in touch can result in a cumulative loss of capabilities. Unless there are effective means of actively transferring the tacit knowledge from the American subsidiaries/partners back to the home laboratories of the European multinationals, it is the European science base that loses and suffers a cumulative falling behind the frontiers of scientific practice. This in turn could affect Europe's ability to create the high value-added jobs in this sector over the longer run." Sharp, "Science of Nations," 147–148.

22. Pierre-Benoit Joly, "*Bacillus thuringiensis*: A Century of Research, Development and Commercial Applications," *Plant Biotechnology Journal* 9, no. 3 (2011): 283.

23. National Academy of Sciences, *Genetically Modified Pest-Protected Plants: Science and Regulation* (Washington, DC: National Academy Press, 2000), 28.

24. Thomas R. DeGregori, *The Origins of the Organic Agriculture Debate* (Ames: Iowa State Press, 2004).

25. Qaim, "Benefits," 552–557.

26. Clive James, "ISAAA Brief 49-2014: Executive Summary," January 2014.

27. Pierre-Benoit Joly, "Innovating through Networks: A Case Study in Plant Biotechnology," *International Journal of Biotechnology* 1, no. 1 (1999): 67.

28. Joly, "Innovating through Networks," 68.

29. Monsanto divested itself of its chemical operations, which were reconstituted in 1997 as Solutia Inc. Solutia was later acquired by for $4.7 billion by Eastman Chemical Company, which itself was spun off from Eastman Kodak in 1994.

30. Office of Technology, *Assessment, Biotechnology in a Global Economy* (Washington, DC: Congress of the United States, 1991), 3.

31. Office of Technology, *Assessment*, 3.

32. Margaret Sharp, *The New Biotechnology: European Governments in Search of Strategy* (Brighton, UK: University of Sussex, 1985).

33. James F. Oehmke and Christopher A. Wolf, "Measuring Concentration in the Biotechnology R&D Industry: Adjusting for Interfirm Transfer of Genetic Materials," *AgBioForum* 6, no. 3 (2003): 134–140.

34. Lawrence Busch, "Can Fairy Tales Come True? The Surprising Story of Neoliberalism and World Agriculture," *Sociologia Ruralis* 50, no. 4 (2010): 331–351.

35. Prabhu L. Pingali and Greg Traxler, "Changing Locus of Agricultural Research: Will the Poor Benefit from Biotechnology and Privatization Trends?," *Food Policy* 27, no. 3 (2002): 223–238.

36. Gemma Farré, Koreen Ramessar, Richard Twyman, Teresa Capell, and Paul Christou, "The Humanitarian Impact of Plant Biotechnology: Recent Breakthroughs vs Bottlenecks for Adoption," *Current Opinion in Plant Biology* 13, no. 2 (2010): 219–225.

37. For a historical review of the evolution of the framework, see Emily Marden, "Risk and Regulation: US Regulatory Policy on Genetically Modified Food and Agriculture," *Boston College Law Review* 33, no. 3 (2003): 733–787.

38. National Academy of Sciences, *Introduction of Recombinant DNA-Engineered Organisms into the Environment: Key Issues* (Washington, DC: National Academy Press, 1987), 6.

39. National Academy of Sciences, *Recombinant DNA-Engineered Organisms*, 6.

40. National Academy of Sciences, *Agricultural Biotechnology Strategies for National Competitiveness* (Washington, DC: National Academy Press, 1987). This report built on an earlier study, National Academy of Sciences, *Genetic Engineering of Plants: Agricultural Research Opportunities and Policy Concerns* (Washington, DC: National Academy Press, 1984).

41. National Academy of Sciences, *Field Testing Genetically Modified Organisms: Framework for Decisions* (Washington, DC: National Academy Press, 1987). This report built on an earlier study, National Academy of Sciences, *Genetic Engineering of Plants*.

42. John N. Hathcock, "The Precautionary Principle: An Impossible Burden of Proof for New Products," *AgBioForum* 3, no. 4 (2000): 255–258.

43. Secretariat of the Convention on Biological Diversity, Cartagena Protocol, 3.

44. Secretariat of the Convention on Biological Diversity, Cartagena Protocol, 8.

45. Lucia Roda Ghisleri, Arturo Anadón, Miguel Á. Recuerda, Pedro Díaz Peralta, Fernando González Botija, Anselmo Martínez Cañellas, Alejandro Lago Candeira, Enrique Alonso García, and María Rosa Martínez-Larrañaga, "Risk Analysis and GM Foods: Scientific Risk Assessment," *European Food and Feed Law Review* 41, no. 4 (2009): 235–250.

46. Robert Falkner, "Regulating Biotech Trade: The Cartagena Protocol on Biosafety," *International Affairs* 76, no. 2 (2000): 299–313.

47. Ellen van Kleef, Øydis Ueland, Gregory Theodoridis, Gene Rowe, Uwe Pfenning, Julie Houghton, Heleen van Dijk, George Chryssochoidis, and Lynn Frewer, "Food Risk Management Quality: Consumer Evaluations of Past and Emerging Food Safety Incidents'," *Health, Risk and Society* 11, no. 2 (2009): 137–163.

48. Lynn Frewer, Chaya Howard, Duncan Hedderley, and Richard Shepherd, "What Determines Trust in Information about Food-Related Risks? Underlying Psychological Constructs," *Risk Analysis* 16, no. 4 (1996): 473–485.

49. Peter Jackson, "Food Stories: Consumption in the Age of Anxiety," *Cultural Geographies* 17, no. 2 (2010): 147–165.

50. Sarah Lieberman and Tim Stuart Gray, "The World Trade Organization's Report on the EU's Moratorium on Biotech Products: The Wisdom of the US Challenge to the EU in the WTO," *Global Environmental Politics* 8, no. 1 (2008): 33–52.

51. Noah Zerbe, "Feeding the Famine? American Food Aid and the GMO Debate in Southern Africa," *Food Policy* 29, no. 6 (2004): 593–608.

52. Ilona Cheyne, "Life after the Biotech Products Dispute," *Environmental Law Review* 10, no. 1 (2008): 52–64.

53. E. Jane Morris, "The Cartagena Protocol: Implications for Regional Trade and Technology Development in Africa," *Development Policy Review* 26, no. 1 (2008): 29–57.

54. John E. Losey, Linda S. Rayor, and Maureen E. Carter, "Transgenic Pollen Harms Monarch Larvae," *Nature* 399, no. 6733 (1999): 214.

55. Richard L. Hellmich, Blair D. Siegfried, Mark K. Sears, Diane E. Stanley-Horn, Michael J. Daniels, Heather R. Mattila, Terrence Spencer, Keith G. Bidne, and Leslie C. Lewis, "Monarch Larvae Sensitivity to Bacillus thuringiensis-Purified Proteins and Pollen," *Proceedings of the National Academy of Sciences* 98, no. 21 (2001): 11925–11930.

56. Around the same time, controversies erupted over the claimed discovery of Bt genes in local corn in the Oaxaca region of Mexico (later repudiated by the journal *Nature*, where it had been improperly published) and the detection of Bt genes of StarLink corn bred in the United States for animal feed in the human food chain.

57. Ann M. Showalter, Shannon Heuberger, Bruce E. Tabashnik, and Yves Carrière, "A Primer for Using Transgenic Insecticidal Cotton in Developing Countries," *Journal of Insect Science* 9, no. 22 (2009): 1–39.

58. David Zilberman, Holly Ameden, and Matin Qaim, "The Impact of Agricultural Biotechnology on Yields, Risks, and Biodiversity in Low-Income Countries," *Journal of Development Studies* 43, no. 1 (2007): 63–78.

59. Carl E. Pray, Jikun Whang, Ruifa Hu, and Scott Rozelle, "Five Years of Bt Cotton in China: The Benefits Continue," *Plant Journal* 31, no. 4 (2000): 423–430.

60. Marcel Kuntz, "Destruction of Public and Governmental Experiments of GMO in Europe," *GM Crops and Food* 3, no. 4 (2012): 262.

61. T. W. Sappington, K. R. Ostlie, C. Difonzo, B. E. Hibbard, C. H. Krupke, P. Porter, S. Pueppke, E. J. Shields, and J. J. Tollefson, "Conducting Public-Sector Research on Commercialized Transgenic Seeds: In Search of a Paradigm That Works," *GM Crops and Food* 1, no. 2 (2010): 1–4.

62. Kuntz, "Destruction," 262.

63. S. Gómez-Galera, R. M. Twyman, P. A. Sparrow, B. Van Droogenbroeck, R. Custers, T. Capell, and P. Christou, "Field Trials and Tribulations: Making Sense of the Regulations for Experimental Field Trials of Transgenic Crops in Europe, *Plant Biotechnology Journal* 10, no. 5 (2012): 511–523.

64. Kuntz, "Destruction," 263.

65. Ronal J. Herring, "Science and Society: Opposition to Transgenic Technologies: Ideology, Interests and Collective Action Frames," *Nature Reviews Genetics* 9, no. 6 (2008): 458–463; Klaus Amman, "Genomic Misconception: A Fresh Look at the Biosafety of Transgenic and Conventional Crops. A Plea for a Process Agnostic Regulation," *New Biotechnology* 31, no. 1 (2014): 1–17.

66. T. Bernauer, T. Tribaldos, C. Luginbühl, and M. Winzeler, "Government Regulation and Public Opposition Create High Additional Costs for Field Trials with GM Crops in Switzerland," *Transgenic Research* 20, no. 6 (2011): 1227.

67. Jörg Romeis, Michael Meissle, Susanne Brunner, Denise Tschamper, and Michael Winzeler, "Plant Biotechnology: Research Behind Fences," *Trends in Biotechnology* 31, no. 4 (2013): 222.

68. Jikun Huang, Ruifa Hu, Carl Pray, Fangbin Qiao, and Scott Rozelle, "Biotechnology as an Alternative to Chemical Pesticides: A Case Study of Bt Cotton in China," *Agricultural Economics* 29, no. 1 (2003): 55–67.

69. Shahzad Kouser and Matin Qaim, "Impact of Bt Cotton on Pesticide Poisoning in Smallholder Agriculture: A Panel Data Analysis," *Ecological Economics* 70, no. 11 (2011): 2105.

70. Kouser and Qaim, "Impact of Bt Cotton," 2111–2112.

71. National Research Council, *The Impact of Genetically Engineered Crops on Farm Sustainability in the United States* (Washington, DC: National Academies Press, 2010).

72. W. D. Hutchison, E. C. Burkness, P. D. Mitchell, R. D. Moon, T. W. Leslie, S. J. Fleischer, M. Abrahamson, et al., "Areawide Suppression of European Corn Borer with Bt Maize Reaps Savings to Non-Bt Maize Growers," *Science* 330, no. 6001 (2010): 222.

73. Hutchison et al., "Areawide Suppression," 222.

74. K. M. Wu, Y. H. Lu, H. Q. Feng, Y. Y. Jiang, and J. Z. Zhao, "Suppression of Cotton Bollworm in Multiple Crops in China in Areas with Bt Toxin-Containing Cotton," *Science* 321 (2010): 1676–1681; Yanhui Lu, Kongming Wu, Yuying Jiang, Yuyuan Guo, and Nicolas

Desneux, "Widespread Adoption of *Bt* Cotton and Insecticide Decrease Promotes Biocontrol Services," *Nature* 487 (2012): 362–365.

75. Eric W. Bohnenblust, James A. Breining, John A. Shaffer, Shelby Fleischer, Gregory Roth, and John F. Tooker, "Current European Corn Borer, *Ostrinia nubilalis*, Injury Levels in the Northeastern US and the Value of Bt Field Corn," *Pest Management Science* 70, no. 11 (2014): 1711–1719.

76. Mike Mendelsohn, John Kough, Zigfridais Vaituzis, and Keith Matthews, "Are Bt Crops Safe?," *Nature Biotechnology* 21 no. 9 (2003): 1009.

77. Alesandro Nicolia, Alberto Manzo, Fabio Veronesi, and Daniele Rosellini, "An Overview of the Last 10 Years of Genetically Engineered Crop Safety Research," *Critical Reviews in Biotechnology* 34, no. 1 (2014): 77.

78. Lu et al., "Widespread Adoption," 362–365.

79. Bruce E. Tabashnik, Aaron J. Gassmann, David W. Crowder, and Yves Carrière, "Insect Resistance to Bt Crops: Evidence versus Theory," *Nature Biotechnology* 26, no. 2 (2008): 199–202.

80. Tabashnik et al., "Insect Resistance," 510–521.

81. Bruce E. Tabashnik, "Evolution of Resistance to *Bacillus thuringiensis*," *Annual Review of Entomology* 39 (1994): 47–79.

82. G. Sanahuja, R. Banakar, R. M. Twyman, T. Capell, and P. Christou, "*Bacillus thuringiensis*: A Century of Research, Development and Commercial Applications," *Plant Biotechnology Journal* 9 (2011): 283–300; National Research Council, *Impact of Genetically Engineered Crops*.

83. Bruce E. Tabashnik and Fred Gould, "Delaying Corn Rootworm Resistance to Bt Corn," *Journal of Economic Entomology* 105, no. 3 (2012): 767–776.

84. Lin Jin, Haonan Zhang, Yanhui Lu, Yihua Yang, Kongming Wu, Bruce E. Tabashnik, and Yidong Wu, "Large-Scale Test of the Natural Refuge Strategy for Delaying Insect Resistance to Transgenic Bt Crops," *Nature Biotechnology* 33 (2015): 169–174.

85. Brian Dowd-Uribe and Matthew A. Schnurr, "Briefing: Burkina Faso's Reversal on Genetically Modified Cotton and the Implications for Africa," *African Affairs* 115, no. 458 (2016): 161–172.

86. For analysis of the case for crop-based universities in Africa, see: Calestous Juma. "Education, Research, and Innovation in

Africa: Forging Strategic Linkages for Economic Transformation," Discussion Paper 2016-01, Belfer Center for Science and International Affairs, Cambridge, MA: Harvard University, February 2016; Calestous Juma, *The New Harvest: Agricultural Innovation in Africa*, rev ed. (New York: Oxford University Press, 2015); and Calestous Juma, "Building New Agricultural Universities in Africa," HKS Faculty Research Working Paper Series RWP12-026, June 2012.

87. David Baulcombe, Jim Dunwell, Jonathan Jones, John Pickett, and Pere Puigdomenech, *GM Science Update: A Report to Council for Science and Technology* (London: UK Council for Science and Technology, 2014), 28.

88. Chidananda Nagamangala Kanchiswamy, Daniel James Sargent, Riccardo Velasco, Massimo E. Maffei, and Mickael Malnoy, "Looking Forward to Genetically Edited Fruit Crops," *Trends in Biotechnology* 33, no. 2 (2015): 63–64.

89. N. J. Baltes and D. F. Voytas, "Enabling Plant Synthetic Biology through Genome Engineering," *Trends in Biotechnology* 33, no. 2 (2015): 120–131.

90. S. Satyajit, A. S. Vidyarthi, and D. Prasad, "RNA Interference: Concept to Reality in Crop Improvement," *Planta* 239 no. (2014): 543–564.

91. Carolyn Y. Johnson, "Harvard, Yale Scientists Develop Technique to Make GMOs Safer," *Boston Globe*, January 22, 2015; and Daniel J. Mandell, Marc J. Lajoie, Michael T. Mee, Ryo Takeuchi, Gleb Kuznetsov, Julie E. Norville, Christopher J. Gregg, Barry L. Stoddard, and George M. Church, "Biocontainment of Genetically Modified Organisms by Synthetic Protein Design," *Nature* 518 (2015): 55–60.

92. Kevin Esvelt, "Strategies for Responsible Gene Editing," Project Syndicate, January 25, 2016, https://www.project-syndicate.org/commentary/crispr-gene-drive-editing-rules-by-kevin-m--esvelt-2016-01.

93. Kevin M. Esvelt, Andrea L. Smidler, Flaminia Catteruccia, and George M. Church, "Concerning RNA-guided Gene Drives for the Alteration of Wild Populations," *eLife* (2014): 2, http://dx.doi.org/10.7554/eLife.03401.

94. Oliver Tickell, "Pandora's box: how GM mosquitos could have caused Brazil's microcephaly disaster," *Ecologist*, February 1, 2016. The author of the article withdrew the claim but maintained the need for caution over the release of genetically modified mosquitoes.

95. David Baltimore, Paul Berg, Michael Botchan, Dana Carroll, R. Alta Charo, George Chruch, Jacob E. Corn, et al., "A Prudent Path Forward

for Genomic Engineering and Germline Gene Modification," *Science* 348, no. 6230 (2015): 36–38.

Chapter 10

1. Chris D'Angelo, "The Oceans Will Contain More Plastics Than Fish by 2050," *Huffington Post*, updated January 20, 2016.

2. Soon after, in December 2015, the FDA approved the use of transgenic chicken to produce a drug in its eggs that can be used to treat a rare disease. The chicken is not intended for human consumption, unlike AquAdvantage fish. However, just like the salmon, the chicken is considered to be an "animal drug" by FDA standards. See Rachel Becker, "US Government Approves Transgenic Chicken," *Nature*, December 9, 2015.

3. I first met Elliot Entis in February 1996 at meeting I hosted to start negotiations for what became the Cartagena Protocol on Biosafety of the Convention on Biological Diversity. My job as executive secretary involved meeting different constituencies represented at the meetings I was hosting. This meeting was naturally dominated by difference stakeholders with strong views on nearly every aspect of transgenic crops. The atmosphere was tense. That was the first year of the first commercial release of transgenic crops in North America. Entis belong to a class of his own. He was eager to learn how the outcome of negotiations on crops was likely to affect his vision and business on transgenic fish. I continued to follow developments regarding transgenic fish directly from Entis, who on several occasions would come to speak to my students. In most of his presentations he encountered diverse views, many of which were openly hostile. He would engage every argument with remarkable empathy. It was largely from these exchanges over the years that I decided to include a chapter in this book on transgenic fish. My interactions with Mr. Entis have been strictly academic. I have had no financial interests or exchanges with him and no connection to his business activities.

4. Dave C. Love, Jillian P. Fry, Michael C. Milli, and Roni A. Neff, "Wasted Seafood in the United States: Quantifying Loss from Production to Consumption and Moving Towards Solutions," *Global Environmental Change* 35 (2015): 1116.

5. Emmanuel Chassot, Sylvain Bonhommeau, Nicholas K. Dulvy, Frédéric Mélin, Reg Watson, Didier Gascuel, and Olivier Le Pape, "Global Marine Primary Production Constrains Fisheries Catches," *Ecological Letters* 13, no. 4 (2010): 501.

6. Boris Worm, Edward B. Barbier, Nicola Beaumont, J. Emmett Duffy, Carl Folke, Benjamin S. Halpern, Jeremy B. C. Jackson, et al., "Impacts of Biodiversity Loss on Ocean Ecosystem Services," *Science* 314, no. 5800 (2006): 787–790.

7. Chassot et al., "Global Marine Primary Production," 501.

8. Bernice Lee et al., *Resources Futures: A Chatham House Report* (London: Chatham House, 2012).

9. Lee et al., *Resources Futures.*

10. C. L. Hew, G. L. Fletcher, and P. L. Davies, "Transgenic Salmon: Tailoring the Genome for Food Production," *Journal of Fish Biology* 47 (Supplement A) (1995): 1–19.

11. Personal communication with Elliot Entis, September 2015.

12. Norman Maclean and Richard James Laight, "Transgenic Fish: An Evaluation of Benefits and Risks," *Fish and Fisheries* 1, no. 2 (2000): 146–172.

13. Shao Jun Du, Zhiyuan Gong, Garth L. Fletcher, Margaret A. Shears, Madonna J. King, David R. Idler, and Choy L. Hew, "Growth Enhancement in Transgenic Atlantic Salmon by the Use of an 'All Fish' Chimeric Growth Hormone Gene Construct," *Nature Biotechnology* 10, no. 2 (1992): 176–181.

14. Food and Drug Administration, *Briefing Packet: AquAdvantage Salmon*, Veterinary Medicine Advisory Committee, Food and Drug Administration Center for Veterinary Medicine, September 20, 2010, 109. http://www.fda.gov/downloads/AdvisoryCommittees/CommitteesMeetingMaterials/VeterinaryMedicineAdvisoryCommittee/UCM224762.pdf (accessed October 27, 2013).

15. William M. Muir and Richard D. Howard, "Possible Ecological Risks of Transgenic Organism Release When Transgenes Affect Mating Success: Sexual Selection and the Trojan Gene Hypothesis," *Proceedings of the National Academy of Sciences* 96, no. 24 (1999): 13853–13856.

16. Food and Drug Administration, *Briefing Packet.* http://www.fda.gov/downloads/AdvisoryCommittees/CommitteesMeetingMaterials/VeterinaryMedicineAdvisoryCommittee/UCM224762.pdf (accessed October 27, 2013).

17. Veterinary Medicine Advisory Committee, *Briefing Packet: AquAdvantage Salmon* (Washington, DC: Food and Drug Administration

Center for Veterinary Medicine, September 20, 2010). http://www.fda. gov/downloads/AdvisoryCommittees/ommitteesMeetingMaterials/ VeterinaryMedicineAdvisoryCommittee/UCM224762.pdf (accessed October 27, 2013).

18. Rachid Ganga, C. Wall, S. Tibbetts, M. Bryenton, A. Peters, D. Runighan, D. A. Plouffe, J. T. Buchanan, and S. Lall, "The Effect of Partial Inclusion of Plant Protein in Diets for Genetically Engineered Diploid and Triploid Atlantic Salmon *Salmo salar* on Growth, Feed Utilization, Body Composition and Ammonia Excretion," *World Aquaculture Society Meetings* (2013). https://www.was.org/meetings/ ShowAbstract.aspx?Id=28627 (accessed October 27, 2013).

19. National Research Council, *Animal Biotechnology: Science-Based Concerns* (Washington, DC: National Academy Press, 2002); Alison L. van Eenennaam, William M. Muir, and Eric M. Hallermann, *Is Unaccountable Regulatory Delay and Political Interference Undermining the FDA and Hurting American Competitiveness? A Response to Tim Schwab's "Is FDA Ready to Regulate the World's First Biotech Food Animal"?* (Washington, DC: Food and Drug Law Institute, 2013).

20. Pew Initiative on Food and Biotechnology, *Issues in the Regulation of Genetically Engineered Plants and Animals* (Washington, DC: Pew Initiative on Food and Biotechnology, 2004).

21. See, for example, Michael Bennett Homer, "Frankenfish ... It's What's for Dinner: The FDA, Genetically Engineered Salmon, and the Flawed Regulation of Biotechnology," *Columbia Journal of Law and Social Problems* 45, no. 5 (2011): 83–137.

22. Neil A. Belson, "US Regulation of Agricultural Biotechnology: An Overview," *AgBioForum* 3, no. 4 (2000): 268–280.

23. The FDA considers the recombinant DNA (rDNA) of genetically engineered animals a "new animal drug" (section 512 of the FD&C) because it is an "article intended to alter the structure or function" (as described in the FD&C) of the animal.

24. Food and Drug Administration, *Comment on Proposed Regulations and Submit Petitions* (Washington, DC: Food and Drug Administration, page last updated October 20, 2014). http://www. fda.gov/RegulatoryInformation/Dockets/Comments/default.htm (accessed January 20, 2016).

25. The appendix of the Environmental Assessment (EA) 35 of AquAdvantage Salmon states explicitly that the FDA consulted with

the National Marine Fisheries Service of the National Oceanic and Atmospheric Administration (Department of Commerce) and the US Fish and Wildlife Service of the Department of the Interior about the "no effect" finding of the environmental assessment and the scientific data underlying it. According to the EA report, both agencies agreed with the "no effect" determination. See Center for Veterinary Medicine, "AquAdvantage Salmon: EnvironmentalAssessment," FDA, November 12, 2015, http://www. fda.gov/downloads/AnimalVeterinary/DevelopmentApprovalProcess/ GeneticEngineering/GeneticallyEngineeredAnimals/UCM466218.pdf.

26. Van Eenennaam, Muir, and Hallermann, *Unaccountable Regulatory Delay*, 3.

27. Max H. Bazerman and Don Moore, *Judgment in Managerial Decision Making* (New York: Wiley, 2008).

28. Daniel Kahneman and Amos Tversky, "Prospect Theory: An Analysis of Decision under Risk," *Econometrica* 47, no. 2 (1979): 263–292.

29. Alison L. van Eenennaam, Eric M. Hallerman, and William M. Muir, *The Science and Regulation of Food from Genetically Engineered Animals* (Washington, DC: Council for Agricultural Science and Technology, 2011).

30. Van Eenennaam, Muir, and Hallermann, *Unaccountable Regulatory Delay*.

31. Personal communication with Elliot Entis, September 2015.

32. Center for Food Safety, *Food Safety Review*, Winter 2013, 1.

33. Center for Food Safety, *Food Safety Review*, Winter 2013, 1.

34. Center for Food Safety, *Food Safety Review*, Winter 2013, 1.

35. John Fiorillo, "Alaska's Don Young Pulls a Fast One with GM Salmon Vote," *IntraFish*, June 17, 2011. http://www.intrafish.no/global/news/ article288627.ece (accessed October 27, 2013). The author of this chapter testified before a congressional committee arguing that the United States served as a role model for emerging nations and needed to make decisions based on evidence.

36. Alaska Department of Fish and Game, "Commercial Fisheries." http://www.adfg.alaska.gov/index.cfm?adfg=fishingcommercial. main (accessed October 27, 2013).

37. Brady Dennis, "Genetically Altered Salmon Are Safe, FDA Says," *Washington Post*, December 21, 2012. http://articles.washingtonpost.

com/2012-12-21/national/36017637_1_ronald-stotish-aqu-abounty-technologies-atlantic-salmon (accessed October 27, 2013).

38. Van Eenennaam, Muir, and Hallermann, *Unaccountable Regulatory Delay.*

39. Food and Drug Administration, "Preliminary Finding of No Significant Impact: AquAdvantage Salmon," prepared by the Center for Veterinary Medicine United States Food and Drug Administration Department of Health and Human Services, May 4, 2012, 5. http://www.fda.gov/downloads/AnimalVeterinary/DevelopmentApprovalProcess/GeneticEngineering/Genetically EngineeredAnimals/UCM333105.pdf.

40. Jon Entine, "White House Ends Its Interference in a Scientific Review," *Slate*, December 21, 2012. http://www.slate.com/articles/health_and_science/science/2012/12/genetically_modified_salmon_aquadvantage_fda_assessment_is_delayed_possibly.html (accessed October 27, 2013).

41. Elliot Entis, "Market Introduction of Transgenic Aquaculture Products: An Overview of Societal Issues," in *Environmental Strategies for Aquaculture Symposium Proceedings*, ed. Ronald E. Kunnen (Ames, Iowa: North Central Regional Aquaculture Center Publications Office, Iowa State University, 2002), 35–42.

42. Entis, "Market Introduction."

43. Letter by Barney Frank, Member of US Congress, to Margaret Hamburg, FDA Commissioner, November 22, 2010.

44. See letter to President Obama, September 14, 2012. http://aquacomgroup.com/wordpress/wp-content/uploads/2012/09/Hindering-innovation-in-food-production-091412-1-3.pdf.

45. Personal communication with Elliot Entis, September 2015.

46. Robert H. Devlin, L. Fredrik Sundström, and Rosalind A. Leggatt, "Assessing Ecological and Evolutionary Consequences of Growth-Accelerated Genetically Engineered Fishes," *BioScience* 65, no. 7 (2015): 685–700.

47. Van Eenennaam, Muir, and Hallermann, *Unaccountable Regulatory Delay*, 3.

48. Sabrina Tavernise, "F.D.A. Nominee Clears One Hurdle, but Others Remain," *New York Times*, January 12, 2016.

Chapter 11

1. Frank W. Geels, *Technological Transitions and System Innovations: A Co-evolutionary and Socio-technical Analysis* (Cheltenham, UK: Edward Elgar, 2005).

2. Erik Brynjolfsson and Andrew McAfee, *The Second Machine Age: Work, Progress, and Prosperity in a Time of Brilliant Technologies* (New York: Norton, 2014), 257.

3. Hasan Bakhshi, Carl Benedikt Frey, and Michael Osborne, *Creativity vs. Robots: The Creative Economy and the Future of Employment* (London: Nesta, 2015), 6.

4. Martin Ford, *The Rise of the Robots: Technology and the Threat of a Jobless Future* (New York: Basic Books, 2015), 248; James Bessen, *Learning by Doing: The Real Connection between Innovation, Wages, and Wealth* (New Haven: Yale University Press, 2015).

5. David A. Mindell, *Our Robots, Ourselves: Robotics and the Myth of Autonomy* (New York: Penguin, 2015); and Murray Shanahan, *The Technological Singularity* (Cambridge, MA: MIT Press, 2015).

6. Bessen, *Learning by Doing*, 205.

7. Eric J. Topol, *The Patient Will See You Now: The Future of Medicine Is in Your Hands* (New York: Basic Books, 2015), 257–274.

8. Rachel A. Parker and Richard P. Appelbaum, eds., *Can Emerging Technologies Make a Difference in Development?* (New York: Routledge, 2012).

9. Michael S. Carolan, "Science, Expertise, and the Democratization of the Decision-Making Process," *Society and Natural Resources* 19, no. 4 (2006): 1339–1341.

10. Wiebe E. Bijker, Roland Bal, and Ruud Hendriks, *The Paradox of Scientific Authority: The Role of Scientific Advice in Democracies* (Cambridge, MA: MIT Press, 2009), 167.

11. Michael J. Feuer and Christina J. Maranto, "Science Advice as Procedural Rationality: Reflections on the National Research Council," *Minerva* 48, no. 3 (2010): 259–275.

12. Peter D. Blair, "Scientific Advice for Policy in the United States: Lessons from the National Academies and the Former Congressional Office of Technology Assessment," in *The Politics of Scientific Advice: Institutional Design for Quality Assurance*, ed. Justus

Lentsch and Peter Weingart (Cambridge: Cambridge University Press, 2011), 297–333.

13. For a review of the principles and structure of science and technology advice, see Calestous Juma and Yee-Cheong Lee, *Innovation: Applying Knowledge in Development* (London: Earthscan, 2005), 140–158.

14. For an outline of the elements of science and technology advice, see National Research Council, *Knowledge and Diplomacy: Science Advice in the United Nations System* (Washington, DC: National Academies Press, 2012), 13–20.

15. Calum G. Turvey and Eliza M. Mojduszka, "The Precautionary Principle and the Law of Unintended Consequences," *Food Policy* 30, no. 2 (2005): 145–161.

16. Marc A. Saner, "An Ethical Analysis of the Precautionary Principle," *International Journal of Biotechnology* 4, no. 1 (2000): 81–95.

17. Lisa F. Clark, "Framing the Uncertainty of Risk: Models of Governance for Genetically Modified Foods," *Science and Public Policy* 40, no. 4 (2013): 486.

18. Jan Nill and René Kemp, "Evolutionary Approaches for Sustainable Innovation Policies: From Niche to Paradigm?" *Research Policy* 38, no. 4 (2009): 668–680.

19. Frank W. Geels and Johan Schot, "Typology of Sociotechnical Transition Pathways," *Research Policy* 36, no. 1 (2007): 399–417.

20. Adrian Smith, Jan-Peter Voß, and John Grin, "Innovation Studies and Sustainability Transitions: The Allure of the Multi-level Perspective and Its Challenges," *Research Policy* 39, no. 1 (2010): 435–448.

21. Anil K. Gupta and Vikas Chandak, "Agricultural Biotechnology in India: Ethics, Business and Politics," *International Journal of Biotechnologiy,* 7, nos. 1/2/3 (2005): 212–227.

22. Calestous Juma and Ismail Serageldin, *Freedom to Innovate: Biotechnology in Africa's Development* (Addis Ababa: African Union and New Partnership for Africa's Development, 2007).

23. Mariana Mazzucato, "Financing Innovation: Creative Destruction vs. Destructive Creation," *Industrial and Corporate Change*, 22, no. 4 (2013): 851–867.

24. Joseph A. Schumpeter, "The Creative Response to Economic History," *Journal of Economic History* 7, no. 2 (1947): 155.

25. Joseph A. Schumpeter, "The Seventh Chapter of the Theory of Economic Development," trans. U. Backhaus, *Industry and Innovation* 9, nos. 1–2 (2002): 116.

26. Schumpeter, "Seventh Chapter," 116.

27. Sabrina Safrin, "Anticipating the Storm: Predicting and Preventing Global Technology Conflicts," *Arizona State Law Journal* 44 (2014): 899–953.

28. Mirella Kleijnen, Nick Lee, and Martin Wetzels, "An Exploration of Consumer Resistance to Innovation and Its Antecedents," *Journal of Economic Psychology* 30, no. 3 (2009): 244–357. For a discussion on ideas, see Bernard Barber, "Resistance by Scientists to Scientific Discovery," *Science* 134, no. 3479 (1961): 596–602.

29. The bill read, "Autonomous vehicle operators must be a licensed driver who possesses an autonomous vehicle operator certificate issued by the DMV. The operator will be responsible for monitoring the safe operation of the vehicle at all times, and must be capable of taking over immediate control in the event of an autonomous technology failure or other emergency. In addition, operators will be responsible for all traffic violations that occur while operating the autonomous vehicle. These operator requirements create the safeguard of a driver who is capable of taking control of the vehicle when needed." California Department of Motor Vehicles, "Summary of Draft Autonomous Vehicles Deployment Regulations," December 16, 2015: 2.

30. Bob Sorokanich, "California Proposes Tightened Regulations on Autonomous Cars," Roadandtrack.com, December 17, 2015.

31. R. Rycroft and D. Kash, "Path Dependence and the Modernization of Agriculture: A Case Study of Aragon, 1955–1985," *Technology Analysis and Strategic Management* 14, no. 1 (2002): 21–35.

32. Marie-Laure Djelic and Sigird Quack, "Overcoming Path Dependency: Path Generation in Open Systems," *Theory and Society* 36, no. 2 (2007): 161–186.

33. Bennett Alan Weinberg and Bonnie K. Bealer, *The World of Caffeine: The Science and Culture of the World's Most Popular Drug* (London: Routledge, 2002), 77.

34. Selma Akyazici Özkoçak, "Coffeehouses: Rethinking the Public and Private in Early Modern Istanbul," *Journal of Urban History* 33

(2007): 965–986; Brian W. Beeley, "The Turkish Village Coffeehouse as a Social Institution," *Geographical Review* 60, no. 4 (1970): 475–493.

35. Lawrence E. Klein, "Coffeehouse Civility, 1660–1714: An Aspect of Post-courtly Culture in England," *Huntington Library Quarterly* 59, no. 1 (1996): 30–51.

36. Jeffrey T. Schnapp, "The Romance of Caffeine and Aluminum," *Critical Inquiry* 28, no. 1 (2001): 244–269.

37. Christian Schubert, "Is Novelty Always a Good Thing? Towards an Evolutionary Welfare Economics," *Journal of Evolutionary Economics* 22, no. 3 (2012): 586–619; Christian Schunbert, "How to Evaluate Creative Destruction: Reconstructing Schumpeter's Appproach," *Cambridge Journal of Economics* 37, no. 2 (2013); 227–250.

38. Mariana Mazzucato, "Financial Innovation: Destruction vs. Destructive Creation," *Industrial and Corporate Change* 22, no. 4 (2013): 851–867.

39. Christopher Henke, *Cultivating Science, Harvesting Power: Science and Industrial Agriculture in California* (Cambridge, MA: MIT Press, 2008), 4.

40. Maarten Crivits, Michiel P. M. M. de Krom, and Joost Dessein, "Why Innovation Is Not Always Good: Innovation Discourses and Political Accountability," *Outlook on Agriculture* 43, no. 3 (2014): 147–155.

41. For a detailed account of market activists, see Hayagreeva Rao, *Market Rebels: How Activists Make or Break Radical Innovations* (Princeton, NJ: Princeton University Press, 2009).

42. William Leiss, *In the Chamber of Risks: Understanding Risk Controversies* (Montreal: McGill-Queens University Press, 2001), 292.

43. Thomas J. Holmes and James A. Schmitz Jr., "Resistance to New Technology and Trade between Areas," *Federal Reserve Bank of Minneapolis Quarterly Review* 19, no. 1 (1995): 1–17.

44. Stephen L. Parente and Edward C. Prescott, "Barriers to Technology Adoption and Development," *Journal of Political Economy* 102, no. 2 (1994): 298–321; Mancur Olson, *The Rise and Decline of Nations: Economic Growth, Stagflation and Social Rigidities* (New Haven: Yale University Press, 1982).

45. Robert L. Langer and Ralph Weissleder, "Nanotechnology," *Journal of the American Medical Association* 313, no. 2 (2015): 135–136.

46. Christopher Foster and Richard Heeks, "Analyzing Policy for Inclusive Innovation: The Mobile Sector and Base-of-the-Pyramid Markets in Kenya," *Innovation and Development* 3, no. 1 (2013): 103–119.

47. Topol, *Patient Will See You*, 6.

48. Topol, *Patient Will See You*, 257–274.

49. Jacqueline W. DePasse and Patrick T. Lee, "A Model for 'Reverse Innovation' in Health Care," *Globalization and Health* 9, no. 1 (2013): 1–7.

50. Jeremy Rifkin, *The Zero Marginal Cost Economy: The Internet of Things, the Collaborative Commons, and the Eclipse of Capitalism* (New York: Palgrave Macmillan, 2014).

51. Christopher Foster and Richard Heeks, "Conceptualising Inclusive Innovation: Modifying Systems of Inovation Frameworks to Understand Diffusion of New Technology to Low-Income Consumers," *European Journal of Development Research* 25. no. 3 (2013): 333.

52. Joanna Chataway, Rebecca Hanlin, and Raphael Kaplinsky, "Inclusive Innovation: An Architecture for Policy Development," *Innovation and Development* 4, no. 1 (2014): 33–54.

53. Peter N. Thomond and Fioina Lettice, "Allocating Resources to Disruptive Innovation Projects: Challenging Mental Models and Overcoming Management Resistance," *International Journal of Technology Management* 44, nos. 1–2 (2008): 140.

54. Michael A. Hiltzik, *Dealers of Lightning: Xerox PARC and the Dawn of the Computer Age* (New York, HarperBusiness, 2000).

55. See, for example, Rachel Schurman and William A. Munro, *Fighting for the Future of Food: Activists versus Agribusiness in the Struggle over Biotechnology* (Minneapolis: University of Minnesota Press, 2010).

56. Kenneth A. Oye, Kevin Esvelt, Evan Appleton, Flaminia Catteruccia, George Church, Todd Kuiken, Shlomiya Bar-Yam Lightfoot, Julie McNamara, Andrea Smidler, and James P. Collins, "Regulating Gene Drives," *Science* 345, no. 6197 (2014): 626–628.

57. Gary E. Marchant, Braden R. Allenby, and Joseph R. Herkert, eds., *The Growing Gap between Emerging Technologies and Legal-Ethical Oversight: The Pacing Problem* (Dordrecht: Springer, 2011).

58. Nick von Tunzelmann, "Historical Coevolution of Governance and Technology in the Industrial Revolutions," *Structural Change and Economic Dynamics* 14 (2003): 365–384.

59. Cass R. Sunstein, "Empirically Informed Regulation," *University of Chicago Law Review* 78, no. 4 (2011): 1350.

60. Nathan Cortez, "Regulating Disruptive Innovations," *Berkeley Technology Law Review* 29, no. 1 (2014: 277.

61. Anne Lewis, "The Legality of 3D Printing: How Technology Is Moving Faster Than the Law," *Tulane Journal of Technology and Intellectual Property* 17 (2014): 303–318.

62. Lucas S. Osborn, "Regulating Three-Dimensional Printing: The Converging Worlds of Bits and Atoms," *San Diego Law Review* 51, no. 2 (2014): 553–621.

63. Deven R. Desai and Gerard N. Magliocca, "Patents, Meet Napster: 3D Printing and the Digitization of Things," *Georgetown Law Journal* 102, no. 6 (2014): 1691–1720.

64. Jeffrey P. Baker, "The Incubator and the Medical Discovery of the Premature Infant," *Journal of Perinatology* 5 (2000): 321–328.

65. Richard F. Hirsh and Benjamin K. Sovacool, "Wind Turbines and Invisible Technology: Unarticulated Reasons for Local Opposition of Wind Energy," *Technology and Culture* 54, no. 4 (2013): 725.

66. Maria Paola Ferretti, "Why Public Participation in Risk Regulation? The Case of Authorizing GMO Products in the European Union," *Science and Culture* 16, no. 4 (2013): 377–395.

67. Paul Slovic, "Perceived Risk, Trust and Democracy," *Risk Analysis* 13, no. 6 (1993): 675–682.

68. Karin Zachmann, "Atoms for Peace and Radiation for Safety: How to Build Trust in Irradiated Foods in Cold War Europe and Beyond," *Technology and History* 27, no. 1 (2007): 65.

69. Stig Kvaal and Per Østby, "Sweet Danger: Negotiating Trust in the Norwegian Chocolate Industry 1930–1990," *History and Technology* 27, no. 1 (2011): 107.

70. For an account of social reaction to coffee consumption and its characterization as "junior alcohol" in south India, see A. R. Venkatachalapathy, *In Those Days There Was No Coffee: Writings in Cultural History* (New Delhi: Yoda Press, 2006).

71. Kenneth T. Andrews and Neal Caren, "Making the News: Movement Organizations, Media Attention, and the Public Agenda," *American Sociological Review* 75, no. 6 (2010): 841–866.

72. Otto L. Bettmann, *The Good Old Days: They Were Terrible!* (New York: Random House, 1974).

73. Eric Hobsbawm and Terence Ranger, eds., *The Invention of Tradition* (Cambridge: Cambridge University Press, 2012).

74. A. Bhalla, D. James, and Y. Stevens, eds., *Blending of New and Traditional Technologies* (Dublin: Tycooly, 1984); and Nathan Rosenberg, "Technology and Employment Programme on Technology Blending," Working Paper, World Employment Programme, 1986.

75. Paul Bellaby, "Uncertainties and Risks in Transitions to Sustainable Energy, and the Part 'Trust' Might Play in Managing Them: A Comparison with the Current Pension Crisis," *Energy Policy* 38, no. 6 (2010): 2624–2630.

76. Francis Fukuyama, *Trust: The Social Virtues and the Creation of Prosperity* (New York: Free Press, 1996).

77. Guido Möllering, "The Nature of Trust: From Georg Simmel to a Theory of Expectation and Suspension," *Sociology* 35, no. 2 (2001): 403–420.

78. Adam Burgess, "Mobile Phones and Service Stations: Rumour, Risk and Precaution," *Diogenes* 54, no. 1 (2007): 125–139.

79. Adam Burgess, "Real and Phantom Risks at the Petrol Station: The Curious Case of Mobile Phones, Fires and Body Static," *Health, Risk and Society* 9, no. 1 (2007): 53–66.

80. Jeffrey L. Meikle, *American Plastic: A Cultural History* (New Brunswick, NJ: Rutgers University Press, 1997), 147.

81. Meikle, *American Plastic*, 147.

82. Nils J. Nilsson, *Understanding Beliefs* (Cambridge, Mass: MIT Press, 2014).

83. Douglas Powell and William Leiss, *Mad Cows and Mother's Milk: The Perils of Poor Risk Communication* (Montreal: McGill-Queens University Press, 1997).

84. Joseph J. Corn, *The Winged Gospel: America's Romance with Aviation* (Baltimore: Johns Hopkins University Press, 1983), 74.

85. Pushker A. Kharecha and James E. Hansen, "Prevented Mortality and Greenhouse Gas Emissions from Historical and Projected Nuclear Power." *Environmental Science and Technology* 47 (2013): 4889–4895.

86. W. Brian Arthur, *The Nature of Technology: What It Is and How It Evolves* (New York: Free Press, 2009), 216.

Index

Surnames starting with "al-" are alphabetized by the subsequent part of the name.